SPAIN AND THE INDEPENDENCE OF THE UNITED STATES

SPAIN AND THE INDEPENDENCE OF THE UNITED STATES
AN INTRINSIC GIFT

⚜

Thomas E. Chávez

Thom E. Chavez

7 Nov. 2006

Santa Fe, NM

University of New Mexico Press
Albuquerque

Library of Congress Cataloging-in-Publication Data

Chávez, Thomas E.
Spain and the independence of the United States : an intrinsic gift /
Thomas E. Chávez.— 1st ed.
p.   cm.
Includes bibliographical references and index.
ISBN 0-8263-2793-1 (cloth : alk. paper)
1. United States—History—Revolution, 1775–1783—Participation, Spanish.   2. United
States—Foreign relations—1775–1783.   3. United States—Foreign relations—Spain.
4. Spain—Foreign relations—United States.
I. Title.

E269.S63 C47 2002
973.3'46—dc21
                                                            2001006449

Publication of this book has been supported in part by a generous grant
from the Program for Cultural Cooperation between Spain's Ministry of Education,
Culture and Sports and United States Universities.

Dedicated to the Memory of

My Daughter

Captain Christel Angélica Chávez, USAF

(1974–2002)

and Her Great Uncle

Fray Angélico Chávez

(1910–1996)

Priest, poet, historian, and artist
who, with his five brothers and a sister,
served in the armed forces
of the United States of America
to help preserve the freedoms and independence
that Spain helped secure.

CONTENTS

᪐

PREFACE

Spain helped the United States to achieve its independence from England. This is not well known in the United States, although it is known and documented in Spain. Spanish historian Francisco Yela Utrilla published a book-length monograph on the subject in 1925 and he included letters of the founding fathers of the United States that he translated into Spanish. The title explains his book: *España ante la Independencia de los Estados Unidos.*

My own interest in, and understanding of, the significance of Spain in the independence of the United States began in a serendipitous way. As a beginning curator in the Museum of New Mexico's history museum, the Palace of the Governors, I rummaged through the uncatalogued artifact collections in the basement. Like any young curator or historian, such busy work seemed akin to a treasure hunt. Little did I realize that one discovery would lead me on a multi-year quest. I found a box carelessly placed among other unrelated items. This box contained three silk flags, with oil-painted insignia that was very detailed and colorful. A letter inside the box explained that the enclosed flags were banners of Spanish regiments that fought in the War of Independence. The banners were sent to the State of New Mexico as gifts from the Spanish government on the occasion of the two hundredth anniversary of United States independence.[1] (See plates 1, 2, and 3.)

An inquiry to the Spanish embassy in Washington, D.C., and a subsequent visit to the National Archives, resulted in a journey that has been a form of personal fulfillment, because, like many citizens of the United States, I claim a Hispanic heritage. Hispanic families in the United States range from recent arrivals, to people whose ancestors settled in what is today the United States, before Jamestown or the puritans and the pilgrims.[2] As the story of Spain's multifaceted role in the early history of the United States unfolds, it becomes clear that all people of Spanish heritage, in some way, can claim participation. The more recent arrivals, especially those people from Mexico and Cuba, can as fully *participate* in 4th of July festivities as any other Americans. The salient point is that all Hispanics helped with American independence as a result of Spain's policy during the colonial period.

The bicentennial of the birth of the United States in 1976 gave rise to an opportunity for Spain to reintroduce its role in the early history of the North American country. Probably the least-heralded and most valuable contribution is a multivolume set of catalogues, documenting the manuscripts pertinent to United States independence in the various Spanish archives. The title of this set of books is *Documentos relativos a la independencia de Norteamérica existentes en archivos españoles*, and I am grateful to Señor José Remacha, who gave me a set. At the time, Señor Remacha was the cultural attaché for the Spanish embassy in Washington, D.C. His gift became the basis for almost two years of research in Spain. The catalogues proved to be an invaluable asset, though I soon learned that not all the pertinent archives, much less documents, were included in the set. In fact, the amount of available material in Spain is overwhelming.

Faced with such abundance of primary source material, I came to realize, to my regret, that I could not do the definitive history on the topic. The documentary material is so plentiful in Spain that there is enough work to last many historians a lifetime. So, I compiled an overview with new information, along with the already-known facts, all of which was placed in a context that included Spain. In addition, topics that should be of further interest and require more research are noted in the citations.

I also chose to concentrate on the Spanish archives, especially in Seville and Madrid. An interesting project would be for a historian, armed with the documents and information in Spain, to delve into the British and American archives. I do not believe the outcome would change the narrative history, as laid out in this book, but the motives of each nation would, perhaps, become more clear. In short, a more balanced understanding of the independence of the United States would emerge.

Archives in the United States, including the National Archives and Library of Congress, on the national level, and the Historic New Orleans Collection, the Newberry Library in Chicago, and the Missouri Historical Society in St. Louis, have material important to United States independence. On the international level, the national archives of Cuba and those of the viceroy of La Nueva España, Martín de Mayorga, in the Mexican National Archives in Mexico City, will provide much additional information. As this book notes, the war that resulted in the independence of the United States was not localized to the thirteen colonies, so even the national archives in such seemingly remote places as Argentina, Guatemala, Nicaragua, Venezuela, and Portugal could prove fruitful.

American historians have begun exploring material on this topic in Spain's archives, although, for the most part, they overlooked this abundance of resources for almost the first century and a half since 1776. Current historians such as Light Townsend Cummings, Gilbert C. Din, and Eric Beerman have been producing quality work, on topics ranging from Spanish observers to biographies of Spanish individuals who had a role in the "Revolutionary War." Nor can the earlier contributions of Jack D. L. Holmes, Abraham Nasatir, Troy S. Floyd, and John Francis McDermott be ignored, for they worked at a time when this history of Spain in North America was considered, at best, an appendage to the history of the United States.

Throughout the research, the writing, and the rewriting of this book, the irony of who—which people and what countries—made possible United States independence became obvious. With this in mind, I have tried to connect yesteryear to today without disrupting the historical narrative. The result is that many people, like myself and family, have a claim to this country's history—from its beginning—and, as the dedication indicates, we still contribute to the patrimony of the United States.

On the other hand, this book is somewhat of a throwback, in that it does not follow the dictates of "new history" that documents "just plain folks as well as culture" with emphasis on topical discussions. As an individual who has worked for over twenty years in the museum profession, the importance of material culture as a source of information for piecing together the past is obvious. The ranks of museum curators include people from all the humanities disciplines, who commonly employ their varied views to create an interdisciplinary approach. These people practiced what has become "new history" before it became fashionable on university campuses.

I believe that a traditional history that concerns itself with geopolitical views is still valuable. In the case of this book, the value is tremendous, for it includes a whole segment of this country's population that has been disenfranchised from the country's birth and, therefore, from its history.

The story of Spain's role in the revolution of Britain's North American colonies is not widely known in the United States. It is my hope that this necessary traditional history will be a small step on the long road toward creating a better understanding between peoples in the United States, if not the world.

Certainly, the experience and support that I received from the Daughters of the American Revolution (DAR), the Granaderos de Gálvez, and the respective governments of Spain and the United States indicate that this is a subject of wide interest. Various chapters of the Daughters of the American Revolution have invited me to give talks and each chapter has been very receptive. In their national magazine, they featured an article that I wrote, and I am especially grateful to the Lew Wallace Chapter in Albuquerque, New Mexico, for it arranged for me to receive the DAR "Distinguished History Award Medal." In addition, the DAR changed their membership rules to allow the descendants of Spanish soldiers into their ranks. *New Mexico Magazine*, a popular publication, has also published an article on the subject as a part of its special quincentenary issue.

I hope that this book will lead to a major traveling exhibition, created from the artifacts, illustrations, and new information made available. To date, the National Park Service has put up some displays, but these have been relatively small and site-specific. A national traveling exhibition, meant for a wide audience, is an unfulfilled goal that I would like to achieve.

As the director of the Palace of the Governors, the state history museum, and part of the Museum of New Mexico system, I have been blessed to work with a great staff. Without them, this professional bureaucrat could not even begin to research and write history, something for which I am formally trained.

Without the benefit of sabbaticals and with only a few weeks' vacation each year, time and expenses could have been a handicap toward completion of this book. Fortunately, I received financial assistance throughout the project. The Fulbright Fellowship program and la Comisión de Intercambio Cultural entre España y los Estados Unidos, as it is called in Spain, was the first and largest grant. Special appreciation goes to Thomas Middleton, María Jesús Pablos, and María Carmen Rodas, whose efficient operation made my ten-month stay in Spain one of the most professionally productive times of my life. Those three people have been a godsend to anyone who has traveled to Spain on a Fulbright Fellowship. They are articulate, efficient, helpful, and enthusiastic about their work. José Remacha and the Spanish embassy then arranged for me to receive a grant-in-aid from the Dirección General de Relaciones Culturales y Científicas, from the Spanish Foreign Ministry (Ministerio de Asuntos Exteriores). This support provided me with funds to spend three more months in Spain to write what would become the first six chapters of this book. Señor Remacha has been a special inspiration for this project.

The late Mrs. Harry Bigbee, to whom I dedicated the article in *The Daughters of the American Revolution Magazine*, supported a second research trip of another three months and the purchase of a computer to help expedite the project. Before she passed away, she read early partial drafts of the manuscript. Her astute comments and suggestions are included in this final product. The support, and more importantly, the interest of Mrs. Bigbee, her husband, Judge Harry Bigbee, and her daughter Elizabeth Bigbee Sheehan, have been a great encouragement to me. People like the Bigbees make the struggle to complete a project like this worthwhile.

The Granaderos de Gálvez in El Paso, Texas, took an early interest in the research for this book. They have hosted me for a number of lectures and supported my work with a small grant, which was made at a perfect time. Special thanks go to Dr. Lorenzo G. LaFarelle and Sheldon Hall of the Granaderos, whose interest and help are appreciated.

My father, Judge Antonio E. Chávez; uncle, the late Fray Angélico Chávez (to whom this book is dedicated); wife, Dr. Celia López Chávez; and colleague, Dr. Donna L. Pierce, all helped transcribe and translate the reams of documents that I photocopied in Spanish archives. Fray Angélico even did double duty by helping with documents written in French.

Sometimes small gestures are significant. Historian Light Townsend Cummings somehow found out that I had embarked on this project. Dr. Cummings sent me a book about Bernardo de Gálvez that he had helped publish, and he wished me well. Then Dr. Oakah Jones, who is a model historian, sent me an unpublished article that he wrote. As might be expected, the article was a great help. Dr. Jones then agreed to review and offer corrections for the manuscript. Again, that such a person would help was invaluable encouragement.

Special appreciation goes to my friends, many of whom are omitted here. Ambassador Frank V. Ortiz and his wonderful wife, Dolores, allowed me to use their private library of books. Their generosity was a boon to the research and ideas in the chapters dealing with the Continental Congress.

Jerry Richardson, Richard C. "Doc" Weaver, Dr. Julio Davila, and the late Riley Parker and his widow, Betty Parker, are all supporters of the museum and are such unfettered enthusiasts of history that I was left with no choice but to finish the book. All historians, I suspect, need such people to provide a well-timed "kick in the pants." Another friend, Paul Kraemer, was of special help with his computer knowledge. His assistance saved me at least a month's work at a critical time.

W. Charles Bennett, himself a historian as well as assistant director at the Palace of the Governors, has not only traveled in Spain with me but has also listened to my ideas. It was to him that I first broached the idea of researching and writing a book on Spain in the American Revolution, while we were on a backpacking and fishing trip to the Río Grande Gorge in northern New Mexico in 1982. More importantly, he, along with a very good staff, have made it possible for me to have the time as well as peace of mind even to attempt such a project.

Finally, I would like to recognize additional contributions from my family and to mention some of the ways my life has changed during more than fourteen years of research and writing. My two daughters, Nicolasa Marie and Christel Angélica, who accompanied me for ten months of research in 1987, have grown up to be fine young women. Nicolasa with her son Noé Antonio has made me a grandfather. And, while they were with me for that time in Spain, I met my future wife, Celia López Chávez, in the Archives of the Indies. She, too, is a historian and has been of inestimable help to me in research and translation, as well as commentary on the manuscript. As an added bonus, Celia has turned out to be somewhat of a computer wizard and, happily, has forced me to take advantage of that technology. While helping with my research, Celia uncovered some relevant and heretofore unused documents in Seville and Málaga. She is even a good editor in her second language, which is English.

My parents, as always, are the reason for me to even attempt to research and write history. As with my previous books, they helped enter the first drafts into the computer. Then they edited and questioned. My father secured a research card to assist with research in the Archives of the Indies. He, like my wife, helped at all stages—from the discovery of information to the translation and editing of the final product. My mother, Marilyn Sprowl Chávez, is a silent inspiration, for not only does she help, she also encourages. There is nothing more inspiring for a son than to make a mother proud. In reality, my immediate family, staff, and friends are a constant reminder that nothing occurs in a vacuum. This book is truly a team effort.

So, to all these people, including my brother Mark, who lived with me for a good portion of the creation of this book, my sisters Carolyn, María, and Roberta, and the many friends and colleagues who are not mentioned here, this is your book, for it is our creation, our history.

A Telling Episode

O n 12 November 1784, William Carmichael, the recently appointed United States minister to Spain, put quill to parchment to write an innocuous letter to the Spanish minister of state, José Moñino y Redondo, conde de Floridablanca. Carmichael made a request on behalf of General George Washington, who had "retired to the country life." Looking for ways to improve life at Mount Vernon, Washington had asked a friend who dealt in international trade to locate and purchase, as Carmichael wrote, a "Jack Ass of the best breed in Spain."

The friend apparently ran afoul of a Spanish law prohibiting the exportation of the desired animal. Carmichael subsequently learned of the problem and decided to resolve the matter by writing to Floridablanca. Washington, Carmichael wrote, "perhaps gave these orders without knowing that a permission was necessary." Would Floridablanca inform him of the proper procedure "for the extraction of an Animal of this kind?"[1]

Unknown to Carmichael, his English usage of "Jack Ass" for mule translates in Spanish to "stallion ass"—a prize breeder, which is how Spanish authorities translated Carmichael's letter. As was his custom, Floridablanca passed the inquiry to his king, Carlos III, and waited for an answer, which upon receipt he then shared with Carmichael. His Majesty could not condescend to permitting the exportation of the requested "Burro Garañon," or stallion ass. The king could not give one of his prize breeders, but, on the other hand, he desired "that this request from such a commendable person be satisfied." Therefore, Carlos III ordered Floridablanca to send Washington not one but two of the offspring mules in case one perished in transit across the Atlantic.[2]

Washington, writing to Floridablanca, was more than gracious in expressing his appreciation for the king's generosity:

My honor is due to his Catholic Majesty for the honor of his present. The value of it is intrinsically great, but is rendered inestimable by the manner and from the hand it is delivered. Let me entreat you therefore, Sir, to lay before the King my thanks for the Jackasses with which he has been graciously pleased to compliment me and to assure his majesty of my unbounded gratitude for so condescending a mark of his Royal notice and favor.[3]

Washington could not have been surprised by the gift,[4] for he knew that the same king had been generous in his support of the fledgling United States. Spain, under Carlos III, had been instrumental in the American victory in the recent War of Independence.

Neither Washington nor Carlos III had any way of understanding just how appropriate the jackass controversy was to Spain's role and aid to the American Revolution. Spain had spent at least five years sending more than the requested supplies and money to help the American rebels succeed in what must have appeared to be an impossible dream. Spanish men from the peninsula and throughout the Americas fought in the conflict. "The Revolutionary War," as the conflict is called in the United States, used funds collected from people living in the present states of Louisiana, Texas, New Mexico, Arizona, and California. In fact, an important percentage of financial support originated in New Spain, now called Mexico. Eventually, thousands of Spanish troops fought British troops throughout the Americas. But, as we shall see, diplomatic circumstance, the sorry episode of John Jay's bias, and a language barrier all conspired to bury Spain's gift to the United States as deeply as the story of Washington's Spanish mules.

A General Setting

The watershed for Spanish and others' involvement in the American Revolution is the Seven Years' War (1756–1763), also known in America as the French and Indian War. This war, in Spanish history, has its roots in the turn of the eighteenth century.

In October 1700, one month before his death at the age of thirty-nine, Carlos II, the last Habsburg king of Spain, made his final will, bequeathing the Spanish kingship and all its empire to Philippe, duke of Anjou, his half sister's younger grandson. King Carlos was incapable of siring children and had no younger brothers, so he could only pass succession through his sisters. One sister, the empress Margarita María, had married Leopold I, the Austrian Habsburg emperor; the other, María Teresa, was the queen of France and wife of Louis XIV. At issue was a French Bourbon succession versus an Austrian Habsburg succession; the choice could upset the European balance of power.

The decision of Carlos II in favor of a Bourbon regime has been judged by most historians to have been wise, although his contemporaries were not so certain, for it meant a change in dynasties. When the grandson of France's Louis XIV ascended to the Spanish throne as Felipe V, the other European powers feared the prospect of a single family ruling both Spain and France. Louis XIV's jubilant exclamation, "now there are no more Pyrenees," only increased their apprehension and strengthened their determination to oppose the new Bourbon power bloc.

Thus, in 1702 a grand alliance was formed to annul the succession, reduce the extent of Spanish and French domains, and support the rival candidacy of the Austrian archduke Karl, who was proclaimed King Carlos III of Spain at a ceremony in Vienna in 1703. For the next twelve years, the War of the Spanish Succession and its North American counterpart, Queen Anne's War, dragged on. All the great European powers were engaged. Spain became embroiled in a virtual civil war from which Felipe V emerged victorious. However, the European alliance did succeed in severing from Spain her remaining continental possessions. Great Britain kept Gibraltar and the Mediterranean island of Minorca. Spanish Italy and the Spanish Netherlands passed to the Austrian Habsburgs.

Spain emerged from the war with its American possessions intact and a Bourbon regime that survives even today. And despite the early fears of a Bourbon power bloc, the new Spanish dynasty developed separately and independently from France.

After the death of his first wife, María Luisa, Felipe married the Italian, Isabella Farnese, niece and stepdaughter of the duke of Parma. As in every family, quarrels occurred.[5] The first dispute arose within the Bourbon family, from Spanish sentiment that France had been too lenient in negotiating the peace of the War of Spanish Succession in 1713–14. Spain reoccupied its Mediterranean possession, Sardinia, and invaded Sicily in 1719. In the process, it became a nemesis to France. The ensuing conflict spilled over to the Americas, where Spain lost the port of Pensacola on the Gulf of Mexico. The state of war created a scare throughout the Spanish viceroyalty of New Spain. The Spanish-Americans expected an invasion from the French base in the "Illinois Country" in the Great Lakes region. The viceroy in Mexico City ordered the governor of New Mexico, his northernmost province, to send an expedition north onto the plains in search of French intruders. Oto and Pawnee Indians, possibly with their French allies, ambushed the subsequent expedition in present-day eastern Nebraska. The battle resulted in defeat for the Spanish, and redefined French and Spanish borders in North America.[6]

The War of Polish Succession (1733–1736) followed the conflicts of 1702–1720. This dispute pitted France and Spain against Austria and its allies, the most important of which was Great Britain. Spain sought to regain its possessions in Italy, succeeding sufficiently to reinstate Spanish Bourbons on the thrones of Naples and Sicily. Because Great Britain loomed ever more prominently as the archenemy of their overseas empires, a Family Compact, or mutual assistance pact, was signed between the French and Spanish Bourbons at the inception of war in 1733.

Despite its European interests, Spain's territories across the Atlantic Ocean remained its primary concern. The financial stability of the empire continued to depend on the natural wealth of the Americas as well as control of the West Indian trade.

Great Britain had been granted specific trading privileges in Spanish-American ports as early as 1714, but by the 1730s had exceeded the legal limits through illicit trade. Spanish measures to curb British excesses sometimes reached the point of absurdity, as when, in 1739, a shipmaster named Jenkins exhibited in London his detached ear, which he claimed had been cut off by a Spanish naval officer. Skeptics noted that Jenkins had two perfectly good and attached ears under his wig. Nevertheless, Great Britain acknowledged its intention to expand its Indies trade at the expense of Spain's New World viceroyalties when it declared war against Spain. The "War of Jenkins's Ear" quickly became part of the War of the Austrian Succession, or King George's War (1740–1748).

The War of the Austrian Succession broke out after the Austrian emperor Charles VI died in 1740, leaving his possessions to his daughter, María Theresa. Frederick II of Prussia saw an opportunity to gather territory at the expense of a financially insolvent Austrian empire and seized the Austrian province of Silesia. France joined the struggle in an attempt to gain territory, and Spain still had interest in regaining more of its former Italian possessions. As a result, Spain signed a second Family Compact with France in 1743. With peace in 1748, Felipe V's son, Don Carlos, was recognized as king of the two Sicilies, while his older half brother was awarded the duchies of Parma and Piacenza. Thus satisfied, Spain ended its pursuits in Italy.

Great Britain sided with Austrian archduchess María Theresa principally to counter French influence on the continent. Great Britain was already fighting against France and Spain overseas. The War of Jenkins's Ear had become an emotional issue in Spain as a struggle against a condescending and aggressive naval rival that illegally sought to occupy Spanish territory in the Americas. A huge British expeditionary force sacked Portobelo in Panama and attacked some Venezuelan ports. British forces laid siege to Cartagena, but the Spanish defenders repulsed them. One Manila galleon with a cargo of silver was lost off the Philippine Islands, and various coastal towns on the Pacific seaboard were attacked. But Spain's fortifications, fleet, and merchant marine were able to repel Great Britain's offensive. England's design to detach the Americas from the Spanish monarchy failed, for the Treaty of Aix-la-Chapelle, which ended the war in 1748, left the Spanish empire intact while canceling British trading privileges in Spanish territory. Chief among those privileges was the *asiento,* a slave trade quota.

The war set the stage for almost forty years and three subsequent wars in which the Americas would become a focal point for the conflicting imperial ambitions of Britain, France, and Spain.

The three nations had extensive colonial holdings, which they tried to use in the strictest mercantile sense. Colonies existed to benefit the mother country—to garner wealth and therefore power, which translated into a well-trained and well-equipped navy and army. So much expense and effort was put into the military that, on many occasions, opponents would avoid clashes to protect their investment. One officer wrote that eighteenth-century warfare was not the art of defending places but of "surrendering them honorably after certain conventional formalities."[7] To become powerful, a country simply needed to sell more than it bought and control as much territory as possible. The country that could keep the most hard specie, gold and silver, would be the most powerful. In previous centuries, Spain used its hard specie for other European ventures. Carlos III's reforms tried to increase wealth from the colonies while closing the flow from Spain to other parts of Europe.

Obviously, then, all three countries competed worldwide. By the 1750s, the Bourbon-Habsburg rivalry was supplanted by a growing French-British rivalry. Indeed, a European balance of power was measured in terms of maintaining the military equality of France and Great Britain. The same split extended to North America, where both sides recognized that the alliances, if not friendship, of Indians would be a helpful factor in the game of frontier muscle flexing.

War did not end conflict but led to more hostilities. Austria's desire to avenge the loss of Silesia in the War of Austrian Succession was the main cause of the next conflict, which broke out in 1756. Complex alliances, national vendettas, and ambitions gave rise to the Seven Years' War, referred to as the French and Indian War in North America, and sometimes called the Great War for Empire. In the North American theater, this war was a prelude to the American Revolution.

At first, the main cause for the war revolved around an Austro-Prussian rivalry and Russia's ambition to make territorial gains at Prussia's expense, then the emphasis shifted to the Anglo-French competition. The two countries' colonies shared common borders in North America while they, with Spain and Holland, competed in the West Indies. French and English colonists desired the Ohio River Valley. The French had been there first, but this fact was of no importance to the aggressive and more numerous English colonists.

In 1754, the Ohio Company—with the blessing of the Virginia legislature, which claimed the Ohio River Valley as its own—sent a colonial militia into the valley to capture the recently established French outpost, called Fort Duquesne, at present-day Pittsburgh. The expedition was led by a young Virginian, whose inexperience showed, for the effort failed miserably. He attacked a peaceful French party and then at Fort Necessity was surrounded and attacked. After one-third of his men suffered casualties in a daylong battle, the twenty-two-year-old George Washington was forced to surrender.

The loss annoyed the British government and confirmed in the minds of the English the belief that the American colonists were useless fighters. The British government took matters into its own hands, sending a second expedition to take Fort Duquesne. Contrary to expectations, the British force met the same fate as Washington's militia. Both of these expeditions, plus innumerable minor clashes, made up a legacy of violent, albeit unofficial, confrontation.

Official hostilities began in 1756 when war broke out in Europe. France sided with Austria and Russia, while Great Britain joined Prussia. Spain stayed out of the fracas until the end. Frederick II of Prussia won some startling early victories, but superior numbers and logistics eventually wore him down. Luckily for Prussia and Frederick, Empress Elizabeth of Russia died and was succeeded by her son, Tsar Peter III, who, unlike his late mother, admired Frederick. As the war ended, Peter III offered mild conditions for peace.

France and England also had declared war on each other, less over their European alliances than because of their ambitions on the North American continent. France won a number of early victories as its soldiers and Indian allies proved themselves to be much more prepared for frontier warfare. This changed when William Pitt, a determined man with a single-minded clarity of purpose, took over the war effort as Great Britain's de facto prime minister. Pitt, under the patronage of the duke of Newcastle, the real prime minister, retained almost absolute power and redefined England's priority as the Americas. He recognized that winning overseas necessitated cutting off the French supply system. To fulfill this strategy, Pitt subsidized Prussia to keep France's attention divided between Old and New Worlds. Secondly, Pitt wanted to use his country's naval superiority to Britain's advantage by defeating the French navy.

France's strategy evolved to where it intended to invade England; a French fleet gathered at the two ports of Brest and Toulon, where they outfitted for the pending invasion. Pitt ordered the British navy to lie in wait for the embarkation of the French fleet. Two ensuing naval ambushes resulted in French defeats and the elimination of France's ability to supply its American forces. As William Pitt knew, the naval battles decided the fate of both Great Britain and France's empires. In the end, France lost Canada, its territory in Africa and India, and most of its West Indies possessions.

As a last attempt to avoid a complete loss, France turned to Spain for help. Don Carlos, who had recently been crowned king of Spain and who would go on to be fairly successful in foreign affairs, inherited the problem of British affronts to his overseas empire. Britain constantly harassed Spain's merchant marine fleet and overseas ports. As a result, Carlos III allowed himself to be persuaded to help France in 1761, when he agreed to the Third Family Compact, which drew Spain into the end of the Seven Years' War. Unfortunately, Spain was not prepared, so it shared France's defeats. Spain lost Havana in the West Indies and Manila in the Philippine Islands. The losses shocked Spanish officials into realizing how vulnerable the empire had become to foreign invasion. Although Spain succeeded in retaking Manila, the whole episode was an early education and one of Carlos III's few blunders in foreign affairs. The king and his advisors would remember the lesson.

In 1763, France and England agreed to terms of peace for North America in the Treaty of Paris. Great Britain gained all of Canada and India from France. Spain lost Florida, which included all the territory of present-day Florida on the gulf coast, to Louisiana. Great Britain divided this area into East and West Florida. France, under Louis XV, ceded to Great Britain all of its territory east of the Mississippi River except New Orleans. France had given Louisiana to Spain as compensation for its loss of the Floridas. Louis XV found Spanish possession of Louisiana more palatable than allowing the vast territory to fall into the hands of Great Britain.

A war-weary Great Britain had to give up some of its recently won territory to end the hostilities. Great Britain returned the islands of Guadeloupe and Martinique in the West Indies to France, and Havana to Spain. The British government apparently and inexplicably felt that inclusion of these islands as well as Cuba, as part of the British Empire, would hurt existing British trade in the Caribbean. The merchants in England completely disagreed with this uncharacteristic move and the cession provoked a storm of protest. The returned islands were far more valuable, they protested, than Canada's "acres of snow," which England kept.[8]

When summarizing the war's consequences, Spain, as a participant on the losing side, did not fare too badly. Spain lost Florida to Great Britain and Uruguay to Great Britain's ally, Portugal. On the other hand, Spain gained New Orleans and the Louisiana Territory, a part of which it already claimed. Great Britain retained rights to harvest wood in Central America. Irrespective of the results, Spain lost the war, and Great Britain, which managed to maneuver itself into a precarious position in North America, would continue with its aggressive American activities.

France was a big loser and, financially strained from the war effort, waited for an opportunity to strike back at Great Britain. Great Britain, by its victory, removed the French threat to its colonies. However, subsequent attempts to extract payments for the war from its own colonies created a situation in which colonial relations became strained enough to lead to disaster for Great Britain and opportunity for France.

Spain resented its losses and Great Britain's continuous intrusion into Spanish overseas territories and trade. Carlos III concentrated on reforming his military. He started building up his navy. The king and his advisors reorganized Spain's New World governmental administration, which immediately started paying dividends from increased revenues that helped to fund the new military.

The new army incorporated French and Prussian military innovations. A modern system of organization using brigades, regiments, battalions, companies, and squadrons was implemented. Men without aristocratic connections received promotions, although such advances were the exception rather than the rule. Officers went through training, some at French military academies. Through constant attention, reexamination, and adjustment, an effective armed force began to emerge throughout the Spanish empire. While building its military, Spain remained cautious about reengaging Great Britain in war.

With the throne's attention, economic and administrative reform began to pay dividends in the Spanish colonies. Intracolonial trade was permitted and direct trade was opened to a number of ports in Spain, ending the Cádiz monopoly on American commerce. Carlos III's reforms initiated an economic regeneration throughout Spain as well as in its colonies.

The Peace of Hubertusburg, signed in 1763, officially ended hostilities in Europe. The treaty called for no territorial change in Europe. Merely by surviving, Prussia surfaced as a European power and a potential barrier to Russia's apparent desire to have more influence in Europe. For the rest of the world, the treaty was a truce; the principals of the worldwide conflict knew that peace was far from permanent.

Some Key Personalities

After nearly a half century of inconclusive warfare, an era of revolution was about to dawn with the rebellion of thirteen British colonies. Carlos III's Spain would eventually become a deciding factor in this initial disturbance. Spain's involvement included a number of individuals who assisted in the birth and independence of a fledgling North American country calling itself the United States of America.

Spain's effort in the struggle was overseen by José Moniño y Redondo, the conde de Floridablanca, the minister of state. Described as clever and astute by admirers and as devious and wily by detractors, Floridablanca concocted a strategy of patience before committing his country to war. With a better grasp of reality than Charles Gravier, the comte de Vergennes, his French counterpart, Floridablanca gathered resources to build his naval fleet and land forces while isolating England through diplomacy before involving Spain in the American war. After Spain declared war on Great Britain on 21 June 1779, he oversaw an aggressive effort.

Floridablanca stuck to a plan of action that would achieve Spain's stated goals. From the very beginning of negotiations with France, Floridablanca and his predecessor, Jerónimo Grimaldi, the marqués de Grimaldi, consistently made clear what Spain wanted in exchange for its alliance with France to help the rebelling colonies. As reiterated on many occasions to all the interested parties, Spain wanted Gibraltar, Minorca, the Floridas (especially Pensacola), Jamaica and the Bahamas. British establishments on the east coasts of Mexico, Honduras, and Campeche needed to be eliminated.[9] Adhering to those goals, Floridablanca strove for the achievement of each objective until the making of peace in 1783. Only the thirteen colonies, by winning their independence, were more successful than Spain as a result of the war. At the war's end, Spain had everything but Jamaica and Gibraltar.[10]

By refusing to recognize the rebelling British colonies, Floridablanca was very careful not to send mixed signals to Spain's own colonies. Nor did he want to alienate or alarm Great Britain before Spain joined in the engagement. He almost succeeded in gaining Spain's objectives at the diplomatic table, thus negating any need to go to war.[11] In maintaining Spain's diplomatic etiquette, Floridablanca insisted that all official business with the Americans be handled through Spain's minister to France, stationed in Paris. For this reason, Pedro Pablo Abarca de Bolea, the conde de Aranda, became a prominent person in the American colonies' attempt to arrange aid prior to, and during, the war.

In the course of his ambassadorship in Paris, Aranda became fond of the fledgling colonies and their struggle. Lacking Floridablanca's patience, Aranda recommended an early and open Spanish commitment to the colonies.

The Spanish aristocrat participated in the Paris peace negotiations in which he proved to be an excellent advocate for Spain. Despite his legendary wine cellar and polished silver place settings, he failed to impress John Jay, who emerged as the key negotiator for the United States. But then, Jay was operating from a different and secret agenda.[14]

Many people had influential roles in the story of Spain's assistance to the American Revolution. For example, the marqués de Grimaldi, who preceded and handpicked Floridablanca as minister of state, oversaw the initial secret aid to the colonies. He set the governmental tone and policy that Floridablanca inherited and continued.

No history of the Americas, much less of Spain's role in the American Revolution, would be complete without José de Gálvez, Carlos III's minister of the Indies and patron of his own nephew Bernardo and older brother Matías, and the man who had overall responsibility for Spain's wartime activities in the Americas. His policy was obviously aggressive and, as it turned out, correct. Not surprisingly, then, he was a man highly qualified for his position when war broke out.[13]

José de Gálvez was born in Macharavialla, near the city of Málaga, in Andalucía, Spain on 2 January 1720. (See plate 5.) He spent his youth in his hometown until his early teens, when the bishop of Málaga, Diego González Toro, singled him out to study theology. Until González Toro's death in 1737, Gálvez lived and studied in Málaga. When his patron died he exchanged his ecclesiastical studies to take up law. After studying at the University of Salamanca and, possibly, the University of Alcalá, Gálvez went to Madrid to practice his vocation.

Within a short time, the young lawyer developed a reputation for his work in international law. One legendary story about Gálvez relates that he won a case for some foreign clients against the Spanish government. Word of his closing arguments quickly made the rounds of Spanish officialdom. King Carlos III became interested enough to summon the lawyer into his presence. "By what right do you argue against your King?" inquired his majesty. "Señor, antes que el Rey, está la ley;" "Sire, above the King, is the law" came back the reply.[14]

For whatever reason, Gálvez soon had backers in influential positions. Like many others, he found himself moving up in the governmental ranks. Early in his career, he impressed the conde de Aranda, who would become the Spanish minister plenipotentiary to France, the marqués de Grimaldi, and the conde de Floridablanca. At times, too, Gálvez conflicted with these knowledgeable and strong-willed men. This appears especially so with Floridablanca,[15] although their rivalry, if it deserved to be characterized as such, did not interfere with their respective performances and their common ultimate goal of defeating Great Britain.

In February 1765, Gálvez was appointed visitor general of New Spain; to give him more authority, he was made honorary member of the Council of the Indies. The new job was perfect for the forceful and energetic Gálvez. He traveled to New Spain within the year, taking his nephew Bernardo with him.[16] As part of his reforms of New Spain, Gálvez turned his attention to the northern frontier and problems with hostile Indians. He initiated a number of projects, as well as inspections along the frontier. Later, as secretary of the Indies, he used his New World experience to initiate a whole governmental reorganization in New Spain, into what was called "Las Provincias Internas," the internal provinces.

In answer to Madrid's concern that Russia was attempting to intrude upon the Spanish empire by expanding down the west coast of North America, Gálvez organized and supervised the settlement of Alta California. Then, his loyalty to his king was demonstrated when he did not hesitate to help carry out Carlos III's 1767 order to expel all Jesuit priests from the Americas.[17]

Gálvez's good work won him royal favor. After his return to Spain in 1772, he fulfilled various special assignments until early 1776 when, upon the death of the elderly minister of the Indies, Julián de Arriaga, he was promoted to the vacant position, which he held with various degrees of authority for the rest of his life.[18]

As minister of the Indies, Gálvez took great interest in the war against England. At the war's inception, Floridablanca wanted to attack the British stronghold at Jamaica, while Gálvez opted for concentrating on the Gulf Coasts. Floridablanca acquiesced and the strategy worked out.[19] Gálvez's influence, with Floridablanca's cooperation, was crucial to the success of the whole American wartime operation.

There is no doubt that José de Gálvez's energetic management style, if not his French connections, and his blatant nepotism made enemies, which may have caused some problems. Some officials resented Gálvez. On the other hand, José de Gálvez's political problems were a small price to pay for the culmination of his successful strategy. The only standard we have with which to measure José de Gálvez is provided by looking at what did happen and what role he had in making it happen. By that standard, Gálvez was a great minister who made a very significant contribution to the American colonies.

Another important figure assisting the colonies in their struggle for independence was José de Gálvez's nephew, Don Bernardo de Gálvez, also born in Macharavialla, Spain.[20] He helped through his diplomatic, financial, and military exploits against Great Britain in the Mississippi River Valley, the Gulf Coast, including the Floridas and Louisiana, and in the Gulf of Mexico. From 1776, when he became governor of Louisiana, until 1783, when the American Revolution ended, Gálvez's patience, audacity, appreciation of frontier people, diplomatic knowledge, and military skill greatly contributed to the eventual British defeat.

He arrived in Louisiana with royal instructions with which he personally agreed. They reflected the commitment of Carlos III to restore Spain's international prestige and grandeur through economic reform, government efficiency, political restructuring, and innovation in colonial enterprise. Gálvez also had to strengthen defenses and gather intelligence against the British.

Although he did not advocate republican or democratic principles that the Revolution came to symbolize, he was representative of the enlightened spirit of eighteenth-century regeneration and reform. More importantly, his monarch very much wanted to recoup the losses of the recently concluded Seven Years' War. The North American rebels not only provided the opportunity, but also had the demonstrated potential of becoming a future and lucrative trading partner.

Long before Spain actually declared war on Great Britain in 1779, the colonials received aid from Carlos III. In 1776, Spain dispatched one of its largest fleets ever to the Americas, where it smashed British smuggling operations along the Brazilian coast and retook Uruguay from the Portuguese, Great Britain's allies. Thus, Bernardo de Gálvez's subsequent instructions and actions took place in the context of a continuing global struggle.

Before declaring war, Spanish aid focused on Gálvez's covert activities in New Orleans, where he received his support and encouragement from Havana. Through the efforts of Oliver Pollock, an Irish-American merchant and agent from Virginia, Gálvez succeeded in supplying the successful campaigns of George Rogers Clark, who fought the British in the trans-Allegheny regions.[21] Supplies originating in New Orleans under Gálvez even reached Washington's army. Finally, he covertly protected American sympathizers.

By the time Gálvez received word of Spain's declaration of war in mid-1779, he had built up his military forces and, in anticipation of war, had set up a network of friends and spies who gathered information and cooperated with American military movements. Worried about defending his positions, Gálvez decided that the best strategy would be to drive the British forces out of Pensacola, Mobile, and the posts they occupied on the banks of the Mississippi River.[22]

He immediately marched out of New Orleans and captured Fort Bute at Manchac and Baton Rouge. Natchez surrendered with the capitulation of Baton Rouge. At the same time, his men in and around St. Louis allied with American irregulars to thwart a British attack on St. Louis in May 1780. In 1781, a Spanish militia of Frenchmen marched to present-day St. Joseph in what is now Michigan, on Lake Michigan, to capture and sack a British fort.[23] Gálvez then masterminded a successful land and sea attack on Mobile and, eventually, Pensacola, his most important victory.[24]

After Pensacola, Gálvez helped plan strategy for military operations against the British in the Gulf region from Guatemala to Yucatán, and for the taking of Nassau, on the island of New Providence in the Bahamas. During all the fighting, Spain continued to funnel money to the colonies. Payments amounting to hundreds of thousands of *pesos fuertes,* each worth about $30 by today's standards, originated in Mexico and were shipped to Havana to be transferred to the colonies, sometimes via French carriers.

Gálvez's colorful story attains a richer brilliance when, in 1777 in New Orleans, he married Félicité de St. Maxent d'Estrehan,[25] a beautiful French Creole woman whose father spied on the British for him. That his men and subjects, as well as allies and enemies, admired his ability and humanness is evident from the documents. At one point before the siege of Pensacola, when his network informed him that the town's people were starving, he ordered a shipload of food and supplies sent to the

British stronghold. He later went on to become an enlightened viceroy of New Spain (Mexico), where he initiated the building of Chapultepec Castle. He died as viceroy in Mexico City, when he was only forty years old, on 30 November 1786.

Spain's victories under his leadership made the British defeat more definitive and helped the United States gain maximum concessions, especially in the West, during the subsequent peace treaty negotiations in Paris. Spain removed the British threat from the south and west of the colonies. Gálvez's activities diverted British men, supplies, and attention away from the colonies, thus aiding the cause through strategy—a strategy about which Bernardo de Gálvez and George Washington concurred.

Much of what Gálvez accomplished, and most of what Spain contributed to the defeat of Great Britain and the ultimate success of the rebelling colonies would not have been possible had it not been for Captain Francisco de Saavedra de Sangronis, born in 1746 in Seville in the Province of Andalucía in southern Spain and educated at the College of Santo Tomás and at Sacro Monte de Granada, where he received a doctorate in theology. He wrote his dissertation on establishing the year of Christ's death.[26] Saavedra gave up his ecclesiastical career to pursue a military vocation and, eventually, became an administrative servant.[27]

As was the practice under Carlos III, bright young men quickly found themselves in favor with the court. So it came about that Saavedra quickly moved up in the governmental ranks. He became secretary to the embassy of Portugal in 1776, and in 1779 obtained a seat on the Council of the Indies, Spain's governing body for the Americas. As one of the secretaries of the Council he worked for José de Gálvez.

After Spain declared war, Saavedra, who was known for his loyalty and ability to work with egotistical men, received a special job to travel to Havana in 1780 and meet with all the military officials of the *junta general,* the General Committee of War. As a royal commissioner from the court of Madrid, his mission was to convince the committee of the king's will. In short, Saavedra had instructions to tell the committee that the king wanted them to embark on more aggressive plans of action. In particular, they were to put into action Bernardo de Gálvez's ideas for attacking the West Florida coast. Despite resistance, Saavedra succeeded in getting the committee to move. He even personally organized a subsequent expedition that included a French contingent to reinforce Gálvez's siege of Pensacola.

After Pensacola had been taken, Saavedra continued to play a key role in the war. When Bernardo de Gálvez was awarded a promotion to field marshal in charge of all the forces in the Caribbean theater, Saavedra became his major strategist as well as principal liaison to the French forces. He endeared himself so well to the French that the minister of state, the comte de Vergennes, wrote the French ambassador to Spain that Saavedra was a man of true merit and should be treated as much a friend as if he were himself Vergennes![28]

At the request of France, Bernardo de Gálvez reassigned Saavedra to help the French naval commander, Comte François-Joseph-Paul de Grasse. Saavedra was instrumental in forming French strategy for the nine months leading up to, and including, the important battle at Yorktown in which the British army was defeated by the combined French and American forces.[29]

Saavedra had a threefold role in the victory at Yorktown. He had a major role in designing the strategy, he secured Bernardo de Gálvez's permission to release the French fleet to sail north, and he was instrumental in raising the funds in Santo Domingo (now Dominican Republic) and Havana to pay for the participation of the French land and naval forces at Yorktown.[30]

The war did not end with Cornwallis's defeat at Yorktown. Saavedra immediately traveled to Mexico City to inspire the out-of-favor viceroy Martín de Mayorga to be a little more generous and timely with Mexico's silver and supply shipments to Havana and Guatemala where Bernardo de Gálvez's father, Matías, led the effort to defeat the British in that area.[31] After returning to the islands, he shuttled between Spanish and French ports gathering information, arranging for supplies, and creating a plan for a massive allied attack on the last British stronghold in the Caribbean, the island of Jamaica. Saavedra created a plan of attack so large that, if followed, it would have compared to some of the allied operations of World War II. His strategy called for a Spanish-French amphibian force drawn from Europe as well as from the Americas. The invasion of Jamaica would have included seventy-five ships-of-the-line, the battleships of the period, and twenty-five thousand troops.[32]

Described by contemporaries and subsequent historians as valiant, intelligent, and sagacious, Saavedra would go on to become a Spanish national hero.[33] After his work in the Caribbean, he became finance minister of his native Spain and then, from Spain's point of view, achieved his greatest fame when he organized and led resistance against Napoleon's forces during the French occupation of Spain after the turn of the century.[34]

The father of Bernardo de Gálvez, Matías, also significantly contributed to the Spanish war effort, for he was arguably as successful as any commander in the war. Like his brother and son he, too, was born in Macharavialla. Born in 1717, he devoted his life to serving his king. His presence, sense of fairness to those in his charge, devotion to his country, and energy all hint that his son's achievements were due, at least partly, to the father's example.

Matías de Gálvez was the oldest of four brothers, including the influential José. Miguel, educated in law at the University of Salamanca, became Spain's minister plenipotentiary to Prussia, where Frederick the Great received him. He later became minister to Russia. The youngest of the four brothers, Antonio, became commanding general of customs in the Bay of Cádiz and eventually achieved the rank of field marshal. While sailing in a Catalonian ship for Cuba, where he would have joined his brother and nephew in the struggle against Great Britain, his ship was unceremoniously captured by Moroccans. As a prisoner in Morocco, he arranged for his own release and then negotiated with the sultan for peace between that North African country and Spain.

Miguel's adopted daughter, Doña María Rosa de Gálvez, reputedly the illegitimate child of Carlos III, became a widely read poet and playwright. She spent her life living on the fringes of the court and became a mistress to Manuel Godoy, minister of state and the strongman of King Carlos IV.[35]

Like his brothers and son, Matías de Gálvez successfully pursued a professional career in the service of his country. He quickly advanced through the ranks to become a captain general. His first command assignments took him to the Canary Islands, a critical Atlantic site for Spain's American commerce. He served in the islands as governor of the Paso Alto Castle in Tenerife and as second general in command of the archipelago. His consistent good work made his brother José's patronage an easy task.[36]

José arranged for Matías to be appointed president of the Audiencia of Guatemala. Matías subsequently became the captain general of Guatemala, to which he was appointed in April 1779.[37] His move to America was critical, for Guatemala, which basically corresponded to Central America as it is known today, was one of the flash points in the Spanish empire where the British had become a major menace. British timber cutting, illicit trade, and smuggling had become a significant drain on Spanish Central American revenues as well as a source of income and strength to the British. Matías de Gálvez had instructions to put an end to Great Britain's presence in the region while initiating or continuing various governmental reforms to increase revenues, especially from Guatemala's many mines.[38]

Guatemala had many similarities to Louisiana, for one of Spain's stated motives for entering into the Revolutionary War was to stop contraband trade in both areas. After the War of Jenkins's Ear, and through the Seven Years' War, the British intrusion continued. Great Britain legally occupied the Mosquito Coast in the 1740s and, from several legal operations along the coast, conducted illegal trade throughout Central America.[39]

Guatemala became an integral part of Spain's desire to recover hegemony along the entire coasts of the Gulfs of Mexico, Honduras, and Campeche. As stated above, Spain sought to purge Great Britain from its American empire.[40]

Gálvez arrived in Guatemala in June 1778.[41] He inherited a task already set in motion, for Spain had gone to great efforts to document Great Britain's entrenched illicit activities. Spanish agents had gone into the Central American jungles to spy on British activities and negotiate with Indian tribes for their alliance. These men would emerge from the jungles months later with detailed information of British activity. Spain constructed the fortress of San Fernando de Omoa on the Bay of Honduras in the 1750s as a bastion against foreign intrusion. Omoa became a symbol of Spain's official stance versus Britain. In addition, Spain embarked on an expensive, ambitious and unsuccessful goal to raise and train a Guatemalan militia of forty thousand men.[42]

The new governor and captain-general soon had his chance to prove his mettle, for not long after Spain declared war, Great Britain launched an offensive up the San Juan River to divide the Spanish empire in Central America.[43]

The immediate need to stop the British offensive resulted in an outburst of energy that brought in supplies and aid from almost every quarter in the Spanish-American empire. Thus backed, Gálvez successfully counterattacked and checked the enemy's advance. Then, in a startling series of moves, Gálvez organized a succession of attacks on various British positions.[44] In 1782, Gálvez personally led his forces in the attack and defeat of the British-held island of Roatán, Honduras,[45] and then with the cooperation of officials in Havana, he put together an even larger force of fifteen hundred regulars and militia in an armada that included two ships-of-the-line, six frigates, and a number of smaller ships. With this force, in August 1782, Gálvez successfully turned back a British attack on the Río Tinto and along the Mosquito Coast.[46]

As a result of his efforts, the gulfs of Honduras and Campeche were freed of illicit British trade. More important to the war effort, Gálvez succeeded in fulfilling his role in an overall Bourbon plan of creating a global diversion for British strategists so that they could not concentrate their forces in any one theater. The Spanish strategy was especially effective in helping the "rebelling English colonies" achieve victory. Great Britain could not afford the luxury of concentrating on its rebellious colonies. The allied effort of Spain and France forced Great Britain to face some hard decisions.

Unlike most everyone else, Diego María de Gardoqui Aniquibar did not have a governmental career. Rather, he worked in the private sector and accepted assignments from his government. As a successful heir to a prominent Bilbao banking and merchant family, Gardoqui used his company to help Spain send aid to the colonies. He also clandestinely outfitted American privateers, including John Paul Jones, who on Benjamin Franklin's advice sought Gardoqui's help.[47] Gardoqui's ability to speak English was invaluable. In early 1777, he was called upon to intercept and diplomatically convince the unwelcome American commissioner, Arthur Lee, not to continue to Madrid but to return to Paris.

At the war's end, the Basque banker reluctantly agreed to leave his firm, Gardoqui e Hijos (Gardoqui and Sons), to accept appointment as Spain's ambassador to the United States in 1785. Nine years later, this man who spent his life in finance and business, and then as a diplomat, understated in a report he wrote in October 1794 while staying in the Royal monastery and palace of San Lorenzo del Escorial, that Spain's contribution to the United States in their struggle for independence has been very important and, perhaps, even a decisive factor.[48]

Juan de Miralles y Trajan and Francisco Rendón both preceded Gardoqui as Spanish diplomats to the United States. Because Spanish diplomacy did not recognize the rebelling colonies, Miralles and, then, Rendón maintained the status of "observers."[49]

Miralles's assistant, Rendón, continued without disruption after the former's death. Like his predecessor, Rendón developed a good friendship with General Washington.[50] His invaluable reports to his government helped weigh Spain's decision to declare war on Great Britain. Rendón, as did Miralles, kept the Americans informed about the covert aid originating in the Spanish empire. Thus, although not formally proclaimed, Spain was a friend to the colonies.[51]

A good portion of the initial aid was transported through the Spanish port of New Orleans. The governor of Louisiana, Luis de Unzaga y Amezaga, who served from 1770 to 1777, ran a cautious administration that was adept at placating a French-American town recently taken over by Spain. He became a close and trusted friend of Virginia's agent, Oliver Pollock. Unzaga and Pollock set the stage for Bernardo de Gálvez's more noted efforts for the American struggle west of the Alleghenies.[52]

The governor and captain general of Cuba, Diego José Navarro, played a key, somewhat controversial, role in Spain's Caribbean activities. All Spanish aid, monetary and otherwise, generally had to be coordinated from Havana under his authority.

Navarro's resolve in the face of the Gálvez family's influence must be considered brave, even though history has shown that his fears for Havana were unfounded. While defending Havana, working with the French, and taking the offensive in the rest of the Caribbean and Central America, Navarro had to abide by a policy with regard to Florida and Louisiana about which he had doubts.[53]

The man behind Spain's contribution to the success of the independence of the United States is the man who agreed to send George Washington two mules: Carlos III, the king of Spain. Of all the eighteenth- and nineteenth-century Spanish Bourbon kings, Carlos III was by far the most enlightened, energetic, respected, and liked by his subjects. He loved the outdoors and the hunt. His slender, long-necked, small-headed appearance made him look a little unregal, especially when he smiled.[54] He was well read and informed. Nor was he provincial, for he had lived in and ruled the newly independent kingdom of the Two Sicilies for twenty-five years before becoming the king of Spain. Although he was not a fan of democratic principles, Carlos III (See plate 4.) was an enlightened and benevolent ruler who had an uncanny knack of surrounding himself with intelligent ministers, and then demonstrated his confidence in them by allowing them to govern. His reign still brings fond memories to the Spanish.

Under Carlos III, the home administration benefited from the annual treasure fleets. The local economy showed upward trends in almost all the provinces on the peninsula. Even Carlos III indulged in the good times. He built a new royal palace, among many other buildings, in Madrid and expanded his winter palace in Aranjuez. He and some of his ministers sat for a couple of official portraits executed by a young Spanish artist named Francisco Goya. (See plates 7 and 22.)

Nor was Carlos III unaware of some of the early leaders in the British colonies. He knew of Benjamin Franklin before the famous American ever arrived in Paris. The king's youngest son corresponded with Franklin.[55] Carlos III was a man who cared primarily for his country, but he was also a person who, as Bernardo de Gálvez wrote to Patrick Henry, was concerned about other peoples: "All the world knows of the generosity of my Sovereign and that his principal interest will be the glory of having facilitated his aid to a nation in need."[56]

Aranda, Spain's ambassador to Paris, was not as enthusiastic about the credit Spain would receive in return for its aid when he wrote to Carlos III in 1783 about the newly created United States of America. He predicted that the new country would grow into a world power and conveniently forget the help it received from France and Spain to get started.[57] In Spain's case, Aranda projected correctly. Spain's contribution to the birth of the United States deserves an acknowledgment as profuse and sincere as that which George Washington gave to King Carlos III for the gift of the two mules.

Spain's participation in the United States bicentennial commemoration, and the quincentenary anniversary of Christopher Columbus's first voyage, have begun an awareness of the reality of Spain's crucial role in the birth of the United States. United States independence, as we know it today, probably would not have happened without Spain.

ONE

From Defeat . . . and Victory, to 1777

I believe you will be able to see their resolve.

Anonymous Spanish observer
to Don Felipe de Fonsdeviela y Ordeano,
the marqués de la Torre, 1776

adrid, the geographical center of Spain, hardly looked like a major European city in 1759. Established as the seat of government in the sixteenth century by King Felipe II, the capital grew slowly on a mesa above the Manzanares River and then around a town square called the Plaza Mayor. The maze of narrow streets seemed to have no purpose. Madrid appeared to be a town that no one wanted to accept as the capital of Spain.

In that year, Madrid became the seat of a new king, Carlos III, the second son of Spain's first Bourbon monarch. He would bring rapid change to the capital and the empire.

Carlos III grew up in Naples where he ruled for twenty years. Upon the death of his half brother, who had been king of Spain, he sailed from Italy to inherit his new position, with more than a few Italian advisors and a head full of enlightened ideas. His solid record in Italy hinted of a new era for Spain, unlike, it seemed, the rule of his two predecessors to the throne. Carlos III was received without protest, although eventually his Italian advisors came to be disliked.

Carlos III was a king who instilled trust in his subjects. When he left Naples, the people came out in mass to cheer his banner-bedecked armada as he departed for Spain. (See plate 6.) The scene was befitting a world leader or, more to the point, a beloved man who had just become king of an empire that extended around the world.

However, not everything went well, for the new king almost immediately committed Spain into the Seven Years' War as an ally to France. The war was already lost and Carlos III's decision did not change the outcome but only humiliated his new country. He nevertheless fulfilled Spain's commitment to a treaty of alliance between the related ruling families of Spain and France known as the Bourbon Compact.

Now, in 1763, he needed to announce that the war had ended and peace had been achieved. The king knew that royal proclamations could be a cause for public celebration. The people did not need much of a reason to join in festivities, for almost anything would do to divert attention from the humdrum passage of daily life. Besides, although Spain was on the losing side of the war, the king could rationalize that he had added to his empire a vast new territory known as Louisiana. And, although he lost Florida, he retained Havana, which previously had been lost in battle.

The proclamation was read in public, not in Madrid's Plaza Mayor but in a new royal park called *Buen Retiro,* which was short for the "Good death of Christ." Perhaps because the war never really hit home, but was fought in distant lands, the people did not feel ambivalent about celebrating a conflict that had been lost. After all, if anyone in Madrid bothered to think about it, or had enough information at their disposal to consider this newly proclaimed peace, they could have rationalized that the cost of peace was relatively small. So celebrate![1]

Even while the people mulled over the new peace, the king and his advisors were ferreting out the lessons of the recently completed war and planning for the next confrontation. Great Britain had taken some Spanish territory and had moved into other Spanish domains. Worse, Spain was too weak to defend itself throughout its vast empire. The victorious British were in a position to flex their commercial and military strength without opposition. Spain's problem in the Americas was exacerbated because France, the ultimate loser of this recently completed war, was no longer a major factor. With the exception of a few holdings in the Caribbean, France lost all of its New World possessions. This left Spain and Great Britain as the major competitors for American territory and trade.

An obviously weak Spain needed time to strengthen itself as well as to develop a policy with which to deal with Great Britain. Spanish colonies would need to play a role by becoming more efficient for the mother country. Above all, time was needed.

This concept of time, specifically the patience necessary to take advantage of time, was a lesson that Carlos III learned from the Seven Years' War when he hurriedly committed his unprepared country. He would prepare his country for the next war with more patience.

France became a problem, for that country had been the big loser. After some initial success, Great Britain's naval strength and larger colonial population proved too much for France. The French wanted revenge and patience was not a part of their national attitude. Spain would have to deal with its impatient neighbor and ally on the diplomatic and familial levels. The Bourbon monarchs would have to cooperate closely.

Unexpectedly, some of Great Britain's American colonies entered the scenario. Britain had expended a great amount of energy and money protecting its colonies during the Seven Years' War. Like Spain, Great Britain wanted its colonies to help pay the national bill. This led to resentment and eventually rebellion in thirteen of its colonies. Neither France nor Spain had expected the rebellion and both found it initially confusing, as well as a potential opportunity for the fulfillment of their plans. At the same time, Great Britain's problems would be an enticement for haste on behalf of France. Spain would work harder to stay focused on its goals, which initially were to recoup territory lost during the earlier war.

In the eighteenth century, Spain's losses to Great Britain included the Floridas, the island of Minorca in the Mediterranean Sea, and Gibraltar. Meanwhile, France wanted to reclaim its lucrative fishing enterprises off the Newfoundland and New England coasts, and wanted to regain a foothold on its lost holdings in India.

For the most part, Carlos III wanted his country to regain its leading status in the world community. To do this he would continue to build on the reforms of his father and brother, who had begun to reverse the downward trends they inherited from the Habsburgs, who had ruled Spain up to the beginning of the eighteenth century. Since 1702, the Spanish army had undergone reforms based on the Prussian ideal of a military force. Now Carlos III concentrated on his army in Spain while initiating preparations for reform of his forces in the Americas. In total, he had the largest land fighting force in the world, but it was debt-ridden and dispersed over Spain's extensive territories.[2]

To achieve his goals, he needed to reform his own bureaucracy, change the medieval attitudes of his people, and turn Spain's overseas possessions into lucrative colonies. The colonies, especially the Americas, were a key to turning Spain around.

If the Americas ceased to be a drain on Spain's economy and could meet even a portion of its potential, the colonies would pay for Carlos's reforms as well as pay for some of the expenses caused by Spain's European entanglements. When that happened, Spain would be ready to start building its strength in anticipation for the conflict everyone expected.

As Spain embarked on its rejuvenation, dealing with Great Britain as a future enemy while reforming the colonial system became a key part of the strategy. To correct the economic deficit in the Americas, Spain needed to eliminate Great Britain's presence, including Great Britain's legal wood-cutting operations and settlements, as well as its illegal smuggling activities in Spanish territory. British raiding and smuggling were most proficient in the West Indies including the Gulf of Mexico, and the Caribbean Sea from the gulf coast of Florida through the west coast of Mexico, to the tip of the Yucatán Peninsula and south, to include Guatemala. Spain's plan was quite simple. They had to recoup all that the British had taken as part of the settlement in the Treaty of Paris in 1763—in Florida, the West Indies, especially, and along the Mississippi River. This plan was a matter of national security.

Kingston, on the island of Jamaica, was among Great Britain's lucrative and legal holdings. Other West Indies possessions included the island of New Providence in the Bahamas and trading rights on the Mosquito Coast along the west coast of Honduras.

Great Britain also had designs on solidifying its colonial holdings and maintaining the claims of the colonies along the east coast of North America that their western borders extended across the continent. Such claims conflicted with Spain's possessions, which included Louisiana, a territory that began at the west bank of the Mississippi River. Thus, British subjects and soldiers had moved into the Ohio River Valley, the lower Mississippi River, the Floridas, the Mosquito Coast, Río Tinto in today's Honduras, and as far south as the Platte River in Argentina. Smuggling was pervasive and costly to Spanish trade within the Spanish colonies.

In Guatemala alone, estimates indicate that as much as half of the export value in trade was being lost annually to illicit activities.[3] By 1770, even Spanish settlers on the Mississippi were buying and selling from British "floating stores" that had bypassed Spanish New Orleans. The new English settlements at Natchez and Baton Rouge on the Mississippi River became centers of British smuggling. Furthermore, British smugglers operating out of Portugal's colony of Brazil and along the Río Plata were reaping untold profits at Spanish expense.

Spain correctly suspected that Great Britain had plans to capture New Orleans. As a result of the Seven Years' War, Great Britain secured the free navigation of the Mississippi River as well as its east bank. The proximity of British settlements at Pensacola and Mobile in British West Florida, as well as Baton Rouge, Manchac, and Natchez heightened Spanish anxiety. British General Thomas Gage, stationed in New York, planned to move on New Orleans, but a 1770 conflict over the Malvinas or Falkland Islands interrupted the scheme.

Although long neglected by Spain, the establishment of French and English naval stations in the Malvinas resulted in a quick Spanish protest through diplomatic channels. France acquiesced but Great Britain refused to abandon the islands. A Spanish contingent from Buenos Aires landed near the English base in June 1770 and forcibly evicted the intruders. This set off a wave of diplomatic activity that distracted the Spanish as much as the English.[4]

In addition to loss of money, Great Britain's New World presence caused problems with Spain's Indian relations. British subjects, also anticipating conflict, actively tried to subvert Spain's Indian alliances. This was of great concern to Spain because such activities disrupted the stability of the involved areas.

Obviously some kind of strategy was needed, for Great Britain had to be dealt with immediately, while Spain needed time to strengthen its own economy. Spain could not prevent Great Britain's intrusive tendencies. Areas would have to be identified, local leaders assigned, and policy established to train militia and troops to defend those areas. In addition, Spain needed to reestablish and maintain its traditional Indian alliances. To do this, they needed to make contact with the Indians and keep an accounting of British activities among the various tribes. Importantly, if war broke out, strong alliances among pertinent tribes could be crucial.

An emphasis on naval power was implicit and significant in all of Spain's strategy, for without it the army was useless. Great Britain, which had a large and modern navy with innovations such as copper-plated hulls that made the ships move faster, could overwhelm either Spain or France, if they did not increase their naval power. Neither of the allies could defeat Great Britain by itself. On the other hand, the term defeat was an illusive concept. None of the principals could defeat the other, in the sense that the military strength of one country or the other was so advantageous that it could invade the other and beat it soundly. Besides, such warfare was a waste of resources. Rather, war was waged on the diplomatic table where countries used various influences, including military, to maneuver themselves into an advantageous position. The number of ships-of-the-line, eighteenth-century battleships, determined how powerful the military card would be. At the end of the Seven Years' War, Great Britain had all the advantages, but this would be changed considerably if Spain and France teamed up. Great Britain's advantage could even be overcome with time.

Great Britain had some weaknesses as well. Primary among these was its economy, for an enormous national debt had been compiled during the previous war. The colonial contribution, or lack of aid, was an obvious target for Great Britain's ministers in their search for revenues. They knew, for example, that in 1763 and 1764 the American customs service cost nearly four times as much as it collected. Such hard financial facts, combined with the less than sterling performance of colonial troops during the war, made the colonies a prime target for British corrective action.

Great Britain had to send troops to the colonies to fulfill William Pitt's strategy of winning the war at home by stressing the colonial frontier. Like Spain, England wanted to shore up its economy by making the colonies pay off through revised policies and more efficiency. Unlike Spain, some of Great Britain's motives seemed to be punitive, or so it appeared to the colonials. British favoritism for its "Sugar Islands," the West Indies, also rankled the northern colonies.

Members of Parliament and the government in London did not hesitate to express their opinions that the colonial effort during the war was less than enthusiastic. England had trouble recruiting colonial troops; they encountered colonial suspicions, a lack of cooperation among the different colonies and, in their estimation, a very poor grade of soldier. All this perplexed the English. British General James Wolfe described his American Rangers at Quebec as "the worst soldiers in the Universe."[5]

A series of laws, codes, and appointments followed, and these only alienated the colonies. British incomprehension of their own people in the Americas led to the point where the mother country declared its subjects in open rebellion, closed all the colonial ports, and sent troops, including paid Hessians, who were hired from the area of Hesse in what is today Germany, to occupy the recalcitrant colonies. Great Britain's attempt to strengthen itself created an opportunity for its enemies to move back up to the competitive table, for its colonial troubles not only tended to offset its naval strength, but also drained resources which provided France and Spain with that valuable luxury of time.

France did not share the colonial concerns of Great Britain and Spain, for it lost its large land holdings and was quickly losing its taste for colonization. France's secretary of state for foreign affairs, the comte de Vergennes, had a young king to advise in Louis XVI. Like the rest of his countrymen, Vergennes dearly wanted to embarrass Great Britain. France would go to war with England less as a quest for gain than for revenge for past indignities. Unlike most of his countrymen and his king, Vergennes understood that a huge amount of work and effort would be necessary to prepare France for a confrontation with its enemy. France's economy could not afford the expenses required. Vergennes, for example, needed to completely revise the shipyards. France's bureaucracy would have to gamble that when the time was right, it would have reduced its debt enough and built its strength to succeed. Hopefully, the spoils of victory would repay the country for its risk, through increased trade from India, the Spanish territories and, possibly, the former English possessions. As England's problems with its American colonies became more obvious, Vergennes believed that American trade would be France's great gain, and it would be at the expense of Great Britain.

To succeed, Spain's help would be needed. As the French ambassador in Madrid wrote to Vergennes, "Be sure, Sir, that in whatever manner France is dragged into the war, Spain will follow."[6] And, after France entered the war and lost an anticipated element of surprise, Vergennes himself expressed to his king a similar thought. Although by then, Spain again agreed to fulfill the Bourbon Family Compact and had given assurances that France could count on Spanish support, France and the rebelling colonies had to pay. Spain always anticipated entering the conflict, but proved to be much more adept at holding its cards.

With the transfer of Louisiana to Spain and the loss of Florida to Great Britain, Carlos III's patience was tested from the beginning. Florida, more properly called Las Floridas after Great Britain established two colonies (East and West Florida), was a daunting loss. Spain's desire to control its trade and destiny in the West Indies dictated that the Floridas be part of the empire. Otherwise, foreign commerce and settlement would be a severe threat to Spanish enterprises. The importance of the Floridas was all too obvious to the participants in the mercantilist world. "I am certain" that the English want the coasts of Florida, "not solely for defense against their enemies but for offense," wrote Juan Joseph Elegio de la Puente, a Spanish observer, in 1777. He added that the Spanish territories would be held hostage "beginning with Louisiana."[7] In a separate letter on the same day he argued that with possession of the Floridas, Spain would control the whole gulf coast from Florida to Mexico thus gaining sole possession of both banks of the Mississippi River and its navigation. Spain also would gain control of the Bahama Channel, a key sea passageway into the Gulf of Mexico between Florida and Cuba.[8]

In Spanish minds, it was clear that the acquisition of Louisiana made Florida important. On the other hand, the new territory of Louisiana needed to be secured, and here the policy of patience became the rule. Louisiana's population was mostly French or some variation of French, with the addition of various other types of people, mostly merchants and adventurers who came down the Mississippi River from the North American interior or from other parts of the world via the high seas.

The three thousand inhabitants, most of whom lived in New Orleans, did not easily accept Spanish administration. Indeed, it was not until Louisiana's second governor, Alejandro O'Reilly, an Irishman turned Spaniard, arrived with two thousand troops and suppressed open resistance in 1768 that the populace accepted Spanish rule. Although he executed five rebellious leaders, his suppression was not overly harsh for the time. Nevertheless, O'Reilly's hard-nosed success, in part, earned him the nickname "Bloody O'Reilly."[9]

Foreseeing such problems, Carlos III vacillated before accepting the colony. The populace in New Orleans did not know about the transfer of sovereignty for a year and a half after the Treaty of Fontainbleu, which was signed on 3 November 1762. They were not told until October 1764, and the first Spanish governor did not arrive until 5 March 1766, three years and four months after the treaty.[10]

Until the administration of Louisiana's third governor Luis de Unzaga y Amezaga (1709–1791), the primary concern was establishing Spanish authority. Great Britain made no secret of its plans to expand down the Mississippi River to open up western trade through New Orleans. As elsewhere in the Americas, Great Britain's unabated aggressive commercial and military policies concerned Spain. Spain did not openly react to the British threat until the 1770s.

Ironically, Spain decided to do something about Great Britain's arrogance and aggressiveness at about the same time as the British colonies became impatient with their mother country. From this moment, Great Britain would be engaged in a series of global confrontations, which forecast a less than positive future.

In March of 1766, the Spanish secretary for the Council of the Indies, the governmental body that oversaw the Americas (Indies), sent a packet to the captain general of Havana containing some information originating in London about an English spy. A British agent, who was a French citizen named Pottier, had been dispatched to the Spanish colonies to collect intelligence. If found, he was to be arrested.[11]

In the same month, Madrid sent another letter in which England's trouble with the colonies appeared severe enough for Carlos III to want his subjects to "be on alert for any incident and to proceed with caution."[12] All of this did not come as a complete surprise, for Fray Balío Julián de Arriaga, the minister of the Indies, had warned the conde de Ricla, the captain general of Havana, six months earlier. Arriaga also instructed Ricla to prepare for possible trouble. The king ordered Arriaga to make sure that the various governors of the colonies maintained discipline and caution to avoid any surprises from the English, "even though there is no motive for suspicion in this a time of peace."[13]

Also, commensurate with the rise of Spanish concern for British intrusion and designs on its territory, Spanish officials began receiving news of discord between Great Britain and its colonial subjects. Spain still saw the British American colonists as British subjects, and suspect. So a breach in the British colonial system, if true, did not necessarily mean that the colonials had stopped being British. On the other hand, the breach could be an opportunity for Great Britain's enemies. But there was the possibility that as the "rebels" or "foreign Americans," as they were sometimes referred to in Spain, became serious about their complaints, they might not pose as much a threat to the Spanish colonies as they had before. Again, Spain would proceed with caution and try to avoid surprises.

In 1768, the captain general of Havana followed a policy of forbidding free access to Spanish ports. Specifically, British ships were to be discouraged from entry into the ports. If entry was a matter of necessity, such ships would be allowed to dock, but the stay was to be "as brief as possible." All foreign subjects would be extradited.[14]

Spain already understood that there was a difference between the English and the Americans. British colonials had been trading in the Caribbean. The English colonies had learned to subvert the British mercantile system through their own illegal activities in the West Indies.

As the breach between Great Britain and its colonies grew, Spanish subjects easily and, it seems, without hesitation, reported a growing rift between the *realistas* (royalists) and rebels. The Spanish government suspected the rebels even though they wanted them to succeed.

The strategic location of New Orleans at the mouth of the Mississippi River and as the Spanish capital of Louisiana became key to Spanish strategy. The elderly Luis de Unzaga y Amezaga was assigned to take over from the brash O'Reilly as governor of the vast, if sparsely populated, Louisiana. O'Reilly, who was sent to Louisiana as a short-term governor to suppress resistance, had done his job well. A new type of disposition was needed to govern in New Orleans's complex situation. Unzaga waited to assume command until O'Reilly departed in March 1770.

A better appointment could not have been made at a more opportune time. Unzaga had to win the confidence of an unruly population, especially the French Creoles, while reconciling between his own government's policies and a pending rebellion of the English colonies.[15]

Unzaga's administration lasted through six key years from 1770 until 1777. His actions were unspectacular but wise. For example, he prudently allowed the indulgence in contraband and illegal trade, for the revenues were important to the citizens of his capital. Frankly, he came to realize, along with his own government, that such trade, especially on the Mississippi River, would benefit the English colonies and not Great Britain. As might be discerned from the British subjects passing upriver to British territory, as well as the establishment of forts at various locales in West Florida and on the Mississippi River, Great Britain still had designs on Spain's new colony. Great Britain gained a foothold by establishing settlements on the banks of the Mississippi opposite Spanish settlements. This caused concern, for here was visual confirmation of Great Britain's plans. Unzaga and his agents kept close watch on what was developing.

In 1771, Unzaga reported in some detail that fifteen families from "la Carolina" had arrived at the new British settlements. The families had traveled downriver from the Illinois country on a *piragua*, which in this case was a long boat, powered by oars.

Another fifty families were expected. Unzaga received the information from the captain of the boat.[16]

These new settlements and the question of their legality concerned the Spanish. Settlements in proximity to New Orleans were an affront to Spain. Unzaga and his superiors correctly understood that Great Britain was establishing a presence that would eventually lead to British navigation of the Mississippi River. The situation was important enough for Unzaga's reports to be forwarded through Havana and on to the king's minister in Spain. And always, Arriaga wrote back on behalf of Carlos III that the court wanted the situation closely watched.

Nothing could be done, for the new settlements had been established on land given to England in the 1763 Treaty of Peace.[17] These establishments, initially two of them, were Natchez and Baton Rouge, both upriver from New Orleans. Manchac, which would become British, was a Spanish fort in 1771.

West Florida became a proclaimed haven for British loyalists who had left the rebelling colonies. Along with their African slaves and those British subjects and merchants who had been there before, these new settlers populated the British settlements. The settlers did not appear to be doing anything illegal, wrote Unzaga, but they posed a threat. Unzaga, no doubt, permitted trade with the settlements under his policy of tolerance.[18] Presumably, the trade provided a conduit for the information he passed on to Spain. Anticipating problems, Unzaga recommended that New Orleans improve its fortifications.[19]

Minister of the Indies, Arriaga, and the new captain general of Havana, Don Felipe de Fonsdeviela y Ordeano, the marqués de la Torre, acknowledged Unzaga's concern, but nothing could be done to impede these settlements. The settlements, they noted, were on land ceded to Great Britain as part of the Floridas. The English governor of Pensacola, the major port and city of West Florida that had belonged to Spain, oversaw the whole British operation on the Mississippi River. Arriaga clearly expressed Spain's position when he wrote that having the potential enemy as neighbors certainly was "not convenient to the interests of the king," but that "there is nothing to do but keep track of things."[20]

As Unzaga settled into his job, he seemed to become more comfortable with the situation and to be more selective about whom he would permit illegal trade. The English population in New Orleans was anything but loyalist. British regulations worked to their detriment and they were trading illegally and contrary to their own government's interests. In short, they sided with the people who would soon lead an open rebellion in the thirteen colonies.

One of these West Indies' merchants was a native of northern Ireland named Oliver Pollock. Pollock left his native country to move to Philadelphia in 1760, but he did not stay long; two years later he was working in Havana where he became a successful West Indies trader. He operated independently and made enough money to purchase his own vessel. In 1768, Pollock moved to New Orleans where he continued to be successful, eventually purchasing a plantation and other lands. In New

Orleans, he apparently endeared himself to the Spanish as well as befriending his compatriot, Alejandro O'Reilly. He also became a trusted friend to the elderly career man, Unzaga. Pollock helped with the seemingly perennial problem of keeping the Continental troops supplied, by drastically undercutting the current inflated prices to sell needed items like flour to the Spanish government.[21] In the course of his life, he became a fierce patriot working for the birth of the United States of America. Unzaga recommended him to his successor as a "faithful and zealous American in whom you might repose implicit confidence."[22]

Unzaga learned from people like Pollock that he could take some liberties with his government's policy to work with the Americans. But, like many others in the Royal Service, Unzaga understood the policy of patience. So, while biding time to allow Spain to repair, especially in places like New Orleans, men like Unzaga were also shaping policy.

The king's ministers repeated the desire to maintain peace. Usually the first points made in their instructions to various officials dealt with the ideal of keeping the peace. Then the emphasis of that particular correspondence followed. Somewhere between the official policy and reality, some discretion was granted to the local official. As the rift between the British colonies and England grew, Spain came to realize that Great Britain's problem was real and serious. Spain came to depend on the judgment of its officials in the field.

Unzaga was the ideal man for his position. He was a seasoned, intelligent official. While he could befriend and work with men like Pollock, he could also refuse American requests to protect their ships from seizure by British ships. The assumption that such ships were protected in a neutral port while on the Mississippi River would not hold up under international law. However, he had no problem discouraging British trade in his colony while covertly accepting American contraband. He changed during his six-year administration as he became more friendly to the American rebels.[23]

New Orleans and Louisiana bordered Mexico, then called New Spain. The province was "face to face to the kingdom of Mexico" wrote Arriaga.[24] Along with the Floridas on its other side, Louisiana made up the north shore, or rim of the West Indies. The captain general of Havana administered the whole area. While he shared concern for the activities of the British, from Jamaica to the Floridas and on the Mississippi River, he also had to be concerned with the rest of the area under Spanish control, especially Havana, the most important city and port of them all.

No one had more concern for the defense of Havana than the naval officials. Any siege of the key port meant a direct naval confrontation. Now less emphasis was being put on defending the city, in lieu of a developing wartime strategy to avoid confrontations. But, when war came, the strategy was to attack Great Britain's forces and possessions throughout the world. This strategy would thus force Great Britain to spread out its forces and overextend its defenses.

The officials in Havana worried. Fear of an enemy attack on Havana was the time-honored and deep-seated basis for all strategy in the area. Navy commander José Solano wrote that Cuba was a key to the communication "with various parts of the king's domain in these West Indies."[25]

Havana had been seized by Britain in the Seven Years' War. Now, British activity in the Floridas not only threatened New Orleans and New Spain, it also posed a threat to Havana. The city, as might be imagined, was a little more sensitive about foreign activity anywhere near its fine harbor. As early as 1766, the policy of discouraging foreign ships from entering Spanish ports spread to other Spanish ports in the theater. Unzaga received such instructions in New Orleans. In this case, foreign meant British and the message was clear—close the ports to their shipping. If a British ship entered a Spanish port the local governor was instructed to seize the ship and return the crew to the closest British port. In addition, all the expenses incurred were to be charged to Britain. The expenses would be presented to London through proper channels. Above all, they were not to trade with foreign ships or let them return to their homeports with certain enumerated cargoes such as hard specie, which meant gold or silver.[26]

To help enforce this strict attitude, as well as prepare for an eventual declaration of war, Unzaga received orders in 1771 to arrange for the formation of a militia in New Orleans. He was to create twelve companies, three of which would be stationed in New Orleans. The other nine companies would be assigned in "the province's districts."[27] Unzaga built on the work done by O'Reilly, for the officers had already been selected from an "inspection" held the previous December. Carlos de Grand-Pré had been named assistant commander of the militia, with lieutenant's pay.[28] Unzaga used the opportunity of forming a militia to help placate the French Creole population; many of the officers he appointed were Frenchmen who became Spanish subjects when Spain took over the colony. In addition, most French would naturally serve Spain because Great Britain was France's main enemy. Many would serve bravely in the upcoming hostilities.

Meanwhile, news from the English colonies forwarded from New Orleans continued to please Spanish officials. Madrid learned as early as March 1766 that the "instability" of the British colonies might lead to some fighting, and even a break from England.[29]

Even misinformation filtered through Unzaga's office. In 1772, the governor received word that New York had been attacked, which did not happen.[30] Nevertheless, Spain was keenly interested in what was happening in England's colonies, and the West Indies became a conduit for news from the north. For example, the new captain general of Havana, the marqués de la Torre, received enough information to compile a fairly detailed account of the Battle of "Bancans," or Bunker's hill. He sent the report, dated 12 October 1776, to the newly appointed minister of the Indies, José de Gálvez, who had replaced Arriaga.[31]

The report included Torre's source material, two letters written by an anonymous Spaniard, probably Puente, living in British-held St. Augustine, East Florida, and two letters from governor Unzaga. The information had been sent from St. Augustine and New Orleans from July through September.

The anonymous informer unwittingly repeated the mistake of misnaming the battle, Bunker's Hill. The battle actually took place on Breed's Hill just south of the namesake locale. The mistake demonstrates that the error of the name had its inception very early after the battle. Nevertheless, he was fairly accurate in other details. The Americans made a grand defense, but lost the battle and suffered three hundred casualties. They killed ninety-three British officers and more than one thousand enemy soldiers were killed or wounded. The actual numbers were 441 patriot casualties and 1,044 British soldiers killed or wounded. He then gave a description of the British forces, listing their numbers and makeup. He noted, "[T]he major part are Russian, Prussian, and German (soldiers) with some Scots and Highlanders." He concluded that under the experienced command of General Lee, the Americans will defend their liberties. If the English go south into Georgia, the informant continued, they will have trouble from the Indians. And, in Charleston, the British will meet "Americans who will make a stand in a weak defensive position," but, he speculated, "I believe you will be able to see their resolve."[32] He was right, for Charleston was successfully defended.

Unzaga added, from New Orleans, that the British were transferring their forces to add troops at Pensacola, New York, and Halifax, and were moving toward Charleston. His sources reported that seven thousand (actually it was three thousand) British troops were being transported by sea to Charleston. He added that he was receiving frequent information, some of which came from Charles Lee of Virginia. Unzaga chose not to comment on the rebels' resolve.[33]

American representatives of England's colonies, specifically Charles Lee, second in command of the Continental army and in charge of the forces in the south, had been corresponding with Unzaga. With the approval of Virginia's committee of safety, which sent an endorsement along with Lee's letter under the care of Captain George Gibson, Unzaga received a request for aid in exchange for colonial help in retaking various English settlements from Manchac north to the Ohio River and then overland via the "Montrepas" and "Gontchatren (Pontchartrain)" lakes to take Mobile and Pensacola, thus neutralizing Britain's power in the area. Lee, who wrote in French, requested a commercial alliance.[34]

George Gibson, whom Unzaga described as a "captain in the first regiment of Virginia in the service of America," presented two questions in writing to Unzaga. Would the king of Spain, "His Catholic Majesty," desire the "acquisition of the town and harbor of Pensacola" and would he "receive possession" of the town and port from the Americans?[35]

Unzaga responded with two letters. He wrote to Lee that he could not grant a commercial alliance without permission "from my sovereign." He reported that he had forwarded Lee's request to Spain and assured the American general that his own desire to comply and facilitate aid would result in a positive response. Unzaga did

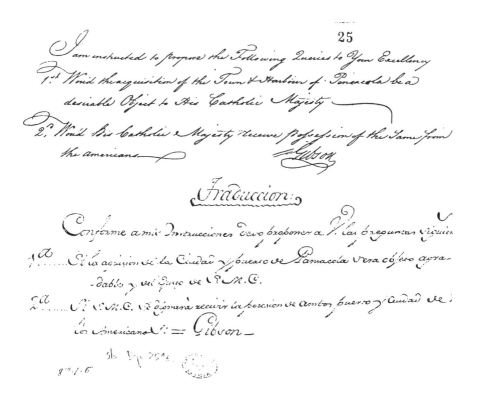

Fig. 1. George Gibson to Luis de Unzaga y Mazaga, Spain's governor of Louisiana (1770–1777). The letter asks two questions regarding colonial cooperation with Spain in taking British held Pensacola. Original in legajo 2586, Santo Domingo, Archives of the Indies, Seville.

indeed endorse the request to José de Gálvez. Unzaga was especially keen on the idea of receiving Pensacola, for with that port in Spanish hands, the British would no longer impede passage from the Gulf of Mexico "to whichever other nation." In his mind, the port of Pensacola had more significance than utility.[36]

Although Unzaga probably was unaware of it, Torre endorsed his assessment in a letter to Gálvez a week after Unzaga had written. Torre wrote that he could not stop British shipping in the channel along the Florida coast. Among other things, the ships provided supplies to the Indians.[37]

Spain's neutrality was at issue here. Spain, and Spaniards, could not overtly impede British ships dealing with Indians in British territory. Nor could Spain actively participate in a siege of Pensacola or any other British establishment that was located in British territory. On the other hand, trade for supplies, if properly handled, was a real possibility and, if the Americans wanted to give Pensacola to Spain in exchange, then the risk was worth the price. According to Unzaga, the Americans planned to conduct a campaign against the British establishments on the Mississippi River and attack Pensacola in the spring of 1777.[38]

After six years experience in New Orleans and a strong friendship with Oliver Pollock, it is no wonder that Unzaga looked favorably upon Lee and Gibson's overtures. Pollock understood and appreciated the Spanish position, so when Gibson arrived with Lee's letters, he was the person who first received the American officer and his men. Pollock also arranged the meeting between Gibson and Unzaga. He translated the English letters to Spanish, and translated during the meetings, for neither Gibson nor Unzaga could speak or read the language of the other. This task was not as simple as it seems, for Pollock had to mask the fact that Gibson, Lieutenant Linn, who was his second in command, and fourteen men were members of the rebel forces—by pretending they were merchants. The group floated down the Ohio and Mississippi rivers from Fort Pitt in Pennsylvania.

By late August or early September, just months after Gibson and his men left Fort Pitt, Unzaga decided to help.[39] Pollock later stated, "Unzaga privately delivered to me gunpowder from the king's stores . . . which I delivered to Captain Gibson." Pollock paid for the powder with a draft dated 21 September 1776 and drawn on the Grand Council of Virginia for 1,850 "Spanish milled dollars."[40]

Thus, within three months after the colonies had declared their independence from Britain, Lieutenant Linn and an American contingent, now bloated to over forty men, departed New Orleans destined for Fort Pitt. Their boat was loaded with nine thousand pounds of gunpowder, stashed in ninety-eight kegs. They traveled upriver to "Arkansas Post," a Spanish establishment where they spent the winter and received another load of supplies before they continued their trip. On 2 May 1777 they arrived in Wheeling, Pennsylvania with their important cargo.[41]

Meanwhile, in New Orleans, Unzaga placed Captain Gibson under mock arrest to avoid suspicion. New Orleans, as was well known, had many British informers. Unzaga "released" the captain along with a Captain George Ord whose vessel had been seized by the British. The two were dispatched to Philadelphia on a ship that Pollock had secured. Not surprisingly, more supplies, including gunpowder, had been stashed on board.[42] Unzaga's action could not have been more timely or pertinent, for during the first two and one-half years of the revolution only the colonial ability to import gunpowder kept them going. The colonies, through their respective governments and through the Second Continental Congress, acted quickly to increase the supply of powder. Local manufacture was not enough. Unzaga's timely shipment saved Wheeling and Fort Pitt from British capture. Without those key bases of operation, George Rogers Clark could not have succeeded in his campaign of 1778 in the Ohio River Valley.[43] Pollock noted that the shipment "was a signal and seasonal supply."[44]

Although the Spanish were not as quick to jump to conclusions as Great Britain's King George III, who stated as early as November of 1774 that "blows must decide whether they [the colonies] are to be subject to this country or Independent,"[45] the Spanish hoped that the rebels were as determined as they sometimes appeared to be. Three years later, Spain's government had no doubt. José de Gálvez addressed the Council of Castile at roughly the same time Pollock and Unzaga were conspiring to supply the Americans. Gálvez did not hesitate to say, "Let us establish indirect and secret intelligence with the American colonies, inspiring them to vigorous resistance."[46]

Unzaga soon received word that Havana would be the base of operations for supplies destined for the rebelling British colonies. Most of those supplies would go through New Orleans and he should begin by shipping whatever surplus he had on hand. In direct reference to the requests of Lee and Gibson, as well as the action already taken by Unzaga, the king wrote his approval and directed that his government follow a policy of cautiously providing secret aid. Spain would pursue the goal of helping the Americans secure their independence. Corresponding instructions were sent to Havana.[47]

By December 1776, Unzaga learned that his long and productive term as governor of Louisiana had come to an end. The young thirty-year-old nephew of José de Gálvez had been appointed to replace him. Unzaga was ailing and had served in the Americas for forty-one years. He brought to New Orleans an efficient administration and maintained calm during the birth of the American Revolution. He could not have prepared the way any better for his successor. Unzaga's final acts in Louisiana were indicative of his good preparation, for he recommended the new governor, Bernardo de Gálvez, to that "faithful and zealous American," Oliver Pollock, and to Gilbert Antoine de St. Maxent, a native of France, citizen of New Orleans, successful merchant, and father of Gálvez's future wife, Félicité de St. Maxent d'Estréhan.[48]

TWO

Posturing Early: The Spanish Lakes and South America, from 1776

. . . the haughtiness of the squadron commanders and governors of their possessions, leaves no assurance about their good faith.

Julián de Arriaga to the conde de Ricla, 1764

*A*t about the same time that Bernardo de Gálvez received his appointment as acting governor and then governor of Louisiana,[1] Spain began to confront Great Britain in a series of global actions. The Spanish government had been chafing at Great Britain's aggressive commercial and military policies for years. The Seven Years' War only exacerbated the feeling, for Great Britain was a poor winner. Perhaps, everyone hoped, the pending confrontation would put an end to such affronts.[2] Spain became more concerned over Great Britain's manifestly anti-Spanish policies. Meanwhile, Great Britain's policies with its own colonies became more troublesome and seemed, to some colonists, to be increasingly intrusive. The year 1776 was crucial for both the Spanish and the colonists.

While remaining calm enough to avoid doing something so rash as to declare war, Spain adjusted its policy to a semi-covert system of simultaneously checking and resisting British expansion and aggression at several points throughout the world. As it had in Louisiana, this new attitude became obvious in the Caribbean. Spain also used the time to try to win diplomatic concessions, such as the return of Gibraltar.[3]

The Caribbean Sea, with all its islands and bordering landmasses, was one of two bodies of water that made up the West Indies. Spain traditionally used the lucrative area for its trade possibilities, natural wealth, and global influence. The Spanish essentially pictured the area as its own, two bodies of water, the shores of which had belonged to their country since the sixteenth century. At first, Spain managed the area from the central location of Hispaniola, which later became Santo Domingo, and then switched to the influential port of Havana. The idea was simple, even obvious when a map of the area could be seen. The northernmost body of water was the

Gulf of Mexico. It was entered from the Atlantic Ocean to the east through a channel, which ran between the southern tip of Florida and the island of Cuba. The North American continent from Florida to the Mississippi River and on through the present states of Louisiana and Texas formed the northern shore. At Texas the shore dipped south to become the eastern coast of Mexico and the western shore of the gulf. The major port of Veracruz is located on this shore. Mexico's coast turned back east to define the southern edge of the area. This jut east and then north is the Yucatán Peninsula, the tip of which is a short hop back to the island of Cuba.

The Caribbean Sea is actually the southeastern edge of these two bodies of water. The "Caribe," as it is called in Spanish, is separated from the Gulf of Mexico by the Yucatán Peninsula and Cuba. Its western shore is the east coast of the Yucatán Peninsula to the Gulf of Honduras, continuing down the Mosquito Coast, which consists of the present countries of Honduras, Nicaragua, Costa Rica, and Panama. The southern boundary is made up of the coast of the isthmus to the South American continent and its northern coast. The city and port of Cartagena is located on this sea's southern boundary on the coast of Colombia, which along with the neighboring Venezuela was referred to as *la Tierra Firme*. A series of small islands dropping down from the major islands of Cuba, Hispaniola, and Puerto Rico formed the eastern boundary. These islands are known as the Leeward Islands for the northern group and the Windward Islands for the southern group.

The Spanish-held islands of Cuba and Hispaniola bordered both bodies of water. Their central location dictated that their major port cities of Havana and Santo Domingo be the seats of government as well as centers of trade. They were the commercial conduits for Spain's greatest source of wealth in the eighteenth century.

From the Mexican port of Veracruz, silver from the rich mines of north central Mexico, along with the rich trade originating in Asia and brought to Mexico on the so-called Manila galleons, sailed through the West Indies on its way to Spain. In Portobelo, on the northern coast of today's Panama, the natural wealth extracted from the mines in Peru and Bolivia was loaded on ships for transport to the mother country. Cartagena was the entry into Peru via land. All the bountiful benefits, such as sugar, coffee, cocoa, wood, new medicines,[4] and dyes traveled through this important area. The West Indies also became a crucial leg in the three-pronged exchange that involved sugar, rum, and slaves.[5]

Ironically, the original goal of Columbus was to sail west to the Indies, meaning the East Indies. Instead, a continent blocked the way and Earth was a lot larger than he expected. This did not prevent England, France, and Spain from searching and competing for a more direct western route to the Orient. Not until the expedition of Meriwether Lewis and William Clark[6] in 1805 through 1806, under the auspices of the United States, did Europeans and their American descendants realize that a direct water route to India, Columbus's old dream, just did not exist.

Nevertheless, that dream paid off with a variation for Spain. Spanish galleons sailed from New Spain and Peru to the Philippines and the port of Manila. The ships

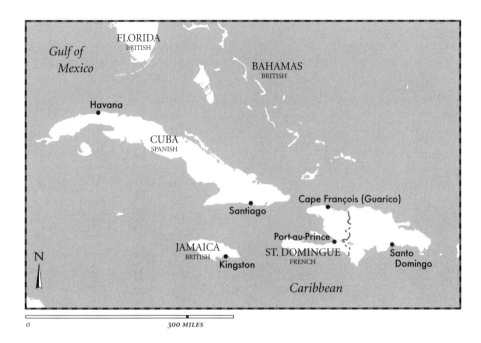

Fig. 2. The West Indies.

returned to the Mexican port of Acapulco where the goods were unloaded and shipped overland, through Mexico City to Veracruz. The "treasure fleet" sailed from Veracruz to Spain, laden with the wealth of American silver mines and East Indies material goods. Many times these fleets stopped in Havana, which had become one of the richest, if not the richest American city. In addition to the obvious trade, Havana could credit a lot of its success to contraband. Oliver Pollock successfully started his career in Havana. He operated independently and certainly not as a subject of Spain, although by the time he had befriended Unzaga he counted himself a citizen of New Orleans. Illicit trade in the West Indies was rampant and it was not limited to one nationality.

Spain, France, Great Britain, and the Netherlands[7] had bases of operation in the West Indies. None officially permitted trade with the others, and Spain, by act of discovery and early exploration, felt that it had the only legal rationale for being there. Things changed through the years. War and diplomatic nuances resulted in the unquestioned legal presence of these nations. Kingston, on the island of Jamaica, provided the English with a good base of operation; like Havana, the British port provided good access to either the Gulf of Mexico or the Caribbean Sea. From Kingston, Great Britain controlled the Floridas and thus controlled good access through the Bahama Channel. Great Britain also had possession of the Bahama Islands, with the major island and settlement of New Providence, which are located

Fig. 3. The Leeward and Windward Islands.

off the east Florida coast and at the entrance of the channel that bears their name. As an indemnity from the Seven Years' War, Great Britain secured timber-cutting privileges in Central America. The lucrative Spanish trade moving through the area was too rich to be avoided and now the British used their possessions to start moving into the Yucatán Peninsula, the Gulf of Honduras, and the Mosquito Coast.

As was evident in Louisiana, Spain kept a close eye on British actions. Many of the letters of warning and caution sent to Louisiana were also meant for other officials in the West Indies. Julián de Arriaga's 1764 warning to maintain discipline and take precautions to avoid any surprise from the British came out of a realistic appraisal of the British in the West Indies at the conclusion of the Seven Years' War. "Although there is no motive," he wrote,

> for the English to commit any hostility in this time of peace [the] arrogance with which they continue to dispute the interpretations in some of the arti-

cles of the treaty and the haughtiness of the squadron commanders and governors of their possessions, leaves no assurance about their good faith.[8]

And the naval concern, as expressed by José Solano, that Havana was the important key to the defense of the West Indies, including New Spain and *la Tierra Firme*, fairly accurately summed up Spain's attitude.[9]

At stake were some of the richest and most populated cities in the New World. Havana, Cartagena, and even Mexico City were larger, wealthier and, in many ways, more advanced than any of the English New World cities in the cold north. Kingston, because of its commerce, possibly was more important to Great Britain than Boston, New York or Philadelphia. And even less argument would ensue over the relative importance of Great Britain's West Indian trade relative to the troublesome and costly North American colonies.[10] Within the context of the Americas, Spain's renewed determination and, as shall be seen, its ability to resist, would force the British government to make some hard decisions about the relative importance of the American colonies. At the time, Great Britain was having enough trouble with the North American colonies. This was a fact that the conde de Aranda would stress during negotiations in 1778.[11]

Aranda worked as Spain's ambassador to France and thus was in a key position to conduct the diplomatic business of Spain with France and England. By the time he was appointed to Paris, Aranda had served a long career. Born in 1719 in Sietamo (Huesca) Spain, the young Pedro Pablo Abarca de Bolea spent most of his formative years in Italy where his father pursued a career as a military officer. At the age of seventeen years, he left school to join the army and within four years rose to the rank of captain while serving in Italy. He fought in the Italian campaigns in the 1740s and was gravely wounded in 1743. He then returned to his native country, receiving a number of positions such as ambassador to Portugal and to Polonia, governor and captain general of Valencia and the prestigious position as the president of the Council of Castile, the most influential political body in Spain. He also spent some time traveling through Europe, and officially retired from the military in 1758. Above all, he was a military man by vocation and profession. He believed in the Bourbon reforms sweeping Spain under Carlos III and gladly helped his king try to consolidate power by expelling the Jesuits in 1767. He helped maintain calm in Castile when opposition to the reforms began to surface. He also helped found the Masons in Spain.[12]

Despite his apparently successful career, Aranda was somewhat of a liability. The handicap of his personality created rivalries for him. One of these people was the minister of state, the marqués de Grimaldi. Aranda at times appeared to be insecure and contradictory, but when he made up his mind he could be very difficult, even explosive. He was known to take the most insignificant question of discussion and use it to turn the conversation into a laborious and ungracious task. Carlos III, who appreciated his loyalty and genius, is reputed to have said about him that, "the count was more obstinate and stubborn than an Aragonese mule."[13]

His appointment to the ambassadorship in France was a reflection of his complex persona. Grimaldi did not want him around Madrid, yet because of his influence and contributions, he could not cast Aranda aside. Sending him to Paris answered the problem perfectly. The appointment would at once exile him, and force him to give up his military and political influence for diplomacy. Aranda accepted the appointment to begin his new career. In the end, he proved Grimaldi wrong, for Aranda would parlay his ambassadorship into a promotion to Grimaldi's position. Nevertheless, Aranda could not change his style and his major contact in the French government, Vergennes, said of the impetuous Aranda: "I have negotiated with the Turks and in this there has been enough said, for although it is true, I have never seen anything like this ambassador."[14]

For the duration of the conflict, Aranda remained the Spanish ambassador to France. Other government officials came and went, but Aranda persisted. Most of the information filtering from London, either common or public knowledge, or from private sources, passed over his desk on its way to Madrid. He was privy to the history of England's desires and Spain's concerns in the West Indies. He was probably aware of the earlier episode when a little over a year after Arriaga had expressed his and the king's distrust of the British, word from London reached Madrid that the British had dispatched Pottier, a Frenchman and resident of Granada in Venezuela, to spy. He was sent on the British ship *The English Parliament*. The plan was to have him travel through the Caribbean and along the coasts of *la Tierra Firme* to "create maps and form intelligence." The London letter also stated the obvious; there could be no doubt that Great Britain had designs on the South American coast.[15]

Within a month after the letter had been written, Carlos III informed his minister of the Indies. Arriaga, in turn, copied the letter and his king's comments and sent them, with instructions for the governor of Havana to share the important information in the letters with whomever he felt pertinent. Everyone was to watch for this individual who had become a British spy. If he was found, he was to be arrested and interrogated, for his majesty was anxious to receive the information.[16]

Great Britain's action was not surprising, even somewhat expected, for at the same time Arriaga sent out instructions for Pottier's arrest, he also mailed the instructions in which everyone was to act carefully and without hostility toward the British. By all means everyone must maintain the appearance of peace and harmony. Of course, this occurred within a couple of years after the loss of the Seven Years' War and Spain still needed time to reorganize.[17]

Spanish policy became more aggressive as administrators began to question the legality of British establishments throughout the empire. Did the Peace Treaty or any other treaty grant Great Britain permission to set up settlements on the Central American Coast and environs?[18] The question no longer was a matter of if, or when, these settlements would be set up. They were being established and Pottier's mission left no question about what Great Britain intended. Unfortunately, Pottier, and others like him, gathered information because Spain's necessity to buy time to strengthen itself gave Great Britain an opening. Following unofficial policy, British subjects moved onto the Mosquito Coast. British maps clearly indicated that Spain's future enemy had collected a lot of accurate information about the Caribbean Sea and Gulf of Mexico.[19]

Upon observing a 1775 map, Aranda deduced that in Jamaica, Britain had the perfect location to direct all the commercial traffic, legal or otherwise, in that part of the world. In his report, Grimaldi added that the major consequence of British settlements on the Mosquito Coast is that they eventually will be able to expand and influence "Mexico, Havana, Yucatán, Honduras with Portobelo, Cartagena, and Caracas, and none more exposed to them than the stretch of Panama so they can separate [corte] the two Americas." The outspoken ambassador continued to predict that the British could accomplish the splitting of the Americas and, perhaps, their other goals within ten years, although, he noted, some had predicted fifty years. He agreed with some prognosticators that Great Britain's ultimate goal was Panama, for from there, the British could accomplish anything.[20]

The question of legality was cleared up. Aranda and Vergennes met over the issue, initially at the request of the conde de Quines, the Spanish ambassador to England.[21] In 1775, Aranda was so sure of the legalities and of Great Britain's plans, he unhesitatingly predicted that an English expedition would be sent to the isthmus. The expedition would not be official, for "that would be an unjust provocation and formal declaration of war." Great Britain, he pointed out, does not need war because of its colonial problems. Therefore, they will claim ignorance to any Spanish protest about the expedition. They will answer that they have not authorized such a foray and that Spain "proceed to extract whoever these aggressors are."[22] Matías de Gálvez, in Guatemala, later noted that Great Britain could cover up its activity with its legal Mosquito Coast activities. The only obstacle left for Great Britain would be to win over the local Indians, for they had always been a major problem for river travel on the San Juan.[23]

Here was food for thought. The isthmus at Panama gave Great Britain access to the Pacific Ocean. Of all the European countries, Spain was the only one sailing across the Pacific and benefiting from its trade and natural wealth. Great Britain's ally, Portugal, traded in the East Indies, but like England, used the traditional route around Africa to get there. With British control of Panama, one of two things could happen. Goods could be shipped overland from the Pacific to the Atlantic seaboard, or was Aranda referring to the eventual possibility of a man-made waterway? In either scenario, England would be an unwelcome competitor of Spain's for the Oriental trade. This development would impact Mexico and the West Indies as well as severely change Spanish revenues at home. But, Great Britain needed to take control of Panama, either through war or illegally. Because of other problems, Great Britain was no more ready for war than Spain, so the latter of the two options could be expected.

During the middle of 1776, Spanish attention seemed to be turning toward the area of Nicaragua and Guatemala. Perhaps there was a twofold reason and perhaps the concern was deep-seated and therefore occurring almost unintentionally. Even the newly appointed viceroy of New Granada, Manuel Antonio Flores, writing from across the Caribbean at Cartagena, appended his concern for the area when reporting Lieutenant Gastelu's voyage of inspection. He commented on his correspondence with the president of Guatemala and the governor of Nicaragua in which he suggested that they should check the San Juan River, its fort, and the settlements of Trujillo and Omoa.[24] He felt that the British could have more in mind than settling the coast and expanding to Panama. If they intended to divide the two continents with a convenient water-land route, then Nicaragua would be a natural place, for, as Flores demonstrated, Spaniards were familiar enough with the terrain to know that it would be a prime candidate.

In fact, Spain had studied the possibility of digging a canal for years. King Carlos I had the area surveyed in 1524. He was especially interested in utilizing the San Juan River. The idea was simple. If ships could sail up the San Juan to its origin at Lake Nicaragua, then there was the matter of digging a canal from the lake to the west coast and the distance of "a little more than four leagues." The actual distance of approximately eleven miles did not seem insurmountable.[25] This passage was considered the easiest of all possible routes, including cutting a canal through Panama. Furthermore, because theoretically less work would be necessary, the task could be more easily disguised.

Because neither country had a desire to enter into war at the moment, Spain, which had been preparing for almost twelve years, could afford to take a stronger stance versus Britain. Carlos III and his ministers shared the desire that Spain would not lose its overseas colonies to Great Britain as had happened to France. Along with Aranda's concern for Panama, there was an equal fear for New Spain (Mexico), for even without the Oriental trade this was a wealthy colony. To protect against an attack by sea, which would come at Veracruz, the king ordered Lieutenant General Juan de Villalba y Angulo to strengthen his forces and build a fortress that would protect Mexico City should the defenses at the port fail.[26]

Spanish governors and military officers filed numerous reports of British activity in the second half of 1775. Englishmen employed Mosquito Indians for six months of the year to catch tortoises for their shell. Black slaves were being used to help in the enterprise.[27] The whole Mosquito Coast operation was being planned from London, although that would not be officially acknowledged. The British intended to establish some influence close to Cartagena,[28] at that time the key to the northern and western coast of South America. By getting close to Cartagena, the British could then establish ties with their Portuguese allies in South America.

In late 1775, Viceroy Flores received two letters from Arriaga, both dated on the same day. The first reiterated that the British settlements were conscious acts. London was actively pursuing the matter of expanding into Spanish territory. Flores needed to act. Therefore, the king wanted an expedition sent out to locate the intruders and evaluate their strength so plans could be made to stop them. Arriaga added that supplies would be sent to help stop these illegal activities. The second letter supplemented the first, for it instructed the governors of all the affected territories to help Flores gather information on the British intruders.[29]

Flores answered that, per his instructions, he would send Don Manuel Guinior to investigate and locate the British positions where they were prejudicing the Indians or subverting trade.[30] He also suggested that the king should notify the king of England of this illegal activity. Maybe with such a complaint, the governor of Jamaica would take action to "correct such a scandalous disorder between friendly nations."[31] Flores thought the problem would be solved much easier at the national level in Europe. His superiors knew better.

By February of 1776, responses to the instructions started returning. The Spaniards easily located the British.[32] Now something needed to be done, for Spain could not permit this obvious affront, which became even more apparent when Flores commissioned two *balandras,* sloops named the *Pacífica* and the *Recurso,* to inspect and chart the coast from the Gulf of Darién north to Honduras. Navy Lieutenant Don Antonio de Gastelu commanded the expedition. He kept a diary of the journey in which he reported that he had no trouble at all encountering British people in Spanish territory. He sailed on February 27th and by the end of April he had spotted one Dutch and three English ships. He also located some Englishmen on the Mulatas Islands, and entered the Río Tinto where he found more English ships, plus many settlers with slaves and supplies from Jamaica and London. He captured one of those ships, which had supplies for war and agriculture.[33] These last supplies were apparently destined for the Mosquito Indians.

Flores was aware that the British seemed to be concentrating on the area and suspected that they were resurrecting Spain's old plan, and the reports indicated that he was right. The governor of the province of Costa Rica told of British settlements at the Río Negro and next to a place called El Piche. This last site had African slaves, plantations, mules, and horses. One of the leaders was a man named Robert Hudson.[34] Another Spanish official from Comayagua wrote that the British had set up "immediately next to our possessions," as was well known, at the Río Tinto and the town of La Cribe.[35]

Spain's government needed to do more than acknowledge the many reports coming in. Again, the officials seemed more concerned for Guatemala, which included Nicaragua and its surrounding areas. Replies back to the officials in the field reiterated that they should strengthen their own defenses, closely watch the British and be prepared for surprise attacks. The governors were encouraged to try to figure out ways to counter British attempts to win over the Mosquito, Zambo, and Mosco Indians. The crown added that it would need to know of any additional intrusion and, if possible, how to take action to stop this illegal action. The various governors had permission to act against intrusion.[36]

Flores knew that activity in Guatemala was further from his domain than if Britain's goal was actually Panama. As he read the various reports, including Gastelu's journal and another Royal Order to keep watch,[37] he took some time to write two letters, one mailed to each of two superiors, Arriaga and José de Gálvez. Arriaga received a standard analysis of the British activities along the Mosquito Coast. Flores emphasized their increasing influence among the Indians.[38] Gálvez, however, received an extended and more detailed letter, for as minister of the Indies, Gálvez was Flores's immediate superior. Flores repeated the information he shared with Arriaga and then went on to add a statement about the lack of military readiness in his viceroyalty. He had a "fixed regiment but on foot" and all the boats in Cartagena had been reduced to two frigates, which were small warships usually carrying between twenty and sixty cannons on a single deck, three *balandras* of war (meaning that they are armed), and one small merchant boat. (See plate 8.) Militia could supplement the troops, but supplies were very short.

In fact, no offensive of any kind could be mounted without additional supplies if the enemy's strength was as reported by Gastelu. At that moment, Flores reported, the British could easily cut off Spain's coastal fortifications because of their superior naval strength in the area.[39] The man who had suggested that something be done at the national level was now reporting that virtually nothing could be done at the local level.

Apparently, Flores was unaware that Spain had decided to be more assertive, although not through diplomacy. Another flash point of British activity was in South America around the Río de la Plata in Uruguay and south toward Buenos Aires in Argentina. With their Portuguese allies, Great Britain had become very aggressive in setting up illegal posts and trade. So while Arriaga and José de Gálvez received reports from the West Indies, they also were mulling over the problem of British aggression under cover of the Portuguese. At stake in this region were the rich Andean silver mines. A canal through Central America would take a lot of time and effort, a minimum of ten years, according to Flores. The threat in South America was more immediate, so the government decided to deal with that problem by concentrating on the Portuguese. By doing so, Spain felt that a strong message would be sent to the international community. Spain had strengthened its forces and was ready to actively resist aggression throughout its empire. Spain not only felt ready to act, but also knew that Great Britain was overextended.

The Spanish government did not simplify matters when the Council of the Indies sent out a change of policy. Henceforth, they would allow trade with France in all Spanish ports. However, trade with the English and Dutch was forbidden.[40] This 1776 policy, in effect, acknowledged that France was an ally in Spain's clandestine confrontation with Great Britain.

To further clarify matters, Carlos III consulted with "his nephew," King Louis XVI of France, to determine which West Indies ports would be involved in direct trade and to make arrangements as to which ships would transport what. The issue of which ports would allow residency of French ministers was also negotiated. Hopefully, this new arrangement would help curb contraband trade, while instilling a feeling of cooperation among the allies, to the detriment of Great Britain.[41] The new policy brought the two Bourbon allies closer together and muddied the waters for British spies.

Aware that Great Britain could not acknowledge its illegal operations, Carlos III and his ministers decided to launch a full-scale attack on the Portuguese and British establishments in South America in 1777. They planned in great secrecy, placing the whole operation under the command of Don Pedro de Cevallos. Cevallos's expedition was described by Francisco de Saavedra as "one of the best organized and best provisioned enterprises that has been prepared in Spain."[42]

The armada left the port of Cádiz on 13 November 1776 with over nine thousand men in one of the largest fleets ever to sail to the Americas. The fleet included seven ships-of-the-line, eight frigates, four smaller ships, and many transports, which carried fourteen infantry battalions and four cavalry squads.[43]

Great Britain was warned not to interfere, because this was an affair between Spain and Portugal. Spain gambled that Great Britain would remain neutral. Aranda's argument that the British could not afford war because of their colonial problems was the basis of Spain's assertiveness. To make sure, London was told that any interference could be reason for a declaration of war, for Spain was trying to defeat some illegal merchants and correct some Portuguese affronts, neither of which had anything to do with Great Britain.[44]

While the large fleet sailed into the south Atlantic, another squadron sailed up the Iberian coast to make a point with Portugal and its pro-English, anti-Spanish minister of state, Sebastiao José de Carralhoe Mello, the marquís de Pombal. The Spanish squadron entered the Tajo River and anchored in front of Lisbon. Pombal, who actually ran the Portuguese government, hid his surprise and anger, doing the only thing he could do. He received the Spanish officers with full decorum. Nonetheless, the point, if not the insult, had been made.[45]

The more important part of the strategy was the armada heading to the Río de la Plata. Cevallos's forces achieved brilliant success. They moved down the Brazilian coast smashing British smuggling operations and then took Uruguay from the Portuguese, thus securing the Río de la Plata and the city of Buenos Aires. Great Britain could do nothing to oppose Cevallo, for as predicted, care had to be taken not to allow this to grow into a full war. Great Britain needed time and, coincidentally, was distracted when its thirteen colonies declared independence.

The move was bold and calculated, for Carlos III did not want war any more than did the English Parliament. He did want to negate Portugal,[46] which had become a staunch British ally, and he wanted to make a gesture indicating that Spain's passivity could not be assumed any more.

Spain's actions to the Río de la Plata were not what Viceroy Flores desired or expected, but Spain's actions were successful. With the military action in South America, Spain put Great Britain on the defensive for the first time in living memory. As in a great chess match, Flores's part of the board was left unattended to execute a move elsewhere. The movement of the forces into the South Atlantic possibly could explain his lack of supplies, ships, and men.

Although no one in the West Indies would learn of the success of Spain's bold move in South America until the second half of the following year, 1778, they all were aware of the action. As a result, a greater burden fell on these officers and government leaders to maintain an even stronger vigilance. The success in the south would trigger a renewed vigor for expelling the British in Central America, while the revolution in North America continued to open options to Spanish strategists.

Meanwhile, the local officials had to take care of their own business. In February of 1777, Pedro de Carbonell, the governor of Panama, issued instructions to Lieutenant Colonel Don Francisco de Navas to sail up the Mosquito Coast and inspect the English settlements. Navas was to determine the strength in fortifications and troop numbers. However, Navas's long instructions, amounting to sixteen pages, emphasized that the goal was to contact "El Rey," the king of the Mosquito Indians, to develop a friendship and alliance that would separate the Indians and their trade from the British.[47]

The Caribbean would not be forgotten, nor would the idea that Great Britain might attempt to create a canal. This was obvious when, in 1778, Spain learned that a British naval captain presented a plan to use the San Juan River and Nicaragua Lake as the basis of a transcontinental waterway to the Bay of "Papagayos" and the South Sea. The report quickly attracted the crown's attention in Spain and was forwarded to the West Indies with instructions to inspect the feasibility of the idea.[48] The king's concern resulted in renewed energy toward the expulsion of the British from Central America.

THREE

Independence and the Common Foe

... to communicate, treat and conclude with his most Catholic Majesty, the King of Spain ... a treaty ... for the just purpose for assistance in carrying on the present war between Great Britain and these United States.
Congressional appointment signed by John Hancock,
president of the United States Congress, 1777

... each according to their interest.
The conde de Aranda to Grimaldi, Paris, 1777

*O*n 2 July 1776 the Second Continental Congress passed a motion that had been proposed by Richard Henry Lee a full month before. The resolution read, in part, "that these United Colonies are and of right ought to be free and independent states." Two days later, the Congress passed a second resolution that expanded upon the first. The second declaration of independence eloquently states the colonies' philosophical position and cleverly listed the failures of the British government. The colonial representatives laid every grievance at the feet of King George III and did not place any blame with the Parliament. The declaration was a culmination of ideals first expressed six months previously by Thomas Paine in his essay titled *Common Sense*. Until Paine's essay the colonists had appealed to the king and blamed Parliament, but Paine correctly argued that the king had sided and even sanctioned Parliament's devious action. Monarchy itself, he asserted, was an absurdity and one honest man was worth more to society and God, "than all the crowned ruffians that ever lived."[1]

Obviously, support of this attitude was not the reason for either France or Spain to ally themselves with the rebel cause. Vergennes would end his career in disappointment when he came to realize that his policy of supporting the colonies gave birth to a revolution in his own country that destroyed both the government and king he loved dearly. The declarations of independence were reported in the Spanish press as news of little interest. *La Gaceta de Madrid* ran two articles, in August and

September, in which notice was made of the event.[2] The colonial choice of words and their audacity probably raised some Spanish eyebrows, for the Spanish government, as well as the press, knew the colonies' earlier position. In fact, the appeal in which the colonials petitioned King George III and the Parliament, denying that the latter body had any authority over them, but nevertheless agreeing as a matter of expediency to submit to Parliament's acts for the colonial regulation of trade, seemed a much more logical position to the Spanish press.[3]

In another petition from the Second Continental Congress, the rebels suggested to George III the idea that Englishmen in America and in England should be able to retain their brotherhood in loyalty to a common king while maintaining separate parliaments or governments. The same petition accused the sitting members of Parliament and the prime minister as "being those artful and cruel enemies who abuse your Royal confidence and authority."[4] All these petitions implied a threat of separation while maintaining hope for reconciliation. Spain and France observed the situation and did not find most of the colonial activities philosophically or even politically objectionable.[5]

As has been demonstrated, Spain had no illusions about what was happening in the English colonies. By the time the colonies declared independence, fighting had gone on at Lexington, Concord, Boston, and Charleston. Fighting for independence actually began before the declarations and Spain kept abreast of the conflict.[6] Not only was Spain keeping informed, but it also quickly contributed to the cause, and followed a policy of helping the insurgents prior to any knowledge of the declarations of independence. Unlike any other European country, Spain also engaged in conflict with British subjects and a British ally in its 1776–1777 expeditions to South America and Portugal. Without an official treaty of allegiance or a declaration of war, Spain participated in the conflict very early on the side of the colonies. Eventually, France formally recognized the upstart colonies and Spain declared war on England.

Each of the two major countries and the Americans who eventually joined forces against Great Britain had its own agenda. Each had to give something up and only one considered independence for the colonies a top priority. This goal, of course, belonged to the colonies. From the beginning of the war the colonial leaders knew that their goal of independence would succeed only as a part of a grand international conflict that involved diplomacy, expenditures, and fighting beyond the home front.

Unlike the radical Thomas Paine, the new country's leaders quickly backed off from openly stating the idea that a monarchy was absurd, for they needed to attract aid from governments that had kings. Some of the patriots even hoped to establish a monarchy in the new country they were struggling to form. These men knew that both Spain and France had an interest in extending aid to the upstart colonies. They also had some ideas as to why. The Seven Years' War left a legacy well known to the Americans. They knew that France, a traditional foe of England, hoped to regain some of its losses if not its prestige.

Colonial merchants had been trading in Spain's ports and those of other countries throughout the West Indies. Spain's desire to secure Florida and thus its hold on the Gulf of Mexico was painfully obvious, for that also meant closed navigation of the Mississippi River. The United States wanted free navigation to stimulate Western trade as well as growth. Spain saw western expansion from the English colonies, whether they were independent or not, as a threat to its own territory, which stretched from the Louisiana Territory through Texas and New Mexico to the just-settled far western area called Alta California. In a note to his grandson, Benjamin Franklin demonstrated his comprehension of Spain's position vis-à-vis the young United States.

> Should Spain be disinclined to our cause from an apprehension of danger to her South American dominion cannot France be prevailed on at our request and assurances not to disturb theirs to guarantee to that Crown her Territories there against any molestation from us?[7]

Spain wanted terminal limits on the United States' territorial claims and to achieve that goal would close the Mississippi to free navigation and recover the Floridas. In short, Spain expected a confrontation with Great Britain for its own reasons. The intent was to recoup all that had been lost in the Treaty of 1763 and to retain what had been gained.[8] George Gibson's letter of inquiry about Spain's position, relative to retaking possession of Pensacola in West Florida if the American rebels succeeded in capturing the port, resulted from colonial knowledge of what Spain desired.[9]

France wanted to replace England as the primary trading partner of the former colonies. Vergennes and his royal master also hoped to regain the fishing rights that their country had before the Seven Years' War. They needed to restore Newfoundland and France's old possessions around the Gulf of St. Lawrence.[10]

Europe was another matter, for the recent war had broken a traditional balance of power between France and England. As Great Britain's prime minister, William Pitt well knew that France, through the use of the Bourbon Family Compact, intended to regain an equal position of power in Europe. The compact meant that France would attempt to become an integral European player, with Spain's aid.[11] This was a goal totally oblivious of American independence, save for the opportunity to weaken Great Britain.

There was no ideological conformity among the allies: the reformist Spain, a revengeful France, and the rebelling English colonies. They shared a common foe and each country in its own way sought to break the advantage that Great Britain had gained. On Spain's behalf, there was a royal commitment from Carlos III to restore the country to the respectability and grandeur of yesteryears.[12]

The colonials knew exactly what securing aid for the maintenance of their revolutionary war would entail. There was no illusion. Congress would have to consider the objectives of both France and Spain, because France would not commit without Spain's backing.

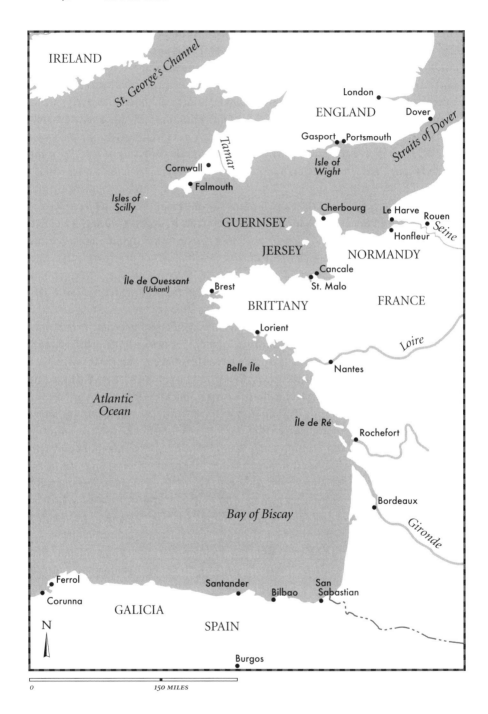

Fig. 4. The Coasts of England, France, and northern Spain.

On 29 November 1775, seven months prior to the declaration of independence, the Continental Congress set up a Committee of Secret Correspondence with the task of seeking and receiving foreign aid. This committee was fairly successful, for it dispatched Silas Deane to Paris where he arrived on 7 July 1776. The committee also sent George Gibson to New Orleans where, as noted, he successfully received enough Spanish supplies to save Forts Pitt and Willing from defeat.[13] An added benefit came back from Madrid. A Royal Order dated 24 December 1776 instructed all the responsible officials, including the governors of Havana and Louisiana, to quickly supply the *"Americanos"* with what gunpowder and rifles or muskets, *"fusiles,"* were available. The governors were to ship the supplies on the free merchant ships.[14]

Although the Committee of Secret Correspondence could not receive credit, Grimaldi and Vergennes, the respective foreign ministers of Spain and France, began to work together to form a coordinated allied front in opposition to Great Britain. José de Gálvez's arguments for establishing secret contact with the American colonies to help them divert Great Britain might have entered the equation.[15] Spain's interest in regaining Minorca in the Balearic Islands and Gibraltar required that the Bourbon allies use some diplomatic clout as well.[16]

Grimaldi and Vergennes did agree to further help the insurgent colonies by setting up a dummy company named Roderique (Rodriguez) Hortalez et Cie in May 1776. They also agreed that Pierre Beaumarchais, the author of "The Barber of Seville," would manage the company, the purpose of which was solely to launder money and supplies to the English rebels in America. Both countries contributed an initial million *livres* worth of munitions and supplies to start the company.

As neutrals, neither Spain nor France could openly give aid to the rebelling subjects of a third country. Such an act would be an obvious provocation of war and the time was not right for such a conflict. However, the appearance of a private, non-government related firm doing business was a different matter. If the company's activities were discovered, both countries could disavow duplicity in the operation. Nonetheless, Spain was contributing on two fronts, through New Orleans and Beaumarchais's company, when word of the colonies' declaration of independence reached Europe.

After independence, the colonies did not see a need for continued secrecy, for they had declared themselves a country. Instead, Congress wanted treaties, first with France, a country that the Americans correctly assumed would be most open to their overtures. Along with the already-stated reasons for France's anxiousness, Congress realized that Louis XVI's government would be more receptive simply because France did not have any major colonies. In fact, France had grown tired of the colonial enterprise.

To help Deane with his negotiations, Congress sent two more commissioners to Paris. Arthur Lee, who was in London, and Benjamin Franklin, who was in Baltimore, received appointments to Paris to press for a treaty of alliance with a European country, preferably France, and to secure more supplies. Franklin immediately sailed from Philadelphia and became the senior member of the diplomatic team.

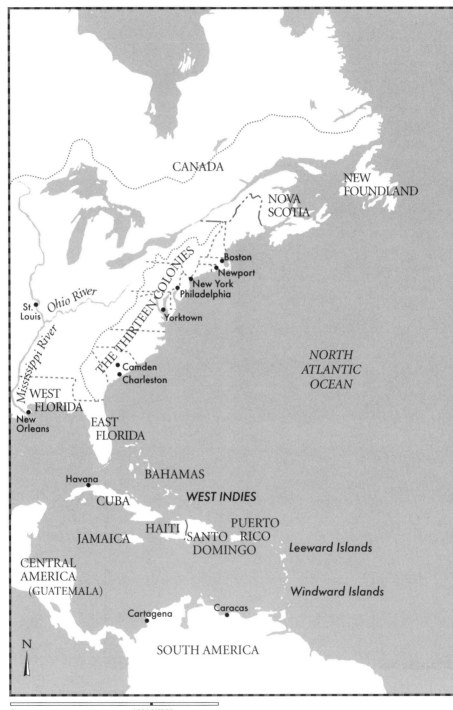

CANADA

NEW FOUNDLAND

NOVA SCOTIA

THE THIRTEEN COLONIES

- Boston
- Newport
- New York
- Philadelphia

Ohio River

St. Louis

Mississippi River

- Yorktown

- Camden
- Charleston

NORTH ATLANTIC OCEAN

WEST FLORIDA

New Orleans

EAST FLORIDA

BAHAMAS

Havana

CUBA

WEST INDIES

JAMAICA

HAITI

SANTO DOMINGO

PUERTO RICO

Leeward Islands

CENTRAL AMERICA (GUATEMALA)

Windward Islands

Cartagena

Caracas

N

SOUTH AMERICA

0   1000 MILES

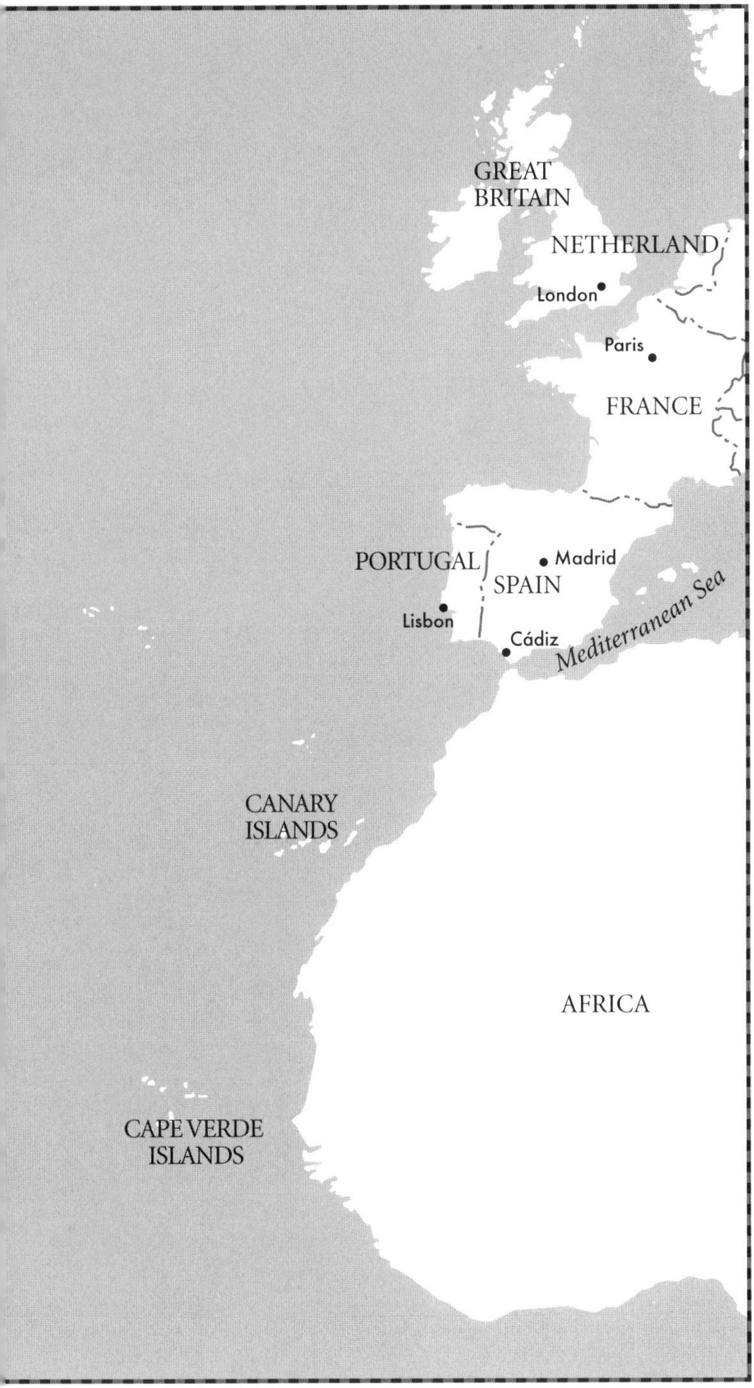

Fig. 5. The West Indies in relation to Europe and America. Adapted from Tuchman, The First Salute.

Franklin had begun an informal relationship in 1774 with King Carlos III's youngest and favorite son, Don Gabriel de Bourbon. Franklin, while in London, fulfilled a request through the Spanish embassy to send the prince a glass harmonica, which the American had recently invented. Franklin also sent instructions on how to play the instrument. Apparently, to thank Franklin, the prince sent Franklin a book that he had translated. The book arrived right after the United States' Committee of Secret Correspondence was formed to attract foreign aid and alliances.[17]

Franklin immediately used the opportunity of the gift to write a letter to his royal friend to thank him and note that their respective countries should be friends.

It seems therefore prudent on both sides to cultivate a good understanding that may hereafter be so useful to both; towards which a fair foundation is already laid in our Minds by the well-founded popular opinion entertained here of Spanish Integrity and Honor.[18]

The new commission with its senior member, whom the Spanish ambassador Aranda always referred to as "Doctor Franklin," entered a favorable environment for their business. Deane, who had been in contact with the French government and with Aranda, was aware of the aid going through New Orleans. At the very least, he knew that both Spain and France had an interest in the Americans' cause.

Aranda anxiously waited to see what proposals from Congress Franklin would bring with him.[19] Now that the colonies formally had broken away from the mother country, diplomacy would become interesting. The threat of England and her colonies settling their differences was not as preeminent as before.

Aranda had advance word of Franklin's appointment and departure for Europe. Although Franklin arrived in France in December of 1776, Aranda became a little bit perplexed when he could not get information about Franklin's overdue arrival in Paris. He suspected the French government of sequestering the American commissioner. This unexplained delay and Vergennes's apparent embarrassment when the high-strung Aranda confronted the French minister in Versailles, increased Aranda's anxiety when he heard of a curious problem involving a shipment of supplies to the colonies. A ship called the *Amphitrite* had embarked from Le Havre "carrying officers and supplies to the Americans." Two days later, the port officials received a ministry letter asking that the supply be detained and, if it had departed, to send a ship in pursuit to order its return. The assembled pilots in the port were unanimous in their reply that too much time had elapsed to catch the ship.

Aranda asked Vergennes about the matter. The answer, wrote Aranda, "left no doubt about the timidity which reigned, and that the manner in which the pending matters with the insurgents was not entirely plain and clear." Could Franklin's mysterious whereabouts be connected to the ship incident? Or, is it possible that France, an ally, had decided to keep the negotiations secret to avoid suspicions and therefore notified Franklin "not to present himself in Paris?" Vergennes replied to Aranda that he did not know when Franklin was expected to arrive and that he was overdue. Vergennes, like Aranda, was waiting.[20]

Actually, Franklin's ship, the *Reprisal,* was diverted from its destination at Nantes and had to anchor in the Bay of Quiberon. Rather than wait, Franklin rented a fishing boat to take him and his two grandsons, William Temple and Benjamin Bache, to Avray, France. From there he traveled in a coach to Nantes, where he arrived on December 7th. Eight days later, he left for Paris, but stopped over in Versailles on the 20th. He entered Paris the next day.[21]

In the meantime, Aranda learned from Grimaldi that the Spanish court was considering "aiding the Americans directly." Aranda, who was still waiting for word of Franklin, scheduled another meeting with Vergennes on Sunday morning, the 20th, to avoid "the countless other people who might get in the way." Aranda pointedly stated that Spain was interested in supporting the colonies and that his country had already contributed one million *tours* pounds. Now that France had solicited Spain for more aid for the Americans, Aranda stressed that Spain should not be "kept in ignorance" of anything pertinent to the insurgents. Furthermore, he added, if France insisted on such actions of secrecy, the Spanish court "undoubtedly . . . was thinking as to how to help the colonies by different means." Spain would act independently if France chose not to cooperate in the sharing of information. Aranda's words got Vergennes's attention, for the French minister divulged that Franklin had arrived, presumably at Versailles, the day before, which would have been December 19th.[22]

Finally, on 28 December 1776, Aranda received a letter from the American commission, announcing that they had been directed by "the united provinces of America to cultivate the friendship of the Courts of Spain and France." They asked to meet with the Spanish diplomat on the next day.[23]

After Aranda learned from Vergennes that he had already met with Franklin, the Spaniard set a time for seven in the evening on the requested day, which again was a Sunday. The meeting would take place after dark at his house.[24] Thus, within the elegance of the Spanish ambassador's residence, Benjamin Franklin, Arthur Lee, and Silas Deane began talks with Spain. The conversation was amiable, with Franklin trying to placate Aranda for the inconvenience his travels had caused. Franklin thanked Aranda for the asylum that Spain was giving American ships in Spanish ports and hoped that the policy would continue. Aranda assured him that there would be no change.

Aranda apparently was a little frustrated because "Franklin speaks very little French, Deane much less, and Lee none."[25] The three Americans offered Aranda nothing new. The ambassador had met with Barbeu DeBourg the previous June in Paris. DeBourg was a secret agent for the American colonies which, at that time, had not declared independence. DeBourg asked for clandestine aid and Aranda used the opportunity to garner information from the colonies. The American agent assured Aranda that he was in direct correspondence with Franklin.[26] Now that the Spaniard was face to face with Franklin, he was disappointed. He told Franklin that he was surprised that his message comprised nothing more than a request for good relationships, "when in the situation in which they found themselves anyone might judge that his coming was directed foremost at seeking aid and soliciting such aid with other proposals dear to the Courts which they sought," when "thus far the Colonies were not peaceable possessors of their freedom." Franklin, no doubt, sharing the shocked reaction of many before him when dealing with Aranda, replied that he had more to propose in a memorial (report), which, at the moment, was being copied. The meeting closed with Franklin's assurance that he had the full powers from Congress to negotiate and treat in all the pertinent matters.[27]

On Saturday, 4 January 1777, Aranda, Franklin, and Lee held a second meeting. Aranda took the liberty of arranging for a translator, the conde de Lacy, the Spanish ambassador to "the Court of St. Petersbourg" (Russia) who was lodging at Aranda's house. Lacy was fluent in English; his presence would help Aranda avoid the pain and frustration of dealing with the Americans' poor French.[28] A long discussion followed, in which Aranda was told that the United States sought a treaty with both Spain and France, "each according to their interest." Franklin did not seem to be fully aware of the aid already being sent by Spain. In fact, he acted as if he were not aware of any aid from Spain or that the colonies had received dry goods, arms, and munitions from the dummy company. Franklin revealed that his priority for the United States was bronze cannons and warships. If need be, he would placate Aranda's apparent displeasure over his hesitation to meet, and reveal his plans with the Spanish ambassador by sending a commissioner directly to Madrid.

In reply, Aranda explained that Spain wanted to avoid all appearances of duplicity, which was why they were again meeting after dark in a neutral country. Spain also wanted to help, but in coordination with France, so diplomatic discussions would be better if held in Paris. Nevertheless, if desired, Aranda would make the proposal to Madrid. Franklin and Lee chose to follow Aranda's lead.

Aranda then invited the two commissioners to ask him whatever else might be on their minds. Surprisingly, they did not ask whether Spain would be willing to help out, the feasibility of securing a treaty, or even information about Britain. According to Aranda, the first inquiry was whether the rumors were true that Russia was going to join the dispute through a treaty of alliance with England. They wanted to know the method by which they could launder "six cargoes" that the Continental Congress had sent to Cádiz, Spain, but addressed to the English business house of Buick and Company. The cargoes were payment for supplies from France. Aranda had no information about Russia outside of "public news in gazettes." On the matter of securing the cargoes, he answered that something could be worked out, "so that justice could be done without delay."[29]

Four days later, Franklin and Lee personally delivered all the papers spelling out their positions. The papers included the promised memorial, which, according to Aranda, only proposed goodwill and reciprocal commerce. Spain needed to work to adapt the proposals and also to make the Americans understand that dealing with the Spanish colonies was the same as dealing with Spain. For example, if Spain opened up commerce in places other than the peninsula, "she would give up her national commerce as lost." Aranda, the mercantilist, realized that trade agreements could be made, but not with Spain's possessions in America.

Aranda, who quickly became an advocate of the colonial cause, also noted to Grimaldi that the Congress "did not wish to come humbly begging." For example, he noted, when asking for warships they offered to pay for them "and want nothing for free."[30]

The Spanish ambassador wrote and conducted himself with the same self-confidence that had irritated some of his colleagues back home. His demeanor also came from a long and successful career, an awareness of position, and his social class. He had scolded Grimaldi earlier for being too timid as the king's minister. At least one historian has credited Aranda's criticism of Grimaldi as the cause for Spain's expedition to South America.[31] Aranda, as he confronted Vergennes and then questioned Franklin, dealt from a strong hand. When France heard about the colonies' declarations of independence, Vergennes proposed a plan wherein France would attack England while Spain could attack Portugal. Aranda relayed Vergennes's idea to the Spanish government. The French quickly backed off from the proposal when they heard that the British had taken New York. France needed Spain's alliance and Aranda, who distrusted the French and expressed his distaste for the Bourbon Family Compact as being beneficial only to France, would be sure to maintain a cautious posture.[32]

In both of his accounts of these initial two meetings with the American commissioners, Aranda's anxiety could be interpreted as curiosity. He was also noncommittal. He was to the diplomatic world of that period what Daniel Webster was claimed to have been to American politics in the next century—intelligent, born to his profession, a staunch patriot, and a totally confident taskmaster.

He mailed both of his reports with all the proper attachments, but he did not limit himself to an impartial review of his diplomatic escapades; he rambled at length venturing his opinion on what Spain should do and why. The idea that diplomats could think for themselves enough to offer different plans of action to their respective home offices is an odd concept today. But before the technological revolution, information took time to get from one place to the next and, on many occasions, related messages passed one another on the high seas or dirt roads, arriving too late to accomplish their goal. Diplomats and other officials had the authority and were expected to act as well as advise.

Franklin's arrival gave cause for Vergennes to raise some of the issues that had been previously negotiated between him and Grimaldi. He, too, was anxious to humble Britain, but advocated a policy of forcing the enemy to make the first move. This was too passive for Aranda, who noted that France, with the acquiescence of Spain, wanted to fake invasions of England, Ireland, Portugal, and Gibraltar by massing land forces at various locations. By doing this, Britain would be forced to counter for each of the possibilities.

Aranda noted that the locations delineated by Vergennes for the invasions of Portugal and Ireland were wrong and the English would know it. A land invasion of Gibraltar was impossible, for everyone knew the rock must be seized by sea and that any invasion of the British islands must involve a serious buildup of sea forces. The mere presence of troops in France or Spain, without ships, did not pose a threat to England. Therefore, Aranda postulated, the expenditure to feint such attacks would not be worth the effort. Besides, he questioned France's grasp of reality. This plan, the problem of Franklin's mysterious arrival, and France's anxiety for entering into war for no real delineated reasons save a desire to ruin Britain, raised questions for Aranda. He understood "that there is a struggle between the knowledge of what should be practiced by a Power like France and the brevity of her actual spirit sustained by the hope of private conveniences."

France, he felt, believed it would gain solely through the colonies' independence, because then France would gain all the trade, which would benefit that country's West Indies ports as go-betweens. Aranda recommended that Spain should develop its own plans, help the colonies for good reason, and then France would have no choice but to follow along.

The only true course was not to pick at England and hope for colonial independence, but "to destroy England forever, for it would be an insurance against future dangers." An opportunity to accomplish this, he felt, has not come up in centuries and may not happen again. Spain, unlike France, can act as a solitary country with full awareness not to drag Austria, Prussia, Russia, Denmark, and Holland into the conflict. Spain should devise its own plans that include France, but not wait for France, which, in turn, is waiting for a provocation. Opportunity must be grasped. France, the enthused Aranda wrote, "tries to dissuade Spain from the coldness it accuses her of; and likewise does not share information so as to keep her ready to take advantage of her for its own ends and urgencies."

Spain has more at stake in this confrontation than France. Just the "immensity of possessions to guard in America" is enough to interest Spain. The two Bourbon sovereigns, united in a common cause based in reality, have an opportunity to correct a major problem now.[33]

Aranda wrote a second letter on the same day. He apparently wrote it after he took some time off to develop his thoughts. He had devoted most of his effort to France's position and reasons why Spain should take the lead. Now, he wanted "to explain to the king the present picture of the Monarchy, and that of his future interests."

Spain must focus on what is hers, for after the success of the revolution of the British colonies, Spain will "remain alone, hand in hand with another Power in all that is *tierra firme* in North America." Aranda had no doubt that Spain would share the continent with the newly independent United States, a country that will continue to grow "because of the attraction which the laws of the new domain offer." But as most of the founders of this country were peaceful, "many being Quakers," Aranda foresaw a nation much more peaceful than England. With the defeat of England, one of two enemies (referring to Portugal), would be eliminated. By dealing with the opportunity of the colonial rebellion, Spain will gain in the Americas and in Europe.

In the Americas, Spain would prefer to avoid future foreign territorial claims, "inland and to the rear of the Colonies" along the Mississippi River, Florida, and control of the Bahama Channel along both coasts. In Europe, Spain could go after Gibraltar and the port of Mahon on Minorca without threatening the rest of Europe. All this could be accomplished through the signing of an early treaty with the colonies, which would be an act of war. Spain must agree to help the colonies, if not by declaring war then by offering to help by whatever means a favorable treaty could accomplish. The colonies are anxious for such an arrangement "to relieve themselves of their problems, avoid unnecessary risk," and by such an arrangement they would agree and commit to helping their allies "until a general peace would be agreed upon by all."[34]

By forming a treaty when independence for the colonies was not assured, when there was still some risk, the colonials would appreciate Spain all the more and gladly settle any future differences. But if the treaty were "deferred to the time when she had survived her difficulties, neither her good will would be so well disposed nor her urgencies serve to help gain a better advantage for us." Hidden means and secret aids, in the end, meant little after the fact.

Aranda stated the obvious. Spain had a lot at stake in this conflict with Great Britain. The new "United Provinces," as they were sometimes called, early on wanted nothing for free and had already offered future trade, land, and military help as collateral.[35] The Americans committed themselves to a struggle in a larger theater in exchange for winning their liberty, and with this attitude neither of the Bourbon monarchs had a problem. None of the countries opposed to Great Britain went into the conflict unaware of the aspirations of the others.[36]

But the main issue was, at what cost? War is a major expense and not just in hard currency. Aranda argued that the war would not require "the utmost activity or adventurous gestures." The process of war with an already wounded and hurt Great Britain would, by attrition, bring about the effect desired. While almost repeating the colonial strategy of avoiding major conflicts and wearing down the British Lion, Aranda argued that Great Britain could not win. Franklin informed him, he claimed, that almost a third of the British naval manpower had been lost because these men had become American sailors—men now opposing Great Britain. This impacted Great Britain's merchant marine, because the government had to replace the losses. Unsaid here is that Great Britain's long tradition of impressing seamen to keep its crews up to full complement and sometimes over, resulted in forces full of people who were, at least, neutral to Great Britain's causes. Aranda insisted that because of Great Britain's lack of good crews, no resources from the Americas for building additional ships, and the economic impact of the loss of colonial trade, Great Britain found itself in the worst situation it had been in "since she took upon herself the domination of the seas." This time, Great Britain's enemies could not have been in a better position.

Spain could impose choices on this weakened country. England could be forced to negotiate about Gibraltar or Minorca, either of which would be a loss. War, in which England had to face a stronger opposition, would prove successful to Spain and France. War would destroy the already weakened commerce and economy of the British islands and would be so devastating that a decisive battle or invasion of England would be unnecessary. Civil dissension at home would pressure the British government "to sacrifice some losses, even if they were sensible."

Aranda concluded that, without great risk, Spain could strike immediately to "produce the desired fruit from the war with the British Crown." He hoped that his "Most Catholic Majesty" would give his report some consideration and share the report with his "wisest Ministers" who could examine the proposals.[37] His request was fulfilled, for the conde de Ricla, José de Gálvez, and Grimaldi received copies and wrote their reactions to Aranda's ideas.[38]

Also in possession of information from the Americas provided to them by Gálvez, the three ministers individually commented on Aranda's reports in early February. All disagreed with Aranda's anxiety to enter into a treaty with the colonies. None felt that the time was right to go to war. Nor did they feel that Spain should be seen as an aggressor. Gálvez postulated that the opportunity would still be available in the spring or later and as of now "we have in our favor the just cause and Divine Providence on our side." All the other monarchs in Europe knew this, but they also did not want to see the colonies succeed against a fellow monarch.[39] All agreed that Spain should not be the aggressor, but should send secret aid. Grimaldi, for example, noted that the latest reports from the colonies indicated that the insurgents are "defending badly" and "have abandoned important ports and fortifications," although he never expressed doubt about the final outcome. He also noted that neither he nor the king had received the memorial about which Franklin had spoken, and that alone would indicate that Spain should not enter into a treaty.[40]

Spain, Grimaldi continued, needed to include in any treaty with the colonies the regaining of what was lost in the previous war. Here, he was reiterating Aranda's sentiment about Florida. He took exception to Aranda when he concluded that it would be "imprudent and inopportune to enter into a treaty with the Colonies at the present moment."[41] Ricla, whose report had a feeling of being more anti-American, succinctly stated that Vergennes was too anxious and Spanish aid was more important than a treaty at this time. He added, somewhat caustically, that when the colonials started winning some battles then Spain could consider a treaty.[42] Ricla and Gálvez expressed caution on how Spain proceeded because, no matter what Spain did, they did not want to cause a major European War.[43] Given the history of the last century, this was indeed enlightened thought, even if, at the moment, sustaining the colonies and eventually winning concessions from England must have appeared to be impossible.

Two days later, on 4 February 1777, the elderly Grimaldi scratched a reply to Aranda. Grimaldi had announced his retirement,[44] but remained in office until the king's appointed replacement, the conde de Floridablanca, could return from his assignment as envoy to the Vatican. Grimaldi must have enjoyed the moment, for, with the king's approval and the concurrence of the ministers' opinions, he was writing an answer to Aranda that the ambassador would not like, but should have expected.

Spain, he said, should strive for a just and offensive war against that common and natural enemy of the house of Bourbon. England must be seen as the first aggressor, for no one should overlook the circumstances of the rest of Europe. Of Aranda's two major points, first that Spain should enter into war with England before it attacks Spain, and second that it would be convenient to make a formal treaty with the American Congress, Grimaldi answered that one action could not be considered without the other. A treaty was an act of war and a declaration of war would make them an ally of the colonies. If France and Spain entered into a treaty with the colonies, then their aid would no longer be secret and the colonies could use the alliance to convince Great Britain to give up. Therefore, any treaty with the colonies has the potential of doing more damage than good. Furthermore, the Spanish king has special considerations that he possesses in the Indies that are larger and more important than the English colonies. The king must be sure not to help set an example for a future rebellion of his own provinces. The British colonies actually have little to offer for the moment.

Assuredly, Spain and France will gain from the split between Great Britain and its colonies, said Grimaldi, but the split will heal because in time the issue of independence will be replaced by business considerations and cultural ties. Spain had to deal with this reality, and as the war progressed, Spain, like the new United States, understood what it was getting into. Grimaldi, on behalf of the king, demonstrated a more accurate grasp of the future than did Aranda.

Grimaldi then considered the question of preparation, for it is one thing, he said, to prepare for immediate war if we are attacked, and another to enter when we are ready. England, he noted, had more ships-of-the-line ready to sail and was piling up enormous expenses. In both cases, it would be prudent for Spain and France to wait. On the first part, to allow the allies to distribute their ships and troops as well as build up strength and, on the second part, to let Great Britain weaken itself. Here, Grimaldi implied that the last point was being accomplished because of the colonies. Thus, Spain could enter the war from a position of strength. Grimaldi, like most of the Spanish officials, had a curious way of mixing policy statements with actual detail. So while expressing concerns over entering the war, he asked Aranda to find out from Vergennes if the French had sent a fleet to their major West Indian port of Guarico or to Cap Français on the island of Saint Dominque, now Haiti, to unite with twelve Spanish ships-of-the-line to deter any British intent in that area.

If, for any reason, the scenario changes, which was likely within a few weeks, the government could reconsider. Otherwise, Aranda should assure the colonial commissioners that His Catholic Majesty has ordered aid for them and wishes them well in their endeavor.[45]

Internally, at least, Spain had fairly well defined its course. None doubted that, at some point, they would be in a conflict with Great Britain. Certain goals had been defined. In the Americas, Spain wanted to retain what territory it had and regain what it had lost: the Floridas, exclusive control of the Caribbean, and an end to British smuggling in Central and South America. In Europe, Spain wanted the return of Gibraltar and Minorca and the neutralization of its two major enemies, England and Portugal. In addition, control of the Mississippi River and the Bahama Channel loomed as somewhat nebulous questions. The problem of joint fishing rights for France off the Newfoundland coast,[46] as well as future trading privileges with the United States hovered on the horizon.

The policy of patience, using time to gain strength, was still in place, and in fact, was being aided by Great Britain's colonial problems. Spain should continue to help Britain's colonial problems grow by sending aid to America until the time came when Spain and France were ready and they could claim British provocation. At all costs, a war in Europe should be avoided. Unlike France, Spain did not anticipate future good relations with the new American country.

Spain, as it should, was looking out for its own interests, which included maintaining a vast empire and rebuilding its economy. As part of the scenario, Spain would determine its own schedule of when and how to be involved or, more accurately, to take advantage of this opportunity. Spain did not want to confront the wounded lion but to nibble at it. With France's cooperation, the maxim of *divide et impera* was developing. Spain had a realistic view of the situation. The American revolution revealed a weakness in the British empire that could be exploited through the relative strengths of the Bourbon monarchies. In the end all would gain, including independence for the colonies, but success depended upon Spain's cunning.[47]

The colonials felt a little more pressed for action than either Spain or France. They were actually fighting and as the Battle of Breed's (Bunker) Hill indicated, munitions, especially gunpowder, were crucial—for then, as now, the lack of ammunition spelled defeat. In 1776, New York had been lost, but Washington re-crossed the Delaware River to win a morale-boosting victory, which was followed by another at Princeton before he retired his decimated army to winter quarters at Morristown. The American commissioners in Paris needed to make arrangements, or so they thought, before the winter snows thawed and the spring campaigns began.

Perhaps misunderstanding the nuances of Aranda's comments, the American commission did not wait for an official reply, but decided to follow up its meetings with the Spanish ambassador by sending Arthur Lee to Madrid. He left on 7 February 1777 and Aranda sent word of his trip in advance. Spain did not want to create any unnecessary problems in Europe by accepting a foreign emissary who, from the European point of view, represented a people whose independence was not yet accomplished. France's acceptance of the commission was enough. Spain could work through its Paris office, but for the insurgents to assume more at this point was presumptuous and could create a crisis.

Orders quickly went out to intercept Lee and prevent him from getting to Madrid. He was not to be arrested or treated rudely, just detained. Grimaldi, still waiting for Floridablanca, decided to diffuse the situation himself. He recruited Diego de Gardoqui, a young Basque banker who had some knowledge of English, to help him intercept Lee.[48] Gardoqui's firm had done business with England for years, and since at least 1765, had been doing business with the British American colonies.[49]

In 1775, the firm began supplying Massachusetts through an arrangement with Eldridge Gerry. Gerry's correspondence to Gardoqui included accounts of the rebellion, so the Spanish businessman had a good idea of what was happening. Gardoqui would be Grimaldi's interpreter. With the help of a letter written in English by Gardoqui and sent ahead, they were able to meet with Lee in Burgos, in north-central Spain.

Gardoqui's letter prepared Lee for what he would hear from the two Spanish officials. He was told that going to Madrid would check Spain's desire to help and would hurt his country in the highest degree. Lee could not stay in Madrid undetected. If Lee could wait outside of Madrid, Gardoqui and Grimaldi would meet with him under disguise and in secret.[50]

In a series of secret and awkward conferences, Grimaldi explained Spain's position in detail to the anxious American who, perhaps, exhibited his impatience when he refused to leave Spain until he heard from the king. Both Grimaldi and Gardoqui informed Lee that Spain's current refusal to go to war by no means precluded aid to the United States. Lee then heard the surprising news that Spain had stockpiled gunpowder and clothing at New Orleans and Havana. Actually, Bernardo de Gálvez in New Orleans had two thousand barrels of gunpowder, lead, and clothing waiting to be picked up for the colonies.

In addition, Gardoqui and his father José, both prominent men in their hometown of Bilbao, were at that moment collecting supplies. Their private company, Gardoqui e Hijos, would be making a shipment destined for the colonies that winter.[51] Lee could not have been more pleased with the news. The amount supplied to the colonies throughout the war still has not been calculated. Gunpowder produced in France and partially paid for by Spain, as well as that produced in Mexico[52] wholly at Spain's expense, would be the major factor in the colonists' success for the first half of the war for independence.[53]

Lee was asked to wait in the town of Victoria, where the Court would send him official notice of their position. As Grimaldi and Gardoqui continued to meet with him, they revealed that Spain, through Aranda, would approach Holland about extending credit for the colonial cause. Gardoqui also delivered the official letter when it arrived. The Spaniards convinced Lee to keep the proceedings secret.

In March of 1777, the American commission received further instructions that resulted in correspondence being sent to Vergennes and Aranda. Aranda's letter, signed by Franklin, did not contain the detail of Vergennes's letter. Nevertheless, the important points did not conflict. The United States understood that dealing with one or the other of the two countries was as if dealing with both. An outbreak of war in Europe was a major consideration and, of course, Congress understood that "for the sake of Humanity" they "would not for the Advantage of America only, desire to kindle a War in Europe, the extent and duration of which cannot be foreseen." This, of course, meant that Congress was willing to tie its goal of independence, even subvert it, to the goals of Spain and France.

The Americans agreed that they would join an allied force to attempt the conquest of "Canada, Nova Scotia, Newfoundland, St. Johns, the Floridas, the Bermuda Islands, Bahamas, and all the West India Islands in possession of Britain." In the case of the "Sugar Islands," or the West Indian Islands, the United States, with enough advance notice, would provide 2,000,000 "of dollars" and six frigates of not less than twenty-four guns each. If Spain joined the war, Congress would declare war on Portugal "and continue the said war for the total Conquest of that Kingdom." Also, the possession of the Floridas with all its cities and ports including Pensacola shall become a part of the Spanish empire, "provided the inhabitants of the United States shall have the free Navigation of the Mississippi." Franklin closed his letter to Aranda stating that the stipulations were subject to modification by the Spanish government.[54]

The French copy of Franklin's letter was dated at least a week before the Spanish copy and two other differences should also be noted. The French letter requested that France use its influence in Europe to prevent any further transportation of foreign troops into the rebelling colonies. The Americans wanted to curb Great Britain's use of Prussian troops, popularly called the Hessians. Also, the United States pledged not to approach any other government without first consulting with France, nor would Congress "take a step" to negotiate a peace "without consulting His Majesties Ministers." In a postscript, the commission noted that they had no doubt that Britain would acknowledge their independence at that very moment, but with certain provisions. Then came the veiled threat. Because the United States desired peace and independence, and if France could not help or give any indication of help within a certain period of time, the commission wondered if the French government had any ideas on what the conditions for peace and independence should be.[55]

Franklin signed the Spanish letter because he wanted to officially inform Aranda that he had been appointed "Minister Plenipotentiary to the Court of Spain," but that he understood why his official presence in Madrid "is not at present thought convenient." Franklin and Congress would do nothing that might "incommode [sic]" a country "they so much respect." He would remain in Paris until circumstances dictated otherwise.[56]

If the different dates indicate that the letters were delivered one before the other, which is a safe assumption, no explanation is given as to why. Nevertheless, the presence of the original French letter written in English and its translation into Spanish in the National Archives in Spain, indicate that Vergennes shared his correspondence with Aranda. The two countries did indeed cooperate.

A subsequent letter from Aranda to Floridablanca helps make sense of the matter. Arthur Lee had returned to Paris with word that Spanish aid had come from resources heretofore unknown by the American commissioners. His Catholic Majesty had helped beyond the known amounts going through France.[57] Lee believed that the commission would receive some official correspondence that would facilitate aid from Holland. He therefore met with Aranda to receive the documents. That very day, Aranda received a report of Lee's escapades in Spain, but the packet contained nothing relative to Holland. According to Aranda, he had to tell Lee to be patient and not worry, because, if Grimaldi told him he would receive such documents, there would be no problem.[58] Lee then recounted the meetings in Burgos and Victoria, even to the detail that Grimaldi shared with him about how Spain was fulfilling General Charles Lee's requests through New Orleans.

Benjamin Franklin then officially presented his credentials of office as minister to Spain, along with the new congressional proposals. The papers instructed that Franklin was "to communicate, treat and conclude with his most Catholic Majesty, the King of Spain . . . a treaty . . . for the just purpose for assistance in carrying on the present war between Great Britain and these United States."[59]

Aranda had no problem getting the commissioners to agree that their presence in his house in Paris, much less in Spain, could be a problem. They should be "aware of the caution with which Spain had to proceed while it remained at peace with England." Franklin handed his credential of office to Aranda, who tried to give it back, suggesting that a copy would suffice. Franklin insisted on returning the document because "he wanted the presentation to be in proper form."[60] Aranda acquiesced and a week later mailed to Spain all the documents, including Franklin's April 7th letter.[61]

Now everything was in place. The diplomats had met and ideas were exchanged. Each country had an idea of the other's position as well as potential. Benjamin Franklin, the Americans' senior member, had been assigned to Spain and the parties agreed upon the idea of Dutch aid. All exchanges between Spain and the colonies would be done with discretion and in Paris. The American commission had done well in its first four months in Europe.

The new Spanish minister of state, Floridablanca, if anything, was more conservative than his predecessor Grimaldi. The American commission and its successors would have to deal with this man for the rest of the war. Aranda, their direct contact, was enthused to the point of illogic about going to war and totally defeating Britain. In contrast, Floridablanca was rational in calculating what could and could not be gained. He tended to listen to all arguments, even repeat them so the proponent knew that he understood the issue before choosing a course, which invariably was a policy of patience and reason.

Floridablanca was, above all, a Spanish patriot and had a clear-minded view of a very turbulent period. He came from a middle-class background and a legal career. As a provincial attorney he won the attention of Carlos III. His unyielding loyalty and uncanny ability to succeed, at least in his opposition to the Jesuits and the Office of the Inquisition, advanced his career until, at the age of forty-nine, he received the appointment of minister of state. To put him in perspective, he was no more a chauvinist for his country than people like John Jay and George Washington were for their country.

Floridablanca's policy came down to continuing that of Grimaldi and of his king. They shared the goal of taking the proper amount of time to build Spain's strength, while pleasing the Americans. They would always argue the cause for their own country. Floridablanca, like Aranda, had proposed and even believed that most of the goals of all the parties could be accomplished diplomatically. Perhaps he was struck with the idea when he read the veiled American threat to France. Just what were the proper conditions for independence? One thing is certain. The Americans presented a problem and Floridablanca accepted the task of finding a solution.[62]

In the meantime, he had to catch up with the negotiations in Paris and help negotiate a new peace with Portugal. King José I of Portugal died on 22 February 1777, which meant that Spain's nemesis, the marqués de Pombal, lost his influence, with the ascension of Queen María Francisca. A new treaty was being negotiated in the Spanish town of San Ildefonso. The new monarch was a little more disposed toward Spain, possibly because she was the daughter of Carlos III's sister. In fact the new queen's mother used the opportunity to spend time in Spain working on the negotiations, which lasted into October. Floridablanca and his Portuguese counterpart, Dom Francisco de Souze Continho, signed a preliminary agreement, which Carlos III ratified in San Lorenzo del Escorial on 11 October 1777. The two neighboring countries no longer considered themselves enemies.

Although not everyone was pleased and some people were uncertain of the outcome during the negotiations, Spain obviously fulfilled a post-1763 goal to eliminate Portugal as Great Britain's ally and Spain's enemy.[63] The new treaty weakened Great Britain, for it lost its only European ally.[64]

Apparently diverted by the Portuguese relations and satisfied that, for the time being, nothing new could be done for the Americans but to send supplies, Floridablanca and Aranda did not devote much time to a potential treaty and alliance with the rebels. Nor, for that matter, did the American commissioners in Paris.

Aranda did expend some effort in March when he wrote a fifty-page manuscript describing the state of affairs for Floridablanca. He mostly reiterated the chronology and progress of negotiations up to that point. He did note that Great Britain might be vulnerable because most of the British land troops had been sent to the colonies. Because of this, France considered the possibility of invading the British Isles.[65]

By early June, Congress had received a report from its commission in Paris. In a testament to the importance of the information that Lee brought back from Spain, the Congress's Committee of Commerce immediately dashed off a letter to Bernardo de Gálvez in New Orleans. They wrote that their agent to Madrid had met with "a person of consequence" who "assured him" that Spain would supply blankets, clothes, and military supplies. The goods would be made available in New Orleans and some of the supplies would be shipped from Havana. They requested that Gálvez notify them when the supplies became available.

The letter was very friendly, thanking Gálvez for his past favors and indicating that Oliver Pollock had spoken highly of him and Spain. Congress acknowledged the fact that New Orleans, a Spanish port, was admitting American shipping. Importantly, they gave a very truthful account of the revolution. Both sides, they reported, are preparing for a new campaign. General Washington is waiting for General Howe, commander of the British forces, to move before he acts accordingly. The two armies are "nearly equal in numbers," but the British are better "disciplined, armed and uniformed." Nevertheless, the Congressional letter boasted, the Americans are more versatile, better marksmen, and they fight for a better cause. Furthermore, the American troops will be supported "by the militia of the country . . . that has already participated in the glory of routing such a formidable enemy."

The letter also reported that General Horatio Gates had prepared to engage the British, who were led by Generals Guy Carleton and John Burgoyne. Great Britain intended to march south out of Canada, thereby cutting the colonies in half and replenishing British troops in New York. While the Americans expected some American desertions, they had no doubt about Gates's ability to stop the British. The packet included some newspapers for Gálvez's perusal.[66]

Whether Bernardo de Gálvez or his government realized it, the Congressional committee had been very frank. Their letter demonstrated that they understood the British military strategy. Great Britain intended to use its troops in New York to feint south while Burgoyne completed a pincers movement by striking from Canada. In addition, the committee correctly predicted the outcome, for that year's campaigns ended "with much honor and success for America."[67]

In April, Aranda relayed to Floridablanca an arrangement about which Congress was unaware at the time of their committee's letter. An agreement had been worked out in which an amount of three million *livres* would be sent to the colonies. This amount would be in addition to the two million *livres* sent through Roderique Hortalez et Cie that Spain and France had arranged. The letter does not spell out the source of this money, the total of which "should permit Congress to attend to its urgent matters," but implied that Spain and France once again had raised the money.

Here, Aranda almost casually went into a detailed account about Vergennes who, according to the Spaniard, ordered that all Aranda's mail be opened. Nevertheless, this apparently was so commonplace that Aranda felt that he should merely be aware of the problem but say nothing.[68] Such were the times. All the governments suffered from intrigue. Not even the new American government avoided the problem.[69]

Floridablanca answered Aranda with a long letter, in which he reviewed the ambassador's actions up to the present. He approved Aranda's answers to the Americans and the French. He agreed that Aranda should meet with the Americans as little as possible to avoid unnecessary complications. He appreciated Franklin's agreement to stay in Paris. He had read the American proposals and seemed most impressed with the idea that they were open to suggestions and counter proposals.

He then gave Aranda a general summation of the aid that Spain had sent to the Americans from June of the previous year. While not giving amounts of aid, he commented on all the different points through which the aid passed. Floridablanca knew that Aranda did not know of some of the transactions. For example, the king directed trade through the Spanish colonies because he knew the Americans were in urgent need of the supplies. Other aid originated in the northern Spanish port of Bilbao where the company of Gardoqui and Sons helped. More than 70,000 *pesos,* over two million of today's dollars, already had been sent from Bilbao. Spain was preparing to send more support.

Floridablanca expected additional aid to materialize from Holland. He heard that Holland had agreed to an initial minimum amount of 50,000 *pesos.* Spain, Floridablanca noted, was effectively getting aid to the colonies. America had a friend, even though, "for various political considerations," there was no official treaty. The U.S. Congress and the American deputies should not suffer any anxiety on Spain's behalf. So, in addition to all this aid, Floridablanca assured Aranda that the new plan to send another three million *livres,* equally contributed by the two courts, would meet the king's approval.[70]

Floridablanca's assurance, followed by a second American memorandum presented by Benjamin Franklin in July, inspired Aranda to dash off another long letter in which he repeated many of the same ideas that he sent to Grimaldi. The memorandum did not really add anything new, and perhaps its timing and that of Aranda's second appeal to go to war had more to do with Floridablanca's earlier decision to wait through the spring.

Aranda reported that France was willy-nilly backing into war and Spain would have to follow just to shield its ally. France probably could not avoid war, despite all the infighting, for he heard that the French ministers "squabble for weeks, for days and, even, hourly sometimes animated." Aranda now argued that England was not getting any weaker, the war would probably end within the next year, and Portugal was no longer a problem. Why not act? If part of the British fleet in America could be surprised, the land troops would be rendered useless. Aranda was right about the importance of the British navy. He was also right in stressing the vulnerability of the British American fleet. Eventually, the allied strategy would be to neutralize that fleet.

France, he reported, is so obviously embroiled that Great Britain can pick its moment. The British ambassador already had complained about France's harboring of American ships and crews in her ports. France's action had made things so bad, from the British point of view, that brazen Americans leaving French ports even attacked British coal barges along the British coast.

Aranda noted that even France could not reply to British complaints except to complain about British affronts. Nor could France stop aiding American ships because the sale of booty had become an integral part of the coastal economy. The

French government actually had no control over the matter. Aranda recommended that Spain should get involved, for, in his opinion, Spain could no longer ignore the situation.[71]

Apparently, Aranda had an inkling of the extent of the problem American warships and privateers had caused by their use of French ports. The Americans did not care to understand the gravity of their actions. The extent and audacity of their raiding and then using French neutrality for protection had just about driven Great Britain into war with France. Even the ship that transported Franklin and his two grandsons to France managed to capture two British ships on the way. The booty, of course, was dispersed in France. And, Aranda's feelings notwithstanding, France was not prepared for war.

Vergennes warned the American commission that the American raiding activities forced France to violate existing treaties then in place with Great Britain. With the exception of Franklin who cautioned his colleagues to be patient, Vergennes's plea went unheralded.

Nothing could be more perplexing to Vergennes then to hear that three American warships had embarked from French ports on a successful raiding foray and then hurriedly took refuge in France because the British navy was in pursuit of them. The incident enraged the British public, and aroused European opinion.

Vergennes had to do something. Initially, he wanted to expel the ships from port. This would surely result in their immediate capture. But, although frustrated with the Americans, he did not want to alienate them, so he decided to order the small fleet sequestered.

Like his earlier warning, his good gesture went unheeded, for on 17 July 1777 American Captain Gustavus Conyngham sailed from Dunkirk in the cutter *Revenge* that had been purchased for him by William Hodge. American use of Dunkirk was especially embarrassing because France and Great Britain had designated the city a demilitarized port, with a British commissioner in residence there. Conyngham, who already had been arrested once for raiding from Dunkirk, immediately violated his written orders to sail directly to America.

Conyngham apparently acted on secret orders sent to him by Silas Deane, who was frustrated by what he perceived to be the commission's lack of success and wanted to draw France into the war. Deane sent his secretary, William Carmichael, whose activities throughout the war raised some eyebrows, to meet with Conyngham to deliver the official orders. Carmichael had some secret instructions, for Conyngham never attempted to sail to America, but started capturing British ships. The American exacerbated the problem by using a crew consisting mostly of Frenchmen. When one of his prizes was recaptured, the episode became a major scandal. Great Britain threatened immediate war with France. Vergennes had William Hodge arrested. France was on the brink of an unwanted war.[72]

Vergennes believed that war was inevitable and said as much to his ambassador in London. Fortunately, the crisis passed, but not before some difficult diplomatic exchanges. Great Britain, like France, almost let itself be drawn into an unwanted conflict. France did not appreciate the problems caused by the Americans, and the American commission split over this and other issues.[73]

As Floridablanca knew, Aranda did not have command of all the facts. Nor did Aranda consider the relative strengths of countries. Despite his praise of British "talent and courage," he seemed to underestimate them as a foe of Spain. He appealed to a man who noted the omissions of his argument more than the other commissioners. Floridablanca had enough confidence in his country's position to stand pat and not rush into a formal commitment.

Problems came up now and then. A policy of support had been initiated; now the two sides needed a plan. In September, Aranda informed the American commissioners that henceforth they should deal directly with Diego Gardoqui for shipments to the colonies. It was thought that this move would help keep accounts clear, facilitate shipments, and would be more deceptive. The American commission hired a banker of the French court, referred to as Mr. Grand, to handle their affairs. He approached Aranda with a proposal for presenting Spain with a plan of remittance. Aranda would not reply to the plan until he could get it translated into Spanish. He also refused to reply to Grand's verbal translation. Instead he forwarded the document to Floridablanca.

Floridablanca and Aranda shared a concern "about the considerations of the excessive expenses which Spain had noticeably borne, and still did, the great amount which it indirectly had been contributing to the advantage of the Americans with her armaments and preparative measure," without any kind of formal agreement for remittance.[74]

The memorandum must have been a curious message for Floridablanca, for Spain had sent aid, matching France, and then sent more. Yet Deane, Lee, and Franklin criticized the efforts of Spain and France, hoping that they could encourage even more aid. Their own account, attached to the missive, showed that the Americans had established a line of credit for the amount of 7,730,000 *livres* and they wanted an additional loan of two million more! Of course, the Americans proposed to pay back Spain and France with tobacco, indigo, potash, and rice. Unfortunately, the treachery of some of their own crews and the British blockade prohibited them from making payments, for the time being. They needed more uniforms and were ready to sell eight ships-of-the-line. Ironically, while complaining that their country had not received everything promised them, they admitted that they knew that some shipments had been sent directly from Spanish ports "the value not yet known to us." The Americans' concern for Spain's friendship lacked logic when considered in context of Spain's actions.[75] Perhaps the new arrangement, whereby they would deal directly with Gardoqui, would improve matters.

Had they known more of what was happening at home, perhaps the three Americans in Europe would have been a little more positive toward Spain. Congress received a letter from Bernardo de Gálvez in New Orleans in which he informed them that he had supplies waiting for them. Because "there is not a single person here well enough versed in the Spanish language to produce a correct translation of the letter," they had to depend on a corresponding letter from Oliver Pollock. Not only did Gálvez have supplies on hand, but also he expected more to arrive monthly![76]

Robert Morris and William Smith informed Gálvez that they had appointed Pollock to be the agent for Congress. They charged Pollock to charter or buy ships to arrange for shipments to travel up the east coast and unload their cargoes wherever they found it safe. The two congressmen asked Gálvez if he would be so kind as to help with Pollock's expenses. Congress would repay him in full. Like their representatives in Paris, they complained about the effectiveness of the British blockade, which prevented repayment for shipments to Spain.

As in the past, the Congressional letter contained a narration of the military events going on at the time. The British had occupied Philadelphia, "which has occasioned us to be here [York]," but they are surrounded by Washington's army. In the north, the American General Horatio Gates confronted General John Burgoyne. Burgoyne had been authorized to march south form Canada via Lake Champlain and the Hudson River to New York, thus splitting the colonies. Congressmen Morris and Smith had just received word that the British general surrendered to a complete victory for the Americans. Now, Gates could march south to join Washington, and victory is "almost a certainty."[77]

News of Gates's victory at Saratoga on 17 October 1777 reached Europe as early as 3 December 1777.[78] On December 13th, in Paris, Aranda commented to Franklin about Burgoyne's defeat and stated that he believed that "the moment had come" for Spain to act.[79] The Americans had reason for their enthusiasm, for they had ruined the British strategy to cut them in half. In addition, the Americans had achieved an important victory. Surely there would be positive aftereffects. So far as the fighting in the English colonies was concerned, the battle opened a new stage in the war. A parallel scenario would follow in the diplomatic saga.

FOUR

Floridablanca and the Policy of Patience

> *. . . [to] have more clarity about their [the British] designs and make our decisions without rushing.*
>
> The conde de Floridablanca to Aranda, 1777

$\mathscr{G}$eneral Gates never marched southward to join Washington in a great victory over General Howe. Instead Howe's army, as Congressmen Morris and Smith noted, occupied Philadelphia and stayed in snug quarters for the winter. Washington and the remains of his army spent a miserable winter at Valley Forge. Obviously, victory was not as forthcoming as the colonial leaders would want the Spanish to believe.

The following spring the Continental army thawed out enough to be rejuvenated with the arrival of long-awaited supplies, a good portion of which originated in Spanish territories. Even then, the army could not perform a military miracle, although it prepared by training under the forthright Prussian, Baron Frederich von Steuben, who reorganized and drilled the army. Though stronger, the army remained weak and undermanned. Sir Henry Clinton, who replaced Howe as commander of the British forces, embarked on a new policy, which dictated not taking chances. He marched his army back to New York, the best north Atlantic seaport on the continent. His new emphasis would be to keep New York and make an occasional foray into the south. Washington wanted to strike at Clinton's army as it returned to New York. The attack, under the leadership of General Charles Lee, was bungled and the British successfully moved into New York. Washington followed them and set up camp at the city's perimeter at White Plains, where he stayed for the next year and a half.

When Great Britain lost the battle at Saratoga, the Parliament realized, perhaps for the first time, that they might not win the war. The British Parliament decided to deal with the Americans and authorized a commission, headed by Lord Carlisle, to make an offer to end the rebellion. This, in itself, was cause for enthusiasm, to the point of striking a medal commemorating Burgoyne's surrender to Gates.

Unfortunately for the British, the offer to repeal or suspend every disagreeable act passed since 1763 was a couple of years too late, for Parliament failed to offer the one thing the colonists now desired, which was independence. Congress, its military forces, and even the majority of people had invested too much in their enterprise to settle for less. Yet they understood that Great Britain's eagerness to end hostilities and keep them within the British family gave them a tool that would help them achieve their goal.

Word of London's desire to end the war was exactly what Vergennes did not want to hear. If Great Britain succeeded, it would come out of the disturbance as strong or stronger than before, and France's opportunity to inflict a crippling blow on its traditional enemy would be lost. If England and its recalcitrant colonies could settle their differences, France would not even have the advantage of partaking in some of the colonial trade. Nor could Spain or France anticipate payments on the credit they had extended to the colonies. Franklin and his colleagues already implied the possibility of settling with London in at least two written memorials.[1] The commission did not miss the opportunity of this advantage.

Change in national relationships occurred, but not as commonly believed, for the Battle of Saratoga did not immediately change everyone's opinion. France did, indeed, seem to note Great Britain's reaction to Saratoga, but Spain, with the very stable Floridablanca at the helm, maintained its patient course.

Carlos III and his ministers had been preparing for an anticipated confrontation since the previous war. The government had been sending instructions in expectation of war. Every official in the Spanish empire had received such instructions long before Saratoga. For example, a missive dated 25 November 1776 ordered the governor in New Orleans to spy on the British, keep abreast of the events in the English colonies, strengthen the defenses, curtail and end smuggling, build up the militia, and devise ways to clandestinely aid the rebels.[2] In August, two months before the so-called pivotal battle at Saratoga, Spain had decided to follow France's lead and sent some observers to the colonies. They needed more information to cover plans for all possibilities. The king wanted two representatives to go to the colonies. One would observe the political situation and the other would keep tabs on the military. The two men especially needed to keep track of the colonial relationship with its mother country, for this, above all, was becoming the key to Spain's participation.[3]

The selection of the two individuals who would help to gather information in the colonies was left to Diego Joseph Navarro y Valladares, governor and captain general of Havana, who on 11 November 1777, reported to José de Gálvez that he had selected Don Juan de Miralles y Trajan to be Spain's unofficial liaison to Congress. Miralles was a businessman and resident of Havana, who had some command of the French and English languages. Among Miralles's listed attributes were his connections and familiarity with the towns and trading centers of Caracas, Cartagena, Puerto Rico, Santo Domingo, and Havana. Don Juan Elegio de la Puente, Miralles's brother-in-law,[4] received the appointment to observe the American military activities. Puente had been an accountant for the treasury and had lived in East Florida before that territory became British. He had a brother in Georgia. While Navarro did

not note the fact, Puente also had written a fourteen-page history of Florida, apparently to bolster Spain's historical claim to the area. Both men, Navarro felt, had the
experience and knowledge to fulfill their respective jobs without losing time.[5]

Navarro apparently appointed Puente to please José de Gálvez. Puente first traveled to Florida in 1764 when he presented himself to the British governor as a native
of St. Augustine. He wrote the history of Florida later that same year that attracted
Gálvez's attention, for the minister sent a copy of the history dated 4 May 1778 to
Governor Navarro.[6]

Neither of the men had been appointed as a reaction to the outcome at Saratoga,
although both men probably left for the colonies aware of the battle. They could have
heard the news from Spain. Bernardo de Gálvez, in New Orleans, received word from
Congress and subsequently passed it on in March of 1778. James Willing had taken the
correspondence from Smith and Morris overland from the east coast and then downriver to New Orleans.[7] Gálvez did not hear about Saratoga for months after word
reached Europe. It is possible that he could have received the news faster via Europe.
Obviously, no one in the West Indies had the latest news from the colonies, which is
a good reason why Spain wanted some representatives in the rebelling colonies.

Both Miralles and Puente entered the colonies by different routes. Miralles
traveled by sea up the east coast, eventually landing at Charleston, South Carolina on
9 January 1778.[8] Puente, who acted more like an undercover agent than a diplomatic
observer, traveled to his familiar East Florida under the pretext of a fishing trip. He
was in Florida by late December.[9]

Miralles had extensive instructions. The Spanish government did not want to
create a diplomatic scandal, so, as they did with the American commissioners in
Paris, they instructed Miralles to exercise caution. First, he was told how to get to the
colonies, and then what to do once he had safely arrived among the Americans. To
help prevent detection by the British, Miralles was put on board a ship, called *Nuestra
Señora del Carmen,* carrying tobacco to Spain.[10] Miralles handed the captain specific
instructions including the exact longitude markings of when to turn north and than
turn west after passing through the Bahama Channel. The captain was to be put in at
the first opportunity, when Miralles would fake illness or "by another excuse that
your prudence dictates" manage to be left ashore. The *Carmen* would then sail on to
its destination at Cádiz. After Miralles figured out whether he was among friends or
foes, he would make his way to the Congress. His instructions warned him to be careful, for the people could easily deceive him and ruin his mission.

If he succeeded and found himself secure among the Americans, he was to send
his reports directly to José de Gálvez. His primary order required that he establish
direct communication with Congress to help expedite any forthcoming negotiations.
His instructions, numbered "nine" and "ten," dealt directly with Spain's main concern,

> to investigate and inform yourself in detail of the actual state of war and of
> its progress, their respective forces, of the disposition in which both, or

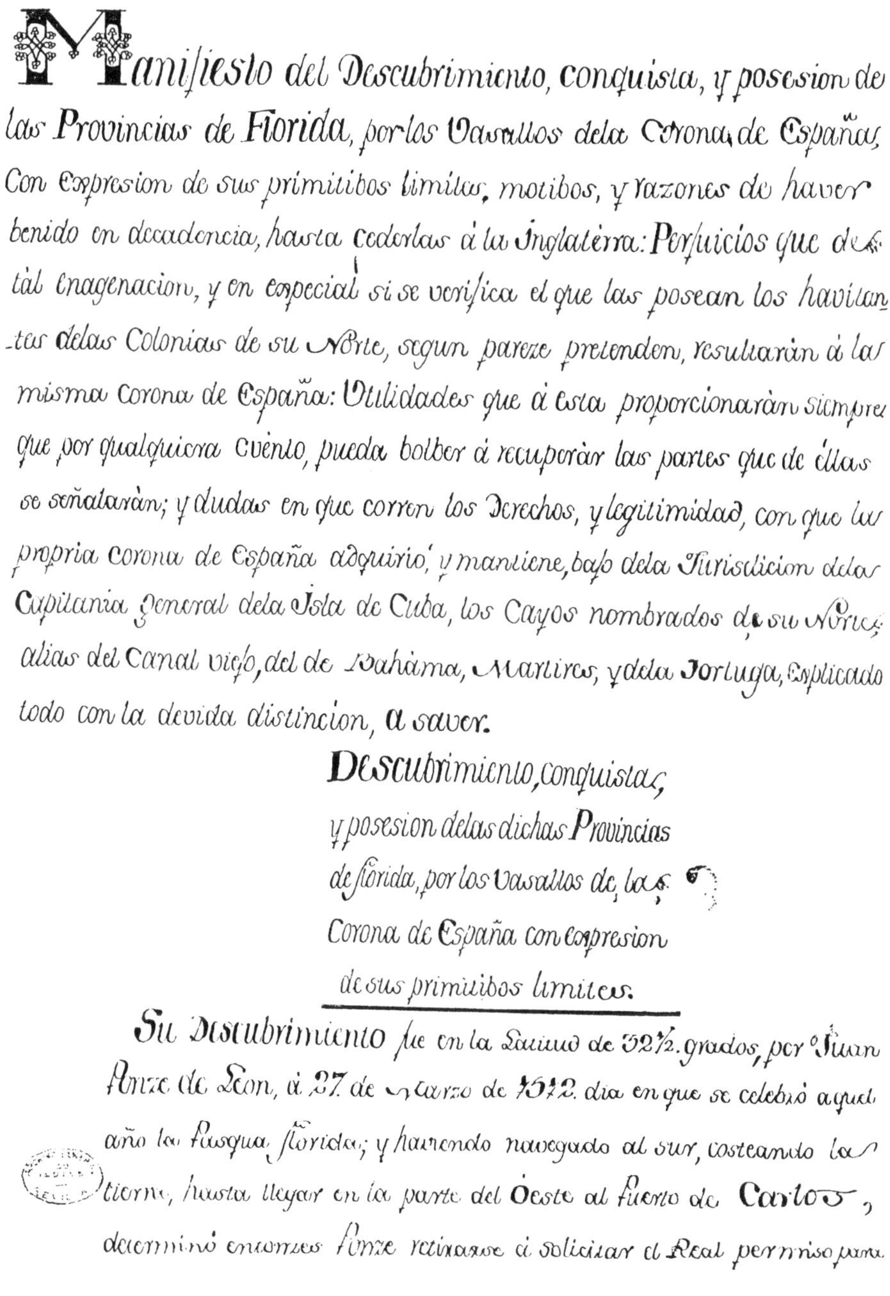

Manifiesto del Descubrimiento, conquista, y posesion de las Provincias de Florida, por los Vasallos dela Corona, de España, con expresion de sus primitibos limites, motibos, y razones de haver benido en decadencia, hasta cederlas à la Inglaterra: Perjuicios que de tal enagenacion, y en especial si se verifica el que las posean los havitan-tes delas Colonias de su Norte, segun pareze pretenden, resultaràn à la misma Corona de España: Utilidades que à esta proporcionaràn siempre que por qualquiera Cuento, pueda bolber à recuperar las partes que de ellas se señalaràn; y dudas en que corren los Derechos, y legitimidad, con que la propria Corona de España adquirio, y mantiene, bajo dela Jurisdicion dela Capitania General dela Jsla de Cuba, los Cayos nombrados de su Norte, alias del Canal viejo, del de Bahama, Martires, y dela Jortuga, explicado todo con la devida distincion, a saver.

Descubrimiento, conquista, y posesion delas dichas Provincias de florida, por los Vasallos de las Corona de España con expresion de sus primitibos limites.

Su Descubrimiento fue en la Latitud de 32½. grados, por Juan Ponze de Leon, à 27 de Marzo de 1512. dia en que se celebrò aquel año la Pasqua florida; y haviendo navegado al sur, costeando la tierra, hasta llegar en la parte del Oeste al Puerto de Carlos, determinò entonzes Ponze retirarse à solicitar el Real permiso para

Fig. 6. First page of Juan Elegio de la Puente's "History of Florida," 1778. Original in legajo 1598, Santo Domingo, AGI, Seville.

whichever of the two are ready to continue or abandon it, and whatever hurt-
ful intention toward Spain and her possessions in America they might intend.

and,

you should focus your vigilance in finding out if the colonial rebels try to
make an agreement with the Royalists, the how, when, and with what
agreements, in order to advise with the best anticipation. And, more important, if by chance the royalists should plan some expedition against Spanish
or French possessions . . . , please get this valuable information to the
authorities in Spain or Havana as quickly as possible.[11]

Miralles was to set up business as a merchant dealing in African slaves and supplies. He would be paid and supported by the Royal Treasury. Thus, he could avoid
British suspicion. Also, his instructions insisted that he spare no expense. Miralles's
extensive instructions to cover his mission reflected Spain's belief that international
affairs had become very delicate. War loomed larger.

The instructions even specified what Miralles needed to do if the British blockade succeeded in intercepting his ship. He would answer inquiries about his ship's
strange location by stating that the customary prevailing winds required a change in
course. His superiors felt that the excuse sufficed, for Spain's neutrality prevented
Great Britain from doing anything to a third party merchantman on the high seas.[12]

Puente corresponded with José de Gálvez before Miralles successfully landed at
Charlestown. Apparently writing from St. Augustine and sending his letters through
Havana, Puente argued that Spain should invade East Florida before the Americans
took it from Britain and turned on West Florida or Britain kept it, to use West Florida
for centers of aggression in the Gulf region. He also assured Gálvez that the Indians
in Florida would side with Spain. Furthermore, all the American people and shipping
that he had encountered had been very friendly. While he claimed to have many
reasons to favor the Americans over the British, he argued that Spain still should
focus on Florida, no matter who wins the rebellion.[13]

Long after both Miralles and Puente left on their respective missions, news of
Navarro's choices and actions reached the Court and received royal acknowledgment
as well as approval. Then, in March 1778, Navarro informed Bernardo de Gálvez that
the two observers had successfully arrived at their destinations. Miralles presented
some letters of recommendation to George Washington and the United States
Congress that were immediately acknowledged. Puente stayed in St. Augustine where
his ensuing long silence worried Navarro.[14]

Although France also had an official observer in the colonies, Vergennes, for some
reason, became fearful of Parliament's conciliatory temper that might produce an
accord between the belligerents. Yet Vergennes understood that Spain needed to be a
part of whatever strategy he followed, especially if he went to war. Saratoga and the

British reaction reinforced his attitude toward war, for he did not want to see England become reconciled with its colonies. He wanted to enter into a treaty of commerce and amity with the colonies, which meant war with England. Therefore, any treaty with the colonies required guarantees insuring that they would stay at his country's side and Spain would join France in the conflict. Without such guarantees, a treaty with the colonies meant problems, for France could not take on the British alone.

The first guarantee did not pose a problem. The colonies already agreed to pay the price for France's alliance. They would continue to fight until all the allies agreed to peace.[15] A treaty could be signed declaring France and the United States allies. This would prevent the Americans from making a separate peace.

The second guarantee became a more difficult issue, for Vergennes's Spanish counterpart, Floridablanca (see plate 7), was not as impressed with the preeminence of an English-American settlement, nor was he infatuated with the idea of going to war just yet. Vergennes's frantic requests and Aranda's pro-war position resulted in two very pointed and clear letters from Floridablanca. He gave detailed reasons why Spain would not go to war. Instead, he added, Spain would take some time to gather more information to "have more clarity about their [the English] designs and make our decisions without rushing."[16]

Fully aware of the plans going on in London, Floridablanca predicted that they would come to nothing. He did acknowledge Vergennes's desire for Spain and France to proceed together and formulate a plan based on their goals and concerns. Carlos III and his minister of state agreed that the time was at hand for Spain's position to be explained "with plain frankness without concealing any of our ideas or misgivings."

Basically, Spain could afford to wait and did not feel any urgency to rush into war. Spain had an array of options before it and, like a good chess player, could foresee some of the opponent's possible moves. The Spanish government first questioned whether the situation was so pressing in the colonies that they would need an immediate alliance, further aid, or for the European countries to negotiate a favorable peace for them. Floridablanca considered the possibility that negotiations would be a small price to pay for the Americans' friendship. But what if the British cabinet changed over, bringing in new people who would call for war against Spain? In this last case, Spain would be better off to have some kind of agreement with the colonies waiting in the wings. The various officials residing in Paris would have to be forewarned and instructed. Here, Floridablanca alluded to hearing that France already had presented the American commissioners with some formal propositions.

Meanwhile, Spain wanted to hear from its emissaries. Floridablanca noted that it would be a matter of "good policy" to have the latest and most accurate information about the state of affairs in the United States. Nevertheless, war could break out unexpectedly, so France and Spain should develop a plan of action for both their defense and offense. Such a plan necessarily required that Spain's fleet and land forces safely return from Buenos Aires. This meant that Spain would delay entry into the conflict. The two countries, Floridablanca continued, needed to determine how their respective fleets could be used to achieve their objectives of defeating England and aiding the colonies.

Spain had to consider the defense of its vast empire. Floridablanca specified Havana, Puerto Rico, Santo Domingo, and the coast and Province of Caracas as places of importance. He reminded France not to forget that its West Indies possessions, especially Martinique, needed protection. The two countries had to determine how and with what resources they needed to defend these ports without deemphasizing their overall objectives. Such planning required a determination of how many troops, warships, and supplies would be needed and when they would be provided. Finally, they needed an agreement as to where all these resources would be deployed.[17]

Negotiations were going on in secret, so that England could not anticipate a declaration of war even though Parliament and the king expected the possibility. The indications were too obvious to avoid. Port privileges, secret but not unknown aid already supplied to the colonies, West Indies activities in preparation for war, and the expedition to South America all pointed to a pending Franco-Spanish alliance in opposition to Britain.[18] Spain still had not given up its advantage of determining the time and place to enter the war. Floridablanca would be careful not to negotiate that advantage away.

The clever Spanish minister suggested that all the sides should secretly agree that the treaties would not be observed until they can "carry into effect the measures and precautions conducive to assure the voyages of the fleet and expedition from Buenos Aires, along with the defense of the Isles" (West Indies) important to both Spain and France. Floridablanca knew that the fleet was not expected back from its successful foray until July, so he needed to create an interim plan.[19]

Floridablanca preferred to call the Bourbon participation in the conflict a form of protection. He tried to avoid military terms. As protectors, the two crowns must stipulate that the colonies will not be abandoned until they are "recognized as an independent state." On the other hand, good planning requires that all the partners list their objectives to avoid misunderstanding and "gradually formulate a scale of operations." The interruption or extinction of English trade to its North American colonies was of no consequence to Spain, although the government recognized that this was a goal of France. France's other goals to invade the British islands and regain a presence of some type in Newfoundland were not Spain's priorities.

Here, Floridablanca could not have been more honest and open about Spain's aspirations, for he and his government appreciated the objectives of France and the colonies. But Spain felt that neither country's goals could be accomplished without Spanish participation. So, to assure their success, Spain would extract a price. Floridablanca wrote:

> Of herself Spain has no other objectives than to recover the shameful usurpations of Gibraltar and Minorca, and to cast out of the Gulf of Mexico, the Bay of Honduras, and the Coast of Campeche, those [British]

settlers which trouble her no end. There it is necessary to concentrate on where we will begin [the plan], should it be convenient and better for us to act separately than together, reciprocally supporting the purpose and expansion of one ally with the plans of the other.[20]

No matter how the plan turned out, the colonies would be expected to help achieve those goals, "even though it be only the diversion of forces." Floridablanca wanted Spain's plans and aspirations told to the Americans even though "this frankness" was risky because they would place a confidence in a "People who have so many relations of Nationality, kinship, and even interests, with Great Britain."[21]

The minister's final consideration dealt with the sobering thought of war in Europe. There was some fear that Turkey, a weak ally of France's, might suddenly want to expand and cause some unneeded problems. Floridablanca knew full well that European peace depended on a precarious balance of powers among the various European nations. France used its alliance with the relatively weak states of Sweden, Poland, and Turkey to counter the expansionist tendencies of the stronger and unfriendly states of Russia and Prussia. France's rivalry with England, as has been explained, was an age-old matter of vying for European supremacy, and now equality. Turkey, like a number of the weaker countries, had the potential of throwing all of Europe into war by disrupting the balance, thus forcing France and its ally, Spain, to make "a prejudicial and shameful peace" with England to avoid greater losses. The two countries, continued Floridablanca, should strengthen their position by asking the Dutch if they wanted to join in the alliance. They, too, were discontented with the British.[22]

Obviously, Floridablanca was neither devious nor conservative. He expressed no distaste or concern over the actions of the colonists against their monarch. He exhibited the thoughts and actions of an intelligent and efficient minister. He saw through many of the immediate problems to larger considerations. When, on the eve of war, many people became emotional, Floridablanca remained calm. His clear vision of what was good for Spain and how that could be parlayed into help for the rebelling colonies, and for France, eventually would result in success for Spain and its partners.

A conference of Spanish ministers was called to determine a consensus about what should be done. Aranda concluded that Spain and France should arrange plans of action based on the different circumstances. At the least, the arrangements should be contingent upon the independence of the English colonies.[23]

Anxious about what London might be doing, Vergennes became perplexed with Floridablanca. Perhaps influenced by Franklin, although there is nothing to verify that, he answered Floridablanca's inquiry about France's specific goals.[24] France wanted nothing more than to gain trade with the colonies and deliver a damaging blow to England. Spain, he added, wanted much. He also reported to his king about "Spain's gigantic demands."[25]

Aranda apparently tried to placate Vergennes by telling him that for Spain's part he understood that France had no interest in Spain's desire for Gibraltar, Minorca, and even less for Spain's problems in the West Indies.[26] The Spanish government became aware of Vergennes's frustration and, at the same time, suspected Vergennes. Floridablanca felt that Spain had not heard the full extent of Vergennes's private negotiations with the colonies. While he correctly surmised the situation, his fear for a negative impact on Spain was unnecessary. Nevertheless, he instructed Aranda to be careful in what he said to Vergennes.[27]

Vergennes had some important scenarios to consider. He had a window of opportunity in which to face Great Britain. For the moment, France had the advantage of choosing when and where to begin hostilities. This offset the slight superiority Great Britain enjoyed in naval power. Great Britain could sail sixty-six ships-of-the-line while France had fifty-three ready to go. Relative strengths were measured by these battleships of the day that carried more than sixty cannon and as many as three gun decks. Vergennes needed to be careful in choosing his time. He wanted to use his advantage of surprise while not alienating the rest of Europe. Also, France needed a pretext to blame England for actually starting hostilities.

France knew that England had another fourteen ships-of-the-line that only needed crews. They would be manned in the spring when sailors could be taken from the arriving merchantmen. Vergennes had to figure out a plan of action that would take place before Great Britain could go to full strength.

France had to defeat Great Britain in one well-planned campaign. If France did not succeed, Spain's navy of fifty ships-of-the-line and its land army in the Americas would become indispensable. Vergennes completely understood his risk and the importance of Spain.[28]

France had to gamble that its extensive alliance system would not draw it into a war in Eastern Europe. As Vergennes contemplated how to defeat Great Britain, Maximilian Joseph, the Elector of Bavaria, died, leaving no heirs and a likelihood of a disputed succession and war. If Austria should decide to take over Bavaria, Prussian balance of power would be disrupted and that would be dangerous to France. Nonetheless, Vergennes elected to concentrate on his plans, while hoping that Prussia and Russia would maintain equilibrium in Eastern Europe.[29]

Although the French ambassador in Madrid, Armad Marc, the comte de Montmorin, believed that Spain would have to follow France into the conflict, Vergennes knew better. After consulting with his king, he wrote to Floridablanca. Louis XVI wanted to secure connections with the Americans, but did not want to alienate his uncle, Carlos III. Therefore, France would be willing to help Spain recover Gibraltar, the island of Minorca, and help expel the British from the Gulf of Mexico. Montmorin delivered the letter to Floridablanca who, according to the French ambassador, flew into one of his famous, if not feigned, temper tantrums. Nevertheless, Montmorin continued to predict that Spain would have to join the conflict.[30]

Vergennes decided to act without the assurance that Spain would join the conflict. Vergennes understood that Floridablanca did not feel obliged to join France.

Nor would Spain consider any kind of overt act until its treasure fleet arrived. Floridablanca did not feel a pressing need to go to war. He knew that the colonies would not make up with London, money was on its way from the West Indies, the armed forces were gaining strength, and with a policy of patience, the Spanish government was maneuvering into a strong diplomatic position. Let the French guess at Spain's true feeling. Floridablanca was content to wait and, when ready, he would extract a high price from France.

On 6 February 1777 France entered into two treaties with the United States, thus becoming the first foreign country to recognize the new American country. Vergennes received almost everything he wanted. The United States received everything they could possibly want, and Spain remained in a very favorable position. In case of war, which was inevitable between England and France, neither the colonies nor France could make peace without consent of the other. France, which had lost any desire for further colonizing, renounced all future territorial claims in the North American continent. Both countries agreed to maintain the independence of the United States. In return, the United States gave up exclusive control of when to end the war, or so it seemed.

Vergennes needed two treaties, especially the second one of alliance. The first treaty of commerce and amity would result in war. The second treaty protected France from a colonial change of heart. But Vergennes's rush to enter into a treaty necessitated risk. The United States, as well as France, needed Spain, and Floridablanca's unwavering position worried Vergennes. Perhaps realizing Spain's demonstrated willingness to help, while depending on the Bourbon Family Compact and hoping to placate the Spanish, France and the United States decided to include a clause in their treaty that permitted Spain to enter the conflict as a full partner. This meant that Spain would be considered an equal and its goals would have to be part of any negotiated peace. This also meant that the United States or France could not sign a peace without Spain's agreement. Spain had no requirement to join the fighting, but knew if that was its desire, the conditions were set. The clause, article thirteen, was written at the end of the treaty and kept secret. The allies did not want Great Britain to know.

The Americans willingly agreed to pay this open-ended price to assure their independence. No one doubted that Spain's eventual involvement made the United States' independence not only a matter of time, but secure.[31] Now France's treaty of commerce and amity meant that France recognized England's colonies as an independent country. France, therefore, had committed an act of war against Britain, who now had more to deal with than the troublesome colonies.

Word of the Franco-American treaties reached London in late March 1777, a little earlier than expected. England and France withdrew their ambassadors. Floridablanca was not surprised; he sent a message through Montmorin reassuring Vergennes that Spain would live up to its obligations, without defining what he perceived those obligations to be. He cautioned that France should not expect to dictate when and how Spain would become involved. He succeeded in convincing

Montmorin of his sincerity in this matter, for the French ambassador added that Spain would merely be of peripheral help if forced into the conflict.[32]

At the time of signing the treaties, France had hoped to delay hostilities but not to lose the element of surprise. Vergennes and his strategists believed that by the time the news of France's alliance with the United States had traveled to the United States and back to Britain, three months would pass. Britain would not learn of the alliance until sometime in April or May, not March. They planned for France to have some time to prepare its navy as well as try to get Spain involved. At the very least, Vergennes felt that France's action had checked any attempt of the British Parliament to come to a reconciliation with the colonies.

None of the parties had illusions of an easy victory. Great Britain completely changed strategies, in order to fight a more cautious war. They redistributed their forces, abandoning the north down to New York and concentrating on the south, where they surmised the population would be more favorable to them. For the moment, Great Britain held only New York City, Philadelphia, and parts of Rhode Island. They needed to consolidate forces, for they did not have the troops or ships necessary to fight in the colonies and in the West Indies. They wanted to withdraw from Philadelphia and concentrate in New York. In addition, they feared an invasion of England. Finally, Great Britain did not want to provoke Spain.

George Washington hoped that the French fleet would counteract the British fleet, which had kept him at a great disadvantage. The British naval blockade had been fairly effective. Meanwhile, Great Britain freely used this excellent and safe source of transportation. British land forces and their supplies could be transported without fear of the kind of molestation that led to Saratoga, and they could strike anywhere along the coast, raiding almost at will. Importantly, Washington dared not risk an all-out assault without his own naval support.

Thus, while Henry Clinton, who had replaced Howe as commander of the British forces, planned to march back to New York, where both Lee and Washington would face him in a stalemate, the French came up with a plan. Despite British fears, France did not care to invade England by itself. An invasion had enormous technical problems, not the least of which was that France had no ports in the English Channel that could harbor ships-of-the-line. Transporting the required number of men and material from other, more distant ports would not result in the kind of quick strike Vergennes had in mind.[33]

However, while checking the British by threatening an invasion with the main part of the French navy, Vergennes could use the Toulon fleet to sail to North America. France earlier had offered the Toulon fleet to Spain as an enticement to enter the war and a gesture of goodwill. Spain refused the offer. Now the fleet was available for Vergennes's plan. Echoing Aranda's strategy, Vergennes ordered the Toulon fleet of twelve ships-of-the-line and five frigates to sail, with secret orders to open hostilities upon its arrival in America. With the proper execution, France would surprise and successfully capture Great Britain's American fleet of twelve smaller class ships-of-the-line, thereby stranding 33,756 British troops and ending the war.[34]

For the moment, Vergennes did not concern himself with Spain, for he was ready to launch his gamble, which he expected would result in a quick victory, without the aid of an ally. By the end of March, Spain had been informed of France's plans to surprise the British fleet in America. Vergennes pointed out the advantages of France's scheme to Spain. In doing so, he also demonstrated that he clearly understood Spain's position. A French attack of the English fleet, at or around New York, would draw British forces from the West Indies, thus permitting the Spanish treasure fleet safely to return to Spain. The plan kept Spain, which carefully maintained its neutrality, from being implicated, while it created advantageous opportunities for Floridablanca's country to become involved. Floridablanca, on behalf of his king, approved France's plans.[35]

Spain tried to negotiate with London, which, on occasion, seemed willing to avoid war through diplomacy. Floridablanca hoped that Great Britain would be willing to make concessions, even turn over Gibraltar, to avoid an unfortunate expansion of the hostilities in its colonies and keep Spain out of the fray. Lord Weymouth, one of Great Britain's secretaries of state, made overtures to Spain's chargé d'affairs in England. Would Spain, he wanted to know, mediate the Anglo-French dispute? Floridablanca agreed. France protested, but had to appear to go along. Spain's mediations hit an impasse when Great Britain asked Spain to have France retract its American treaties. The Spanish chargé reportedly replied that Spain "could not suggest such an indecent proposal." Then, when Britain refused to consider turning over Gibraltar, Floridablanca endorsed France's plans to surprise the British.[36] Great Britain, in effect, sacrificed the American colonies for Gibraltar.

France's fleet sailed on April 13. Vice-Admiral Charles Hector, the comte d'Estaing, commanded the expedition, which successfully embarked without arousing British suspicions. Once the fleet had distanced itself from the continent, France used a small British provocation to declare war, and the first major skirmish occurred on July 27 in European waters. No ships were taken, but much damage was inflicted, and there were one thousand casualties. Nevertheless, the Toulon ships safely sailed on their way to New York.[37]

D'Estaing opened his sealed orders and failed in his mission. Clinton had started transferring his army from Philadelphia to New York. He transported his army's supplies by sea, arriving in New York on July 1, a week before d'Estaing's arrival. The British secured the port with a blockade of nine ships-of-the-line at Sandy Hook. For some reason, d'Estaing chose not to force the issue and, instead, directed his ships and four thousand men to the Delaware capes,[38] thus aborting the plan to eliminate the British fleet.

Washington and his officers were still heartened. The American general proposed using the new French troops to help General Lee recover Newport, Rhode Island, which was the last British presence in New England. However, disappointment followed when a storm shattered d'Estaing's fleet, forcing the French commander to leave his as well as the American troops unprotected. In the face of new British reinforcements rushing across the Atlantic under the command of Admiral John Bryon, the French retreated while their ships were being refitted in Boston. This was hardly the surprise Vergennes envisioned.

In November of 1778, d'Estaing used his refurbished fleet to collect his force and sail for Cap Français. As Spain warned, France needed to consider its other interests when entering the risky business of war. For the moment, and with the element of surprise lost, the French high command felt that protecting their West Indies trade had a higher priority than aiding a very disappointed George Washington. At least d'Estaing kept his fleet intact.[39]

France, like the other European countries, placed more value on the West Indies. French forces laid siege to British Dominica on September 8 and five days later British Admiral Samuel Barrington took the French port of St. Lucia. Before he would return to Europe, d'Estaing captured St. Vincent and Grenada.[40] But without a major French victory, Britain maintained naval superiority in Europe as well as the West Indies. At the same time, French forces were losing so badly in India that, within the year, France lost everything in that theater.[41]

If the importance of Spain had not been obvious before, it certainly became so now. Spain had the naval force and the West Indies presence to make a difference. With Spain in the war, d'Estaing would not have worried about the southern ports, for Spain could have protected that interest. Indeed, this very scenario repeated itself three years later, but with two differences. Spain joined the war so the French fleet was free to help the allied land forces in the north.

Without a quick victory, suffering the predicament of defending themselves rather than aiding the colonies, and waiting for Spain to answer their call for help, the French fleet and men stayed in Cap Français for almost a year. In the fall of 1779, the first French ships that had sailed to help the colonies achieve independence, returned to France. The new French alliance, so far, had been less than successful.

Spain proved to be uncannily correct in its strategy. Saratoga did not mean a quick colonial victory and an end to the war. France found itself in a position that Spain had forewarned. Meanwhile, Great Britain had been stalemated, so Spain benefited from the commodity it wanted most—time.

The *flotilla* to South America returned, and Mexico was producing silver to support the upcoming effort. Spain continued to prepare, while the war stagnated. In Paris, Aranda and the United States commissioners focused on Spain's continuing aid, for all of France's assets would be needed to fund its own effort. Spain's aid to the colonies became even more important.

Just a few weeks before the signing of the Franco-American treaties, Arthur Lee went to Aranda's house one evening to acknowledge that the United States had received a shipment of supplies and money.[42] The shipment passed through Havana. Aranda and Lee were unsure whether the shipment was valued in *reales* or *livres* because seventy-five *livres* equaled 120 *reales*, (5 *livres* equaled 8 *reales*) which, when added, could be a major difference. Aranda went to see Vergennes to make sure everyone was in agreement about which denomination had been promised. Apparently the value was in *livres*, and this was the first of three equal shipments that had been scheduled.

Aranda was also a little concerned that Lee knew of Havana's role in the matter. The ambassador felt that there had been a serious security leak that could result in British repercussions.[43]

Nuances aside, Carlos III and his government followed a policy of helping the American colonies. Arthur Lee received assurances that Spain would continue to do what it could.[44] The United States Congress reflected this attitude, for it continued to ask Spain for aid.

Even as France entered the war, Patrick Henry, or Patricio Enrique as the Spanish translated his name, wrote from Virginia that his state, in particular, and the "confederation of the states of America," in general, were very appreciative of Spain's help. Nonetheless, the British naval blockade was making the war difficult because the colonists were having trouble importing supplies. The colonists, wrote Henry, needed "woolens, especially blankets and tarps, and munitions." Spain's neutral status with the strategic city of New Orleans already helped alleviate the problem. In early 1778, Henry therefore asked Bernardo de Gálvez in New Orleans if Spain would allow the Americans to set up a fort in Spanish territory on the Mississippi River to help facilitate supplies up the river.

Next, Henry wanted Spain to ship to Virginia one hundred and fifty thousand pistols, the value of which could be considered a loan. If agreeable, Gálvez should decide a convenient location for the transfer "in New Orleans, Havana, Cádiz or somewhere else." In return for Spain's help, Henry offered "the gratitude of this free and independent country, the commerce of one or all of its rich products, and the friendship of its brave inhabitants." But the real plum was at the top of his letter, for he inquired whether the reduction of the English settlements in West Florida would meet with Spain's approval. He heard that the English living on the Mississippi had become a nuisance. If Spain approved, the Americans could "easily obstruct the English."[45]

Colonel David Rogers was entrusted with Patrick Henry's letter. He carried it down the Ohio and Mississippi rivers to New Orleans where he delivered it in mid-October 1778.[46] Rogers met with Gálvez to discuss particulars of the proposals before a reply was drafted. For the matter of supplies, Gálvez noted that perhaps Henry was unaware that some had been sent just recently. Governor Gálvez wanted to send more, but his in-house stocks currently were depleted. Nevertheless, he would send Henry's request on to Havana.

Spain could not acquiesce to establishing a foreign fort on its territory and Gálvez did not have the authority to approve one. Without saying no, he denied the request by insisting that the British be removed from the river first. So, if the Americans wanted to try to force the British out, they would get no opposition from

Spain. Neutralization of the British settlements would help open the river to free access so that Spain and the United States could transport supplies more efficiently. Again, rather than commit everything to writing, Gálvez "had several conferences with Colonel Rogers regarding the state of the war, and other subjects, all of which he will inform you [Patrick Henry] upon his arrival in Virginia."[47]

In Havana, meanwhile, Navarro had to oversee all the West Indies activities, including the supervision of getting supplies and aid to the United States. He began to feel pressure from different areas. In agreement with d'Estaing's concern for defending the important West Indies ports, Navarro worried when he heard that London had ordered Clinton to move south. The governor was convinced that Great Britain's ultimate goal was Cap Français and the French settlements on Santo Domingo Island. Such a strategy, he feared, could expand into aggression against Spanish possessions. Bolstered with the news that the Regiment of Navarra was on its way to reinforce his own troops, Navarro alerted all the Spanish officials to prepare defenses. He expressed confidence that they could withstand an attack.[48]

Even while so threatened, Navarro kept supplying the colonies, per arrangements made in Paris. The Spanish viceroyalty of New Spain (Mexico) was producing and shipping supplies to be smuggled into the United States through Havana as well as New Orleans. Government officials in Mexico City and at Veracruz kept up with the progress of the rebellion and happily cooperated with Navarro. France was also pleased with Spain's generosity while receiving supplies for themselves at Veracruz.[49]

In the midst of all this activity, Navarro had to maintain the appearance of strict neutrality. Spain's noncommittal posture was the screen for all its clandestine activity with the colonies. Now that France had entered the war, the governor and captain general of Cuba was reminded to be careful in his relationships with the belligerent nations. Navarro, for his part, conveyed Spain's policy throughout the West Indies. He also exemplified the comprehension of Spanish policy and fears that permeated throughout Spanish officialdom. Navarro corresponded with Antonio María Bucareli y Ursúa, a former captain general of Cuba who had become the viceroy of New Spain, expressing his concern for France's commitment to the American colonies if war broke out in Europe. Citing the ambitions of "Germany and the Prussians" over Silesia and the potential of Russia joining the fray, Navarro parroted the concerns of many Spanish officials, including Floridablanca.[50]

Maintaining neutrality was difficult while secretly supplying the United States and supporting France. When representatives from either of the two allies acted foolishly, as did Arthur Lee when he tried to go to Madrid, they further confused as well as threatened matters. Another example occurred when a British ship in the West Indies captured a ship flying a Spanish flag. The captured ship's captain was French and the crew consisted of almost every nationality except Spanish. The captain produced papers, which amounted to a note from Bernardo de Gálvez, dated a year-and-a-half earlier. Gálvez had granted permission for a different captain to leave New

Orleans. Prudently, Navarro could only conclude that the note did not pertain to the captured captain, his ship or its contraband.[51]

The United States preferred that Spain give up its neutrality and join the war. But the Americans did not need prodding to praise the Spaniards for their support. Robert Morris and William Smith wrote to Bernardo de Gálvez on at least three different occasions expressing their pleasure with Gálvez and Spain.[52] Patrick Henry, in his aforementioned letter, wrote of Spain's "friendly help" supplying the colonial army on various occasions.[53] George Washington unabatedly praised Spain in a letter to Navarro in early 1779. The American general thanked the Cuban captain general and his country for the "estimable care [and] the cordial and affectionate" demonstrations of friendship and support. Washington would "always desire" to talk of the "great estimation and appreciation that comes from Navarro's good will and of the respect with which those who are so happy to merit a place in the friendship of His Majesty." He "only wanted to express gratitude" for the help that Spain had "honored" him.[54]

Spain's help not only "honored" those fighting in the United States, it also aided allies in Europe. Now that France's seaports were no longer neutral, Spain's ports became important. With France in the struggle, Benjamin Franklin received permission to recommend to U.S. captains to put themselves under the care of Gardoqui's company at the northern Spanish port of Bilbao. They could unload their booty in exchange for supplies required for raiding the English coast. Any excess from the sale of the captured goods would be sent to the United States. John Paul Jones was one of many American captains to follow Franklin's advice. Using his family's banking firm as a cover to protect Spain's neutrality, Gardoqui worked directly with the U.S. commission in Paris.[55]

The real question was when would Spain enter the war and under what circumstance? As seen, there was a difference of opinion, even within the Spanish government. The Americans and the French wanted, indeed needed, Spain. While American praise and appreciation for Spain's help was real, the underlying motive was to enlist the resources of Carlos III into the war. Navarro, when forwarding a packet of letters, including Washington's, that originated with Miralles in Philadelphia, noted that Congress had resolved to cede to Spain all of the land of West Florida. To get this land, the United States would assign three thousand troops to help Spain.[56]

Miralles, writing from the United States, noted that the Americans were still trying to scare Spain into a treaty. The American "politicians" reported to him that Great Britain had embarked on a policy to grant independence to the insurgents and create an alliance with its former colonies to invade and take France's West Indies possessions. Great Britain's enticement to the colonies was independence and at least partial occupation of France's former possessions. But, added Miralles, this scheme should not be taken seriously.[57]

Aside from Aranda's lengthy letters, the most interesting report came from Marcos Marreno Valenzuela, the Spanish ambassador to London, who wrote a detailed twenty-seven-page report to José de Gálvez in November of 1778. The ambassador tediously weaved an argument to impress his government with the importance of the American rebellion. He correctly observed that the rebels were not the type of people one normally associates with revolutions, but were the natural leaders of the colonies. They had formed a union among the various colonies using their common histories, culture, and desires. This, in itself, was unprecedented. In addition, the rebels formed a government and planned well. In Marreno's mind, the rebellion would not fail. France already had joined the conflict, as would other European powers, and they should, Marreno said. The future economic wealth of the new country and the potential for trade was enticing enough to fulfill the colonial requests for aid. On the other hand, the rebels had formed an army and would form a navy because of their shipbuilding industry and inheritance from England. The new country, a descendant from England, would share that sovereignty's natural aggression. Therefore, Marreno added, Spain needs to be a friend to curb the future appetite of the United States for Spanish colonies and to demonstrate to its own colonies that the Spanish government understands the plight of the English colonies and, unlike Great Britain, shares its colonies' aspirations. He detailed the American industries, Indian relations, and diplomatic agenda, and he fairly accurately forecast how Europe both needed and would benefit from the new American nation. He also echoed some of his countrymen by noting that the youthful ambition and culture of the United States would be a problem to Spain's American possessions.[58]

At the very least, the rebellion's certain success was assured by Britain's lack of forethought, for they forgot that they were dealing with people who considered themselves equals and not subservient to the English. And the opportunity for European help was an epoch-making event because Europe had become irretrievably connected to the riches of the Americas. The independence of one country, even if not rich like the Spanish colonies, would forever change the relationship between the two continents. For example, the old mercantile system would end. The United States would open trade with whomever it wanted. Asia and Africa were available and none of the European countries could prevent this new country's future success. At least, Spain could learn from Britain's example to improve its own colonial relations.[59] Marreno summed up his "reflections" in his cover letter.

> The rebellion of the English colonies and the results by their independence that they have proposed, will be one of the most worthy objects to occupy Your Excellency's superior talents for assuring to the King and his subjects, as Europeans and as Americans, the advantages that surely have resulted, from the assertive providence's, change everything as we know it, requiring Your Excellency's untiring applications.[60]

The ambassador was not in a minority opinion among Spanish officialdom, for Carlos III had been steering a very clear course. Marreno's view once again demonstrated the forethought of many Spanish officials. Another neutral view was allowed publication in Madrid in 1778. Francisco Alvarez, whose real name was Don José de Olmeda y León, of Madrid, Spain, wrote a small book in which he described each "English colony" by county. He gave a brief history and description of each colony, commenting on cities, people, religions, commerce and so on. He noted that New York was guarded by Fort St. George, and that Charleston was a good port because it could receive ships of over two hundred tons. Not once did he refer to the rebellion or even a problem between the colonies and England.[61]

No country wanted Spain to give up its neutrality more than France, and among the French, perhaps Montmorin had come to understand best the difficulty facing his country. As his opinion of Floridablanca matured, he understood that Floridablanca's faked tantrums and confusing letters had maneuvered Spain into an ideal position. When Floridablanca complained that France had no interest in seeing Spain get Gibraltar and Minorca, which he followed with the observation that Spain had little interest in Jamaica and Florida, except for Mobile and Pensacola, Montmorin began to comprehend Floridablanca's strategy. Spain, with all its treasure ships safely in homeports and the return of its South American fleet, would allow Britain to buy its neutrality. Montmorin clearly realized that his country would have to make some serious offers.[62]

As Floridablanca forthrightly requested that Great Britain make some offers or risk war, Montmorin warned Vergennes not to alienate the powerful Spaniard. Montmorin, like every French official, knew the cold facts: France had sixty-six ships-of-the-line and Great Britain now had ninety. He correctly predicted that Spain would not declare war until sometime in 1779, and would not officially recognize the United States until peace.[63] Montmorin, like Floridablanca, knew that France's treaties covered as much as Spain required and that recognition of the United States would accomplish nothing more. In fact, such an act for Spain would have been diplomatically foolish. Not only did Spain have to make sure not to send bad messages to its own colonies, but it also did not want to run the risk of driving other European nations into Great Britain's camp.

Great Britain again hinted that Gibraltar and Minorca might be available, but quickly backed off. George III would not comply with any offers to Spain. He stubbornly believed that his country would defeat Spain, France, and the recalcitrant colonies.[64]

With Montmorin's urging and Vergennes's desperation, France needed to prod Spain into a larger commitment. Floridablanca suggested that the two countries mount an invasion of England with a joint fleet of sixty ships-of-the-line. Vergennes, perhaps not sensing Floridablanca's attempt to assess his anxiety, countered with a proposal for an invasion of Ireland. Floridablanca then told Montmorin that Gibraltar was too strong to attack unless France and Spain could distract Great Britain's forces to the Americas, specifically the West Indies. Then they could feint an attack of Gibraltar and have the British so diverted, they could invade England.[65]

Vergennes saw all this as getting nowhere. Along with his ambassador in Madrid, he sensed that Floridablanca wanted specific deals. Vergennes then made a telling request of his king.

> If it is a fact that His French Majesty cannot struggle long on equal terms with the English and that a prolonged war, which would not be exempt from disadvantages, could entertain the ruin of his navy and even his finances, and finally that His Majesty reduced to his own means would be less able to make his enemies feel the need of peace than if he were acting in concert with a strong ally, then the most natural consequence is that everything invites him to take some risks in order to activate such a desirable alliance. I will not dissimulate, Sire, that the views and pretension of Spain are gigantic, but it is necessary to consider that the time one uses to countervail against them will be lost for the establishment of combined operations which one cannot hasten too much to prepare.[66]

France could not defeat Great Britain without Spain's full support, as Vergennes argued, so Louis XVI had to acquiesce to Spain's demands. This meant that the secret clause of France's treaty of alliance with the United States would come into effect. Neither France nor the United States would sue for peace until the respective goals of each were met, and now Spain's had been fulfilled. Both France and the United States needed Spain to achieve victory and guarantee United States' independence.

Louis XVI did not take long to agree with his minister. Bolstered with the knowledge that a settlement was in process in Germany, the king gave Vergennes permission to proceed on Spain's agenda. Vergennes, in turn, sent some ideas to Montmorin while instructing him to negotiate a treaty with Spain. Montmorin received Vergennes's letters at the end of 1778.[67]

Floridablanca and his country had anticipated war for years. Spain and its colonies had been preparing for armed conflict since the last war. Spain and its agents had been gathering intelligence on the future enemy, which, coupled with the gathering of money and buildup of forces, gave credence to the policy of patience. By 1778, the viceroy of New Spain and the government in Cuba had organized an intelligence system that cost 53,000 *pesos* per year. Havana and Guatemala became centers of espionage. The Spanish empire was braced for war. With London's failure to respond to Floridablanca's diplomatic efforts, a declaration was forthcoming. Spain's policy of taking its time to gain strength was ready to pay dividends.[68]

FIVE

Duplicity in Favor of the Americans, 1777

Is Spain a neutral nation in respect to yours [The United States] *and Great Britain?*

Bernardo de Gálvez to Captain James Willing, 1778

While Floridablanca kept trying to succeed at the negotiating table, anticipation of Spain's entry into the war gathered momentum each day in the Spanish colonies. Great Britain simply could not be allowed to expand into Spanish territory. Spanish American officials had been preparing for war with a sense of urgency since 1777.

Gathering information became a paramount part of Spanish strategy. Spain needed to know the extent of British operations and influence upon the Indians, within and outside of British territory. A strategy had to be developed in anticipation of war, a strategy that, at once, would check British expansion and expel them from their legally held settlements in West Florida and the Caribbean—and their illegal settlements in Central America. Great Britain could not be permitted to cut a waterway between the Atlantic and Pacific oceans without resistance from Spain.

Thus the officials of Louisiana, Florida, and Guatemala had the key tasks of preparing defenses, planning offenses, and overseeing covert operations. This responsibility fell into the respective hands of Bernardo de Gálvez in Louisiana, and his father, Matías de Gálvez, in Guatemala. Both men operated under the patronage of José de Gálvez, the uncle of Bernardo and brother of Matías. And both men faced similar problems, although Matías did not have the close proximity of the American colonies.

In January 1777, Bernardo officially took over Louisiana from Unzaga's very competent administration. He did not take over immediately, but met and worked with Unzaga for weeks before Unzaga left. He operated closer to Spanish officials in Havana, in this case Diego de Navarro, as well as various military officers responsible for the Spanish West Indies, than did his father, who seemed to be more secluded in Guatemala.

Bernardo de Gálvez also inherited his predecessor's friendship with Oliver Pollock, the agent from Virginia, and Gálvez was even more open to helping the American cause. Gálvez's marriage solidified his position among his own population and his personality was perfectly suited to his position.

With the allegiance of his own people and the accessibility of American rebels, Bernardo de Gálvez had a ready-made situation to take advantage of New Orleans's geographical proximity to British West Florida and the rebelling colonies. Spying on the future enemy would be a relatively simple task.

Bolstered with instructions to gather intelligence, from the day he became governor of Louisiana, Bernardo de Gálvez quickly set up a system of information gathering that would complement the already large amount of intelligence he was receiving from American patriots. By taking advantage of his predecessor's connections, and with the help of funds from Havana, Gálvez proceeded to get details of the colonial conflict, garner news of British strengths and weaknesses in West Florida, and learn of any British plans for Louisiana.[1]

His major threat became his primary objective. Pensacola was a strategic port held by Great Britain. From there, Great Britain could easily launch an attack on New Orleans, which, if successful, meant the loss of Louisiana and, with Jamaica, the tightening of a British noose around Havana. On the other hand, Gálvez thought in offensive terms. In his mind, the question was not how to defend Spanish interests, but what were the British doing to impede his planned offensive?[2]

The governor of Louisiana was a key player in the developing allied theory and strategy to divide and conquer Great Britain. At what cost would Great Britain retain its hold on New York or Jamaica or Pensacola or Gibraltar? If the combined forces of the United States, Spain, and France could threaten, if not actually attack, various points of the widespread British empire and avoid a direct confrontation, perhaps the allies would nibble their way to victory. The potential for this strategy had been demonstrated by Spain's naval foray to South America. Spain succeeded there because Britain could not come to Portugal's aid.[3]

Bernardo de Gálvez became a major distraction to the British. His preparation for aggressive action would force Great Britain to make some hard decisions. With the Spanish navy looming, Great Britain would not be able to concentrate on North America. Even George Washington understood the advantage of a navy and its deterrence. More importantly, like Vergennes and Montmorin, Washington understood the importance of getting Spain into the war. He wrote that without the Spanish navy, "I fear the British Navy has it too much in its power to counteract the schemes of France."[4] "The English," he wrote to Congress, "are now greatly superior to the French by sea . . . and will continue so unless Spain interposes."[5] Washington prophesied that victory would be achieved only when "France and Spain should unite and obtain a decided superiority by sea."[6] In New Orleans, Gálvez continued his preparation for the reality of that event.

Naval strength not only provided military superiority, it provided versatility.

The ability to move on water would dictate a victor. Until Spain entered the war, the advantage belonged to Britain. Gálvez, a key, even if his role was not already defined, prepared for an offensive that included siege by sea. Most of his initial information came to him through his dealings with Oliver Pollock and the American colonists who talked to his many officers in New Orleans and at their bases. The Americans were more than willing to provide information in exchange for aid. They also seemed to reciprocate Gálvez's authentic friendship. For Spain's part, the feeling was mutual. Gálvez, in his Royal Orders dated 24 December 1778, needed to solicit the "British Americans." Furthermore, if the rebel colonists wanted to capture the British settlements on the river and in West Florida, Spain would be happy to receive them "as if in deposit" for the aid now being sent. Gálvez also acknowledged that he was intimately aware of "how much my predecessor [Unzaga] participated" with the Americans "led by the General Charles Lee." The supply system had been set up. Gálvez would transfer the supplies as they arrived from Havana, and all was to be done under the greatest secrecy.[7]

As early as 1777, Gálvez had become familiar enough with his position to become active in information gathering. Thus, at the same time the American Committee of Secret Correspondence, with Benjamin Franklin, was meeting in France, and a year after Spain had begun supplying the Americans in New Orleans, the correspondence to and from Gálvez begins mentioning "trusted men," some known, others not, who were being sent into British territory.[8]

In 1767, Spain established a base called Fort San Gabriel de Manchac, which was four hundred yards across the Bayou Manchac from the British-built and maintained Fort Bute. Lieutenant Raimundo DuBreüil commanded the small contingent for a short time in late 1777 and early 1778. He then took permanent command from 28 September 1778 until his death in 1780.[9]

The British built and occupied forts at Manchac and Natchez after the French and Indian War, for they obtained from France the left bank of the Mississippi River down to the Bayou Manchac. By 1768, they had abandoned the two posts. Spain, nevertheless, kept a small garrison at Fort San Gabriel and with reason, for in 1778, British strategy changed again and sent troops back to the area.[10]

Lieutenant DuBreüil, along with his colleague at Galveztown, Sub-lieutenant Francisco Collell, would provide Bernardo de Gálvez with important information about British strengths and movements. Their information, and then service, would be invaluable to Gálvez's future success.[11]

In late February 1777, a packet of seven letters, sent from the Royal Court then residing at El Pardo outside of Madrid, was mailed to Bernardo de Gálvez. All the letters told of a Spanish merchant who was on his way to New Orleans. The Royal Officials made it clear to Gálvez that Don Miguel Antonio Eduardo was a very special person who would be sailing on a mail transport, a packet boat from La Coruña in northwest Spain.

Bernardo's uncle José had concocted a plan to send Eduardo to New Orleans, disguised as a merchant. Eduardo had been a public interpreter in Havana and was sent on an ill-fated mission to Philadelphia in 1776. His flawless English, experience, and private status would expedite the secret aid. He would deal directly with the rebels, thus absolving the Spanish government of any appearance of complicity.[12]

Eduardo traveled as a merchant, probably with connections to Gardoqui's company, to act under the utmost security as an agent expediting the movement of supplies to the American insurgents. He would be paid by the Royal Treasury and operate out of New Orleans, where he would help the Americans prepare for the capture of Pensacola as well as the other English settlements on the Mississippi River. The arms and munitions that he was accompanying were destined primarily for Spain's Indian allies. Finally, Gálvez was informed, if Eduardo were captured, Spain would claim no knowledge of him.[13]

Eduardo, with his letters and supplies, did not arrive in Havana until late April or early May 1777 and, after a four-day trip, arrived in New Orleans on May 13.[14] The marqués de la Torre, then in his last year as captain general of Cuba, and Gálvez, who dutifully reported that Eduardo had arrived and immediately left "for the River," were already making plans in regard to the British settlements. Torre, acting on recent policy, was busy arranging for Colonel Antonio Raffelin to head up a group of Americans to spy on Jamaica from French Cap Français. He also had set up a system of informants in East Florida, centered on Don Luciano Herrera, who had lived in St. Augustine since 1763.[15]

Soon after Eduardo sailed into New Orleans, Bernardo de Gálvez received a report, from someone other than Eduardo, that the Americans were coming "this summer" with four to six thousand men to dislodge the English from the Mississippi River and Pensacola. Gálvez did not believe the report even though he knew that the British had the same information and were preparing for the attack. For his part, New Orleans's miserable state of defense needed some work.[16]

On the same day, Gálvez sent a separate letter to his uncle, José Gálvez, complaining of Eduardo's nebulous responsibilities. First his selection, and then what he was doing were so obvious that, Bernardo reasoned, the British figured him out in Havana before he ever departed for New Orleans. Second, the method of his payment was wrong, for it was obvious and slow in Havana. Meanwhile, many people who knew him previously immediately identified the agent. The governor suggested that Eduardo should return to Havana.[17] Nevertheless, Eduardo continued in New Orleans.[18] Gálvez knew that his uncle's scheme was doomed, so he modified the plan. Following standard policy, the governor declared that the royal warehouse had a surplus on hand and that the excess would be offered at public auction. He then arranged for Santiago Toutant Beauregard, a New Orleans merchant whose brother Bartolomé already had been recruited to watch the British, to purchase everything with funds provided by the government. The surplus, of course, was the shipment destined for the rebels. Thereafter, Beauregard replaced Eduardo as the merchant shipping goods from Havana to his New Orleans warehouse and subsequently to the rebels.[19]

Gálvez did not seem to want Eduardo's assistance. Gálvez had been dispersing the supplies to the Americans with little trouble and less fanfare. Also, as he would demonstrate, Gálvez preferred that Spanish forces lead in the attacks of British settlements in West Florida.

Rather than wait on one of the "official" spies, Gálvez sent an acquaintance of "confidence" to Pensacola to get a firsthand account of the enemy's stronghold. Gálvez was so secretive that the person's name does not appear in his correspondence. Nor did the governor tell his subordinates or even the treasury officials. He personally paid the man seventy-six *pesos* and six *maravedíes,* which he claimed was "a small expense for the service."[20] Although the agent was not an engineer, he was well prepared, for he filed an impressively detailed report.[21]

The spy described the fort at Pensacola as being in shambles, with the armaments in various states of disrepair. He reported that the soldiers amounted to about eight hundred and fifty men in Pensacola and only forty-nine stationed at Mobile. Poor construction of the fort's walls led him to predict that they could only stand three or four months without support. Sand and bundles of brushwood made up the batteries, cannon embrasures, and towers. The last were "musket-proof only" and the embrasures so unstable that they collapsed during construction. When they were tested against cannon fire, the bundles immediately caught on fire. The report continued that the embrasures "are so unstable that one hour of fire from their own cannons would destroy them without doubt."

The report included the caliber of all fifty-eight cannons that made up Pensacola's artillery. Of these, six or seven were beyond repair and only twenty-eight or thirty had been mounted. The British also had seven mortars to hurl bombs and rocks. A shipment arrived with a supplement of twenty-five cannons of four- and six-caliber along with munitions. Unfortunately the shipment did not include any four-caliber balls. In addition, the spy noted, they also received three bronze cannons. In all, Pensacola received less than a fourth of what they ordered. Furthermore, most of the artillery was nautical armament and not of much use on land.

The fort itself was round, and divided in three sections with four towers. The embrasures in front were four feet thick while the side facing the sea "is badly-constructed." Nevertheless, the British officials in Pensacola and Jamaica believed that war with France and Spain was inevitable. This was six months before the Franco-American treaty. Pensacola had been ordered to prepare and Governor Lord Peter Chester had taken the warning seriously. An attack was expected. If Pensacola was lost, the British government decided to retake it "in any event and at any cost." Great Britain saw Pensacola as the key to gaining and maintaining the interior and frontiers of Florida.[22]

Bernardo de Gálvez realized that Pensacola was vulnerable and that Britain recognized the port's commercial and strategic value with its proximity to the Mississippi River and Bahama Channel. Britain would sacrifice its other Florida establishments to defend Pensacola.[23]

Gálvez's trusted man also commented on a congress of Indians held in Mobile. About twenty-five thousand Indians, including men, women, and children from the Creek, Choctaw, and Chickasaw tribes attended. The British superintendent stressed upon the Indians not to let the Americans pass through their lands. He threatened that if the Indians permitted the Americans into their lands, the Americans would take the lands, "make themselves masters," make the Indians slaves, and "throw all the natives out of the area, as they did with the Cherokees." The Indians agreed to the superintendent's proposals, no doubt realizing the truth of his comments while not understanding the difference between Englishmen and the inhabitants of their rebelling American colonies. Receiving gifts seemed to be more important to them.

Gálvez's man surmised that, argument and gifts notwithstanding, the Indians "had no intention of opposition or hostility towards the Americans." Here, Gálvez pointed out that some five hundred Creeks had gone to a meeting called by the American superintendent. As a result, about half of the members of the Creek nation who had agreed with the British superintendent were now flying American flags in their villages. Again, the American gifts of flags most likely had no value of allegiance among the Creek Indians.[24]

In North America, Spain always felt that the friendship of Indians naturally favored the Spanish, when it came to choosing between the British and Spanish. Generally, this was true. In those areas where the Spanish had not solidified contact, Spain's attitude was that the British could influence the Indians through promises and gifts, or encourage already hostile tribes to be even more hostile. In both cases, Spanish policy reflected a confidence that the Indians could be won over once the Indians were contacted. So, while Spain would continue to keep track of British activity among Indians, the reports invariably echoed Gálvez's information that there was no cause for great alarm.

Gálvez's informant also reported that spies were rampant in New Orleans. Although all sides denied such activities, spying was normal. Perhaps some of the information's detail attracted Gálvez's attention. His man cited information received by Governor Chester. Unzaga had shipped gunpowder up the Mississippi River. The British suspected Oliver Pollock as having a role as a "supposed agent of Congress," a Captain Hawkins who is a "supposed American commissioner" was freely operating in New Orleans, and that another shipment of goods had gone to the rebels through Philadelphia.[25] This last tidbit was fairly accurate and was a direct reference to Oliver Pollock's ship, which transferred Captain Gibson back to the colonies.

The knowledge, or conjecture, in Pensacola that Spanish New Orleans was shipping supplies to the Americans was not news to Gálvez. Peter Chester had protested that issue to Gálvez in March 1777. Unzaga received a similar letter a few months earlier in November 1776. Great Britain had been spying on activities in New Orleans since 1773.[26] Obviously, secrecy became somewhat of a charade.

Gálvez might have been more interested in Pensacola's reaction to his aggressive stance of seizing British ships involved in illicit trade. Obeying his official instructions of office, Gálvez, unlike his predecessor Unzaga, felt that the time had come to end the practice of smuggling. He decided to use the prevailing trade regulations to seize British and American contraband ships. To make his point, he ordered eleven vessels seized in one night on 17 April 1777.[27]

While these were not large ships, for Gálvez himself wrote to Spain that the majority were useless for navigation and were used only to transport supplies, the act was noteworthy. He realized that his act would help shift trade to the French as well as striking a "blow," while creating somewhat of a surprise to British "clandestine trade."[28]

Indeed, Peter Chester's response began with, "imagine my surprise" when he heard about the incident. He hoped that Gálvez's action and policy was not true, but the next day he learned of Gálvez's public mandate that all British ships be impeded. While contraband trade existed, how could every Englishman be punished for the culpability of a few? Besides, Chester added, he heard that Spanish ports were permitting free trade with the French. Per article seven of the 1763 Treaty of Paris, Great Britain had the right of free navigation of the Mississippi River. Furthermore, Chester demanded "immediate restitution, release and return" of the Englishmen who were "illegitimately incarcerated." He also wanted Spain to pay costs. To make his point, Chester sent Lieutenant Colonel Alexander Dickson and John Stephenson of Pensacola to confer with Gálvez.[29] Gálvez indeed had struck a nerve.

Within a month after Chester wrote his letter of complaint and perhaps even before Dickson and Stephenson delivered it, Gálvez had in his hands a timely report from his spy in Pensacola.[30] How interesting it must have been for the governor of Louisiana to read that despite British spies "so malicious and inflammatory" that they submit reports in which "they do not forget to leave out the most minor circumstance," the British reaction to the confiscation of "merchandise and ships" was mild. The anonymous friend noted in his report that opinion was varied in Pensacola. Some of the council members and "gentlemen lawyers" believed that Gálvez had acted according "to the letter of the law, with justice and equitability, and that all means were taken." To argue otherwise "and to ask for amends are in vain, absurd, and frivolous." Nevertheless, Chester and his advisors would "pretend to feign" that Gálvez had acted contrary "to the privileges that the English enjoy as a result of the last recent treaty of Paris."[31]

Chester's envoys arrived toward the end of July and delivered the governor's letter to Gálvez. The subsequent arguments of Dickson and Stephenson followed the course as laid out by Gálvez's spy. The British envoys remained on board the frigate, the *Atlanta*, which Gálvez quickly pointed out had itself fired upon, as well as detained, neutral shipping. Most of the charges thrown at Gálvez were frivolous if not desperate. Primarily, the British envoys argued that Spain and Great Britain were at peace. By treaty, they both enjoyed free navigation of the Mississippi River and the river was neutral, so Spain could not extend its jurisdiction into that area. Furthermore, custom, under previous New Orleans administrations, permitted smuggling and Gálvez's action was directed solely toward Englishmen. Otherwise, he would have arrested some Spanish merchants who were trading with the English.[32]

Gálvez replied that free navigation did not permit illegal acts, that the river did not provide sanctuary for culprits caught in the act, and that previous law or custom was not his responsibility, nor should smugglers feel safe because they had not been

Fig. 7. Peter Chester, Governor of Pensacola at the time of the Spanish siege. Biblioteca Nacional Madrid. From Reparaz, Yo Solo, *100.*

caught. The only reason Spanish subjects had not been arrested in this case is because they found none at the scene and the English smugglers refused to divulge their Spanish colleagues.

Gálvez bolstered his answers by turning some of the frivolous complaints to his favor. He acted according to Spanish law and all procedures had been followed. In reply to the envoys' suggestions about certain points of law, Gálvez pointedly reminded them that the accused were subject to Spanish law, not British law. In accordance with Spanish law, Gálvez had already pardoned some of the prisoners, who were provided with clothes and means to return to their homes. The occasion, Gálvez noted, was the feast of Pentecost, when by law he personally must release some prisoners who have committed minor crimes. Neither Dickson nor Stephenson knew of the release. Drawing from the information he had from Pensacola, Gálvez pointed out the occasions when Spanish and French ships had been "violated" by British ships even on the lakes by New Orleans.[33]

All of this transpired during the heat of August in New Orleans. From the beginning of the exchange, Gálvez offered the envoys the hospitality of his city "so that you could enjoy more comfort than the river offers." However, he took the moral high ground by protesting the tone of Chester's letter as well as the mission of the two envoys. He would not submit himself to a British investigation that amounted to establishing "a tribunal in my own jurisdiction." He found that attitude to be an abuse of his hospitality. The envoys took the hint and stayed on board the *Atlanta* the whole month, although Gálvez cleverly left the decision to disembark with them.[34]

One little surprise came to Gálvez in a letter from the envoys on August 17. Although they were not sure of the particulars, they heard that an English village was raided by "the crew of a certain corsair . . . belonging to the rebel subjects of His British Majesty," who were armed and equipped by the agent of the rebel colonies, Oliver Pollock, a resident of New Orleans.[35] This was the first official and direct mention of Pollock, his loyalties, and activities to Spanish authorities. Chester, through his envoys, carefully suggested Spain's duplicity in the matter.

Gálvez ignored the insinuation and instead used the incident to accuse the British of using it as a weak defense for "the many violent acts committed by its own forces." How could he be accused of violence "upon the boat owners," the smugglers, when aside from the immediate incident, Dickson and Stephenson could cite only one "and this you impute to be an American pirate armed by the agent of the rebel colonies Oliver Pollock?" How could he be responsible for a ship that is armed and American when its flag is British? He had no knowledge that there was a rebel agent residing in his town nor, as he cleverly put it, "that his name was Oliver." The "other Pollock I already knew," he continued, "as an honest trader born in Ireland." He would be more careful with ships as well as with "this Mr. Oliver, whom I never surmised to be a person of such great importance." Besides, the ship in question was now in possession of the British and they should be careful in accusing Oliver "as a pirate for being a rebel," for as Gálvez understood the incident another person committed the transgression.[36]

As had been predicted, the envoys returned to Pensacola after accomplishing nothing. Chester did not receive satisfaction for any of his demands. If anything, he did learn that his counterpart in New Orleans was a man of resolve as well as clever. Chester's envoys could not even maneuver themselves into the town to collect the kind of information Gálvez's trusted spy had gathered about Pensacola.

Circumstances, although unfortunate, presented Gálvez with another opportunity to interact with Chester and to exhibit another side of his personality, if not the methodology of treating a potential enemy, during this period. Three days before Gálvez penned his longest and final answer to Dickson and Stephenson, he wrote a letter to Governor Chester about a matter that concerned him. Although in a separate letter he stressed that he was not using spies, he heard that Pensacola was suffering from a lack of critical goods because the normal supply ship had not arrived.[37] He therefore gathered together 150 barrels of wheat and ordered one of his frigates to take the foodstuff to Pensacola.[38] The gesture was purely meant as goodwill. Gálvez really intended to help, especially the sick and infirm.[39]

Chester, who appeared to be every bit as much a gentleman as Gálvez, seemed authentically impressed with Gálvez's gesture. Pensacola was suffering with many sick people. Gálvez, who knew from his inside information that Chester had sixty completely incapacitated soldiers, also learned that the suffering had extended to many of the citizens, including the women and children. Under the circumstances of impending war, Gálvez made a generous gesture. That the ship's crew was ordered to stay on board while in Pensacola certified Gálvez's good intents.[40] He easily could have tried to use the opportunity to garner even more information about Pensacola—even if he did not need it.

But the aid was sent in vain, for a British ship of supplies arrived from Jamaica to render Gálvez's gift unnecessary. Gálvez's "benevolent intention," Chester wrote, was "sincerely appreciated." He added that he wanted to praise Gálvez with the highest sentiment for his politics, under the present circumstances. As a gesture of thanks, Chester ordered that two barrels of port beer be sent back to the Spanish governor on the Spanish transport ship.[41]

Gálvez's only motive to send aid to his future enemy was his humanitarian spirit and, as he wrote to his uncle in Spain, "to win good feelings from [his] neighbors."[42] He might have felt that their relations had hit a low when Dickson and Stephenson were in town. Although he did not write his concern, he might have felt that the presence of the *Atlanta,* which was a fully armed British frigate facing New Orleans, was a threat. Nevertheless, he did not back down from his position, leaving the British envoy and their frigate with nothing to do but leave. If Gálvez intended to soothe feelings by sending aid to Pensacola, he succeeded.[43]

The British were so taken by both of Gálvez's actions, their "malicious" spy system failed to note that Gálvez released two of the eleven ships he had confiscated.

Both of the released ships belonged to the rebels.[44] This may have been what he was referring to in his release of prisoners for Pentecost.

Spain's duplicity in favor of the Americans, at this time, is further demonstrated when Gálvez was notified by Lieutenant George Morgan that Fort Pitt had received a shipment of supplies that originated in New Orleans. Morgan also wanted information about Pensacola in anticipation of an American move against the port. Gálvez replied that he was pleased to hear the good news and that further help was Morgan's for the asking, for he was anxious to see Morgan and his colleagues succeed. Gálvez assured the colonial officer that he would do everything he could to keep supplies ready. However, he reported nothing about Pensacola. The governor wrote his letter at the same time that he was arguing legal points with Chester's men.[45] Gálvez proved to be very resilient.

Peter Chester could do nothing about the situation, even though he knew that Spain, and Gálvez in particular, were helping the insurgents. Great Britain wanted to suppress the traffic through New Orleans, but policy dictated caution because, above all, Great Britain did not want to provoke Spain into a declaration of war. Chester, as Gálvez well knew, had to tend to his own defenses.[46]

The Spanish governor was further heartened when he began receiving official reaction to his reports, all of which had been sent to Spain. The king was so pleased with Bernardo's trusted man that he ordered the governor to continue along that vein.[47] In regard to his confiscation of the British smugglers, Gálvez received a letter sent from the monastery of San Lorenzo del Escorial in which Carlos III approved of his attempts to forbid illicit trade and requested, as a matter of secret policy, that all Spanish officials follow suit. The royal letter pointed out that examples could be made of the English.[48] Then after review of Gálvez's reports about Chester, his envoys and the exchange of correspondence between them and Gálvez, the king sent his "approval and sovereign gratitude."[49] Finally, Carlos III completely approved of Gálvez's humanitarian gesture "for the extreme necessity that those neighbors [in Pensacola] were suffering."[50] Eventually, the king ordered that Gálvez be reimbursed for his expense in purchasing the wheat that was sent to Pensacola.[51]

Gálvez's activity perhaps anticipated the swirl of events that began in the late summer and fall of 1777. The news of the battle of Saratoga, the arrival of the United States commissioners in Europe, and a heightened Spanish involvement, with the appointments of Puente and Grimaldi to the United States, all occurred at this time. A British retaliation could be expected. Bernardo de Gálvez did not have to wait long to receive a report of a British "insult" to a Spanish ship. If Gálvez thought that British aggression had reached "a point of intolerable insolence difficult to be borne by a man of honor," he now had to prepare for even more such activity.[52]

At the end of July, the San Pedro Thelmo, a Spanish mail ship, was "extorted" by two pirate "corsarios" under British flags. Another neutral merchant ship suffered the same fate. The San Pedro Thelmo was carrying correspondence between the Spanish and French islands, but had originated from Cádiz.[53] After August, British patrols kept a closer watch on the Mississippi River. As a matter of practice, British confiscation of "contraband" and the ships transporting such aid to the colonies had become a lucrative business in Jamaica, where a special court was set up to determine the guilt or innocence of such ships. That the court and those who captured the ships received the benefits of the ship's cargoes assured a lack of justice not lost on anyone but the British. By the end of December, Bernardo de Gálvez was warning as well as reporting to Spain that, "passing through the Mississippi River, while not impossible, was, at least, very difficult."[54]

Perhaps acting on Gálvez's request for more support for the defense of New Orleans, and certainly in reaction to the Dickson and Stephenson affair and British affronts, Navarro felt compelled to inform José de Gálvez that a packet boat and a frigate named *El Valiente* had been assigned to the Mississippi River before Bernardo de Gálvez began his term. Commander General Don Juan Baptista Bonet, the chief of the navy in the West Indies, agreed with Navarro that two ships were sufficient. Bernardo de Gálvez, for the time being, would not receive the second frigate that he requested. Navarro and Bonet organized and planned the naval activities in the area. They did not feel it was necessary to consult with the new governor.[55] Perhaps the successes in New Orleans were beginning to be tiresome to the hierarchy in Havana.

Plate 1. Photograph of the reproduced flag of the Regiment of Spain given to the State of New Mexico as a bicentennial gift from Spain. Collections of the Palace of the Governors, Santa Fe.

Plate 2. Photograph of the reproduced flag of the Regiment of Navarra given to the State of New Mexico as a bicentennial gift from Spain. Collections of the Palace of the Governors, Santa Fe.

Plate 3. Photograph of the reproduced flag of the Regiment of the King given to the State of New Mexico as a bicentennial gift from Spain. Collections of the Palace of the Governors, Santa Fe.

Plate 4. Carlos III, King of Spain. Painting by Antonio Rafael Mengs. Original in the Prado Museum, Madrid. From Reparaz, Yo Solo, *16.*

Plate 5. Painting of Macharavialla, the birthplace of the Gálvezes. Original in the collections of the Louisiana Arts and Science Center, Old Governor's Mansion, Baton Rouge, Louisiana. From Woodward, Jr., Tribute to Don Bernardo de Gálvez, *frontispiece.*

Plate 6. Carlos III leaving Naples to become the King of Spain. Painting by Antonio Joli. Original in the Prado Museum, Madrid. From Reparaz, Yo Solo, *12–13.*

Plate 7. José Moñino y Redondo, the Count of Floridablanca, Spain's patient Minister of State who orchestrated Spain's participation in the war. Oil painting by Francisco Goya. Original in the Prado Museum, Madrid. From Reparaz, Yo Solo, 37.

Plate 8. Eighteenth-Century Spanish Frigate. Original painting in the Museo Naval, Madrid. From Reparaz, Yo Solo, *89.*

Plate 9. Uniform of the Regiment of Louisiana. AGI, Seville. From Reparaz, Yo Solo, 33.

Plate 10. Portrait of General George Washington. From Blum et al., The National Experience, *133.*

Plate 11. Matías de Gálvez, father of Bernardo, brother of José, commander of the successful campaigns against British forces in Central America, and viceroy of New Spain (Mexico). Oil painting by Andrés López, eighteenth century. Original in the Museo Nacional del Virreinato, Mexico. From Bradley Smith, Mexico: A History in Art, *194.*

Plate 12. Engineer's uniform, 18th-century. Grenadier, Regiment of Aragon. Grenadier, Regiment of Hibernia. Uniform of the 2nd Regiment of Cataluña. From Reparaz, Yo Solo, *176.*

Plate 13. Grenadier, Regiment of Navarra. From Estado Militar de España, *1790; and* Reparaz, Yo Solo, *57.*

Plate 14. Battle of Cape Santa María between Admiral Rodney and General Lángara, 1780. The valiant Lángara made Rodney and the British pay for their victory. Lángara is here shown still fighting on his flagship that is all shot up. Anonymous oil painting. Original in the Museo Naval, Madrid.

Plate 15. Naval commander José Solano y Bote. Original in the Museo Naval, Madrid. From Reparaz, Yo Solo, *145.*

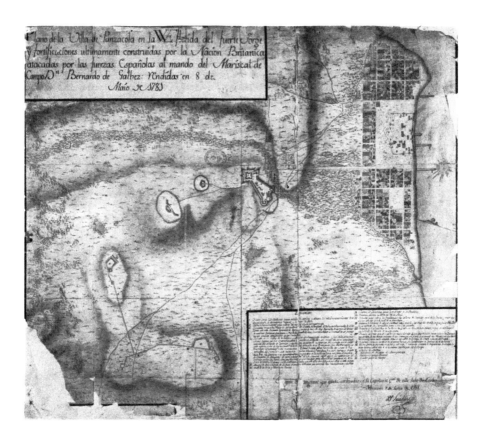

Plate 16. Plano de la villa de Panzacola, del fuerte Jorge y fortificaciones últimamente construidas por la Nación Británica. . . . *By Luis Huet, July 1781. Original in Servicio Histórico Militar, Madrid. From Reparaz, Yo Solo, 169.*

Plate 17. Pensacola under attack. A contemporary sketch. Original in Biblioteca Nacional, Madrid. From Montemayor, Yo Solo, xviii–xix.

E	11 La Iglesia	16 El Castillo bolado de media Luna
A	12 Trinchera delos Españoles	Se Hallaron Madrid en la Librería
ñoles	13 Desembarco	de la Viuda de Miguel Escribano.
	14 Tropa Española	Calle de Carretas N° 8
	15 Tropa Inglesa y el fuerte	Con el Nuevo Gibraltar.
	Jorge	

Contemporary view of the Fort and Bay of Pensacola, depicting the Spanish invasion. (Biblioteca Nacional, Madrid, 1781; Library of Congress.)

Plate 18. Painting of Bernardo de Gálvez with the brigantine Galveztown *in the background. Painting by Algustín Berlingero. Original in the Museo Naval, Madrid. From Reparaz,* Yo Solo, *92.*

Plate 19. Brigantine with sixteen cannons, like the Galveztown. *Drawing by Algustín Berlingero. Original in the Museo Naval, Madrid. From Reparaz,* Yo Solo, *93.*

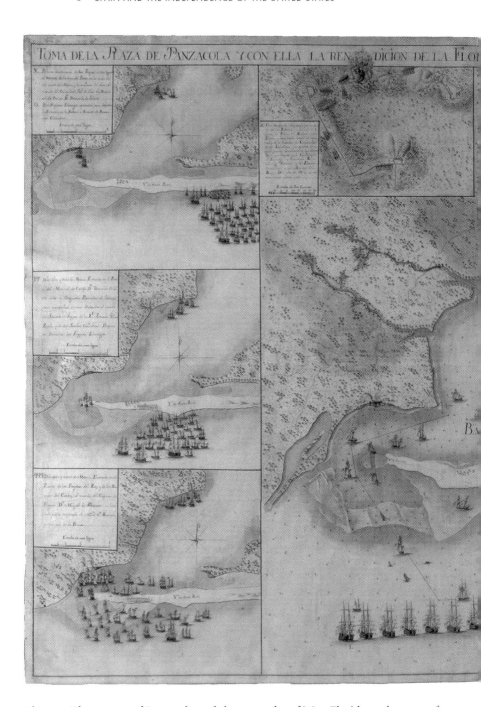

Plate 20. The capture of Pensacola and the surrender of West Florida to the arms of King Carlos III, 1781. Original in the Museo Naval, Madrid. From Reparaz, Yo Solo, 147.

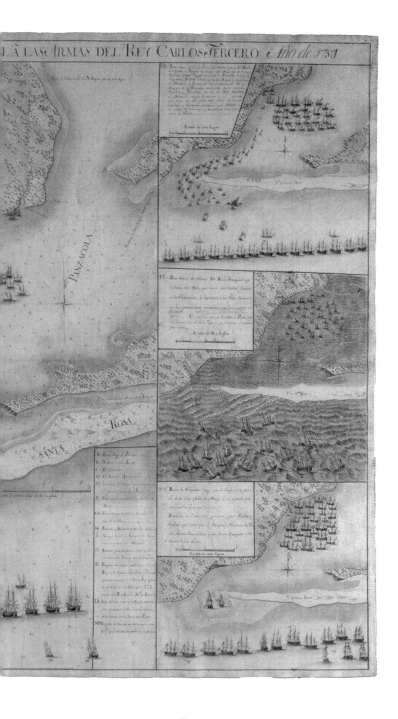

Plate 21. British flag taken by Bernardo de Gálvez with the defeat of Pensacola in May 1781. A portrait of Gálvez is at the top of the frame. Museo Ejército, Madrid. From Reparaz, Yo Solo, *201.*

Plate 22. Francisco Saavedra. The king's emissary and strategist whose quick thinking resulted in the American victory at Yorktown. Oil painting by Francisco Goya. Original in the Courtauld Institute Galleries, (Lee Collection), London. From Reparaz, Yo Solo, 36.

Plate 23. First Marquess, Lord Cornwallis, Commander of the British forces in the last campaign at Yorktown. Engraving by John Jones. Original in the Yale Center for British Art. Photo: Bridgeman Art Library.

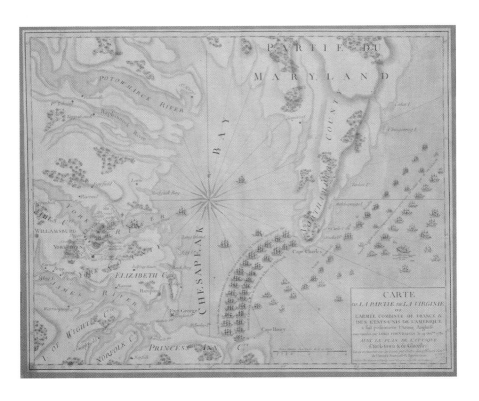

Plate 24. The Siege of Yorktown, showing Williamsburg and Yorktown left of center, naval action of the Battle of the Bay, right of center, and the subsequent blockade of the bay by the French fleet. Original in the Library of Congress. From Tuchman, The First Salute, *208.*

Plate 25. French ships. Watercolor by Rafael Monleon y Torres. Original in the Museo Naval, Madrid. From Reparaz, Yo Solo, 96.

Gen. Bernardo de Gálvez
Battle of Mobile 1780

*Plate 26.
Stamp issued in the United
States commemorating the 1780
Battle of Mobile. Original in
the collections of the Palace of
the Governors, Santa Fe.*

Plate 27. Gálvez family shield, reflecting the many family exploits, especially in the Americas. From Woodward, Tribute to Don Bernardo de Gálvez, *2; and Reparaz,* Yo Solo, *9.*

Plate 28. *Portrait of Bernardo de Gálvez, the Count of Gálvez, commander of all Spanish forces in the Gulf, and viceroy of New Spain (Mexico). Oil painting by Father Pablo de Jesús in 1796. Original in Chapultepec Castle, Mexico City. From National Museum of History: Chapultepec Castle, plate 9.*

Plate 29. Diego María de Gardoqui, Spanish banker, strategist, and diplomat who arranged for aid for the rebellious colonies and, then, became the first Spanish ambassador appointed to the young United States of America. Anonymous oil painting. Original in the collections of the Palace of the Governors, Santa Fe.

SIX

Antebellum Anxiety, 1777–1779

I have, as yet, no accounts by which I may venture to act on the offensive against the subjects of Spain, which I ardently desire.

British Colonel Henry Hamilton, 1779

Navarro formally took office six months after Gálvez, on 11 June 1777. His sense of measured caution contrasted with Torre, his predecessor, who tended to be more of an innovator. Navarro would have some hard decisions to make, but he had help, for he depended on his staff. He was a prudent and calculating, if not stubborn man—a soldier who believed in regulations and who, above all, desired to serve his king. He was not an innovator and believed in an environment where he could freely depend on his consultants. These were Puente, Bonet, and Antonio Ramón Valle, a talented assistant who came from Spain to be Navarro's secretary.[1]

Navarro oversaw Spain's North American policies from his desk. All the supplies going to the colonies were sent from Havana to various delivery points, including New Orleans. He managed the budget for all the aid, subversive activity, and official governmental functions in Louisiana, as well as the Gulf region. Both officially and unofficially, his office would be the conduit for orders and correspondence permeating throughout the Spanish Americas. On some occasions he had to take action with Spanish officials who were not administratively responsible to him. As will be seen, this created friction. He also had to defend Havana. Influential residents of the commercially rich city had clear memories of the recent war in which Great Britain laid siege and captured the city. Since then, the governors and captain generals in Havana were especially aware of the city's defense and worked closely with the various military commanders to assure success in the advent of war. Obviously, the most important of these commanders would be the man in charge of the navy—Bonet.

At that moment, Navarro was being sensible in following Bonet's advice and refusing young Bernardo de Gálvez's request. Navarro encouraged Bernardo's efforts to strengthen the fortifications of New Orleans and fulfilled a request for more cannons.[2] The British also had a presence in the Gulf and Caribbean, about which Navarro received reports from Puente in Florida, as well as representatives of Indian tribes coming to Havana. The information presented the strong appearance of danger to Havana. Sending a warship to New Orleans was not a matter to be taken lightly.

In late December of 1779, Puente dashed off some letters to José de Gálvez exhibiting unbridled enthusiasm for East Florida. The spy felt that the Indians would side with Spain, the Americans would help, and Spain had a historical right to the land. East Florida, in his mind, was the key to Spanish success in the area.[3] Puente's friend, Commander Bonet, vouched for his expertise, which no doubt added weight to his arguments in Navarro's mind.[4]

The arrival of Indians from the "Uchiz" or Creek nation probably had been arranged by Puente to press his point. Transported on a *"goleta,"* the schooner *San Antonio,*[5] the twelve Indians were led by a man named Tunapé. He reported that the English had just sent agents from Pensacola to the different Indian nations in Florida, listed as the Talapucas (Tallapoosa, part of the Creek Tribe), Aquicas, Chicas, Chizcas (Chichas), Allamos, and Chatacas (Choctaws). Tunapé wanted to help the Spanish defeat the British, especially at a fort named Apalache that had been in British possession for eight years. Englishmen surrounded his nation. They prohibited his tribe from fishing in the river they traditionally used. If the Spanish could supply him with arms and munitions, including "a flag with the king's coat-of-arms," the Creek Indians with the Tallapoosa nation, "who always cooperate as brothers" will help defeat the English. In boasting of the two tribes' bravery, Tunapé belittled those Indian nations who had befriended the English, in the process naming the Cahataques (Choctaws), Chicasdes, Cusupuyas, Charchices (Cherokees), Yaches, and Mojoas.[6]

A couple of weeks after Tunapé pledged his nation's cooperation, Navarro reported that a British corsair from Carolina had stopped a Spanish brigantine sailing from Cartagena.[7] Navarro had his hands full.

In Louisiana, Gálvez increasingly attracted Navarro's attention because the area seemed to become a British priority. Great Britain began patrolling the Mississippi with two war ships that, at times, fronted New Orleans. Under any circumstance, such action could be taken as hostile. Besides the affront, the ships stopped all traffic on the river. Bernardo de Gálvez, whether he had the resources or not, was not the type of man to be intimidated. Drawing on the experience and information of his covert operations, Gálvez wrote a letter of protest to Chester and assigned Captain Jacinto Panis to personally deliver and negotiate an arrangement with Pensacola's governor.[8]

Gálvez conveyed that he did not consider the actions of His British Majesty's ships, the *Margot* and *Providence,* to be "a dignified representation" of Chester. He was tired of the insults and wanted to create some kind of understanding.[9] Gálvez understood that Chester was trying to make a point but wondered at what cost.[10]

Gálvez had the opportunity to return Chester's gesture of sending Dickson and Stephenson to New Orleans, when he sent Panis to visit Chester. Before he was through, Panis traveled through British-held Mobile and Pensacola, where he recorded details of the defenses of both places. His plans for the capture of Pensacola were eventually implemented.[11]

Gálvez used the excuse of British taunting on the Mississippi to send Panis to Pensacola. Panis's trip is a perfect example of the kind of direct action and forethought

Fig. 8. José de Gálvez, Minister of the Indies, the Spanish political lightening rod who directed fulfillment of Spain's military strategy in the Americas. From Reparaz, Yo Solo, 14.

becoming rampant in Spanish policy, which Bernardo de Gálvez perfected. Nor would he rely on one source. In a revealing document dated 30 April 1778, Navarro listed the expenses for two men named Joaquín Escalona and Julián Flores. They had been in Pensacola "examining" British warships then anchored in the bay. A report by Puente was connected with Navarro's account. Puente listed the villages and numbers of men, women, and children of the Creek Indians.[12] Between Navarro and Gálvez, British Florida was becoming an open secret.

Perhaps in a surprise move, because of how quickly it happened, Captain James Willing, commanding the Continental ship the *Rattletrap*, sailed down the Mississippi with a detachment of soldiers and attacked the British settlement at Natchez, which quickly surrendered. The inhabitants were made prisoners of war. Willing allowed them to name a committee to draw up the articles of capitulation, to which he agreed. Willing and his men then went on to capture the English posts of Concord, opposite the mouth of the Arkansas River, Arkansas, and Manchac, and some British ships. Gálvez reported that a frigate had been taken at Manchac and a brigantine in the mouth of the river.[13]

Gálvez soon found out that Willing, perhaps flushed with success, had gone on to capture another frigate, the *Neptune,* which was anchored at the village of Arkansas, which was actually in Spanish territory. This forced a reaction from the Spanish governor. Willing had violated Spanish neutrality and almost ruined Panis's mission to West Florida. Willing would have to return the *Neptune,* its cargo, and three black slaves. He would also have to apologize. In these requests Gálvez wrote to Willing that "I will not deviate one single bit."[14]

Willing's activities obviously irritated Gálvez. He reiterated Spain's position of strict neutrality and received Willing's promise "not to get over excited." Instead, the American commander's enthusiasm had placed Spain and "the king's confidence in me" in jeopardy. Willing, when questioned, argued his position and Gálvez had to be very direct. The situation needed to be remedied and, Gálvez wrote to the American captain, he would "employ all" his "facilities" and he expected Willing to "contribute and accede" to his desire. Gálvez went on to quote law, the sense of betrayal he felt, and then specifically laid out where the frigate had been captured. He then queried:

I ask you now, was it Spanish territory, the riverbank on which the brigantine, the *Neptune* had been docked for several days? Is Spain a neutral nation in respect to yours and Great Britain?[15]

He framed the questions so that the answers would be self-evident and followed with the query that how could anyone think the *Neptune* was not protected?[16] Willing's next two letters gave ground. Gálvez would have his way. Interestingly, Willing even argued over keeping the slaves he had captured.[17]

Gálvez's situation was even more complicated, for many of the British citizens fled from their settlements before the United States contingent. They were now helpless before the Choctaw Indians, who raided the British settlements soon after Willing had finished.[18] The citizens mentioned this problem in their articles of capitulation, but the Americans, for some unexplained reason, could not prevent their Indian allies from raiding. Gálvez thus received and granted protection to those who asked. These people seemed horrified at how they had been treated and what had happened to them. They were more than thankful for Spanish protection, for Harry Alexander, the former first magistrate of the River District, wrote to Gálvez that they did not understand how they could have been "most cruelly treated by a Set of people who ought to have thought us the same with themselves; nay even as to our political principles they neither asked a Question nor gave us a choice." He added:

> On the contrary your Excellency has set a noble example of humanity and generosity worthy of that most Excellent Prince whose representative you are; And it is our duty to proclaim to all the world, and in particular to the Court of Great Britain the Beneficent part which you have so generously and seasonably taken.[19]

Gálvez received three such letters of appreciation for his actions. Henry Stuart, the British Intendant of Indians, who took refuge under Spanish protection, wrote the first letter, in which he stated, "I have not words to express my gratitude." Indeed, he was an important person and the Americans wanted him badly.[20] The last undated letter contained the signatures of thirty-six British subjects and residents of Manchac. They, too, appreciated the humane treatment they had received from Gálvez.[21]

While he expended energy seeing to the proper treatment of these people, he had to face two British frigates anchored in his harbor facing his city. Not coincidentally, Chester sent the ships with another complaint and, of course, the usual demands. He ordered Gálvez to capture and turn over the rebel renegades, release the British prisoners, ships, and so on. Specifically, Chester wanted Gálvez to arrest Irishmen who had become American sympathizers. These traitors, claimed Chester, were residents of New Orleans.

During all of this, one of the frigates apparently fired a shot. Fortunately no damage was done. Whether or not the firing was accidental, the incident could have precipitated a conflict neither side wanted.[22]

Meanwhile, Willing camped outside of the city. His greater mission was to meet with Gálvez, deliver more letters from Congress, and receive supplies to take back upriver. Thus, while being rebuffed and scolded for violating Spain's neutrality, he witnessed all the above commotion. He was aghast at the impudence of John Fergusson, the British naval captain responsible for the discharged shot. Willing wanted Gálvez's permission to attack Fergusson's ship. But Gálvez, with a larger picture in mind, prevailed against any such action.[23]

To make sure that there would be no misunderstanding, Gálvez had a public proclamation published in which he laid down strict rules of neutrality. Spain should observe a "perfect neutrality" between the two belligerents.[24] As governor for a neutral country, he could "indistinctly concede to one and the other" his government's hospitality when he felt it was needed. He hoped this simple position would clear up any confusion resulting from the recent events.[25]

In addition, Gálvez wanted to keep the British at bay while he fulfilled Willing's orders for supplies. To do this, he followed international law, while violating his king's instructions to him. He had been ordered to close his port to all British citizens except in cases of emergency. Instead, Gálvez seized the opportunity to cover up his clandestine activities with the Americans, who were technically British citizens, and for genuine humane reasons, violated his instructions to offer sanctuary to British citizens. Gálvez wrote to his uncle, the minister of the Indies, that he hoped that he would receive the king's approval after the fact.[26] Not only did he receive royal approval and appreciation for his "prudence, care and good conduct," but also Carlos III granted him special liberty to continue to act as he saw fit in carrying out policy.[27]

Willing delivered some important documents that included congressional letters confirming the appointment of Oliver Pollock as an agent for the United States Congress. As already mentioned, Gálvez received from Robert Morris and William Smith an account of Saratoga. Willing's instructions read that he needed to pick up more supplies because the rebellion had spread into the Illinois country.[28]

By now France had signed the treaties of alliance with the colonies, Britain was changing its strategy to a more southern emphasis, and everyone in the West Indies seemed certain that Spain and England would soon be at war. Willing's escapades worried Gálvez, for he had British warships in his harbor, British citizens in his town, and people were already tense enough. He hoped that the British would not be provoked into war over Manchac and Natchez. Even when the two British ships weighed anchor and left for Jamaica, the governor wrote that he had his "horse saddled at all hours." Indeed, "all the horses are saddled."[29]

All of Galvez's agents began to report that the British intended to force him, if necessary, to acquiesce to their demands. His people kept watch over the other British corsairs on the lakes around New Orleans. He assigned a schooner solely for that purpose. Although he was short of supplies and he had released the crew that he felt had been wrongly captured, he did not give in to British demands.[30] Perhaps because France's new alliance with the colonies diverted their attention or they just did not feel strong enough to attack New Orleans with Willing's contingent close by, the British threats remained only words. Most likely Chester did not want to be the person who started a war with Spain so, once again, cooler heads prevailed.

Willing's victories were short-lived. British ships transporting soldiers soon sailed for Manchac. By June of 1778, the British made a show of strength with the arrival of over four hundred British soldiers. These were the first British troops sent to the area. Now, the British would invest a little more effort in the area's defense.[31] Lieutenants DuBreüil and Collel kept Gálvez informed of the British buildup.[32]

Gálvez, in noting Great Britain's efforts to maintain its hold on the Mississippi and hearing from his lieutenant governors stationed in the town of St. Louis in upper Louisiana, made sure that the northern part of his new province followed his policies and kept alert for expected British activity. First Francisco Cruzat and then Fernando de Leyba, who took over in March 1778, reported on the potential enemy.[33] Among other things, they reported a British plan to attack Louisiana from the north.[34] Eventually, Gálvez used his own father-in-law, Gilbert Antoine de St. Maxent, to travel upriver where he secretly compiled detailed plans of the newly constructed Fort Bute at Manchac, while overtly checking on some land that he owned. St. Maxent's exact plans would become instrumental in Gálvez's eventual success after war was declared.[35]

The best way to stop any possible aggression from upriver was to help the Americans successfully hold Fort Pitt. Fulfilling Willing's and Pollock's orders for supplies and money was of paramount importance.

Willing had orders to escort the supplies destined for Fort Pitt. He would transport the supplies upriver where they would be used by the Continental troops fighting in the Ohio River Valley. Congress hoped that the supplies were already in storage in New Orleans so they could be sent quickly.[36] As Gálvez found out, the supplies went to George Rogers Clark, who was busy countering the plans and aspirations of British Colonel Henry Hamilton.[37]

Gálvez had the supplies in storage and ready for shipping. By 2 May 1778 a bill of transfer had been drawn up, signed by all parties, and the goods turned over to Willing, who successfully transported the shipment to St. Louis. Lieutenant Governor Leyba immediately wrote to George Rogers Clark to inform him that the supplies had arrived and would be held until Clark sent instructions. Leyba also congratulated Clark on his recent victory at Kaskaskia. Meanwhile a second shipment arrived in St. Louis. Pollock arranged for this second load of supplies to be escorted upriver by a Mr. Besolill. Clark initially did not know whether the supplies were his or were destined for Virginia. He then received assurances that the Congress and Virginia were receiving supplies, via a different route.[38]

Pollock had, in effect, been promoted. He now represented Congress, which hoped to extend the agent's personal credit to cover the many emergencies and expenses that arose. For example, to get the major part of the above order to the colonies proper, he needed to contract for five or six ships to transport the goods. This, too, had to be done expeditiously, for the Congressmen Smith and Morris wrote, "prompt dispatch is very essential and necessary since we are in great need of these articles."[39]

In May 1778, a special request was forwarded to Navarro in Havana. Congress asked him to inquire of Spain whether United States ships could receive permission to trade as well as receive protection in Spain's Cuban ports? Secondly, could the United States assign an agent to Havana?[40] Pollock must have known that U.S. ships could seek refuge in Havana, since the fall of 1776. They could not trade, but were given the same treatment as French and English ships. Navarro answered that the current system of covertly trading through New Orleans was better, and that agreeing to such requests might cause British suspicion. Furthermore, his government wished to maintain its neutral status.[41] In fact, Navarro reiterated the necessity of maintaining the appearance of neutrality in a letter to Bernardo de Gálvez written four days earlier. On top of the American requests and actions and the British reactions, Navarro was aware of the complications of maintaining neutrality now that France entered the war and became one of the belligerents. In addition, Navarro had bypassed New Orleans as an information gathering center because Willing's expedition disrupted relations with West Florida.[42]

Navarro, as well as Gálvez, knew that the United States received all that it had requested in money and supplies. Spain would have no problems extending credit to Pollock to help expedite matters. The Spanish saw this last as an act of aid, not really expecting a payback. Neither Pollock nor Congress had enough money or goods to secure the kind of aid they required. A congressional guarantee, at that moment, amounted to a promise of future trade. Nevertheless, the ever-honorable Pollock assumed the position of personally borrowing money for the cause. Congress, in turn, would reimburse the agent, or so he believed. By the time Spain entered the war in mid-1779, Pollock had resorted to using his slaves for public works in New Orleans, and had mortgaged some of his land to fulfill a request from Patrick Henry, then governor of Virginia. One historian has written that by the end of the war Pollock was $300,000 in debt.[43]

Spanish money and supplies flowing through New Orleans under Bernardo de Gálvez's supervision became so extensive that Spanish money had completely boosted Continental currency and had become fairly commonplace among the colonies. This was especially true in the west where Leyba extended credit to George Rogers Clark. Leyba, about whom Clark noted to Patrick Henry, "interests himself much in favor of the States," got the citizens of St. Louis to furnish credit for Clark's effort, and thus their own eventual defense. Because of Spanish money, Continental currency, in spite of speculators, was sustained at par in the west, while in the east it dropped to twelve cents per dollar.[44]

Gálvez made the decision to extend credit to Pollock and he once again hoped to get approval after the fact. Leyba had no problem following Gálvez's lead. In June 1778, Gálvez turned over 24,023 *pesos* or $72,690 in modern equivalencies, in two payments to Pollock, which was in addition to the value of 26,990 *pesos* worth of supplies that had been assigned to go upriver.[45] Pollock immediately started arranging for ships and began arming the *Rebecca,* a captured British corvette or frigate that would escort the shipment.

Apparently, the *Rebecca* had been one of the ships captured by Willing's men that Gálvez determined was a legal act. Pollock, perhaps for his role in the capture, used the *Rebecca* as his personal ship, which he renamed the *Morris.*[46]

Pollock and another American officer, Captain William Pickles, agreed with Gálvez's position, on their word of honor, that they would abide by Spain's neutrality while in Spanish territory. Pollock had received official permission to outfit the ship under great secrecy and Spanish protection. This was especially dangerous, for Pollock noted that "the fortune of war had cast a small detachment of American troops into his regime" and that Gálvez conceded his government's hospitality "with the attention to the critical situation of such public business."[47]

Based on the list of supplies that went north, rifles and clothing, especially uniforms, became important items in these shipments. In addition, Pollock specifically mentioned gunpowder and, by current standards, some thirty to fifty thousand dollars' worth of blankets that had passed from Spanish to American hands in the last half of 1778. Spain's support of the American colonies before entering the war was unprecedented. Pollock himself would, at the least, receive another two payments in October that totaled 15,948 *pesos fuertes* and, subsequently, 22,640 *pesos fuertes* the following July.[48]

The second set of payments came at a time when Gálvez had received another contingent of American soldiers under the command of David Rogers. Patrick Henry sent Rogers to deliver more letters soliciting additional aid and assistance. Unfortunately, the British had all but closed the river to such activities so that, Gálvez informed Henry, for the time being shipments would have to go through the Gulf of Mexico and up the east coast. Pollock, with a Captain Robert, who also had to swear that he would not attack any British possessions while under Spanish protection, needed to outfit more ships and an escort. Pollock spent his money to arm the *Rebecca*.[49]

Gálvez was convinced that Great Britain would strike its first blow at Spain by attacking New Orleans. His own forces and defenses had not yet been strengthened, so he felt exposed. In July, two of his commanders reported a botched British plan to use Indians to attack Spanish settlements and eventually devastate New Orleans. Lieutenant Juan de la Villebreuve, a Spanish commissioner to the Choctaw nation, reported in early July that the British had devised a plan involving two frigates and 2,450 men, only 250 of whom were English. The majority of the army, which was supposed to gather at Manchac, was made up of fifteen hundred Choctaws, four hundred "Chicachas" (Chickasaws), and three hundred Cherokees. Because the Cherokees and the Chickasaws feared the Americans, the expedition was aborted.[50] This report was confirmed by infantry Captain Carlos de Grand-Pré, who cited the same Indian tribes, and noted that the date for attacking "our establishments" was scheduled "for dawn on August 24." The captain agreed with Villebreuve that the two tribes' lack of interest in the venture killed the plan. He added that he thought "the English certainly have the idea of making trouble against us by using Indians without appearing to have a part in it."[51]

Even Navarro agreed with Gálvez's assessment, for one of his spies wrote from Pensacola that a British ship had suffered an accident in the harbor at Pensacola while they were building up strength. It looked like the British were preparing for something.[52]

As will be seen, the whole English strategy in the American West was to use

Indians against their enemies. Colonel Henry Hamilton planned to use Indians to move down the Ohio and Mississippi rivers.[53] But the great care and patience about which the Spanish officials were constantly reminding themselves to maintain the appearance of neutrality frustrated the British commander. "I have, as yet, no accounts by which I may venture to act on the offensive against the subjects of Spain, which I ardently desire."[54] Eventually, the boastful Englishman wrote Bernardo de Gálvez that he did not appreciate Spain's role in furnishing his rival George Rogers Clark with munitions.[55]

The reality of the force behind Hamilton's words was being confirmed. Villebreuve and Grand-Pré were both trusted officers. Their reports were in keeping with the history of information streaming into both New Orleans and Havana. Navarro, although he did not seem as concerned as Gálvez, did send a detachment of 212 men to New Orleans in May.[56] Gálvez passed all his information to Navarro, adding that he needed more knowledge about Manchac and that a garrison of 695 German mercenaries from the German province Waldeck had been stationed at Pensacola and Manchac. The Germans, along with 170 Pennsylvania loyalists and 313 Maryland loyalists, had been shipped to Pensacola before most of them were transferred to Manchac. They originated in New York, leaving there in October 1778.[57] Gálvez knew this because he received twenty-six deserters in New Orleans. Obviously, Gálvez needed to be concerned about British designs on Louisiana.[58]

With Pollock and the American troops, who were disguised as merchants and innocuous citizens, Gálvez had a nice supplement to his own paltry forces. Not only would he grant permission for American troops to pass through Spanish territory, and thereby past British blockades, he would be happy for them to delay a bit while their transportation was being prepared. As he wrote to José de Gálvez, he lived under the suspicion of a British attack as well as the growing appearance of war so "I have detained the American detachment . . . to have strength available."[59] The Americans apparently stayed in New Orleans through October, for it was not until October 24 that Gálvez fulfilled Pollock's second request for funds, essentially to help fix the *Rebecca*.[60]

Actually, Gálvez knew of the pending arrival of more American troops within weeks after receiving his officers' reports. Willing had started downriver with another contingent, but because of the British buildup above New Orleans, he decided to return to Fort Pitt. He turned his command over to David Rogers, who with seven others, successfully pressed on to the Spanish port to get more supplies.[61] They had rowed down the Mississippi River in a large canoe, avoiding the British. Patrick Henry sent them. This is when Gálvez replied that the British had closed the river, making it next to impossible to transport contraband supplies.[62]

A month later, Gálvez's informers reported that the British had "arrested" two ships at Nátchez. This caused Gálvez to remind Grand-Pré to maintain neutrality and to express his feeling that the British were planning to attack.

Again, on this very busy October 24, Gálvez issued payments to some of his informers.[63] The network kept the governor abreast of all events pertinent to his responsibilities in Louisiana. Gálvez's success in garnering information from the British prepared him for his eventual military successes. Panis's earlier diplomatic mission to Pensacola ostensibly accomplished little, but secretly garnered a lot of information about Pensacola. As Gálvez heard about British buildups, he again sent Panis to Pensacola to protest the constant British insults. In the process, Panis added to the information already available about both Pensacola and Mobile.[64]

Then there was the aforementioned Miguel Eduardo, who as near as can be seen over two centuries later, did very little while in Louisiana. He and his family set up residence in New Orleans, where he received payments of 125 *pesos* on a sporadic basis.[65] Nevertheless, Eduardo appeared at the top of a list in the account of payments for the expense of the "secret commissioner" in the Royal Service, compiled by Gálvez. He received two months' salary by "the Royal disposition." Apparently he had not been paid the previous month. In a letter written by Gálvez, Eduardo was depicted as a person who performed his undefined assignment with "exact punctuality, honor" and "in religious secrecy."[66] At one point, Eduardo did write to José de Gálvez that he traveled upriver around the "Villa de Gálvez" and Manchac. He added that he wanted more money. He apparently received specific assignments. However, constant quibbling over how he would be paid seemed to indicate that he was not the trusted man who went to Pensacola for Gálvez.[67] His commission ended in 1779. By late March, he had returned to Havana. On April 14, Navarro informed his boss, José de Gálvez, that Eduardo's mission was finished.[68]

Among other agents listed on the October 1778 account is a "Guillermo" or William Loyson (Lyson?) who was paid "to discover the plans of the English against Louisiana." He made more than a few trips to Pensacola. Others were paid to find out the same kind of information in New Orleans and Nátchez.[69]

Fig. 9. Signature of Miguel Antonio Eduardo, Spanish spy in Louisiana. AGI, Seville.

As Spain's entry into the war approached, and everyone could feel the tension build and anticipate the moment,[70] Gálvez continued to receive information about British activities. A lot of action was occurring up north in the Illinois country, and the English continued to build up in West Florida. Nevertheless, Navarro reported to Spain that Pensacola appeared tranquil, although the people seemed to be leery of the Americans. However, Gálvez heard from Manchac that Chester had ordered the construction of a series of forts on the Mississippi River. Each fort would have a garrison of three hundred men. To fulfill this quota, three thousand men were in transit to Pensacola on five frigates. By the end of 1778, the reinforcements began to arrive.[71] In late February 1779, Bernardo de Gálvez reported to his uncle José that Pensacola had sent three regiments to the Mississippi River, which was an exaggeration. They had reinforced the new forts under construction, including a new establishment fronting Galvestown. Bernardo felt that the British planned a surprise.[72] In March, Puente reported to Navarro that another fifteen hundred British troops were destined for Pensacola in April 1779. Puente added a sentiment that Navarro knew, which was that war with Great Britain was inevitable.[73] Yet, Bernardo de Gálvez seemed undaunted as he continued to follow instructions building up his own forces and helping the United States.

SEVEN

Illinois to Guatemala: A Benevolent Neutrality and Preparation, 1778–1779

[Leyba] interests himself much in favor of the States.
George Rogers Clark, 1778

*S*et on the west side of the Mississippi River below the confluence of the Missouri River and above the Ohio River, the village of St. Louis hardly appeared to be the place for an experienced Spanish officer and bureaucrat. Founded in 1764 by French traders Pierre Laclede and his young stepson Auguste Chouteau, Laclede's village, as it was popularly called, did not seem to be a town of much importance in a pending world war between Spain and England. Yet, here was a seat of government for Bernardo de Gálvez's administrative assistant, Fernando de Leyba, the lieutenant governor of Louisiana.

Leyba became Louisiana's third lieutenant governor in June 1778. St. Louis, primarily a trading post, did not have any fortifications; in fact, the small village had no defenses whatsoever. There were no hostile Indians nearby, so although the inhabitants received Leyba with enthusiasm, they did not feel a need to construct earthworks.[1]

That attitude would change with Leyba, for he had with him secret instructions, and like other Spanish officials of his time, he was aware of a pending war. Indians would become a threat, but only as allies to the British forces currently under the command of Colonel Henry Hamilton, whom Leyba considered unscrupulous. Leyba worked in coordination with Bernardo de Gálvez and knew that St. Louis had become a sensitive post. Any doubts he had were removed by all the Spanish aid originating in New Orleans that went through his command on its way to the American revolutionaries.

Thus, while helping the Americans, in the process of which he quickly became friends with George Rogers Clark, he kept a close eye on British activities in the Illinois country. He tried to learn their plans and prepare his garrison for attack. He commanded an outpost in a vast territory, the fighting for which could be integral for geographical claims during peace talks.[2]

Among the specifics of his instructions, Leyba sought to develop and maintain friendly relationships with Indians, increase the area's friendly population among settlers, develop an agricultural economy, and raise and train a militia. He was to do this with no aid from New Orleans. His instructions meant that the inhabitants of St. Louis and St. Genevieve, a small Spanish settlement some thirty miles south of St. Louis, would have to change their ways. The people were frontiersmen and military discipline could be an outright shock.

Leyba had the power of governmental authority, although St. Louis's geographical distance from the real seat of power almost made use of it a hollow threat. On the other hand, the proximity of real fighting, Spain's obvious sentiments, and a pending declaration of war instilled a sense of urgency in the lieutenant governor and his people.

Leyba sent his plan of defense as well as a desperate request for two hundred troops to Gálvez, who immediately replied with his appreciation for the plan. Nevertheless, he did not have enough men in New Orleans to spare any for St. Louis.[3] With funding appropriated by the Virginia legislature as well as the Continental Congress, and with credit arranged by Oliver Pollock through the cooperation of Bernardo de Gálvez in New Orleans, George Rogers Clark was able to pursue his plan for securing the Ohio River frontier for the continentals. The redheaded, dark-eyed, impetuous Clark had spent most of his youth exploring, surveying, hunting, and speculating in the territory over which he had been given command. As a twenty-one-year-old, he had traveled down a part of the Ohio River and wintered in the Turkey Creek area in western Pennsylvania above Fort Pitt.[4]

Now, as an American officer, he raised around one hundred seventy-five men and departed from Fort Massac ten miles south of Louisville for a grueling six-day (two days without food) overland march to British-held Kaskaskia, which he surprised and captured on 4 July 1778. The small British garrison surrendered without a struggle. Within the next month, Vincennes and Cahokia, across the river from St. Louis, came under Clark's control—again without resistance. Clark had achieved success, but the job was not complete. Maintaining his small force in the face of a British counterattack from Detroit required more resources from Spanish territory. Fulfilling his ultimate goal of taking Detroit was out of the question, for the time being.

In fact, only around one hundred of his troops were willing to remain with him to secure the area. Distant from his own resources and with a dwindling force, only the support from St. Louis and New Orleans, along with recruitment among the French settlers in the Illinois country, could maintain his position.[5] He must have welcomed the letter from Fernando de Leyba that congratulated him on his recent successes. Leyba also informed the continental commander that supplies had arrived from New Orleans, and then invited him to St. Louis.[6]

Oliver Pollock had extended credit on either the Virginia legislature or Congress to secure the shipment. Gálvez's initial unauthorized approval of Pollock's borrowing had paid off with Clark's success. Leyba quickly sent word to Gálvez, who was pleased. His own officials, meanwhile, told Clark that Pollock could arrange for more supplies.

The system of payment was fairly simple. Clark and Pollock issued bills of credit (to borrow) on Virginia, the amount for which Pollock would pay at least face value. Pollock, in turn, hoped to be reimbursed by Virginia or Congress. This system allowed for supplies to be arranged at a much quicker rate, which was ideal.

However, Pollock, and possibly his friend Gálvez, knew that the system was failing at the reimbursement stage, especially at this moment when Congress had to abandon Philadelphia to the British. Before the Spanish declaration of war in June 1779, or the next year, Pollock had started to mortgage off his land.[7]

Lieutenant Governor Leyba and Colonel Clark had good reason to meet. Leyba had supplies on hand that Clark desperately needed. Moreover, arrangements needed to be made for more. Sometime during the end of July and beginning of August, Clark spent two days and nights at Leyba's house in St. Louis. Clark needed to know whether the supplies in Leyba's possession were destined for Congress or Virginia. If the latter, they were his. The shipment was most likely the same that Pollock and James Willing had received and valued at 26,990 *pesos fuertes*. If so, the uniforms, clothes, blankets, weapons, and quinine were destined for the Continental army, which had just suffered through the winter at Valley Forge.[8]

Clark welcomed the repast arranged by Leyba. The American colonel was the guest of honor for a first night's dinner consisting of many toasts by the thirty guests. It all culminated with a dance that lasted to the morning hours, and the whole event was repeated the next night. Leyba treated Clark "with all the decency in my power." The two men visited at least once more before the end of the year.

They became good friends, exchanging news and information. Clark probably danced with Leyba's sister, Theresa de Leyba, thus initiating what would become an unfulfilled romance. The two met on those rare occasions when Clark visited St. Louis. Duty required Clark to spend long absences from Theresa. After her brother's death before the end of the war, Theresa became forlorn and entered a convent in New Orleans. Eventually, Clark learned of his friend's death and what Theresa had done. He wrote a letter proposing marriage, but, alas, the proposal arrived after she took her final vows to become a nun.[9]

His sister's romance aside, Leyba, like Gálvez in New Orleans, maintained Spain's strict appearance of neutrality. At one point, Leyba refused to help capture some American deserters declaring that by virtue of his country's neutrality, the deserters could seek refuge in Spanish territory. Clark understood and always cooperated with the Spanish official, even sending cordialities to "Madam Lebau" (sic).[10]

As testimony to the authentic relationship between the two men, they wrote to their respective superiors praising each other. Clark reported to Patrick Henry that he was pleased with Leyba. The Spaniard, wrote Clark, "interests himself much in favor of the States . . . more so than I could have expected." He continued that Leyba offered to help raise as many troops as he could.[11] Both Patrick Henry and Bernardo de Gálvez approved of this friendship. Gálvez wrote to Leyba that he hoped their good feelings for one another would be kept up and that Leyba would personally cooperate with Clark. Henry wrote two letters within three days, perhaps to assure that one would get through to St. Louis, in which he expressed his gratitude for Leyba's aid and receptive disposition.[12]

Leyba, or as Clark incorrectly wrote on another occasion, "Leabau,"[13] had been on the job for less than two months when Clark visited him. He, no doubt, shared information with Clark about the situation in the Illinois country. Clark had people spying in the area since 1777.[14] Both men knew that Indians who favored Great Britain inhabited the country. The only significant numbers of settlers from which to draw militia were French, and the British could not depend on them. The two friends understood their respective situations relative to support and supplies and they hoped that New Orleans would continue to send aid. This, of course, became a bit difficult, for, as mentioned, Willing's raids at Manchac and Natchez had resulted in increased British attention in the area, including the two British warships that anchored off New Orleans.[15] Perhaps an awareness of the problems in New Orleans, plus the expectation of a counterattack, dictated to Leyba and Clark that matters could not wait. Leyba gathered supplies from among his own people, extending his personal credit to help Clark and his men. The Spanish official's quick action and generosity came none too soon.[16]

He, like Pollock, lost a large part of his personal wealth, a problem that may have hastened the death of his wife as well as his own. Leyba eventually wrote Gálvez:

[B]ut the coming of the Americans to this district has ruined me utterly. Several inhabitants of this town, who put their property in the hands of these Americans to please me, find themselves in the same situation. . . . I accomplished this [aid] on my own credit with all the inhabitants so that they might provide these Americans with whatever they needed.

The result, Leyba continued, was that he was "overwhelmed with trouble" because of his debts and because Gálvez may not approve of what he had done. Finally, as a result of these problems, Leyba added that his wife "saw her hopes frustrated by the labyrinth of debts in which she found me involved," and "was overcome by such a great melancholy that after only five days of illness in bed," she died.[17]

Colonel Hamilton decided to attack Clark from Detroit. With only 162 men, two-thirds of whom were French-Canadian militia, he set out to undo Clark's gains. Hamilton had no intention of attacking the rebels with his small force, despite Clark's roughly equal number of men. Hamilton counted on adding Indian allies as he moved toward Vincennes. In fact, he gained 350 Indian allies that, he hoped, would more than offset whatever aid the Spanish were giving the intruders.

Hamilton's action was either too eager or, probably, overconfident. The British colonel revealed his attitude when he surveyed the contestants:

The Spaniards are feeble and hated by the French, the French are fickle and have no man of capacity to advise or lead them, the Rebels are enterprising and brave, but want resources, and the Indians can have their resources, but from the English, if we act without loss of time in the favorable conjuncture.[18]

That the British officer depended on his allies, was indicated by his threats to turn loose the Indians. Hamilton would learn that he could not count on his French militia and, as the campaign unfolded, Hamilton's words were far different than his actions.

The British force had no problem retaking Vincennes on 17 December 1777.[19] But Hamilton chose not to press the advantage because he felt that the season with flooding rivers dictated against any more overland marches. In addition, he inexplicably released all his Indian allies and decided to winter in Vincennes with no allies and a small force of men whose loyalty to him was, at the least, questionable.[20]

Hamilton's letter to Bernardo de Gálvez, written at this time, does not make sense, for this is when he threatened to use his Indians against St. Louis, if Leyba and Gálvez did not quit providing the rebels with powder and other supplies.[21] He was bluffing.

Leyba, as yet unaware of the release of the Indians, took Hamilton's threat seriously. His settlement was very weak, with only twenty-four soldiers, a drummer, and an undetermined militia. Any other available men were out hunting. Indians, he noted, preferred to attack weak targets, so he feared the reality of Hamilton's threat more than an attack of British irregulars.[22]

Clark, who had been keeping tab on Hamilton's movements through Leyba's informer and business associate, Joseph María Francesca (Francisco) Vigo, believed the British commander to be mistaken in his confidence and strategy.[23] On 25 January 1779 Clark wrote to Leyba a full report of what he had heard. Vigo had disappeared and he correctly assumed that the informer had been captured. Vigo was released on the promise that he return directly to St. Louis, and because he was a Spanish subject. After returning to St. Louis, he immediately traveled to Kaskaskia and shared with Clark all the valuable information he had gathered about Vincennes.[24] Clark's hunting parties had also secured plenty of information. Hamilton indeed left Detroit for the Illinois country with British, French, and Indian troops. "It is whispered that the enemy is determined to take the garrison and only wait for favorable weather for this March." They will "pay dear" if they try, he added. Any further information from his spies would be sent to Leyba "immediately."[25]

Clark recruited a force of two companies, consisting of 180 men from the French villages. He would not wait, like his counterpart. The new force marched overland nineteen days to Vincennes where, once again, the British capitulated without firing a shot. When hearing of the approach of Clark's army, Hamilton's French-Canadian militia refused to help. Left with only thirty men, Hamilton surrendered on 24 February 1779 and was taken prisoner and transported to Virginia.[26]

Five days later, Clark reported the news to Leyba, expressing his surprise that

Hamilton quit without a fight after "seeing his men's stores [and] strength of fort," and that the feared British commander surrendered "to a body of men not double his number." Clark hoped to give Leyba the details in person and, again, thanked the Spanish leader for his "kindness."[27]

With Hamilton's threats solved, the Illinois country became somewhat calm, if not secured. Hamilton could be replaced and the British had the resources in Quebec to mount another, more serious attack. George Washington kept abreast of Clark's successes. He may have been surprised at Clark's effectiveness. At the very least, he developed a new strategy because, along with Clark's activities, the war had stalemated and the European nations, with Spain's involvement, appeared about to come to terms; this would leave the new United States a vulnerable country pinned to the Atlantic Coast.

George Washington considered an early peace a disagreeable possibility, for the question of peace and independence was also a matter of timing. If peace created an independent United States without Long Island, New York City, most of Georgia, Rhode Island, and an undetermined portion of the Northwest, then his country would have entered into a bad peace. At the time, Britain occupied all the above areas and could have laid claim to them.[28]

In January of 1779, Washington ordered a letter drafted by Alexander Hamilton to a congressional committee in which he repeated his position,

[I]t is not only possible but probable the affairs in Europe may take a turn which will compel [Britain] to abandon America. The interposition of Spain and the union of her maritime force to that of France would probably have this effect.

With Spain in the war, he continued, "England would then certainly be obliged to renounce her American projects."[29]

While, on the one hand, wanting to believe that Spain would enter the war thus establishing, "I hope . . . a decisive turn to our affairs,"[30] Washington did not base his strategy on his hopes. To mitigate the results of a premature peace, he decided to follow up Clark's success and concentrate on the western frontier, where he would gain claims to the territory west of the Alleghenies and south of the Great Lakes. He organized a three-pronged attack using regulars and Indian allies designed to converge in British-occupied western New York.

By the summer of 1779, the campaign began under Colonel Daniel Brodhead and General John Sullivan. Brodhead led a force of 605 continentals and volunteers from Fort Pitt up the Allegheny River. It is a safe assumption that the military success of Washington's plan, in part, stemmed from supplies that originated in Spanish New Orleans. Clark and Leyba were instrumental in transporting supplies up the Mississippi and Ohio rivers to Fort Pitt. As Spain moved closer to a declaration of war and as Pollock ran out of credit, fewer supplies came upriver. In fact, George

Rogers Clark's successes became lost in the larger picture. What supplies could be arranged, went to the Continental army. The Americans' neglect to the Illinois country began to accomplish what Hamilton could not. By the middle of the year, Americans began abandoning their garrisons in Illinois.[31]

While Leyba labored to prepare for the defense of his hamlet as well as helping Clark capture Hamilton and securing the region for the time being, another part of the Spanish American world seriously began to prepare for war. Guatemala, as Spain knew, was an area that needed to be defended. Indeed, armed conflicts between Spanish and English forces constantly flared up before the official outbreak of war.[32] In addition, removing British smugglers, pirates, and legal timber cutters from Central America, a term roughly synonymous with eighteenth-century Guatemala, was one of Spain's declared goals in its negotiations with France.[33] Spain considered the captaincy general and *gobernación* of Guatemala a "domain" whose authority extended beyond its present borders to include most of Central America, a very integral part of its empire.

Like the upper Louisiana area, Guatemala needed to prepare. Unlike Leyba's domain, Guatemala was more accessible to Spanish officialdom, but with very difficult terrain, which had impeded earlier attempts to revitalize the colony.

Guatemala's value to Spain, if only in the mind of José de Gálvez, who had the administrative responsibility of the Americas, resulted in the transfer of José's brother Matías de Gálvez, who moved from his position of general and governor of the Castle of Paso Alto on the Island of Tenerife in the Canary Islands. He had explicit instructions to speed up the defensive organization of the militia, cut contraband, and reorganize the administration. In other words, defend and, once and for all, make the colony cost-effective.

Matías de Gálvez had served a long career as a Spanish official. (See plate 11.) His career was notable for his devotion and not for a brilliant performance. Now sixty-seven years old, he would have an opportunity to perform.[34]

Matías de Gálvez eventually replaced General Martín de Mayorga when the latter received a transfer to the more prestigious position of viceroy of New Spain in Mexico City. Martín de Mayorga served a fairly eventful six-year term (1773–1779) in Guatemala. He had to deal with an earthquake that destroyed the capital, Antigua. He oversaw the establishment of Nueva Guatemala as his new capital of Guatemala and the Kingdom of Central America. The transfer of people and the civil and ecclesiastical offices, despite the constant objections of the archbishop, was a monumental task. His new promotion to replace the recently deceased marqués de Bucareli in Mexico became controversial. Rumors spread that José de Gálvez planned to place his brother in Mexico City and that José may have even arranged for Bucareli's death to clear the way. Then, surprisingly, Matías de Gálvez was sent to Guatemala as the "President elect," eventually to become the governor and captain general while the "mediocre" Martín de Mayorga received the more prestigious position.[35]

One solution to the mystery of Matías de Gálvez's appointment had to do with the growing specter of war. Guatemala was in much greater peril than Mexico. The idea of creating a water route through the continent, thus fulfilling Columbus's dream of a direct waterway to the Orient, was not forgotten by any of the European participants in the new world competition. The mines and other natural resources, coupled with the area's lack of defense, made Guatemala a natural target. And, as history has shown, sending Matías de Gálvez to Guatemala was the correct move.

He arrived in Guatemala on 29 June 1778 at Omoa on the northern coast of Central America. He entered Nueva Guatemala (Guatemala City) where he had arrived by July 17th, and served as commandant-inspector of troops as well as "second commander" of the Kingdom of Guatemala under Martín de Mayorga.[36]

He needed to speed up reforms begun in 1765 under Pedro Salazar y Herrera.[37] He conducted an inspection immediately upon his arrival and discovered that the thirty-thousand-men militia that was supposed to have been organized and equipped, did not exist. In fact, he described the military as a "mere pittance of people" who had no idea why they had been enlisted or what they were supposed to do. The armaments were laughable. What equipment could be located was in a state of disrepair.

Gálvez wrote that he needed arms to fulfill his instructions to reorganize a militia to defend Guatemala. Raising a force without arms would be useless. He asked for ten thousand rifles with bayonets for his infantry and four thousand carbines for his cavalry. In addition, he wanted a corresponding number of pistols, belts, swords, and straps which, when received, would permit him to begin serious training of his new militia. Given the apparent emergency under which he worked, he suggested that arms would need to be sent with "all possible brevity" from the other American "kingdoms."[38]

Gálvez knew that the British planned to attack Nicaragua and try to take possession of its lake of the same name. To counter this possibility, he made sure that Fort Immaculate Conception (Immaculada Concepción) on the San Juan de Nicaragua River was well fortified. He also installed a fleet on the lake that was under the command of Ignacio Maestre whose salary was more than the governor of Nicaragua.[39] In addition, Gálvez made sure that Fort Omoa's bastions were completed, and then appointed a French engineer, Simón Desnaux, to command the fort.[40]

The mountains, jungles, and river valleys with a tropical climate and great "distances between populated areas" all loomed as obstacles before Matías de Gálvez. Nevertheless, with outside help providing the arms, he would "leave no stone unturned, . . . in spite of those obstacles" to prepare troops "for the defense of these vast dominions." Sharing a trait common in his family, Matías de Gálvez would not be discouraged.[41]

Of course, his family connections allowed him the luxury of a positive attitude. He was requesting aid from his well-connected brother, after all. His instructions included much more than arranging for the defense of Guatemala. The long-stated aspirations to change Guatemala's wasteful economy into an efficient, loyal, and financially beneficial operation encompassed more than a military buildup. Nevertheless, the first step in this tall order was defense. With the potential of war, the opportunity to curtail Britain's influence in the area would become reality. Securing the area against foreign intrusion would eliminate a major hindrance to fulfilling the large order of his instructions. Oddly, the instructions concentrated on defense and said nothing about offensive action against the British foe. Instead, as Matías de Gálvez reflected, he needed to prepare for the defense of Guatemala in offensive terms.[42]

Unlike Leyba's plight in St. Louis, Matías's correspondence brought results. His brother, writing on behalf of the king on May 21, replied that His Majesty was aware of the state of the military forces in Guatemala and had granted that the necessary supplies be sent. Matías, now the newly and officially appointed president of the Audiencia and captain general of Guatemala, must have been pleased both for his recent appointment and for the depth with which the officials, wintering in Aranjuez, understood his task.[43]

José de Gálvez instructed Matías, "now more than ever . . . dedicate yourself to complete this important work." José would arrange for six thousand rifles along with three thousand carbines and pistols as soon as possible. Matías de Gálvez could order the swords from a company in Caracas. Yes, the crown was aware that the forces in Guatemala "are reduced to a great multitude of enlisted people without instructions, methods or order." Nevertheless, they must secure the area from enemy invasions.

Further instructions spelled out that Matías de Gálvez should prepare his forces to act defensively through rapid movement to occupy mountain passes, the heights, and create defensive works like trenches and, in important places, fortifications. If urgent help was needed, Gálvez could turn to Havana or the French settlements in the Caribbean. Along with the threat of an invasion of the area, which, oddly, José de Gálvez wrote that he did not think would occur because Britain had too many other problems, Matías de Gálvez needed to watch for English pirates by stationing lookouts along the coastal heights.[44]

Word from Spain was paradoxical. José de Gálvez and the king must have known how close Spain was to a declaration of war. So, on the one hand, the instructions had a sense of urgency and, on the other, José's mistaken belief that Great Britain probably would not invade Guatemala sent a mixed message and even seemed complacent. Matías de Gálvez, like his compatriots in the rest of the Spanish American world, did not share that complacency.

Probably no one felt the pending pressure more than Diego Joseph Navarro y Valladares in Cuba, in whose office the activities of the Gulf of Mexico and the Caribbean Sea were being coordinated.

Both Navarro and Bernardo de Gálvez were appointed to their respective positions soon after the conde de Floridablanca ascended to the minister of state in Spain. These appointments reflected a clear policy change that committed Spain to a relationship of "benevolent neutrality" with the British-American colonies.[45] This was reflected in Bernardo de Gálvez's official neutrality and unofficial aid to the Americans, all of which originated in Havana. The mission of Miralles to the United

States Congress as an observer, also under Navarro's authority, kept with the new policy. A prong of this policy, already started, was the preparation for, and resistance to, British expansion and affronts, including those in Guatemala. Again, the key to this was Navarro.

Like the other participants in the conflict, Spain had its internal differences. As seen in the correspondence between Aranda in Paris and Floridablanca in Spain, Aranda led an influential court faction known as the *Aragoneses* who took a more pro-American and pro-war position. Floridablanca represented a more cautious and chauvinistic approach. Navarro inherited a position that placed him in the "crosshairs" of a number of problems, the origins for which had contrary motives.

These policy preferences manifested themselves throughout the Spanish bureaucracy. José de Gálvez, in charge of the American theater and his Francophile allies, including his family members, felt that England needed to be extracted from the Gulf of Mexico and Caribbean Sea, which they, like all Spanish officials, considered to be Spanish. To this faction, East Florida was not the most important American territory. Louisiana and control of navigation on the Mississippi River were their priorities.

Many other government officials, especially in Havana and Santo Domingo, desired that Spain regain East Florida, which had been a Spanish colony from the sixteenth century until the end of the Seven Years' War. Many Spaniards still lived there. People such as Juan Joseph de la Puente convinced Navarro to make East Florida a priority.[46] The other agent was Luciano Herrera, who stayed in St. Augustine after 1768. He observed British-occupied Florida and sent regular reports to Havana, likely in concert with Puente.[47]

At the same time, Navarro came to depend on another person who did not agree with the Gálvez position, or strictly subscribe to Floridablanca's policy. Juan Bautista Bonet, the commander of the Spanish naval squadron in Cuba, had a clear, if not stubborn, sense that Havana should not fall to Great Britain. Torre no doubt stated Bonet's position to Navarro, for Spain considered the position of captain general of Cuba crucial to enacting official policy in the area, since the end of the previous war.

The port city was the gateway to the West Indies and the most important military command in Spanish America. Havana's importance was reflected by the appointment of a series of competent and influential military commanders, who succeeded in bringing about a military rehabilitation on the island of Cuba after the Seven Years' War.[48]

Navarro's appointment was to one of five such positions in the Spanish colonies. The other captaincy generals were located in Guatemala (now filled by Matías de Gálvez), Venezuela, Bogotá, Chile, and Puerto Rico. Captains general held military and civil command outside the geographic boundaries of viceroyalties, the most important of which was New Spain because of its source of wealth. During the war, Navarro's position would ascend that of the viceroy in Mexico City and his counterparts, for his office was the pivotal position to Spain's West Indies military success, before and during the war.

Navarro and his staff had to consider the various policies and their respective proponents while making decisions based on orders from Spain and the realities of the field. They coordinated logistical problems of major proportions. Money, troops, supplies, and equipment moved in large numbers under Navarro's authority. For example, the supplies and money handled by Bernardo de Gálvez came to him via Havana or because of Havana's arrangement. Now, as war approached, Havana administered an increase in troop strength.

Troops originating in Spain and sent to other parts of the Spanish-American world were being transported into the West Indies with a greater sense of urgency. For example, the regiments of the infantry of Navarra, el Príncipe, and España shared typical histories of troop movement and use. They disembarked from Cádiz in Spain for Havana at the end of 1776. In 1779, before declaring war, Spain transferred the first battalion of the Regiment of España to New Orleans. The second battalion was sent to the same city in July of that year to help reinforce the city's defenses against an anticipated British attack.[49] The rest of the regiment remained in Havana, but would eventually participate in the war at Mobile, Pensacola, and the Bahamas. (See plates 12 and 13.)

The Prince's Regiment, known as the "Tercio de Lombardía" when it sailed from Cádiz for duty in Venezuela, was split between Caracas and other duty stations before transferring to Cuba where it received its permanent name. As happened with the Regiment of Spain, the Prince's Regiment was split up, with a part of it serving under Bernardo de Gálvez on the Mississippi River, and at Mobile and Pensacola.

The Regiment of Navarra had a less complicated history. Unlike the two previously mentioned regiments, the Regiment of Navarra sailed directly to Havana.[50] The regiment of over fourteen hundred men and officers boarded two ships that sailed from the Spanish port of El Ferrol and arrived in Havana at the end of February.[51]

Governor Navarro had to make sure supplies were sufficient for the troops. An example of the movement of supplies can be gleaned from two military inventories sent to Louisiana under orders of Navarro. The lists indicate the types and amounts of items, as well as the painstaking care that Navarro's staff took to keep track of everything from rifles to musket balls, which were counted and noted.[52]

Other troop and supply movements gleaned from the scattered records[53] indicate that Navarro and his staff spent a great amount of time preparing for war. Navarro had to determine where the troops were needed, in the face of reports, orders, policy, and timing. The captain general was responsible for overseeing troop and supply movements, monitoring a system of informers, including their compensation, receiving and harboring ships from the United States in Havana's port, and preparing for many unforeseeable circumstances.[54]

Spanish officials kept abreast of all pertinent information because of an effective spy network and an efficient bureaucracy. Knowledge and warnings about British troop strengths on the Mississippi River, and in Jamaica in 1778, kept officials like Navarro and Bernardo de Gálvez alerted. They used the information to conjecture about British strategy. Gálvez always felt that Great Britain would target New

Orleans. After the 1778 confrontation of the two British warships at New Orleans, he warned Navarro that the threat to his undermanned forces was so imminent that he kept his men on the highest state of alert.[55]

Such justified tension occurred in an environment of factional rivalries over Spanish policy and the complete uncertainty of when Spain would officially enter the war. None of the Spanish leaders in the Americas doubted that Spain would go to war. Gálvez worried that Great Britain would take advantage of its land and sea superiority in the area to surprise Spain by initiating the war. His concern was a minority opinion. Most of the Spanish officials felt that Great Britain did not want Spain in the war and so would not initiate action. Some felt that the British might possibly negotiate a peace to keep Spain neutral. As will be seen, Floridablanca, in part, based his policy of trying to win concessions from Great Britain on this last theory.[56]

In early 1779, Gálvez and Navarro were relieved to know that the French fleet under Vice Admiral Charles Hector, the comte d'Estaing, with twelve ships-of-the-line and thirteen frigates, had sailed into the West Indies.[57] This was the same fleet, incidentally, that so disappointed the revolutionaries when it sailed south from New England in November of 1778. Floridablanca's negotiations with England were partly opportunistic and mostly a ruse. Washington, with his usual penchant for viewing the larger context, understood that reality pointed to Spain entering the war. He planned as well as speculated toward that eventuality.[58]

Everyone, it seemed, except the national government of Spain, had a sense of urgency. Bernardo de Gálvez felt immediately threatened by Great Britain's close proximity to his command. He knew that they were strengthening their forces. Pensacola, he overestimated, had amassed four thousand royal troops.[59] Gálvez initiated an exchange of letters with Bonet that lasted through Spain's declaration of war. The letters reflected the many complexities of fighting in the West Indies. In New Orleans lay the importance of the Mississippi River, the threat of immediate attack, and a key location on the Gulf Coast. In addition, Bernardo de Gálvez did not concur with the *Floridianos* who had gained influence on Navarro and his advisors. Gálvez felt that New Orleans could not be lost, for to do so would result in the loss of Louisiana and navigation on the Mississippi River. With such a victory for Great Britain, the rebelling colonies would be in peril of being surrounded.[60]

Bonet acknowledged the precarious position of New Orleans and, therefore, Louisiana, but argued that Havana had many responsibilities other than New Orleans. Bonet and Navarro concluded that Gálvez would have to do the best that he could under the circumstances.[61] Gálvez wanted more troops and supplies to fulfill his mandate to defend Louisiana. The regular troops would form the military strength that his militia could supplement.[62] Bonet, reflecting Navarro's attitude, did not want to put Havana at risk and, secondly, wanted to prepare for an attack on East Florida. As already noted, the American colonies made overtures about helping Spain take Pensacola, if the latter agreed to enter the war. Also, like José de Gálvez, Navarro did not feel that Guatemala was threatened. The captain general wanted to concentrate in the Gulf of Mexico, not the Caribbean Sea or South America. In practical terms, he did not want to strengthen Louisiana or aid Guatemala, at Havana's expense.[63]

To Navarro's credit, his penchant for order led him to pass on to Spain all of the correspondence between Bernardo de Gálvez and his naval commander in April 1779. In addition, Navarro compiled his own reports. He delineated the British buildup and threat in Florida. Bernardo's uncle, José de Gálvez, was the person who received the packets. As per normal procedure, he would read, study, and condense the contents for his king's consumption. Obviously, Gálvez had some influence on royal decisions. Bonet and Navarro must have realized that the minister of the Indies might not be favorable to their position.[64] After all, they were in opposition to the minister's nephew and brother. José de Gálvez, summering with the court in Aranjuez, penned the expected answer on June 25. Havana, he wrote, needed to place more emphasis on Louisiana. As had already been expressed, relative to Guatemala, the king wanted the officials in Havana to "take the opportunity to assure that New Orleans and, moreover, the establishments of the Mississippi be defended from the invasions that threaten them."[65]

Navarro did not hesitate to fulfill the spirit of José de Gálvez and the king's desire. By the end of July, he informed Bernardo de Gálvez that he would be sending the second battalion of the Regiment of Spain to New Orleans. On August 14, less than three weeks later, the reinforcements embarked from Havana in six transports.[66]

As events developed, Bernardo de Gálvez's position proved to be correct. Correspondence from Pensacola, sent to individuals in New Orleans, warned of a pending English invasion. These letters amounted to private warnings among friends concerned for each other's welfare. An intercepted official document revealed the blunt message that Great Britain intended to deal a blow to the "Dons" of New Orleans. These letters merely reconfirmed what the spy system had already revealed.[67]

With the knowledge that more troops were on the way, Bernardo de Gálvez planned a strategy to attack the British settlements on the Mississippi River. Manchac would be the first target. To this point, he had prepared for defense. Now, he felt secure enough to inform Bonet that he had changed his plans.[68]

EIGHT

Negotiations and the Spanish Declaration of War

A Remonstrance of a very serious and decisive nature.
William Henry Drayton to King George III, 1779

istorians in the United States have criticized Spain for its reluctance to enter into the war earlier. Some historians blame Spain's hesitancy on Floridablanca, who is depicted as somewhat less than agreeable, maybe even underhanded. This false impression has Spain and its minister of state, in effect, attempting to sell out the struggling British colonies.[1]

Floridablanca, as demonstrated earlier, worked on Spain's behalf and with a policy that would not commit his country to war until the treasure ships from the West Indies had safely docked in Spain, and the other countries involved in the war had agreed to Spain's goals. He owed no allegiance to the American rebels, although by now Spain had invested a lot of money in the revolution. He played his diplomatic cards with the cunning of the experienced professional that he was. To have declared war earlier would have been of no benefit, for Floridablanca knew that Spain was not ready.

The Continental Congress did not doubt the integrity of the Spanish government. With open knowledge of Spain's mediation attempts, members of Congress openly stated their trust in "His Most Catholic Majesty."[2] Spain's refusal to consider anything short of independence for the colonies pleased the Americans and, at the same time, created anxiety among them. The new government had confidence in Spain's efforts. Gouverneur Morris, an influential Congressional delegate, published a letter in February 1779 in the *Pennsylvania Packet* in which he explained that independence would become reality because France had joined in the struggle,

and those who know the connection between the Courts of Versailles and Madrid, their enmity to that of St. James, and their national interests, cannot but perceive that Spain will soon be joined in this contest, unless it be terminated agreeably [*sic*] to our interests.[3]

Morris added, perhaps reflecting his interest in business as well as politics, that Spanish aid would make the colonial currency strong.

Everything that Spain had done since the Seven Years' War, clearly pointed to the appropriateness of Floridablanca's policies. He would not bargain away American independence, or leave France to lose a war by not fulfilling the terms of the Family Compact. Nor would he or Carlos III enter another war prematurely.

From the American point of view, Carlos III and his minister became brokers for a "just and lasting peace," meaning independence of the thirteen colonies. Sentiment, although skeptical, leaned toward a negotiated peace. As early as December 1778, when the first reports of Great Britain's refusal to accept United States independence became known, congressional delegates such as Samuel Adams and Henry Laurens quickly noted that Spain was preparing for war and that meant victory.[4]

This common notion was expressed in a letter from Rhode Island's delegates in which they stated that England had sent to Spain a number of conditions for peace, the chief of which was,

> That the King of France should retract the Declaration made last Winter by the French minister to the Court of London respecting the Independence of these States . . . his most extraordinary proposal was received by Spain as a high insult, and in consequence of it everything in that kingdom was in motion [for war].[5]

There can be little doubt that the Continental Congress knew that Spain, one way or another, was working on its behalf.

At the moment, Spain had a great diplomatic advantage. Great Britain, France and the colonies were committed and fighting. Spain could determine the outcome. The Americans and France did not doubt that Spain's allegiance meant victory. Great Britain was uncertain, although a great many British subjects in positions of influence knew that Spain's participation would mean defeat. Some believed that Spain would never make war on another European country over the issue of colonial independence. Others with unfounded chauvinistic confidence had a more extreme view—England would win the war under any circumstance.

Floridablanca, correctly, tried to win a peace diplomatically. He offered Great Britain mediation. Spain insisted that American independence be accepted, for antebellum considerations were not part of the exchange. Great Britain would have to accept the loss of its colonies, or, at least, win them back through a prolonged war. At best, if England considered some of the enumerated concessions to Spain such as the return of Gibraltar and the island of Minorca, Spain would remain neutral.[6]

As the year turned, Juan de Miralles and Conrad Alexandre Gerard, the French diplomat to the United States, reported the progress of Spain's mediation to members of Congress. Gerard even formally suggested that it was time for the Continental Congress to select a delegate to send to Spain to partake in the ongoing negotiations.

The possibility of peace, he noted, was real. In his letter submitted to John Jay, who was the president of the Continental Congress, he stated that Spain was about to offer England a final chance to settle the conflict through mediation. If this offer failed, Spain would enter the war on the side of France and the colonies. The letter was read to Congress on February 12 and it stated that the king of Spain had made "the independence of the United States the preliminary article to a general pacification." Gerard added that now was a great opportunity about which France was in complete agreement. England had no European allies and the results for the rebelling colonies were all beneficial to various degrees. He then enumerated Spain's territorial claims, but noted that if mediation resulted in a quick settlement, "Spain would have no claim upon the U.S." or upon the Floridas.

Gerard urged that "the United States should prepare a person to participate in the negotiations," for if Spain failed to negotiate a just peace, its role, especially with the potential for financial aid, needed to be delineated. A Spanish subsidy would be crucial and welcomed to the continued war, because it "could give the States credit in Europe equal to their wishes" and France needed two years to recover financially enough to "be more competent to war."[7]

No clearer message could be made to the Americans that both Spain and France were working toward independence for the fledgling country. Because Miralles did not have official diplomatic status, Gerard was used to officially express Spain's position. And here, Spain invited a United States diplomat to participate in its negotiations with Great Britain.[8]

Gerard also echoed Vergennes's belief that the war could not be won without Spain. Success of the allies depended upon Spain's aid. This time, Gerard added that the threat of Spain might possibly force a peace and United States independence. If not, Spain's military prowess would force England to, as Samuel Adams put it, "be obliged to withdraw her Attention in a great Measure from America"[9] and thus "leave it in our power with the Spirit of Enterprise" to assure independence.[10]

That "enterprise" included the necessity of bolstering the Americans' faltering and almost worthless currency and credit. Spain would assure the economic strength of the fledgling country. The importance of this is reflected in the many times it was mentioned among the correspondence of the country's leaders. And, in exchange, Spain's territorial requests as well as its interest in American wood for masts, sold at cheap prices for its ships, were worthy of serious consideration.[11]

Spain's position caused a renewed confidence among the leaders in the young Continental government. Peace with independence, in one way or another was now at hand. Many delegates in Congress openly expressed this positive attitude. Just the day after Gerard's letter was submitted to Congress, William Henry Drayton wrote a letter to King George III of England, in which he told the British king that now was the time for him to take the "harsh prescription" and grant independence to the American colonies. Otherwise, the American wrote that he knew that the Spanish ambassador, Pedro Luján Jiménez de Góngora, the marqués de Almodóvar "by order of his master delivered to your Majesty a REMONSTRANCE of a very serious and decisive nature."[12] Now all the participants were aware of the others and the British government could have no misconception about their choices.

Congress continued to receive good news from Spain, which, like Drayton's letter, contained enough detail to indicate an open flow of information. They heard that ships and supplies were gathering, that Great Britain refused to consider independence again, and that money might come from the Netherlands as well as Spain. They fully believed that Spain intended to enter the war, if Great Britain did not overcome its "vanity," "obstinacy," and "wickedness" and agree to Spanish mediation.[13]

Some months later, Spain's April ultimatum to Great Britain, and the negative reply, were presented to Congress. The delegates learned, as they suspected all along, that Spain dealt strongly with Great Britain. The court of Madrid informed London that time was running short. Great Britain should not expect to delay, but give serious consideration to the listed points offered for peace. Great Britain must end hostilities with France and "the colonies" and, within one month, the belligerents must select a location for negotiations. Here, Spain offered Madrid as a site. In addition, the colonies would "be treated as Independent in fact" and they would be represented by one or more commissioners to negotiate the peace.[14]

Despite some individual speculation, the colonials had been kept aware of Spain's intentions. The idea that Spain pressed only for American independence in appearance, but not seriously, does not match the facts. Spain insisted that the colonies be treated as independent until the outcome of negotiations. Importantly, Spain wanted the young country to be treated as an equal to England and France. The Americans and their ally, France, could determine the destiny of the new country, for they each would have commissioners to negotiate with Great Britain.

In fact, Almodóvar, the Spanish ambassador in London, quickly reported that the British government could not accept treating the colonials as equals who would negotiate the treaty.[15] Unfortunately, but not unexpectedly, Floridablanca's effort to negotiate a peace did not work, so he and his king prepared for war.

When, in March 1779, word that Spain had arranged to have the ports of "the two Sicilies," which were under Spanish control, opened to American shipping, Spanish sentiment became obvious.[16] While such an act no doubt had little influence on the war's outcome, it, of itself, served notice to Great Britain. Opening ports in the Mediterranean attracted attention to the body of water where Spain hoped to extract territory from Britain, either during negotiations or during the war. Spain's Mediterranean goal of acquiring Minorca and Gibraltar was well known. For Great Britain, war would be more costly if it required more concessions in the Americas.

The important matter of the appointment of a delegate from the Continental Congress to take part in negotiations was a gracious offer subsequently overlooked by U.S. historians. While Congress understood the opportunity provided by the offer, the appointment apparently became stalled as a result of an important but drawn-out political quarrel in Congress. Disagreement broke out when a rift between Silas Deane

Fig. 10. Nineteenth-century cartoon. The leopard is England and is under attack by
the American serpent, the Spanish lion, and French rooster. Original in the
Maritime Museum, Paris. From Reparaz, Yo Solo, 50.

and Arthur Lee in France reached American shores. Both men were part of the original delegation sent to France. From the beginning, Arthur Lee, a somewhat dour, humorless man educated in England, became the odd man out among the three commissioners. Both Franklin and Deane were outgoing and somewhat gregarious. The relationship between Lee and the other two commissioners decayed into a feud, which resulted in complaints and accusations, and ended by dividing the Continental Congress in a long debate.

Both sides accused the other of incompetence, leaking information to the British, and seeking to promote their personal financial fortunes through business ventures gained from their positions as diplomats. This last charge was probably true, especially of Deane, who was recalled in the summer of 1778, ostensibly to report on the state of European affairs but, in reality, to answer Lee's charges.[17]

Deane's questioning began on 15 August 1778 and lasted into the next year. This only heightened division to the point where Deane's proponents introduced into Congress the message that France and Spain did not trust Lee, because both countries felt that he had provided information to the British, in particular, in advance of his ill-advised attempt to travel to Madrid.[18] The feelings ran so high in Congress that Henry Laurens, an ally of Lee who preceded Jay as President of the Continental Congress, resigned his position in December of 1778, in part to take a more active role in the debate.[19]

A committee assigned to look into the affair brought in its report in late March of 1779. It found the conduct of both diplomats to be imprudent and prejudicial to "the honor and interests of the United States." The committee recommended that both men be removed and a minister or commissioner be appointed to Spain.[20]

In May, Gerard made two additional requests to Congress to send a representative to Spain.[21] Eventually, as news crossed the Atlantic that Spain's latest attempt to have Great Britain take its "harsh prescription" had failed,[22] Congress began to concentrate its attention on more positive matters. The task of selecting a minister to Spain became paramount. However, hard feelings created during the Deane and Lee conflict now manifested themselves and delayed any conclusion in the matter.[23]

Spain's desires, as enumerated with its list of objectives for entering the war, had been known for a long time in France and were now known to all sides. By inviting Great Britain to the bidding, Floridablanca forced France to get serious about agreeing to terms. The colonials would have to follow its ally's lead. The only problem for the Americans was Spain's insistence on sole right of navigation on the Mississippi River.[24] Florida was not of value to the struggling colonies, for it had remained loyal to Great Britain. Spain's other desires were beyond the revolutionaries' ability to guarantee.

While Floridablanca gave Britain a window of opportunity, the real target was France. Louis XVI and Vergennes, especially, had to agree to help Spain gain Gibraltar, Minorca, and the Gulf of Mexico's northern coast.

No doubt, Floridablanca would have considered, maybe even accepted, a serious

British offer, but he never expected such a rejoinder, for he had secretly worked out an alliance with France, while waiting for Great Britain's answer to the final offer.

The whole episode has misled some historians into concluding that Spain was not earnest about entering the war. Some correctly observed that Britain sacrificed its American colonies to keep Gibraltar. Even contemporaries like George Washington understood the events as they unfolded. The general observed in a letter to John Jay that England's failure to take advantage of Spain's offer of mediation "is more strongly tinctured with insanity than she has done in the course of this contest." The only excuse for Great Britain's action, he added, is its "obstinacy."[25] Washington, like Floridablanca, expected England's negative reaction.

In France, Vergennes wasted no time agreeing to Spain's terms. He fully knew, as one historian later wrote, that it was "almost inconceivable that France and the United States could have defeated Britain without Spanish help."[26] Vergennes had been of this opinion since d'Estaing's failure to surprise the British fleet the previous year.

Carlos III and his advisors had nothing left to do but formally enter Spain into the war. As previously noted, Floridablanca's opposition to an alliance with the Americans took precedence over Aranda's position of recognition. Spain, per the secret clause of the treaty already signed by the colonies and France, would assure that military victory included independence for the colonies. This was also specified in a new treaty being drafted in Aranjuez, south of Madrid, that would be signed by Spain and France.[27] On the other hand, Spain feared that immediate recognition of the former British colonies could lead to problems in its own colonies. Spain also had some trepidation that the new country would merely replace Great Britain as an aggressive territorial and commercial neighbor. The Spanish government felt that recognition would exacerbate the process.[28] As later events indicated, Spain's concern was justified.

Amazingly, the Continental Congress kept fairly well apprised of European diplomacy as well as Spain's intentions. As early as February, Congress resolved that the king of Spain was working in their interest and had forced Great Britain either to accept independence as a condition of peace or to face the prospect of Spain going to war with them.[29] Benjamin Franklin wrote from Europe in February that Spain had been negotiating with England for a while, insisting on American independence in fact, if not in appearance. Spain's attempts, he added, had been rejected. The Spanish navy had become strong and prepared for war. Franklin added in a subsequent letter to Patrick Henry that he hoped that "Spain is now near declaring against our enemies."[30] John Adams added that his country needed to pay more attention to Spain. He felt that Spain's assistance was the key to victory and that the Spanish colonies would make excellent neighbors for the new American country. He correctly observed that Spain was "powerful and influential," and the Netherlands had "little influence."[31] Meanwhile, George Washington, who was wintering in Miralles's house in Philadelphia, sent a letter to Navarro in Havana merely to thank the captain general for Spain's continuing help.[32]

For his part, Miralles reported that the Americans would cede any territory con-quered by Spain in Louisiana, and do so without placing any condition on naviga-tion of the Mississippi River. He also relayed a rumor that he did not believe: England was about to grant independence and ally itself to its former colonies. Then the two countries would attack the French Caribbean holdings, which would be ceded to the United States. Miralles's skepticism was correct.[33]

France and Spain also agreed that French troops would fight in the rebelling thirteen colonies while Spanish forces would concentrate in its own territory. Spain feared giving its own colonies any cause for disgruntlement by occupying other colonies. France did not have that problem.[34]

Again, Spain followed a course most beneficial to itself while achieving the goals of its partners. Spain clearly wanted Gibraltar and Minorca in Europe and the British out of the Gulf Coast from Florida through Central America. Britain only needed Spanish neutrality, but never counteroffered to see if Spain would back away from its support of American independence. France took advantage of this opportunity to agree to all of Spain's conditions.

On 12 April 1779 the new Franco-Spanish alliance was signed at the summer palace in Aranjuez. France ratified the treaty at Versailles on April 28. Floridablanca succeeded in entering Spain into the war on Spain's terms. How he must have sensed the irony of impressing upon France his position, for Vergennes earlier had tried to scare Spain into the war. Amazingly, even the treaty provided for one final opportu-nity for Great Britain to accept Spain's conditions. Again, as expected, the British government refused.[35]

France agreed to its new alliance with Spain without consulting the Americans, which, in effect, committed the Americans to Spain's goals. Leaders in the rebelling colonies did not complain; on the contrary, they were happy. Spain formally declared war on 21 June 1779.[36] Spain agreed not to make peace with Great Britain without France's acquiescence. Significantly, Spain consistently recognized that France could not achieve peace until England recognized American independence.[37]

So, without becoming an ally of the rebelling colonies, Spain tied itself to inde-pendence. This was the best of all choices for the Spanish regime and as good as could be expected for the Americans. Subsequent United States historians would condemn Spain's position or even ignore Spain's key involvement in the war, because Carlos III and Floridablanca did not agree to an alliance with the United States.[38] However, from a Spanish point of view, which is all these men were required to have, they could not have done better. In the process, they likely prevented eventual defeat of the colonies and France.

American historian Jonathan Dull, an expert on the revolution and France's role in the war, felt that victory could not have been achieved without Spain.

> Had the French navy been crushed, Britain could have successfully block-aded the American coast and made New York impregnable. Without money

and supplies from Europe, the survival of the United States would have been unlikely. Without the military and naval help, the expulsion of the British from America would have been impossible.[39]

Most contemporaries of the time understood that Spain's declaration was pivotal. Among other advantages, the addition of the Spanish navy gave the allies naval superiority over Great Britain. This would be crucial to the decisive victory at Yorktown.[40] Spain's declaration of war introduced something more important than recognition. It provided a realistic chance at independence.

Word of Spain's action traveled fast to the Americas. In some cases, it appears that a forewarning had been issued to Spanish officials. News of the declaration of war was dispersed through José de Gálvez's office in Spain to Havana and from there throughout the Spanish Americas. Gálvez sent word to his nephew on May 18, while the news was communicated to most of the other principal officials on May 20.[41]

Roberto Ribas Betancourt, the governor of Yucatán, also received a letter from José de Gálvez dated 18 May 1779 in which he was informed of the state of war and given instructions. Gálvez expected the governor to destroy all the English settlements in his area, especially along the coast. In addition, he needed to coordinate efforts with the governor of Guatemala, Matías de Gálvez. Betancourt, like all of his colleagues, expected war and answered José de Gálvez with detailed plans of their preparation.[42]

In Havana, Navarro received a Royal Order dated 18 May 1779 and published it 22 July 1779.[43] Navarro also sent word to Miralles in Philadelphia. Thinking ahead or demonstrating good planning, the captain general of Havana wanted to know if the American army planned to move south to East Florida.[44]

He also sent a letter to the "Governor of Charlestown" in which he asked the governor if he could move troops to Georgia and "directly against the royalists in Florida." Perhaps being a little coy, Navarro than reported to José de Gálvez that he had notified Miralles and the American governor of the declaration, but did not mention his proposals for strategies.[45]

Miralles shared Navarro's desire to see the British defeated in East Florida. However, he kept busy collecting information for his almost daily dispatches to Spain and, perhaps, was anxious to receive an appointment as ambassador, which did not happen.[46] For whatever reason, Miralles waited until November before he made an official presentation to Congress. He informed the American government that the news of the declaration had been sent out in July and that he was instructed by his king to inquire whether the Americans would attack East Florida. Without evidence, it seems that Miralles delayed asking about East Florida while waiting for direction from Madrid, or he understood the virtues of patience and tact.[47] In any case, he pushed for an attack on East Florida.

Navarro dispersed the news throughout the rest of his domains including Trinidad, Cartagena, Santa Fe de Bogotá, and Panama. He also expelled all English,

Irish, and Scottish ships and people from Cuba and ordered that "all individuals and ships from 'the United Provinces of America' be treated well."[48]

Bernardo de Gálvez received word on 21 June 1779, the same day that war was officially declared in Spain. He immediately held a town meeting in which he announced the long-awaited action. Viceroy Martín de Mayorga in Mexico received the royal order and printed it on 12 August 1779 in Mexico City.[49]

Bernardo de Gálvez knew that the news had put in motion the transfer of troops from Havana. He and Bonet had planned the event since at least April. Bonet initially hesitated, for he feared spreading his resources too thin by sending troops to Louisiana, the Mexican coast, and defending the islands while sending supplies to the "northern colonies." However, assurances from José de Gálvez that the king understood Louisiana's importance gave reason for Bonet to prepare the troops for Bernardo de Gálvez in New Orleans.[50]

The official declaration of war listed all the wrongs of British action, and the refusal of Great Britain to negotiate seriously, as the reasons for the declaration. Of course, His Most Catholic Majesty regretted having to resort to this ultimate and worst of solutions, but he was left with no alternative.[51]

One last significant facet of the treaty needs to be noted because it might indicate that the Americans deserve some criticism as a result of the actions of their own diplomats during the peace negotiations. France, and therefore the United States, agreed to continue fighting until Spain secured Gibraltar from Great Britain. As everyone knew, Great Britain's stubborn position over "the rock" was a major reason that Spain entered the conflict. Floridablanca, in a timeless statement, described Gibraltar as "that pile of stones, only a matter of expense and trouble to them [Great Britain], disturbing to us and an impediment of permanent friendship."[52]

The advantage of Spain's open involvement in the struggle ran the gamut in the minds of the Americans. Such benefits included everything from money to the Spanish navy, and Samuel Adams's declaration that Great Britain would have to concentrate on its now formidable European enemies, thus leaving the colonies to "our safe and lasting peace."[53] Unfortunately, Congress did not act quickly appointing an emissary to Spain, because it was still divided over the Deane and Lee affair. The debate continued to delay any agreement as to who would be the commissioner to Spain. Even Gerard became involved when he, perhaps meddling where he should not, leaked the information that the Spanish government found Lee disagreeable and distrustful. William Carmichael, who would become secretary to the future ambassador in Spain, supported those criticisms, adding that Lee's English contact was Lord Shelburne and that Spain was not pleased to hear that when Lee traveled to Spain, he had replaced Franklin.[54]

Neither Gerard nor any of the Congressional delegates knew at the time that Lee audaciously sent two letters to the court of Spain in which he suggested his own strategy for a Spanish victory. "Spain," he wrote, "will need to guard against British privateers" and "the key to a Spanish victory is to secure her commerce from British depredations." He added that the Spanish fleet needed to trap the British fleet in the Mediterranean while the French checked any help in the English Channel and the Bay of Biscay. Only then could "the power of Spain to clip the wings of Great Britain and pinion her forever" be realized.[55]

Lee sent his first letter a couple of weeks before the Spanish declaration of war and his second letter four days after. By any standard of the time, his letters were unusual, especially for a diplomat representing a country seeking recognition. In addition, he knew that he was under investigation. Maybe he was desperate to demonstrate his loyalties. Underlying his strategy for Spain was a completely different set of assumptions than those shared by his colleagues in America. Whereas they saw opportunity, he warned about the threat of English disruption of Spanish commerce. He was the only person to suggest that a major naval victory in the Mediterranean Sea would win the war.[56]

Floridablanca replied to Lee a month and a half after Lee's last letter. The Spanish minister of state merely acknowledged Lee's letters and nothing more. Floridablanca and his government had prepared for war far beyond Lee's imagination. Obviously, too, Lee would not have been a good choice for the Continental Congress to send to Madrid.[57]

With the advantage of hindsight, one wonders whether Spain would have modified its position in regard to United States recognition if Congress had acted quickly.[58] After a series of votes reflecting the political division then rampant in Congress, John Jay emerged as the choice to be the minister to the court of Spain. Jay, who had replaced Laurens as the president of the Continental Congress and, incidentally, backed Silas Deane during the quarrel, was well known to Miralles. The Spanish observer found Jay to be sympathetic to Spain as well as a personal friend. Jay, a New Yorker, had dined with the Spaniard on more than one occasion and knew that the unofficial diplomat had the backing of the royal court, which makes Jay's subsequent disastrous tour of Spain all the more puzzling.[59] Gerard was also pleased with the choice. Jay and John Adams, who received the appointment of minister to negotiate a peace treaty with Great Britain, were named to their respective positions a couple of months after Spain entered the war.[60]

None of the American leaders doubted that Spain's military weight would secure victory. If the general public did not hear of Spain's action by word of mouth, they read about it in the newspapers, for Carlos III's proclamation was translated and published. George Washington read an account given in the newspapers published on August 23.[61] Now, he knew, the war would spread beyond the colonies and independence was a reality.

NINE

European Allies, 1779–1783

. . . dearly sell the enemy the victory.
José de Gálvez to the governor of Havana, 1780

*S*pain had become a different country from the end of the Seven Years' War until its entrance into the conflict that included the American Revolution. The empire had begun to generate funds and build strength. Annual revenues in Mexico alone increased from twelve million to fifty million *pesos fuertes* annually.[1] The military forces had improved enough to do honor to a reformed administration, which was probably the most efficient government of any of the players in the war.

Upon Spain's declaration of war, the fighting took on a distinct worldwide flavor. Fighting broke out in the Mediterranean, with joint French-Spanish forces laying siege to Gibraltar, while seriously organizing for an invasion of England. At the same time, Matías de Gálvez, who had been in Central America for only a few months, was forced into a defensive posture with outnumbered and unprepared troops. Matías's son, Bernardo, began an offense up the Mississippi River. Spanish forces eventually would get as far north as St. Joseph, Michigan.[2] In the Caribbean, plans and preparations were being made to defend Havana as well as the French possessions, so that the French navy could support land troops in the north. Preparations were made for an invasion of the Bahamas and Jamaica, a strategy that Benedict Arnold had suggested to Congress, although there is no evidence that it influenced Spanish planning.[3] France now seriously took up arms to regain lost possessions in India.

All of this was part of a strategy to take advantage of the combined Spanish-French naval superiority, the large Spanish American land force, and the self-confident forces of Great Britain's rebelling colonies. The strategy was obvious and successful, for the allies knew that Great Britain had priorities other than its North American colonies. Only Spain, with its large empire and sixteen years of preparation, could have made such a strategy possible.

The Spanish government ran an empire that reflected its legalistic penchant for filing copies of everything everywhere, and was flexible enough to allow local strategies to be developed by people familiar with the situation. The flow of information kept everyone informed and helped the central administration formulate policies that worked toward eventual victory, and assisted in the local venues.[4]

However, not all went smoothly. As previously described, locales competed for priority treatment, there were differences over strategy, and proprietary jealousies arose. Spain's governmental system had the flexibility to let all the differences not only be aired, but also be known and discussed. Spain brought clarity of vision to the war that focused on goals and an understanding of the means for achieving the end. Spain and France had given much thought and preparation to the war.[5] Coordination, especially, between the two European countries, was necessary for success.

Spain required French help in the Mediterranean. The rebelling colonies and France needed Spain in the Americas. The obvious possibility of coordination among the Bourbons made the threat of an invasion of England real and French activity in India possible. These threats and actions, along with Spanish strength in the Americas, meant less British pressure on its colonies.

The success of the Spanish and French alliance began in Europe and carried on through the Americas to the Battle of Yorktown. Had the two neighboring European countries failed in their alliance, they would not have succeeded in battle. In this larger scenario, the thirteen colonies were a small but important player on the world stage.

Plans for the loosely kept secret to invade England had been formulating since the beginning of 1779. Even the American rebels in faraway North America knew of the pending invasion, although some were confused as to whether England or Ireland would receive the brunt of the combined invasion.[6]

In reality, the American colonists had reason to be confused, because the planned invasion, the strategy for which had been bantered between Spain and France for at least a half a year, never really jelled. Both Spain and France had their respective ideas and limitations. The Spanish, especially Floridablanca, advocated that such an action would surely force Great Britain to give up Gibraltar. However, Floridablanca could not spare land forces. This, he argued, would have to be provided by the French. Spain would supply monetary compensation and some of the necessary ships-of-the-line to escort the invasion.

Ireland was an alternate target. A direct and successful invasion of England would force the rest of Europe against the Bourbon countries. Ireland and a disruption of British channel shipping, with the threat of a mass landing on the English coast, all played into the strategy as it evolved and changed. In addition, the allies believed an attack on Ireland would be less expensive and hazardous. Then France lost confidence in a total invasion. The French fleet was in disrepair, from its shipyards to its crews, and France was disappointed in Spain's inability to provide troops for the venture. France proposed a new strategy to disrupt British commerce by stationing the combined fleet at the entrance of the English Channel, while landing an expeditionary force on the Isle of Wight. In this plan, Spain would provide twenty ships-of-the-line. Floridablanca cautiously agreed to the change. The Spanish minister, like Vergennes, felt that there was a possibility of forcing Britain into an early peace through pressure from its own business community.[7]

The plans reverted back to an invasion of England when the conde de Aranda made a counterproposal to Vergennes for a full invasion and, to the surprise of everyone, Vergennes agreed. All of Vergennes's advisors argued against the idea. Floridablanca continued to adhere to a plan for disrupting commerce. The French ambassador in Madrid wrote that Floridablanca believed that war in Europe kept Great Britain from dispatching forces abroad to attack Spanish possessions in the Americas.[8]

Progress was delayed by weather, disease, and, especially in France, the necessity of gathering crews. Cooler heads and the realities of mounting an invasion contributed to aborting the idea. In addition, Carlos III wanted the mission accomplished by September and he retained the authority to withdraw his forces at that time. As delays mounted, it became clear to everyone that the planned invasion either needed to be canceled or delayed for a year.

The combined naval force did put to sea in August 1779, under the command of the comte d'Orvilliers. The fleet began a search for a British fleet setting sail for America. By the time the British fleet was located, the allied forces were riddled with a mysterious disease that especially decimated the Spanish crews. Hampered by contrary winds and low supplies, the allied fleet returned to port at Brest in early September. Despite the disappointment, the plans and action gave hope to the American colonists, created fear among the English, and resulted in a prize of one ship-of-the-line to the allied forces.[9]

The allies supplied the Americans with up-to-date information. Arthur Lee wrote a very accurate report of the attempted invasion as it happened. On August 10, a month after the Spanish and French fleets embarked, he reported that they had rendezvoused on July 26 off of Cape Finisterre. He continued to inform Congress that the fleet contained fifty ships-of-the-line under d'Orvilliers and that twenty of those were Spanish. The armada included thirty-eight frigates and a multitude of other ships. In addition, a fleet of sixteen Spanish ships-of-the-line had been held in reserve to cruise off the Canary Islands and blockade Gibraltar. Arthur Lee's information was exactly correct. Two weeks later, he reported to Congress that the fleets had not progressed because of adverse winds. Nevertheless, he forecast that Great Britain was "so pressed and kept in check" that it would not be able to send additional troops to the United States nor maintain New York and Rhode Island.[10]

Within days of the declaration, Spanish troops confronted the British garrison at Gibraltar; a small naval assault force attacked the fortress and harbor. Soon thereafter, French forces arrived to join the Spanish force. The siege of Gibraltar began on 11 July 1779 and lasted until the end of the war.[11]

The siege of Gibraltar became the focus of the war in Europe.[12] The British-occupied stronghold is near to, but not at the tip of the Iberian Peninsula that is nearest to Africa. It is one of the two locations for the legendary Pillars of Hercules. Africa is only fourteen miles south, and the close proximity of the two continents forms the Straits of Gibraltar. The two points marked the western limit for trade among ancient Mediterranean peoples.[13]

On June 21, Lieutenant General Joaquín Mendoza notified the British governor of Gibraltar, George Elliott, that he had received orders to cut all communications between the Spanish and British garrisons. Mendoza allowed a few hours for British families to move from nearby San Roque where they had taken up residence. Still, the announcement was a surprise and many possessions were left behind. One group of Englishmen, out on a hunt, had to make their way to nearby Portugal and return to Gibraltar a month later in a rowboat from Faro, a city on Portugal's south coast.[14] Both sides then began to make preparations for a siege. The Spanish contingent of over fourteen thousand men began to dig trenches and dugouts, create breastworks, and mount artillery. In addition, fifteen cruisers commanded by Antonio Barceló maintained a sea blockade. The British defenders, a garrison of never more than seven thousand men, reorganized its defenses, started evacuating citizens to the Moroccan coast under the cover of dark, and began rationing food.[15]

Through the rest of 1779, the actual hostilities were almost nonexistent. Daily bugle calls notified the respective sides that mail could be exchanged. The only evidence of hostility was the blockade.

But the siege successfully cut off most of the food supply, the lone exception being some nighttime smuggling from Morocco. Much of this last source of supply ended up being dispersed through the black market. Gibraltar was caught unprepared, for the British government had not adequately supplied the garrison in anticipation for the war. The black market flourished, as food became scarce and scurvy spread.

Carlos III successfully negotiated with the sultan of Morocco, Mohammad I, to avoid helping the English and to open his ports to Spanish ships. The sultan even contributed a large sum of money to Spain as a pledge of sincerity, although Carlos III did not want overt help from Morocco.[16]

Fortunately for the besieged, the home office in London was concerned enough to recruit one of its old sea veterans out of retirement and give him the commission to break the blockade and supply the garrison. Admiral George Rodney fulfilled his orders. He set sail in late December and engaged and defeated two out-manned Spanish attempts to stop him.

The second of these engagements is worthy of some note, for Lieutenant General Juan de Lángara, apparently caught by surprise, led a squadron of eleven ships-of-the-line and two frigates into a confrontation with Rodney's fleet, which was more than twice as large, with twenty-two ships-of-the-line and fourteen frigates. The valiant but terribly outgunned Spanish lieutenant general continued fighting even though his flagship had been cut to pieces. British accounts describe him fighting despite constant fire from four ships and his ship's masts being blown away. Not until he was severely wounded and his ship had become a barely-floating wreck did he surrender.[17] (See plate 14.)

Lángara's gallant effort, along with bad weather, dismasted one-third of Rodney's ships-of-the-line and scattered most of the rest. In a letter distributed throughout the Spanish realms, José de Gálvez reported on behalf of his king the additional details that two badly-damaged English *navíos*, warships, had entered the port of Lisbon, but were in such disrepair that they could not be fixed. Three other ships "without either masts or fixtures, surrendered to the wind's will or dashed against the rocks." Others of the lesser ships suffered some of the same fate.[18]

Lángara's action was an exception to the rule. Stronger and larger Spanish fleets stayed in port at both Brest and Cádiz. Cádiz was under the command of Lieutenant General Luis de Córdova, whom the outspoken Montmorin called senile. Rodney had to pass both ports on his way to Gibraltar. The French were not close enough to help. Historians, especially from England, have been unable to explain the Spanish strategy of relative inactivity.[19]

The combined French and Spanish forces had more firepower. Perhaps, as one Spanish contemporary expressed the strategy, Spain intended to save its naval assets for other theaters, while maintaining enough of a blockade of Gibraltar to divert the British.[20] That strategy, in effect, allowed Rodney to relieve the garrison in the middle of January, but did not end the siege, for Rodney had been weakened enough to put himself in peril if he tarried.

In a very carefully written and printed letter under José de Gálvez's name, Carlos III countered what he thought would be the misrepresentations of London's press. He noted that part of the Spanish strategy was to use the season of storms, as well as its own navy, to put any British attempt to relieve Gibraltar at risk. This, he continued, is exactly what happened because the bad weather, while preventing a major naval engagement, did wreak havoc on the fleet which, when combined by Lángara's effort, "dearly [sold] the enemy a victory." Meanwhile, the letter confidentially pointed out, the French fleet that was organized to reinforce the French West Indies may have already left Brest—it had—and a major Spanish expeditionary force was preparing to supplement Havana. Both of these armadas would take advantage of Britain's preoccupation with Gibraltar. Spain, he stated was on course toward victory.[21]

Rodney's partial success did create some confusion among Spanish officials. The people who had opposed Floridablanca now used this opportunity to blame him for the lack of defense. Aranda and José de Gálvez were especially vocal. The rift appears to have been personal, rather than a question of strategies and, like most wars, the rapidity of events diverted the attention of the feuding parties.

News of wartime activities in the Americas began to arrive in Spain. Within the first six months, the king received bittersweet information. Havana was secure and not under any immediate threat.[22] Young Bernardo de Gálvez had moved up the

Mississippi River and defeated the British at various settlements and posts by late September of 1779. News of this success and preparations for attacking Mobile and Pensacola had been sent in the last part of September.[23] On the other hand, the early reports from Guatemala painted a darker picture. The enemy had moved fast and caught the undermanned Matías de Gálvez's forces unable to defend themselves. Fort Omoa fell in October. The Royal Court would have heard about the defeat before New Year.[24]

Thus, before and while Carlos III received news of Rodney's attempt at Gibraltar, he learned that his forces had engaged the British in the Americas, an area that was a Spanish priority. Importantly, by the end of February of 1780, he learned that his American leadership felt confident about expanding their success and that his major American port at Havana remained secure. Guatemala continued to suffer setbacks, but was not lost, for Matías de Gálvez was still gathering his forces and showed no sign of breaking.

The king did not overly concern himself with Rodney's partial success, which in his eyes, could be seen as a British failure because the siege was not lifted nor were all the supplies delivered. Or, at very least, as he reported throughout his empire, Rodney's partial success was achieved at a great cost.[25] Instead, he and his advisors decided to continue the siege of Gibraltar as before and concentrate more on the Americas. This strategy would force Great Britain to make some decisions and would placate France, who wanted the war's emphasis placed in the Americas. In addition, and probably key to lack of a more aggressive naval strategy in the blockade of Gibraltar, the new strategy was in accordance with the consistent French desire that Spain maintain its navy and thus the combined Spanish and French naval superiority. So, Spain and France decided to send additional forces to the Americas. Spain agreed to send eight to ten thousand troops with twelve to fourteen ships-of-the-line, and France countered that they would send three to four thousand troops and three or four ships-of-the-line.[26]

In addition, a most significant event took place. Carlos III received word that Commodore Johnson, the British commander on the Lisbon station, delivered an offer from Lord North to the Spanish officials in November 1779. The British government, the message hinted, would consider purchasing peace with the cession of Gibraltar. Great Britain wanted to negotiate. Although the offer was unofficial, Carlos agreed to talk.[27] His belief in negotiations, while tempered with a healthy doubt about British sincerity, was reflected in his letter to the realm. He had José de Gálvez write that Gibraltar

> probably might surrender very soon and we will be able, without shedding of blood, to restore this important *Plaza* to our domain, an accomplishment which up until now the art of war had deemed unbeatable.
>
> The means which had been adopted were the most adequate and efficient for this end.[28]

As one British historian wrote, the mild Carlos III would not want to waste life unnecessarily over something that could be won diplomatically.[29]

It seems that the negotiations, which lasted into early 1781, contributed to a policy of concentrating on maintaining and governing the American possessions that Spain considered its own. Nor does it appear that Spain was willing to sell out American independence for Gibraltar.[30] If Gibraltar was the true goal, then Spain, with France's concurrence, could have concentrated forces and ships enough to secure the fortress. France did offer more ships, but was turned down in favor of the American policy.[31]

Carlos sent Father Thomas Hussey, an Irishman, to act as an intermediary. While in London, Father Hussey had been the chaplain to Almodóvar, the Spanish ambassador. Hussey met with Richard Cumberland, the secretary to Lord George Germain, who was the British secretary of state for the American colonies. The negotiations carried on for over a year until February 1781, when they broke off and Great Britain had to send another rescue mission to bring relief to Gibraltar.

By then, Spain had been encouraged by the continued success in the Americas. Mobile had been defeated and the plans for the siege of Pensacola were complete.[32] The government published the articles of capitulation of Baton Rouge in *la Gaceta de Madrid* in June of the previous year.[33] And, Spanish forces had taken the offensive in Guatemala.[34]

From Spain's point of view, Europe, too, showed positive signs. London suffered an outbreak of riots in June 1780. Known as the Gordon riots, many in Great Britain thought that they heralded a revolution. If nothing else, the riots tended to confirm the allied belief that the English populace would tire of the war if enough pressure could be applied.

Soon after the riots, Spain learned that a huge fleet conveying supplies to British ports in the East and West Indies was about to depart with a weak British escort. Floridablanca pleaded with Carlos to accept a plan to intercept the fleet off the Azores. After some hesitation, the king granted permission. Floridablanca put Córdova, who was at Cádiz, in charge of the task. Córdova moved accordingly and attacked the unsuspecting fleet, eventually capturing over sixty ships, many civilians, and over eighteen hundred officers and men of the royal or East India Company's army. He also captured almost two million pounds' worth of goods. Although not recorded, perhaps Montmorin changed his opinion about Córdova's imputed senility.[35]

As a result of damage inflicted on Rodney's fleet, Great Britain spent most of the rest of 1780 refitting and organizing its American and European fleets. Córdova was able to strengthen his Cádiz fleet by transferring ships from Brest. None of these ships was seriously threatened during their respective moves. In addition, while Spain and France turned their attention to the Americas, Great Britain was not prepared to prevent this new emphasis. Both Spain and France used this time to transfer ships and troops and thus change the course of the war.

France first sent a reinforcement convoy to Martinique under the command of Lieutenant General Luc Urbain du Bouexic, the comte de Guichen. The convoy departed Brest with seventeen ships-of-the-line, over twenty merchantmen, and almost forty transports with two hundred officers and 4,400 troops. The convoy combined with another armada to add three more ships-of-the-line. The departure coincided with Rodney's presence at Gibraltar. The British could not prevent the movement. Eventually, Guichen and Rodney would fight two inconclusive battles in the West Indies, but not until after the troops had been delivered.

A second smaller French convoy left France for India. This force met some resistance and lost one ship-of-the-line and some troops who were being transferred. The rest, including two ships-of-the-line, seventeen or eighteen merchantmen, and transports with most of two battalions of soldiers safely completed the journey to India.[36]

Then on April 18, a Spanish convoy to reinforce the Spanish West Indies left Cádiz. The promised transfer included 146 merchantmen and transports with eleven thousand troops. Only twelve ships-of-the-line were assigned to protect the convoy, which was under the command of José Solano. Perhaps, the small escort was a Spanish acknowledgment that English interference was not expected. Nevertheless, the small escort was a high stakes gamble.

Solano's convoy completed an allied strategy to place the Bourbon partners in a position of overwhelming troop strength in the West Indies. This was an important move. Guichen and Solano successfully gave their respective countries the upper hand in the southern theater of the American part of the war.[37] Had Great Britain been prepared to stop the fulfillment of Spain's plan to send troops to the West Indies, Spain most likely would have been neutralized.

France quickly moved to partially accomplish the same goal in the north. The American colonies suffered some major defeats at Charleston in May and at Camden, South Carolina, in August. The Continental army was reduced to roughly seventeen thousand men and was facing a force of thirty thousand trained British soldiers. The colonies needed help.

France planned to send relief in the form of eight thousand troops under the command of General Jean-Baptiste-Donatien Vimeur, comte de Rochambeau. To assure the safe passage of this army, the expeditionary force was placed under the command of Commodore, the chevalier de Ternay, and divided into two parts. Great Britain, which was now refitting its European navy as a result of the Gibraltar mission, could not prevent Ternay's departure. In addition, the combination of adverse weather and a delay caused by a dispute over back pay prevented the British American fleet from intercepting the French force.[38]

Again, Gibraltar played a role in providing opportunities to the allied nations and helping, eventually, to secure independence for the United States. Perhaps, too, more credit should be given to the conservative naval policies of Spain and France, as well as Lángara's courageous stand.[39]

As Great Britain continued to focus on Gibraltar and the Bourbon allies focused on the Americas, Floridablanca and Vergennes approached Empress Catherine of Russia. France and Spain wanted to keep the other European nations neutral in the war and, if possible, weaken England in the process. The Bourbon kings did not take long to convince Catherine to take the lead in forming a League of Armed Neutrality, an organization of neutral European countries, which, in turn, determined its own definition of free trade with the belligerent nations. Great Britain, and to some extent Spain, stopped and confiscated neutral ships for the slightest suspicions. Spain realized the errors of its ways when it stopped a Russian ship that it thought was trying to aid Gibraltar. With some French prodding, the ship was released and Spain announced a change in policy. At first, all the principal nations, with the exception of Holland, joined the new league. Floridablanca noted that Holland was England's "ancient ally."[40] He was apparently unaware of the checkered history that the two countries shared.

Actually, Holland hesitated only out of fear that its exposed widespread seaports would be easy targets for the British navy. The counter-argument to this was that Great Britain already had enough opposition in the war and the proposed alliance of neutral nations would have the combined naval strength of over eighty ships-of-the-line. Not only would the specter of alienating such a force protect Holland's interests, but also it would allow the League to dictate what goods they could carry on their ships, and preclude the belligerent nations from dictating their own terms. In November 1780, Holland joined Russia, Prussia, Denmark, and Sweden in the League of Armed Neutrality. Great Britain saw Holland's act as a betrayal and prepared for war against the neutral country.[41]

At the same time, Floridablanca and Carlos III renewed negotiations with Mohammed I in Morocco. The sultan agreed to lease to Spain his ports at Tangier and Tetuán, which effectively closed those ports as sources of supplies for British forces. The Bourbon allies continued to isolate Great Britain from potential allies and sources of aid.

Perhaps while trying to counter the formation of the League, Great Britain offered the Mediterranean island of Minorca to Russia, if Catherine would agree not to join the proposed alliance. Spain learned of Great Britain's maneuver, which led to Floridablanca's counter plan—an attack on Minorca to take it away from the British. The minister presented the idea to his king, who was doubtful. Spain, argued Floridablanca, had an opportunity to eliminate the British from their only other Mediterranean base besides Gibraltar. Carlos III acquiesced.[42]

France was informed of the idea, but the French ministers were even more skeptical. Some felt that the island could not be taken. Montmorin felt that too many troops would be needed, and Vergennes could not forecast success without local support on the island.[43]

As a result, the discussions ended, but Spain secretly continued preparations in Cádiz where troops and transports gathered. France learned of the activities and considered the possibility that the goal might be Minorca, but thought it more certain that Spain planned to reinforce the West Indies.[44]

Floridablanca even prepared for the diversionary tactic, as he called it, by sending the marqués de Lorrerich from Palma, a nobleman from the Balearic Islands, to secretly visit Minorca and find out if the inhabitants would side with Spain. With the help of a Frenchman who was married to a Minorcan woman, Lorrerich learned what British Commander General James Murray already knew. The Minorcans would not cooperate with the British, because they considered themselves to be Spanish.[45]

Murray tried to recruit a local militia and failed. He then tried to recruit laborers, masons, smiths, and carpenters to help repair the fortress of St. Philip. Again, he received no cooperation. He became so desperate for help that he even considered recruiting Moors from North Africa.[46]

To complicate matters, the British general did not receive help from London. The Home Office feared losing Gibraltar. Minorca seemed to be a minor consideration. Murray informed his superiors of his problems. His troops suffered from disease and lack of supplies. He described his men as looking more like ghosts than soldiers. Nevertheless, even Murray began to feel that he was not in danger of attack. At one point, he felt secure enough to send some of his own badly needed supplies to Gibraltar.[47] His confidence was misplaced.

With all the necessary information in hand, Floridablanca appointed the duc de Grillon to be in charge of the Minorca invasion. Grillon resigned his position as lieutenant general in the French army to put himself in the service of Spain. Upon his appointment, he wrote to Carlos III that "he would answer with his head, if he did not hand over the place . . . with very little loss of life and at limited cost."[48]

The allied force of fifteen to sixteen thousand men maintained the advantage of surprise by sailing from the more distant ports of Cádiz and Cartagena rather than closer ports. The main part of the fleet took almost a month in transport, during which time it forced a retreat of a British fleet of twenty-one ships-of-the-line. Still the attack came as a complete surprise to the defenders. Murray received no advance information whatsoever.[49]

In late August, the combined force landed on Minorca at two separate locations. The force under the marqués de Aviles easily took its objective, Ciudadela, and the other force under the marqués de Peñafiel occupied Fornells. Between them, they met no resistance, cut the island in half and captured almost half of the British garrison. The allied troops then moved on Port Mahón and captured the arsenal. Among the prizes were 180 cannon and 150 ships.

The victory was exciting, but not complete, for the other half of the British garrison, which originally numbered about twenty-five hundred troops, successfully retreated to the fortress of St. Philip. Grillon, perhaps in his overconfidence, did not include siege arms and equipment among his supplies, so he was not prepared to launch an attack on the fort. With the assistance of a small Spanish fleet under Don

Bonaventura Moreno, Grillon began a blockade that lasted for over two months while he waited for reinforcements and the proper equipment to begin the true siege. The defenders suffered horribly. One of the early bombardments during the siege destroyed the fort's medical stores, which exacerbated conditions. The British suffered from scurvy and typhus, which they called the "putrid fever."[50]

The defenders held out for another three months, making a shambles of Grillon's boastful forecast. On 4 February 1782, Murray agreed to terms of surrender. He had less than six hundred men left, most of whom were in various states of ill health and not fit for duty.[51]

The defending forces in St. Philip included two English and two Hanoverian battalions. They were attacked by a Franco-Spanish force that also included a German brigade.[52] The British home office did make a belated attempt to relieve the defenders. Admiral George Darby planned to send seven ships-of-the-line and seven hundred troops, but changed his mind. He rationalized that his ships were in disrepair and he expected an attack on the homeland. Great Britain never came close to aiding the besieged Murray and his men.[53]

News of the victory at Minorca gratified Carlos III and his advisors. The news spread throughout the empire. More importantly, the victory again demonstrated that Great Britain's concern for Gibraltar created opportunities for Spain and France in other areas. This principle was demonstrated on another occasion when a French fleet captured an English convoy of twenty-two merchant ships with cargoes valued at nearly five million pounds. This capture was accomplished while Great Britain relieved Gibraltar the second time.[54] The expense for the defense of Gibraltar continued to increase.

Spain and France continued to plan and act on the basis of making the British fight a costly and geographically dispersed war. Great Britain kept playing into their strategy. For example, during the occupation of Minorca, Spain and France moved to replace Spanish troops with French troops so that the former could be transferred to Havana. The plans for Jamaica had been forming for some time. France agreed to contribute fifteen ships-of-the-line and four thousand troops. Such planning during the siege of Gibraltar and the taking of Minorca demonstrates that the Bourbon powers steadfastly followed the general strategy to which they had agreed before either entered the war. They would act conservatively, take advantage of Great Britain's obstinacy and the growing unrest of its populace and, above all, spread the struggle worldwide.

Carlos III rewarded Grillon with the command of the siege of Gibraltar where France added another twelve thousand troops, which included the comte d'Artois, the future King Charles X of France and brother of Louis XVI.[55] All of this served to reinforce in British minds the importance that Spain put on Gibraltar. To leave no doubt, the besiegers agreed to a plan of attack formulated by the engineer Michaud d'Arcon, who proposed an attack with specially constructed floating batteries with thick protective roofs. The ten special ships would move close to the defense works and bring havoc on them. Grillon strongly objected to the plan. He was so sure of its imminent failure that he absolved himself of responsibility, in writing, before the attack.[56]

True to Grillon's prediction, the attack proved to be a farce. Contrary winds, rough seas, the accuracy of British gunners, and their use of red-hot shot completely destroyed the floating batteries. In what must have been a spectacular scene the hot shot set fire to the ships, which eventually blew up in explosions that shook the foundations of Gibraltar's buildings. More than forty Spanish and French ships-of-the-line prepared to participate in the battle that began in the morning of 13 September 1782 and lasted for two days. The weather and swelling sea prevented their full participation. Over three hundred and fifty Spanish and French soldiers had to be rescued by British marines. The defenders suffered thirteen killed and sixty-three wounded.[57] Estimates of allied casualties range from fifteen hundred to two thousand.[58]

After the debacle of the floating batteries, the allies satisfied themselves with maintaining the siege to keep Great Britain's attention, as well as to keep Gibraltar on the diplomatic table. A third relief expedition was sent in October 1782. When news of peace ended the siege, the fortress opened for the first time in three years, seven months, and five days.

The defenders, who suffered around five hundred rounds a day from the Spanish guns, lost 330 killed, another 556 from illness, and 161 from incurable complaints.[59] The details represented by those figures give a graphic account of what the historian or reader might casually note. One British contemporary wrote that the doctors were "little better than butchers and are not to be trusted with medicine."[60] The constant bombardment—"during twenty-four hours they discharged 1,263 rounds and the proceeding day 1,948" (about one per minute)[61]—resulted in casualties such as the loss of limbs, the accounts of which reek of misery. "A soldier lost his legs by a shot and bore amputation with firmness but died soon after through loss of blood."[62]

The consistent fire by both sides also bespeaks of the seriousness of the battle. During the siege, British guns discharged about 205,000 rounds of shot and mortar. The allies countered with about 258,000 shots. While neither side suffered heavily from the artillery exchange, the possibility of death lingered and may explain the British casualties from "incurable complaints." Another British account notes, for example, that on 10 September 1782 the enemy fired "about 6,000 shells and shot" and "our loss" amounted to "eight killed and seventeen wounded."[63] One account of an unlucky Englishman who was killed by a long-range shot fired "from more than two miles-and-a-half" hints of the anxiety that the survivors must have felt.[64]

The cost to Great Britain for the defense of Gibraltar far exceeded the listed casualties. Ironically, those who bravely and steadfastly defended the British possession unknowingly did their country a long-run disservice. Combined with the threat of an invasion, the disruption of trade and the loss of Minorca, the British decided to move for an early peace with its colonies.[65] In addition, the European action forced

Great Britain to freeze its European fleet, thus sacrificing its naval parity in the Americas. This parity had been the strength of the British military, which now had the additional problem of facing more French and Spanish troops. This change would result in the pivotal defeat of Lord Cornwallis at Yorktown.

In this context, Spain moved militarily in the West Indies. Coordinated with French help, the West Indies action should have concerned Great Britain more than Gibraltar.

TEN

Central America: An Integral Defense, 1779–1783

. . . to dislocate the English from their hidden establishments . . .
Carlos III, king of Spain, to the governor of Havana, 1781

*I*n Guatemala, Matías de Gálvez had to act, whether his forces were ready or not, for with the outbreak of war, the British did not hesitate. In Central America, Spanish and British forces became entangled in a struggle reminiscent of twentieth-century conflicts in Southeast Asia. Both sides had to survive in harsh conditions and fight with methods far different than their European and North American counterparts. Spanish troops were still involved in traditional defensive and offensive sieges, but there was a difference. Supplies, reinforcements, and especially communications were very difficult to maintain because of the terrain and distance. Both sides could report day-to-day activity during the long siege of a place like Gibraltar in Europe, but this was not possible anywhere in Central America. Reports were filed after the event— explaining a victory or a defeat, or why an action was taken or not. One of the more interesting activities was Matías de Gálvez's strategy of sending reconnaissance patrols to seek out entrenched enemies, English allies who were Black soldiers, Mosquito, Zambo, and Mosco Indians. These enemy allies maintained small posts that protected English sugar plantations and timber harvest camps. Gálvez's patrols withstood extreme hardships of weather, terrain, and the enemy to get information.[1]

Both armies relied heavily on a wide variety of people for their manpower. Gálvez gamely tried to scrape together a force from disparate people and locations. The result was a mixed cadre. He had a regular force of European Spaniards, mulattos, Blacks, and, where he could recruit them, Indians. Great Britain, as will be seen, often used slaves as soldiers and had won over the Mosquito and Mosco Indians. Fighting in Central America during the Revolutionary War is interesting to study and complicated to describe. Actual participation must have been horrible.

The Central American theater was not a sideshow to fighting in other places. The number of troops matched some of the numbers fighting elsewhere, and the locale was geographically and historically significant. If this were not so, both sides, having suffered casualties in the fighting, would have quit the area. Instead, after defeats, each side regrouped to counterattack or to take the offensive. Matías de Gálvez's assignment to Guatemala, in itself, speaks to the area's importance. A member of such an influential family would not have been assigned to such a position if it were not important.

The king continued to reiterate this idea both through correspondence and his personal envoys. Francisco Saavedra, sent to Havana from Spain with explicit instructions, explained to Cuba's leadership that the king's priorities included the defense of Guatemala and that Havana needed to assist with Central America, along with defeating Pensacola, and protecting Cap Français and the treasure fleets.[2]

Carlos III clearly stated his desire in a letter to Governor Navarro. After defeating and securing Mobile and Pensacola on the Gulf Coast, the "second most important objective" was Guatemala, where the goal was "to dislocate the English from their hidden establishments on the Gulf of Honduras, and especially the castle on the San Juan River [thus] impeding [English] intrusion into the great lake of Nicaragua." The king continued that his military needed to take and hold the port of San Juan, defeating "even to the point of exterminating . . . the nations of the Mosquito and Zambo Indians allied as a rule with our enemies."[3] Saavedra warned that Spain could not allow Great Britain to "open access from the North Sea to the South Sea" and separate the Americas.[4]

In accordance with the king's wishes and Matías de Gálvez's requests, money and supplies to help with Guatemala were being sent. Mexico contributed money from taxes collected in Oaxaca, at one time as much as 300,000 *pesos*. Eventually Gálvez would draw on New Spain's viceroy, his predecessor in Guatemala, for one million *pesos,* or thirty million in today's dollars. Peru contributed money and swords. Money certainly reached Central America, for when the British first took Omoa, they were surprised to find two ships in port that contained three million *pesos* meant for Spain and its allies.[5]

Actually, the Spanish assessment of Great Britain's goals was exactly correct. The British had entrenched themselves in the area, especially since the Seven Years' War. Wood harvests for its ships in the West Indies had given rise to English settlements from the north on the Yucatán Peninsula and Campeche to the south along the coast of Belize into the Gulf of Honduras. Along with the many sugar plantations that interspersed the wood harvesting, Great Britain had set up an industry it did not want to lose.

The British saw the Spanish fortress of Omoa as the first step to winning in Central America, and had planned for some time to defeat it quickly once hostilities broke out. Matías de Gálvez knew this.[6] From Guatemala City, Gálvez clearly recognized Omoa's importance to Spanish control over Central America. He called Omoa "the key and outer wall of the kingdom."[7] After Omoa, the British planned to move up the San Juan de Nicaragua River, more commonly called the San Juan River, to gain control of Lakes Nicaragua and Managua. This strategy would result in a British wedge between today's Nicaragua and Costa Rica that would gain access for the British to the Pacific Ocean, along with the opportunity to create a canal. The distance between Lake Nicaragua and the Pacific Ocean is approximately eleven miles.

Upon news of the outbreak of war, Spain moved first. Matías de Gálvez sent reinforcements on board transports to Fort San Felipe de Yucatán, then under the command of Lieutenant Colonel José Rosado. On 15 September 1779 the troops advanced from the fort along the Río Hondo and captured the British Fort St. George (San Jorge), northeast of Belize. The Spanish attackers saw three English frigates, which had been sent to reinforce St. George, but apparently arrived too late, for they never fulfilled their mission. The victorious force took three hundred prisoners, plus women and children, all of whom were transported back to the British at Roatán Island.

At the same time, the British leadership of Governor John Dalling and Captain William Dalrymple, in Jamaica, had ordered Commodore John Luttrell, who was in command of three frigates and two hundred and fifty men, to attack Spanish ships protecting the port of Santo Tomás in the Guatemala Bay of Amatique. But when word leaked out that Gálvez had ordered that port to be abandoned in favor of Fort San Fernando de Omoa in Honduras, Luttrell's orders were changed, to attack Omoa, and the real fighting began.[8]

Luttrell, with the concurrence of Dalrymple, decided not to initiate a full siege. The fort, under the command of Simón Desnaux, could not be taken with Luttrell's two frigates and some five hundred men, including Dalrymple's contingent. In the morning of 25 September 1779, Desnaux ordered his artillery to open fire on the two British ships anchored in front of the fort. The ships returned the favor. Then the two British officers decided to regroup. Dalrymple left for reinforcements at the Río Tinto, while Luttrell continued on to Roatán to replenish his force with the addition of the *Baymen,* another frigate. The two forces then met to travel together to Trujillo, a port on the coast of Honduras, where they prepared for a proper attack on Omoa.

In early October, a British armada of twelve ships and around seven hundred and fifty men left Trujillo. Another five hundred men left the port of Caballos or Cortés, just east of Omoa, to join them. The British fleet quickly unloaded troops who rapidly traveled overland to take the cantonment San Fernando, which was next to Omoa.[9] They then installed two batteries and, with the artillery of three frigates, began the bombardment of Omoa.

Desnaux, who was anxious to receive requested help from Matías de Gálvez, countered with his own artillery and caused some damage on one of the frigates. Nevertheless, the Spanish commander was badly outgunned and outnumbered. The commander refused an offer to surrender, but he was defeated by the ineptitude of his mulatto guards. On the night of October 20, some British soldiers took advantage of the guards' inattention, and scaled a wall and opened the fort's gate. After an hour of resistance, Desnaux and what was left of his force surrendered. Omoa had fallen. The first goal in the British strategy had been won, and the spoils included the aforementioned three million *pesos* found in two boats anchored in Omoa's harbor.[10]

Gálvez immediately wrote to Governor Navarro expressing confidence in achieving an ultimate victory. He stated that if Havana could send some small boats to help attack Omoa by sea, while the land forces attacked, Omoa would be in Spain's hands again.[11] Navarro remained skeptical, answering Matías de Gálvez's stated strategy and requests for aid with an ironic inquiry as to how he lost Omoa in the first place. Nevertheless, Navarro did fulfill Gálvez's requests and dutifully sent copies of the correspondence to Spain. There, José de Gálvez replied that the king wanted help sent to Central America "without losing time."[12]

Matías de Gálvez acted immediately. He moved his headquarters to San Pedro Sula, south of Omoa, and on November 25, he ordered his troops to Omoa. By nightfall, he had surrounded the fort and cut off all water and supplies for the inhabitants. At four in the morning, the two sides began exchanging artillery fire. Dalrymple, now in command of the defense, refused an offer to surrender, claiming that he would fight until the last man. Dalrymple, at the time, did not know the size of the Spanish force. Gálvez, who wanted to get a quick capitulation, resorted to moving his men around and making more campfires than necessary. He also had his soldiers change uniforms to help give the appearance of having a larger force.

A day later, Gálvez offered Dalrymple a second chance to quit, but the British commander refused the offer. Gálvez then threatened his counterpart with continued fighting that might create problems among his mulatto contingents. The mulattos, suggested Gálvez, could run rampant in the heat of battle and he would not be able to control them. Dalrymple remained unimpressed.

On 29 November 1779 Gálvez began his attack at sunrise, but the artillery did not fire as planned, which hindered the siege. Nevertheless, Gálvez's ploys and threats apparently had some effect. That afternoon British rescue ships appeared off the coast and, after sunset, the British evacuated the fort. The Spanish attackers captured thirty defenders. Gálvez's forces did not suffer a casualty, although sickness and exhaustion took a toll.[13]

Gálvez wrote to his brother José to report the victory. His letter reflects pride in the accomplishment of retaking Omoa. His king agreed, for Gálvez received a promotion to brigadier in the Royal army while maintaining his post as captain general of Guatemala.[14]

Gálvez then left Omoa without delay, to prepare for further action against the enemy in Central America. As Navarro and Spain sent more supplies, including one thousand rifles,[15] Gálvez devised a strategy of search and seizure that created a hardship for his men, but was successful for Spain. He divided his forces into three contingents to maximize his effort against the British and their Indian allies. In general, he planned two offenses. One would move along the Caribbean coast against British coastal establishments and the other would move inland to the interior mountains to flush out the Sambo and Mosco Indians. However, another British attack momentarily distracted Gálvez from his plans.[16]

By January 1780, John Dalling in Jamaica was free to organize for the invasion of Nicaragua, which was his main goal. He assigned Captain John Polson to lead a force of one thousand men, drawn from his own sixtieth Regiment, the seventy-ninth Royal Liverpool Volunteers and the Loyal Irish Corps. Two hundred sailors, Sambo and Mosquito Indians, and Black River Volunteers would support them. The force departed from Port Royal on Roatán Island in the Gulf of Honduras on March 4. They arrived at the mouth of the San Juan de Nicaragua River on the 14th of March, and set up a base camp.

One of Polson's officers was a young Horatio Nelson, who was a captain in command of the frigate *Hinchinbrook*. He, with about six hundred men, including Indian allies, followed Polson upriver in Indian dugouts. After twelve days of uneventful travel, they came to the Spanish redoubt called "Platalorma" on Bartola Island. The small contingent of sixteen men was able to hold up the invasion for three hours until an attack led by Nelson ended the confrontation. Two defenders escaped and safely traversed eight miles upstream to warn the Spanish defenders at Fort Immaculate Conception (Immaculada Concepción).[17]

Juan de Ayssa, the commander of the Castle of the Immaculate Conception on the San Juan River, had already heard the rockets exploding and smoke rising over the jungle's trees. He sent two messages to Gálvez in which he reported that a British force was approaching and had already destroyed Fort Bartola, the castle's advance lookout post, but not without a fight. Those fleeing from Fort Bartola warned the main castle. As everyone expected, the British were attempting to gain control of the river and thus take Lake Nicaragua. The thrust was not a surprise.

Nevertheless, Gálvez could not allow the British to succeed. Fully aware of British plans, Gálvez had already moved to Granada, the capital of Nicaragua, by late February in order to strengthen defenses. He furnished logistical support to Fort Immaculate Conception and ordered a patrol of vessels on Lake Nicaragua. When the British siege of the fort began, Gálvez mustered five hundred local militia to construct a stockade at the mouth of the San Juan River and Lake Nicaragua. They called the place Fort San Carlos, in honor of their king.[18]

The Spanish defenders received their first glimpse of the enemy on April 10 at four in the afternoon. By that time, the Spanish Lord Governor had ordered water supplies replenished, the construction of a stockade of timbers to protect the moat, and the burning of a small fort on a hill next to the castle. All the private dwellings, inside the fortress as well as outside, were also burned. In addition, they killed all the livestock, both to stockpile food and to prevent it from falling into enemy hands. Ayssa's orders were carried out with quick efficiency.[19]

For the next eighteen days, a battle ensued in which intrigue, hand-to-hand fighting, and artillery salvos combined with hunger, thirst, fatigue, and the inevitable disease. They were able to retrieve water from a secret spot until the British found

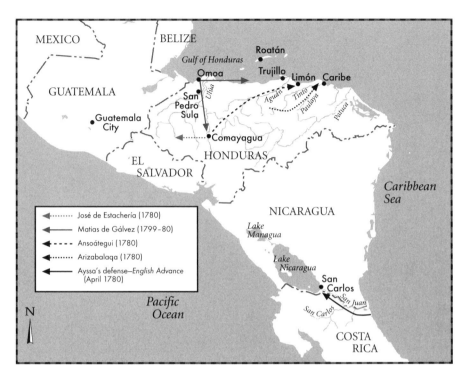

Fig. 11. Early campaigns in Central America.

them at the water hole. A couple of pitched battles were then fought along the river-banks. At another point, the Spanish command learned that the British were low on cannon balls, for they were reusing what the Spanish had shot. This news was of interest, but not of use, because the Spanish were very low in ammunition as well.

Eventually the British set up breastworks within fifty feet of the castle's walls. A Spanish foray beyond the walls resulted in hand-to-hand fighting in which Spanish soldiers used machetes to counter British bayonets. Six enemy soldiers died and one command post was destroyed. The foray also made available some much-needed water. The defense became so desperate that Ayssa commanded, from his rubble of a fort, that vinegar be mixed with the water to make it spread further.

The many artillery barrages continued on a daily basis until the last week of the siege. Ayssa officially reported daily on the deaths of his own men. One officer received a number of shrapnel wounds, on the arm, thigh, and chest. He was given up for dead, but surprised everyone by surviving without leaving his post! On the other hand, a Spanish shot blew up a British emplacement and pieces of the guns and bodies shot up into the air.[20]

As the siege continued, Ayssa ran out of water, ammunition, and space in the chapel to place any more wounded. On 28 April 1780 he ordered an officer to walk

out the front gate under a white flag and request a cease-fire to discuss terms of surrender. Polson agreed to the proposal and hostilities stopped. Ayssa and his brave
men, many of them Blacks and mulattos, had resisted for eighteen days.[21]

Navarro became worried and skeptical about the activities in Central America.
He received reports that Gálvez had recaptured Omoa, but lost the castle on the San
Juan River. At the same time, Manuel Antonio Flores, the viceroy of Santa Fe in
Cartagena, continued to request more troops and supplies to defend against an antic-
ipated attack.[22] Navarro also received news that a 185-ship British convoy had reached
Jamaica. This renewed British strength, theorized Navarro and his advisors, could
lead to a number of dire possibilities, including the feared attack on Havana.[23]

Unknown to the British attackers, Ayssa's defense on the San Juan River had
taken up enough time for Matías de Gálvez to counter with the rapid construction
of Fort San Carlos upriver at the mouth of Lake Nicaragua. The new fortress, one
hundred yards in diameter, had five hundred fresh troops, double walls, and a moat.
It was protected by sixteen cannon on the landside and, on the lake, by a line of
anchored schooners with light cannon.[24] Fort San Carlos, in effect, rendered useless
the British victory at Immaculate Conception, because the Spanish still blocked
their access to the desired lake. Needless to say, when the British troops marched
upriver to be confronted with another fort and a larger garrison, they were
disheartened.

Polson was replaced by Lieutenant Colonel Stephen Kemble, who set up camp
to wait for reinforcements. Kemble was a forty-year-old native of New Brunswick,
New Jersey, who had traveled to Jamaica from New York. He had the confidence of
Dalling, who optimistically kept insisting that reinforcements were on the way.
Kemble, who arrived upriver on June 13, found himself in a terrible situation. He was
camped in a jungle with no reinforcements. His men began suffering from starva-
tion and sickness. Fatalities mounted, first at the rate of a few each week; by early July,
there were six to eight deaths daily. The survivors were reduced to eating bananas and
roasted monkey. Then the rains came.[25]

Back in Kingston, Jamaica, Dalling was out of touch with Kemble's extreme situation. He promised more men, but he never delivered. He wrote that he expected
word of Kemble's ultimate victory at any moment. Finally, the reality of the rest of
the war caused him to give up his illusion. The colonials in North America were
holding their own; the French and Spanish navies outgunned the British, especially
in the Caribbean, and Dalling received rumors of a pending invasion of Jamaica.[26]

On 10 August 1780 Dalling finally wrote Kemble, who had traveled back downriver to secure supplies.

> From the different reports received at home of an intended Invasion by the
> combined powers of France and Spain, from the vast Superiority of the
> Enemy's Fleets to Windward, and from the many fears Government at
> home are alarmed for the safety of this Island . . . and lastly, from the great

delay the Troops have experienced in coming out, together with their very sickly Situation . . . I would now, Sir, have you prepare, with close Secrecy, for a retreat.[27]

Ayssa, who had been taken as a prisoner to Jamaica, learned that the British had planned to establish themselves on the Island of Ometepe in Lake Nicaragua to dominate the lakes and, thus, gain access to both seas. However, Gálvez's quick fortification at "the mouth of the lake" and the prolonged defense of the Castle of Immaculate Conception ruined their plans.[28]

Official word from Spain supported Matías de Gálvez. Supplies must be provided from both Havana and Cartagena to help accomplish "one of the king's principal objectives." The British and their allies must be attacked and discouraged. Eventually, the British must be "cleaned from Guatemala." To emphasize this desire, orders to Havana and Cartagena were sent directly from Spain. Guatemala had become a higher priority.[29]

Left with a hollow victory, few provisions, many sick, and with orders to surrender, the British put up little resistance to the Spanish counterattack and abandoned their strategy of gaining access to the Pacific and splitting the Spanish American empire. On 28 December 1780 a small force of some one hundred and fifty men, under the command of Captain Thomás de Julia, left the new fort of San Carlos to attack the British-held Castle of Immaculate Conception. After a couple of days' siege, involving exchanges of "very live firing," the castle was retaken, along with two hundred prisoners on 3 January 1781.[30] By the beginning of April, Gálvez's forces had pushed the British completely out of the San Juan River from Lake Nicaragua "to the mouth."[31] The campaign up the San Juan River had cost the British three hundred dead and accomplished nothing.[32] Carlos III was very happy to hear this good news.[33]

While Ayssa held out and the second fort was built, Gálvez ordered the execution of his multi-pronged offensive strategy to take the war to the British establishments along the Atlantic coast, up the major rivers, and into the mountains of what is today Honduras. Gálvez, who moved his headquarters from San Pedro Sula inland to Comayagua, in the present country of Honduras, to avoid any threat from the British navy, used the opportunity of the British move up the San Juan River in southern Nicaragua to open his campaign from his new base in the north.[34]

Francisco Saavedra wrote to José de Gálvez that Matías de Gálvez's strategy worked brilliantly, in part because of the brave defense of the soldiers at the Castle of San Juan. Their defense, he reiterated, had checked the British strategy and provided an opportunity for Matías to attack.[35] Saavedra later wrote to Spain, "we should count the defense of Lake Nicaragua as one of the major victories of this war." Great Britain's Middle American plans had been foiled.[36]

Matías de Gálvez was confident of success; he lacked only more supplies and, significantly, smaller ships. He requested this specific aid from Havana on more than one occasion.[37] Although Gálvez was a little miffed at Navarro,[38] the governor seemed more agreeable with Matías's plans and requests, including the small ships, than those of Bernardo de Gálvez, who, at the time, was attacking Pensacola. Navarro had just pleaded with Spain not to abandon Havana as they pushed for offenses in the Americas.[39] Of course, as will be seen, Navarro and his two major officers, Navia and Bonet, were about to be replaced.

Matías de Gálvez later reported to his brother José that his new campaign was a great success. He listed eight enemy establishments destroyed and boasted that the Indians allied with the British now realized the prowess and determination of Spain's soldiers. Furthermore, the British had lost a good source of revenues from the sites that had been rendered useless.

Gálvez then praised his two commanders and their men, urging José de Gálvez to present their accomplishments to the king. Matías's praise of his soldiers' accomplishments hints at the reality of their service, for "they surpassed achievements and difficulties that others at other times thought impossible."[40]

Matías de Gálvez included the reports of his two commanders with his letter of praise. Cayetano Ansoátegui, the commanding general who was put in charge of carrying out the campaign, split his forces. Captain Vicente Arizabalaga received the assignment to take three hundred and fifty men south of Trujillo to the Guanpú River to begin his operation. Ansoátegui kept four hundred and fifty men to go to the Aguán River and then into the mountains to take the war to the Zambo and Mosquito Indians. The journals of these two expeditions speak to the hardships of jungle, mountain, and river warfare.[41]

Ansoátegui traveled out of Comayagua on March 12 and headed in a northwesterly direction for twenty-three days. He described his men cutting their own path through the mountains, presumably to get into the Aguán River basin, which took his force to the northern coast of Honduras at the town of Limón. They took an untraveled route to avoid detection by the British or their allies. All along the way, Ansoátegui sent out reconnaissance patrols to check the many opportunities the terrain provided for ambush. Such a journey in a relatively hot and humid climate was truly worth Gálvez's praise.

Somewhere south of Trujillo, Ansoátegui split his forces, sending Captain Arizabalaga overland due west to the Paulaya River. This created a pincers sweep with the commander's forces moving west along the coast that eventually would meet with his subordinate, who traveled north down the Paulaya and Tinto rivers. They would thus eradicate all the British settlements in northern Honduras, which, coupled with the retaking of Omoa and the successful defense of Lake Nicaragua, would amount to a Spanish victory in Central America.[42]

The western push along the north coast began from Limón. The overland ruse worked, for by Ansoátegui's own admission, the British "could have frustrated all our plans" had they been aware of his presence. Using Black troops as well as regulars, they occupied a number of British "plantations," where the British raised sugar to distill liquor. In the process, they captured British settlers as well as mulatto and

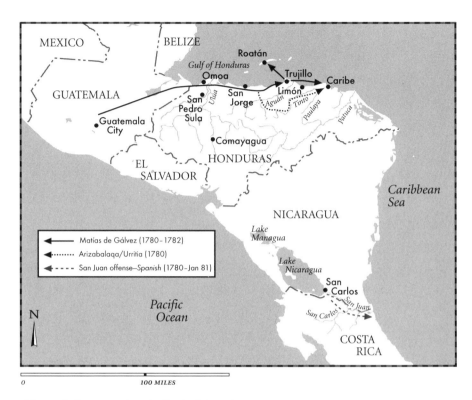

Fig. 12. Later campaigns in Central America.

Black workers. At one point, they captured some small boats, which Ansoátegui sent ahead with some two hundred men. The amphibian force met resistance, but lost only one killed, while Ansoátegui rushed by land to join the battle. Together, the Spanish forced the enemy's retreat into the forest. Many British troops surrendered.

The Spanish force moved to another British settlement called Guepriba, where on a prominent location they found a wood stockade with four cannons. The British troops fired in defense of their position while the Spanish laid siege. After a four-hour struggle, the British "went into a fast and shameful retreat" and, continued Ansoátegui, "my troops entered their trenches and took down the English flag . . . and I have it as a trophy."[43]

The campaign continued in much the same way. Now, with their presence known, the Spanish encountered mostly vacated British plantations and villages. The British, apparently, were producing a lot of liquor and the Spanish commander destroyed the sugar cane fields, dwellings, and, especially, the casks. The last were immediately emptied onto the ground before the Spanish troops had time to think about drinking. Everything was put to the torch.

At Guepriba, for example, the settlement included "well organized" houses "full of elegant mirrors, writing desks, chairs." When the flames engulfed the place, the fire was so intense, he wrote, "it appeared . . . as if the world was ending."[44]

A half a league farther, the troops found the village of Mestrecrio abandoned. They were now within sight of the British-held town of Caribe at the mouth of the Río Tinto. This town was the hub of British commercial activity in the area. In addition, it appeared to be the designated rendezvous point in the Spanish strategy.

Unfortunately for Ansoátegui, when he looked upon Caribe he saw some British ships with more firepower than he could possibly match with his depleted munitions and tired troops. Rather than order a futile attack, the Spanish commander ordered a retreat to Siriboya where he arrived safely with an exhausted force that had suffered only one loss and one broken leg.[45]

At the same time, Arizabalaga traveled overland to the Pauta and Tinto rivers, where on April 6 he began a sixteen-day navigation downriver, using locally made rafts. In the course of his campaign, Arizabalaga and his men had a small battle with some "English Negroes" in which they captured all the enemy canoes and supplies. They then sacked and burnt six British establishments and captured the British "interior governor."[46] Arizabalaga and his men traveled to the mouth of the Tinto River where, like Ansoátegui, they looked upon Caribe. He waited eight days. On occasion he fired a cannon, but received no response. Ansoátegui's contingent was not there. When he heard from some of the prisoners who had fled from Caribe that Ansoátegui had left, he decided to do the same.

His report to Ansoátegui is interesting, for he explained how he waited, hoping to hear that his superior officer would change his mind. Two days after he decided to leave, he received orders to retreat. Nevertheless, Arizabalaga agreed with everyone else that the campaign effectively rendered useless Caribe, the last British post on the coast.[47]

Arizabalaga wrote his report on May 6 and Ansoátegui received it around May 12. By the time Matías de Gálvez had received the reports and recommended the actions of his officers, he also knew that Ayssa's valiant defense had resulted in success on the San Juan River. Although the British would not evacuate the Immaculate Conception castle until 3 January 1781, Gálvez knew that it was inevitable.

Gálvez did not mention in his report a third campaign from Comayagua into the interior. José de Estachería, commander of the infantry of Guatemala, led this unmentioned foray. Whereas the first two expeditions concentrated on the north coast and rivers, Estachería moved into the mountains east of Comayagua to locate Great Britain's Indian allies along the northern Nicaragua border. He successfully confronted the Indians, but, like the other expeditions, he did not stay.[48]

The result of these expeditions was not only to disrupt the British and their allies but also to put them on notice that they were in danger of attack at any time and any place. This, in effect, fulfilled the overall Spanish strategy of forcing the British to spread thin their forces and thus be defeated.

Having made his aggressive point, Gálvez next prepared to attack Great Britain's island base at Roatán. The defense of Lakes Nicaragua and Managua, along with the sweep of the northern coast, had successfully checked the British offensive strategy in Central America. However, neither Gálvez nor the British intended to quit. Gálvez organized for a final push from Guatemala south to Caribe, still in British hands, and on to the island of Roatán. He hoped to extricate all British from the area.

His strategy called for a great number of men and supplies, for, once again, the plan called for overland travel with supplies enough to maintain the men over a prolonged period of time. In addition, he intended to send larger forces sweeping through northern Honduras than he had before and, at the same time, conduct a major assault on Roatán.

With the assistance of Havana,[49] no doubt prodded by Matías's family connections,[50] supplies and equipment began arriving from all over Spanish America. Juan Manuel Cagigal, now the acting captain general in Havana, wrote a pointed letter to the viceroy in New Spain to start supplying not only Guatemala, but Havana and Cartagena as well.[51]

Curiously, Cagigal began to share the same fear of attack that his predecessor felt. He received word from Baltimore through Miguel Antonio Eduardo that the enemy was preparing an expedition in New York to attack Havana or one of the islands.[52] Cagigal, like Navarro, did not want to leave himself defenseless, but, unlike Navarro, would not oppose official policy. New Spain was his solution. The viceroy there owed supplies and could send them directly to Cartagena, Guatemala, and Havana. The royal message to Cagigal was clear. The king did not believe that Havana or the islands would be attacked, so he expected Cagigal to disperse his "excessive" supplies, soldiers, and ships.[53] Matías de Gálvez's success bred official support.

New Granada and Peru continued to send arms and money. Gálvez began to receive small contingents of soldiers from many parts of the Spanish-held Americas. Not satisfied with waiting for aid, he paid local carpenters to build the small ships he needed. Everyone and everything congregated under his command. In some cases, new arrivals joined the expedition while on the march to its first destination in Trujillo. Some continued to arrive after the expedition was in Trujillo.[54]

Gálvez's plan was simple. Move west to Spanish-held Omoa and on to Trujillo, and split his forces in a repeat of the earlier sweep of Honduras. Vicente de Arizabalaga was put in charge of a force of around fifteen hundred men, more than twice the size of his earlier expedition, to march inland again, revisiting the British allies and any surviving British settlements.[55]

Arizabalaga had orders to divide his force, placing half under the command of his second, Captain Nicolás de Urritia. The two columns of approximately seven hundred and fifty men each would repeat the previous year's strategy and converge with full force on the British held establishments of Caribe, the neighboring Quipriva, and any other nearby settlements.[56]

To avoid any misunderstanding at Caribe, Gálvez had the two columns rendezvous at a place called El Embarcadero at the confluence of the Tinto and Paulaya rivers, then move on the British at the Rio Tinto's mouth. With the help of Spanish ships that would blockade the port, the defenders would have no choice but to admit defeat.[57]

Gálvez made sure that the soldiers had more than enough equipment and supplies. He ordered provisions to last for four months. This campaign would not be aborted because supplies ran out. In addition, a greater familiarity of the terrain, the experience gained from the earlier campaign, and Gálvez's determination all conspired to make this new campaign successful.

On 21 December 1781 Gálvez and the nucleus of his force departed from Santiago de Guatemala, the new capital of the "Kingdom" of Guatemala, on a rough overland journey of more than five hundred forty miles.[58] He hoped to gather his forces at San Jorge de Olavebito, some seventy-eight miles (thirty leagues) from the port of Trujillo. From San Jorge, where he arrived on 12 February 1782, he gave Arizabalaga his final marching orders, for the troops, supplies, and naval support all came together as planned. As always seemed to be the case, Gálvez was blessed with good and loyal officers. This trait was reciprocal, for we have seen how Gálvez did not hesitate to praise his men.[59]

Gálvez kept a force of eighteen hundred soldiers, including two hundred "infantry veterans," which he used to secure the north coast "with the idea of covering against the enemy for all purposes while creating a quick notice" to his own naval forces that had gathered at San Fernando de Omoa. The coastal defensive network was the responsibility of Juan de Orea, a veteran and lieutenant of the grenadiers. Orea set out with six hundred men, which he positioned at "proportionate distances" between San Jorge and Trujillo.[60]

While Orea moved on the coast, Gálvez received a dispatch that his troops had pushed down the San Juan River from Lake Nicaragua. They successfully made it to the river's mouth and awaited orders to sail north to join Gálvez. Gálvez decided that they should remain at their important and strategic location.

By 2 March 1782, the coast had been secured to Trujillo, where Gálvez began transferring his troops. He arrived in Trujillo on March 8 and immediately began organizing for an amphibious attack on the island of Roatán, forty-four miles off the coast. A successful attack on that island was crucial to his strategy of ending all British influence in the Gulf of Honduras. Roatán, with its settlement of New Port Royal, was the ultimate and most important goal of Gálvez's current multi-pronged action. The land operations served to divert the enemy, while the thrust took an important British commercial port and the influence that spread from there.[61]

In Trujillo, a general camp of at least twelve hundred men was formed into four divisions. Colonel José Estachería acted as second-in-command. Estachería and his division commanders had a huge logistics task. Within five days, six hundred soldiers, with enough supplies for twenty days, had to be loaded on board ships that left for Roatán on March 12. The armada, which included Matías de Gálvez, perhaps indicating the importance that he placed on the expedition, included the frigates

Santa Matilde, Santa Cecilia, la Antiope, the corvette *Europe,* and an undetermined number of corsairs, six sloops, six schooners, four launches, and eight "small vessels." The armada sailed within sight of Roatán by six in the morning of the next day.[62]

The fleet anchored beyond cannon range of the defenders, even though some futile shots were fired. Gálvez sent Enrique Reinaldo Macdonell, who was second-in-command of the *Santa Matilde* and who spoke English, to go ashore and request surrender. Macdonell left at eight in the morning and returned three hours later with a British request for a waiting period of six hours, which was granted. The Spanish soldiers and sailors noted that the British appeared to be preparing for a defense as they waited for the agreed-upon-time. The British even sunk a mail boat at the entrance of the harbor, to help prevent entry. So it was no surprise when Macdonell, returning for a second time, after the waiting period, brought the message that the British intended "to defend themselves to the end."[63]

Gálvez immediately signaled the attack, but was foiled. Because of high winds, his "two war frigates . . . could not dock." Stuck in strong winds and rough seas, with a good number of his six hundred men none too pleased, Gálvez consulted with his officers aboard the *Santa Matilde,* which had brought supplies from Havana the previous month.[64] The eleven officers unanimously resolved to take direct action and fulfill their mandate to "destroy and dispossess" the British on Roatán. On March 16, the officers, including Gálvez, signed an order in which a new strategy of attack was laid out.[65]

With agreement and resolve, the attack commenced. The two war frigates maneuvered to supply artillery cover for the landing operation. Their object was to silence the enemy guns situated in Fort George and on both points, called "Dalling" and "Despards," of the port's inlet. The maneuvering began at 10:15 A.M., with both sides exchanging artillery fire. By 1:00 P.M., the frigates had "razed the area with such violence and direction," that the British guns were silenced. Gálvez quickly ordered the landing of the troops in launches. Companies of grenadiers and infantry, led by Lieutenant Colonels Joseph Casasola and Pablo de Pedro, and Major General Gabriel Herbias, no doubt anxious to be on land, immediately lowered the British flags at Fort George and over the inlet's two points. Spanish flags were raised in their place.

The two ships maneuvered in closer, within "half a cannon shot" to the main fortress, and began raking the area. Meanwhile, the British had moved some artillery pieces to higher ground and began firing. The renewed exchange continued until sunset when the British petitioned for a cease-fire. Gálvez accepted their complete capitulation the next morning, on 17 March 1782.[66]

The rest of that day was spent gathering spoils, which mostly consisted of weapons. At daybreak of the following day, Gálvez's soldiers were sent to round up all of the slaves who had fled into the mountains. At the same time all the dwellings, buildings, corn and sugar cane fields, as well as the banana plantations, were put to the torch.[67] In addition, a multitude of small boats found in the harbor were burnt and sunk, due to the "illicit trade."

Gálvez and his soldiers left Roatán on March 23 with some three hundred slave prisoners, ten British officers, seventy-one soldiers and one hundred thirty-five British civilians. Others had been sent to Havana. The victorious armada sailed back to Trujillo the next day.[68]

Gálvez did not waste time celebrating, although he did send word of his success to Spain and Havana. He, no doubt, was happy to report that the loss to his own contingent was minimal—some damage to the hulls of two of the frigates, including his own, and the deaths of two men on his ship.[69]

Gálvez needed to return to the mainland. Spanish land forces were closing in on Caribe and Quipriva. Gálvez promised sea support, thus eliminating another reason for the lack of complete success of the earlier attempt to take Caribe. He immediately began resupplying his ships with provisions for another twenty days. In addition, he replaced the veterans of the Roatán success with fresh soldiers, who had been left behind in Trujillo or along the coast.[70]

The convoy of the two frigates, *Santa Matilde* and *Santa Cecilia,* along with twenty-two minor ships, set sail for the Río Tinto during the afternoon of March 27. Arizabalaga and Urritia had converged after undergoing some hardship due to the terrain. They met resistance at El Embarcado, but after a couple of firefights they put the enemy of Zambo Indians and Englishmen to flight. They pursued the enemy, noting their casualties left behind, when they came upon more resistance at the confluence of the Agalta and Paun rivers. There, they encountered some five hundred British, Blacks, and Zambo Indians. Apparently, the rapid fire by the Spanish forces ended any desire for a prolonged confrontation. The enemy suffered a quick thirty deaths, with fifty wounded, before they fled the field of battle. The Spanish suffered four dead and two wounded. Arizabalaga decided to set up quarters and wait for further orders from Gálvez. In the meantime, he would send squadrons into the mountains to hunt down the enemy who had fled. [71]

Arizabalaga wrote Gálvez of his plan the day after Gálvez had set sail for the Río Tinto.[72] Gálvez was off the shore of Quipriva four days later. The sight of his ships provoked some firing from "five or six cannons" that shot "without method or direction," after which the British abandoned their fort after spiking all eight of their cannons so that the Spanish could not use them. A contingent then moved on to the British settlement of around two hundred houses called Mister Crik.[73] They found the place vacated, as Quipriva had been.

A subsequent reconnaissance of Caribe demonstrated that the British intended to leave that port empty as well. Major General Gabriel Herbias and some men sneaked up close enough to observe the inhabitants boarding small boats. The Spanish army, which arrived shortly thereafter, occupied Caribe "without opposition." Again, the cannons were spiked. The settlement consisted of two hundred and fifty houses, some one hundred built of good wood construction. According to the Spanish account, the house of the English superintendent, William Laure, "who had taken shameful flight with his slaves," was especially nice.[74]

By April 13, Gálvez ordered most of his ships, many of which already had returned to Trujillo, to return to Havana, while retaining a sloop and two smaller two-masted ships. He had succeeded in checking the British, reversing two early defeats at Omoa and Lake Nicaragua, sweeping the British from the mountains and along the Mosquito Coast, and winning a big victory at Roatán.[75]

Nevertheless, in part due to a change in Spanish and French strategy, coupled with an unexpected defeat of the French Admiral de Grasse, Gálvez had to relinquish some of the captured territory. A British force under the Irishman, Colonel Edward Marcus Despard, recaptured Quipriva and Caribe. The small Spanish contingent at Quipriva was surprised. All except one were taken prisoner. The one soldier, a Manuel Rivas, escaped to warn the soldiers at Caribe, but the 140 soldiers there were no match for the British force, especially when the British intercepted a contingent of Spanish reinforcements from Trujillo. Despard defeated the Spanish at Caribe on 22 August 1782. The prisoners were sent back to Omoa under an agreement that they would not fight against Great Britain until the end of the war.[76]

Matías de Gálvez, although not happy with the setback, reported to Cagigal, who had fallen into disfavor and was about to be removed. Gálvez wanted more troops to retake Caribe.[77] Cagigal forwarded Matías's request with an impartial summary of the situation.[78] He also requested naval commander Solano to give him an idea of what troops and boats could be made available.[79]

Luis de Unzaga, acting in Cagigal's place in Havana, sent what supplies he could, including a frigate and two or three smaller, armed boats. He also spared 341 men to help, but his aid was too little and too late.[80]

Solano had orders to unite his fleet with the French. He openly feared a British attack on Havana or Puerto Rico and, like Navarro and Cagigal, did not want to leave these two Spanish possessions exposed. Solano did not want to move as quickly as required, so aid to Guatemala as well as his transfer to Cap Français were both delayed.[81] So far as the war was concerned, Solano's delays were moot actions, for word had been sent from Spain to cease hostilities, as required in the preliminary plan for peace that had been agreed to in Paris.[82]

The end of the war came within the year. Matías de Gálvez concentrated on reorganizing Guatemala's administration. He had stopped and defeated the enemy, preventing their attempt to move up the San Juan River and into Lake Nicaragua. At the very least, he had successfully helped fulfill the Spanish tactic of forcing the British to fight in many different areas.

Spanish officials rewarded Matías de Gálvez with his anticipated appointment to the position of viceroy of New Spain in 1783.[83] Upon arriving in Mexico City, he began plans to build a new government palace and embarked on a program to improve his capital city. In his short reign, he started a newspaper called *la Gaceta de México*, created the School of Drawing, and established the Bank of San Carlos. Unfortunately, Matías's tenure was brief; he died within a year of taking office.[84] The only other commander who could challenge the record of his success was his own son who, from New Orleans, mirrored his father's aggressive tactics.

ELEVEN

The Mississippi River and the Gulf Coast—Casting the Dice

In war activity is the origin of good success.
José de Gálvez to the governor of Havana, 1780

. . . it becomes necessary to cast the dice and try one's luck.
Bernardo de Gálvez to Juan Bautista Bonet, 1780

At the outbreak of the war, Bernardo de Gálvez, in Louisiana, was faced with the threat of a quick British attack like his father, Matías, faced in Guatemala. Great Britain wanted to circle the rebelling North American colonies by executing a pincers movement in the west. They planned to invade from the north out of Detroit, or Michilimackinac, in early 1780, retaking everything lost to George Rogers Clark. The initial goal was Spanish-held St. Louis. At the same time, another force, presumably from both Pensacola and Jamaica, would sweep up the Mississippi River. The two movements, when successful, would effectively split the continent from the rebels as well as the Spanish. Moreover, such an action would limit the growth of the colonies if they succeeded in achieving independence.[1]

Unlike his father, Bernardo de Gálvez had been in office with enough time to collect intelligence, raise and train a militia, as well as plan an offensive that would foil Great Britain's plans. Like his father, he would confront the enemy aggressively.

Gálvez planned a rapid upriver sweep to surprise and defeat the British settlements and forts that populated the lower Mississippi River. Gálvez was familiar with Great Britain's plans and he had instructions to move the British out of the Mississippi River in order to thwart Great Britain's strategy. Securing this area would also give more credence to Spain's claim to the lower Mississippi after the war. Some Spanish officials believed that present-day allies would become postbellum foes.[2] Gálvez knew troop strengths and defenses. His own father-in-law had spied and made an exact plan of Fort Bute at Manchac.[3] Willing's sack of Natchez and Manchac a year and a half earlier no doubt aided Gálvez in his preparation.

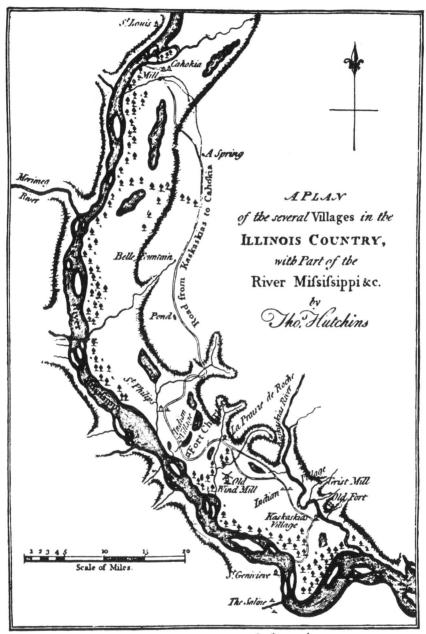

Fig. 13. The Illinois Country in the 1770s. St. Louis is at the very top. Original in Thomas Hutchins, A Topographical Description of Virginia, Pennsylvania, Maryland, and North Carolina, *London, 1778. From McDermott,* Spanish in the Mississippi Valley, *404.*

Fig. 14. The Mississippi Basin after 1777. From Abraham P. Nasatir, Borderlands in Retreat, 28.

Gálvez helped sell the plunder, but protected the British citizens, thus acting humanely and, at the same time, appearing to be neutral.[4] His reports to Havana, noting British reinforcements arriving among the British river settlements,[5] resulted in Navarro ordering the transfer of the Second Battalion of the Regiment of Spain to New Orleans.[6] The additional 631 troops and the supplies, boasted Navarro, would be put to good use against the "establishments of Manchac." With them, Gálvez could now muster a force of over one thousand for his campaign. Navarro theorized that the British were using the imagined threat of an American invasion on their settlements as an excuse to build up forces for an attack on New Orleans. Although he had trouble believing Gálvez's claim that only a third of the existing troop strength in New Orleans was healthy enough to fight, Navarro calculated that the additional troops he sent would give Gálvez a total of 1,200 men. Unfortunately, preparations and adverse weather delayed the convoy and they arrived on the river after Gálvez left.[7]

Bernardo de Gálvez was anxious. He had settled on his strategy before news of the declaration of war reached him. When he announced the news that Spain had declared war to a special meeting of the New Orleans city council, the councilors' enthusiasm matched his own; they were ready.[8]

By at least 17 August 1779 Gálvez sent copies of his plan of operations to both Navarro and Juan Bautista Bonet, the Navy commander for the Department of Havana. He also recommended Jacinto Panis, whose secret mission to Pensacola greatly influenced Gálvez's strategy,[9] to Navarro. Gálvez wrote that the British settlements on the Mississippi River would be the first and most vulnerable objectives. He added that he believed the "English have no news of the plans."[10]

Ironically, Navarro would imply that the plans of attack were his, without crediting Gálvez. His official reports acknowledge the crown's desire to defeat the British on the Mississippi River and to take Mobile and Pensacola. In forwarding what were really Bernardo de Gálvez's plans, Navarro laid out the strategy for an initial strike on the river, after which Mobile and Pensacola became the targets.[11]

In addition, Navarro laid the groundwork for a future rift between him and Gálvez, by arguing strategy with his superiors. His estimates of the required number of troops needed to take Mobile and Pensacola were far less than what Gálvez wanted. Navarro claimed, very early, that Gálvez needed only 3,200 men to "execute the taking of Mobile and Pensacola," a number exceeding his current force, but nowhere near Gálvez's estimate of seven thousand troops. Navarro continued that the defense of Havana needed 3,871 men, not to mention what would be required for fighting elsewhere, such as Campeche, Yucatán, and Guatemala. As well as beginning to counter Gálvez's projections and delaying his plans, the governor of Cuba revealed his great concern for the defense of Havana.[12]

Gálvez, although concerned over the state of his troops, would not let opportunity pass. Informed that some reinforcements were on the way from Cuba, he embarked on a recruiting mission among his own settlements along the river. He needed to supplement his contingent in New Orleans. To this end, he wrote Grand-Pré at Pointe Coupe, DuBreüil at San Gabriel de Manchac, and Collell at Galveztown, informing them of the state of war and telling them to prepare. In addition, Gálvez requested his subordinates to be ready to help provide militia, but he assured those called to service that they would be required only if their service did not cause a hardship on their families.[13] With Gálvez's approval, Collell added thirty-three Americans to his militia company of Spaniards and Frenchmen.[14]

Meanwhile, a major hurricane hit the area. The devastation was great. In New Orleans, many of the transport vessels were sunk or ruined. The town itself had been put into disarray.[15] Most of his soldiers had families and surely were confronted with the many unexpected problems caused by the destructive power of such storms. This was the kind of chaotic situation that required strong and respected leadership.

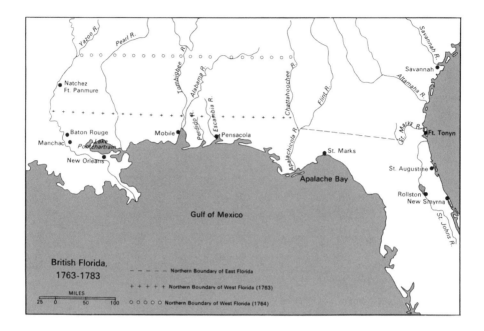

Fig. 15. *New Orleans and environs. From Jack M. Sosin,* The Revolutionary Frontier 1763–1783, *63.*

Armed with reports from men like DuBreüil, who noted that the enemy was inadequately prepared to resist an attack, Gálvez mustered his forces and began the march toward Manchac on August 27. He had with him a truly multiethnic force that included five hundred regular army soldiers, sixty militia, "eighty Mulattos and free Blacks," and nine American volunteers, which totaled 649 men. This army included men from Spain, Ireland, the rebelling colonies, Louisiana, Mexico, Puerto Rico, Cuba, and Santo Domingo (today's Dominican Republic).[16]

Oliver Pollock, destitute from his efforts to raise funds and supplies for American troops, refused Gálvez's offer of a commission in the Spanish army. Pollock preferred to lead the American contingent, taking with them, as Gálvez wrote "the banners of America . . . with us in the field."[17] Gálvez verified that Pollock "attended me in person" until the campaign's successful conclusion.[18] So, with Spanish and American flags unfurled, Gálvez led his troops into battle, attempting a difficult movement across the river and a trek north past marshes toward their first objective, British-held Fort Bute at Manchac.

Commandant Francisco Collell made the initial encounter when he seized some enemy boats on the Amite River some twenty miles from Manchac. He also cut British communications between Lake Marrepas and the Mississippi River, capturing Graham's Fort with its small contingent of twelve soldiers.[19] British Lieutenant Colonel Alexander Dickson, fully aware of the approaching force and the activities on the Amite River, apparently did not realize that a state of war existed and he chose to avoid a major confrontation at Fort Bute. He transferred the bulk of that fort's troops to Baton Rouge on September 3.[20] Governor Chester, in Pensacola, did not send Dickson news of the war until September 9. Dickson's confusion about Spanish hostilities was conveyed directly to Lieutenant DuBreüil, who immediately reported the advantage to Gálvez.[21] The British commander also apparently was not aware of the sickness and fatigue that had reduced his opposition by a third. At dawn on September 7, the Spanish attacked Fort Bute and Spain won its first military victory in the war, without a casualty. The British had one casualty. A British captain, a lieutenant, and eighteen soldiers were taken prisoner. Others fled to Baton Rouge.[22]

Within two weeks, the Spanish force had moved on to, and positioned itself for, a siege of the fort at Baton Rouge, which was protected by a large ditch and 550 defenders. Considering his foe, and the continued depletion of his troops, Gálvez decided against a direct assault. Instead, he faked an attack and ordered his well-placed artillery, under the command of Julián Alvarez, to pound the British fortification.[23]

Colonel Dickson wrote that early in the morning of September 21, the Spanish heavy artillery began firing,

> and after an incessant fire on both sides for more than three hours, I found myself obliged to yield to the great superiority of his artillery, and to surrender the redoubt to his Excellency Don Bernardo de Gálvez, who commanded the troops of his Catholic Majesty.[24]

The British surrendered at three-thirty in the afternoon.

This last victory resulted in the taking of 375 prisoners and eight transport ships, which had brought enemy reinforcements from Pensacola. All the women and children were released. More importantly, the British command met Gálvez's stipulation that Fort Panmure at Natchez also be surrendered. Captain Juan de la Villebeuvre occupied the latter fort on October 5.[25]

The possession of Fort Panmure accomplished all of the campaign's goals. Perhaps one reason for the success of this campaign was the distraction of the British fleet. While Gálvez's forces moved upriver, d'Estaing's fleet sailed to Saint Dominque and intimidated nearby Jamaica, causing the British to keep their shipping at port.[26]

Gálvez spent the next few weeks mopping up against small enemy pockets. A contingent under the American "Captain Mr. Pickle" sailed on the Delta lakes and took at least one British ship. Vicente Rillieux, with seventy Spanish men in a schooner, captured a British ship with four to five hundred men.[27] Rillieux and his men finished patrolling the Amite River, and Grand-Pré successfully led a group of men in taking a British post at Thompson's Creek.[28]

Later that month, the soldiers returned to New Orleans, where the population joyously received them as they paraded through the streets. The festivities ended with a solemn *Te Deum* sung in the Saint Louis Church in New Orleans.[29] The Spanish government, when citing Gálvez for his accomplishments, claimed that the campaign took one thousand English prisoners, eight boats, 430 leagues of land, and closed the Mississippi River to foreign traffic.[30] The citizens of New Orleans enjoyed a proud moment, indeed, but the fighting had just started. The officials, especially Gálvez, knew that Mobile was the next target and that the British were planning an invasion from the north.

One immediate benefit of the early victories was the unexpected interception of British correspondence. More than one letter between British officers and officials among the river settlements and with Pensacola confirmed Spain's understanding of Britain's desire to capture the area. The letters were translated from English and read by Gálvez and his colleagues in New Orleans. Then they were sent to Navarro in Havana, who passed them on to Spain.[31] As the Spanish officials read the letters, they realized more clearly the importance of the Mississippi River campaign. José de Gálvez wrote to Navarro that "the anticipation and action of the Governor of Louisiana" had saved that province. "The King" hopes that such action will be a prelude to other *"mayores,"* major victories.[32]

But Navarro continued to delay, and the king's ministers did not receive Navarro's excuses well. In particular, they found Bonet's slow reactions to Bernardo de Gálvez's request for help to be counterproductive. The outspoken Bonet, who expressed a desire to take advantage of the opportunity to defeat the British along the Gulf Coast,[33] seemed to act in the opposite manner. In a marginal note on one of Navarro's reports to José de Gálvez, Bonet's "apparent opposition to" taking action is mentioned along with the philosophical statement that risks were taken in war and Bonet should learn to act "without hesitation."[34] José de Gálvez must have been a little frustrated with the treatment Bonet and Navarro in Havana were giving his nephew, for his marginal note to the king was a paraphrase of what he had written Navarro earlier: "In war activity is the origin of good success."[35]

Unfortunately, Navarro's hesitation to act as quickly as expected began to cause concern in France. Floridablanca, perhaps not yet aware of all the personal conflicts going on along the Gulf Coast, informed José de Gálvez that he had received various letters from the French government, one of which he sent to Gálvez. The French drew Floridablanca's attention to the inactivity of the military forces in Havana. In the letter forwarded to Gálvez, the French specifically singled out Bonet, whose inactivity, they noted, was contrary to his Royal Orders. Floridablanca was obviously displeased and informed Gálvez that Navarro and company would get a copy of the same letter. He wanted them to see the embarrassment that they were causing their king in Europe. Perhaps such a pointed missive "condemning" their "inaction . . . since the beginning of the war," would prod them into action.[36]

Part of the home government's anxiety had to do with the planning going on among Spain, the United States, and France. Spain's diplomatic observer in the rebelling colonies as well as the French ambassador, the chevalier Anne-César de la Luzerne, received reports via official and unofficial channels regarding merchantmen recently returned from the Caribbean.[37] As everyone at the time knew, the three enemies of Great Britain had felt for some time that Pensacola was important to the overall war effort. Washington mentioned to Luzerne, in a conference at West Point in September 1779, that attacking Mobile and Pensacola would be desirable because the British would have to concentrate their war effort away from the colonies by sending aid to the West Indies. Spain's activity would have the effect of "annoying the commerce of Great Britain and defeating" them.[38] Washington was right, for British units soon began embarking from Manhattan and sailing for British-held East Florida and the West Indies. Gradually, too, the emphasis of the war in the American colonies shifted to the south as London changed strategy. This put a greater burden on Sir Henry Clinton, who commanded the British forces, and a lesser burden on Washington.[39]

Spain wanted American cooperation. On 7 December 1779 Miralles received instructions to petition the American leadership to, at the least, feint a military move south and, at most, invade East Florida. The missive informed him that Bernardo de Gálvez already had defeated the British on the river and, at the earliest opportunity, they would send an expedition against Mobile. "If Miralles is successful," the letter continued, "we hope" that Pensacola would "fall after."[40]

Miralles went to work contacting members of Congress and writing to George Washington in February, exactly when Bernardo de Gálvez began his attack on Mobile. Miralles inquired whether Washington would use his troops in Georgia to divert British attention from Mobile and Pensacola.[41] Washington, already informed of the successes on the Mississippi River, agreed that Spain's Gulf Coast campaign was very important.[42] Washington wrote to Luzerne, who was working in concert with Miralles, that the proposed cooperation was "desirable."[43]

Bernardo de Gálvez and Navarro were advised that the Americans would make the requested diversions. Miralles would concentrate on the time and diversionary strategy.[44] Navarro received at least thirteen letters from Miralles in which the Spanish observer mentioned Congress and Washington's willingness to help. Two of the letters explicitly mentioned American troops moving south into South Carolina and Georgia. Navarro extracted from all the letters and sent them to José de Gálvez.[45]

Although Pensacola remained the ultimate goal, Bernardo de Gálvez felt that he did not have the full cooperation of Navarro. Esteban Miró, Gálvez's personal emissary, could not convince Navarro and Bonet, the latter of whom complained that they could not aid Gálvez, despite the king's early and clear desire that "without delay some form of an expedition composed of sea and land forces should be formed and attack Mobile and Pensacola."[46] They did not want to leave Havana defenseless, and boosted their argument by reminding Gálvez of their mandate to support the operations in Guatemala, where Matías de Gálvez just lost Omoa. Navarro and Bonet were also hampered in extending aid because they had not received expected support from Mexico and the French at Cap Français.[47]

Navarro, possibly feeling the pressure of his superiors' displeasure as well as the pressure of Miró's presence, called a series of meetings with his major officers to discuss strategy. With the exception of Miró, all the attendees, like Bonet, were Navarro's colleagues. Not surprisingly, then, they chose to maintain a cautious course, which meant that they would send some forces to help with Mobile, but not the number requested. Nor does it appear that they were in a hurry to organize the reinforcements. Delaying, in the eyes of others, was a form of inactivity.[48]

Miró kept a detailed diary of his mission to Havana in which he gave a day-by-day account of the litany of excuses for why the fleet could not sail to help Gálvez. The reasons ranged from the weather, to fitting the soldiers with unnecessary capes. When Miró requested that a battalion of the Regiment of Navarra be included in the proposed convoy to Mobile, he was criticized because the commanding officer of the battalion was Colonel José de Ezpeleta, a friend of Bernardo de Gálvez's. Miró thought that Gálvez's desire to have a competent friend at his side was perfectly natural.

Miró quoted Bonet's tirade against the king's orders to quickly take Pensacola and Mobile. Running out of rationales and now confronted by Ezpeleta, Bonet let loose:

What we have with Havana is worth more than fifty Mobiles and Pensacola; it is true that there is an order of the king to carry out the expedition, and I do not know if it would be convenient sometime to disobey the king's orders when it is understood that if His Majesty were here he would do the same.

Miró's reaction to Bonet's resistance is even more telling. Noting that Navarro had agreed and prepared to send reinforcements since the middle of December and now, at the beginning of February, he was still delaying, Miró wrote,

I cannot understand this man, nor why he even promises to help, giving his word to whatever is proposed, and not see anything accomplished.

Miró, like the Spanish officials in faraway Spain, was thoroughly disgusted with both Navarro and Bonet.[49]

Bernardo de Gálvez did not have the forces that he felt necessary to attack Pensacola, but he could go after Mobile, using Navarro's reinforcements. These, with his own contingent, would be enough. Then he could use soldiers from occupied Mobile to help with Pensacola.[50]

So, while his immediate superiors in Havana hesitated and debated, Bernardo de Gálvez began forming his own forces and arranging for their transportation. Perhaps he felt that he could embarrass the officials into supporting him, for he certainly knew that the government in Spain, led by his uncle, sided with him.[51]

Gálvez left New Orleans in the middle of January, with a force of 1,200 men, including regulars and militia. His armada consisted of fourteen ships of various types, none larger than a brigantine. Although they made it to Mobile, bad weather prolonged the journey to thirteen days. In addition, more bad weather interfered with Gálvez's plans. This time a major storm hit just as his makeshift armada appeared off the Bay of Mobile. The weather was "so devastating that the people were only able to save themselves."[52] Tragically, four hundred men were lost in the storm. Gálvez could combat the enemy, but he could do little against nature. Along with the terrible loss of men, his flagship, a brigantine, and another four ships were wrecked on a sandbar.[53]

To most commanders, such devastation would be enough to abort the mission. Gálvez, on the other hand, began reforming his force. He set up camp on the Rio de Perros, three leagues, or a little less than eight miles, distant from Mobile.[54] There, his engineers made scaling ladders from the salvaged remains of the wrecked ships. Fortunately, too, Miró met with some success in Havana, for four ships arrived with reinforcements, apparently including Ezpeleta and Miró.[55] Because of the continuous delays, the preparation process was slow, but when the actual siege began, success came relatively easy.

After spending almost two miserable months at sea and bivouacked in inclement weather, the Spanish attacked the ramparts of Fort Charlotte, which was

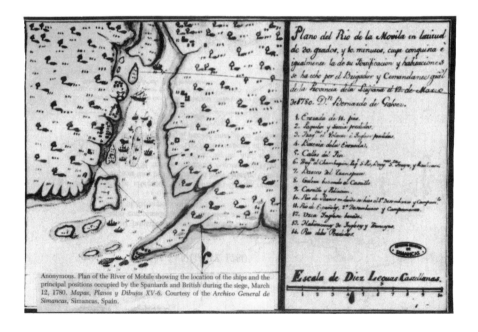

Fig. 16. Anonymous plan of the River of Mobile showing the location of the ships and the principal position occupied by the Spanish and British during the siege, March 12, 1780. Original in Mapas, Planos y Dibujos XV-6, AGS, Valladolid. From Coker and Coker, The Siege of Mobile in 1780 in Maps, *14.*

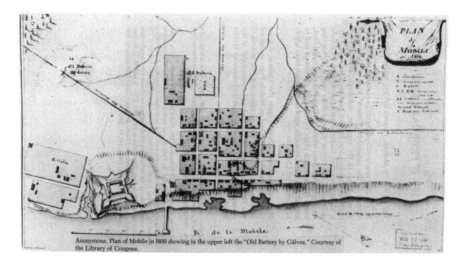

Fig. 17. Anonymous plan of Mobile in 1809 showing in the upper left the "Old Battery
by Gálvez." Original in the Library of Congress, Washington, D.C. From Coker
and Coker, The Siege of Mobile in 1780 in Maps, 44.

defended by at least three hundred men. The attack occurred within the presence of
an enemy contingent of over one thousand strong, from Pensacola under General
John Campbell. The British artillery fired until they ran out of ammunition.[56]
Gálvez, as well as his king, was pleased that Spanish soldiers, "our tired troops, poorly
dressed and saved from shipwreck," garnered a quick victory. The accomplishment
was astounding. Campbell withdrew without fighting, and Fort Charlotte surrendered, with Mobile, on 14 March 1780. The Spanish victors took 307 prisoners and
thirty-five cannons.[57]

Now, only Pensacola remained along the Gulf Coast. Heartened by Campbell's
withdrawal, Gálvez felt that he could get a quick victory. Momentum was on his side
and Pensacola loomed large. "It is impossible to step back," he wrote Bonet, "without
losing most of our reputation." He had the British reeling and he did not want to give
them time to reorganize or build their strength. He was racing with time, for his own
troops, mostly volunteers, had been in the field for eight months under difficult conditions. They would become impatient with a delay and, in addition, if they waited
for summer and got caught in the heat on the sand dunes of Pensacola's beaches, illness would defeat them. Nor did he relish the idea of an unforeseen quick peace without Pensacola, thus losing an opportunity to win West Florida. He wrote to Bonet that
sometimes "it becomes necessary to cast the dice and try one's luck," for "to turn away
. . . from Pensacola is all a retreat." Delay, he felt, meant abandonment.[58]

Bonet and Gabriel de Aristizábal sailed from Havana to deliver more supplies.
Neither one actually landed at Mobile, and therefore limited their exchanges with

Gálvez to letters. They were not as enthused as Gálvez. In fact, Bonet's suggestion that Gálvez use the boats already in his possession to attack Pensacola resulted in Gálvez's comments, given above.[59] Bonet's next letter wished Gálvez well if he wanted to "cast the dice and test luck," but Bonet refused any more immediate help. The protection of Havana remained more important to him. Apparently, upon reading Gálvez's summation of Pensacola's strength, he advised Gálvez not to "risk the glory of all that has been conquered with the incertitude of dice" and suggested that Gálvez take his arguments directly to Havana.[60] Bonet penned two letters to Bernardo's uncle, José Gálvez, explaining why he could not acquiesce to Bernardo's plan for a quick strike on Pensacola.[61]

In a third letter, Bonet complained to José de Gálvez that he could not fulfill a request for more ships at Mobile. Perhaps, he inquired, they could be bought. Then, in a letter sent at the end of August, Bonet cited his "fifty-two years of service and, of these, thirty-two in command" as a basis for his decisions.[62]

Bernardo de Gálvez decided to accept Bonet's suggestion that he go to Havana, for that was his only option at the time. As he pointed out, his convoy did not have nearly the supplies or men that he had requested. Bonet had taken advantage of the situation, for time was limited to form the necessary force to attack Pensacola before the summer heat.

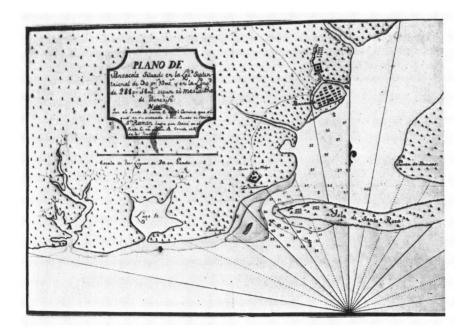

Fig. 18. Map of Penzacola. Original in the Museo Naval, Madrid. From Reparaz, Yo Solo, *75.*

Bonet's advice that Gálvez travel to Havana suggests that he and Navarro felt secure enough to deal with the well-connected, ambitious officer face to face. They were unaware, at the time, that Gálvez's position was about to be enhanced by actions in Spain. As mentioned in previous chapters, Spain used the opportunity of Great Britain's preoccupation with Gibraltar to send a convoy of 146 merchantmen and twelve ships-of-the-line with eleven thousand men under the command of Commodore José Solano (see plate 15). The convoy left Cádiz on 28 April 1780. Once aware of this action, Navarro would be hard pressed to give more excuses for Gálvez's requests.[63] In addition, Juan de Urriza, the intendant of the army in Havana, who seemed to have the confidence of José de Gálvez, received a letter in which he was informed that Francisco de Saavedra de Sangronis had been sent as a special emissary of the king. Urriza was told to "help with all that he asks" while providing him with "all confidence the accounts" of Havana. Urriza answered that he would do as required.[64]

Solano's command demonstrated Spain's determination to live up to its own words about taking risks during times of war. Had Great Britain not been diverted with the defense of Gibraltar, or perhaps the fighting in Central America, or fearing an invasion, Solano's armada could have been intercepted and Spain eliminated as a major player in the war. But Great Britain did not act and Solano successfully transported the troops, thus giving Spain a large superiority of numbers in the West Indies.[65]

José de Gálvez realized that Solano's reinforcements would be important. To make sure, he wrote to Navarro stating that the governor's inability to act after the defeat of Mobile, lost

the decisive moment of defeating the English totally in the Gulf of Mexico making it difficult, perhaps impossible, until the arrival of the Cádiz convoy.[66]

Further recognition of Bernardo de Gálvez's activities and plans soon came through the mails. Pleased with the victory at Mobile, the king promoted him to field marshal and put him in charge of all Spanish military operations on the North American continent.[67]

Obviously, Gálvez was in favor in Spain. Obviously, too, he now commanded greater authority from which to advocate his plans. The fact that his new authority would place any naval forces under his command during a siege grated on Bonet and his navy officers.

Gálvez reached Havana on 2 August 1780 and immediately argued for an expedition to Pensacola in the fall. In addition, he wanted relief for his garrisons in Louisiana and Mobile. A British counterattack was always a possibility.

On the other hand, he had current information, mostly extracted from British deserters, that Pensacola's garrison suffered from sickness, lack of supplies, and discontent. He heard that the fort on top of Barrancas Coloradas (Red Cliffs), which overlooked the bay's entrance, had been almost completely abandoned.[68]

From distant St. Louis, Gálvez received reports stating that the British were planning another attack from the Detroit area. The British planned to take St. Louis[69] and thus, fully expose Virginia to a western attack. Such a strategy also exposed New Orleans from the north.[70]

In fact, Lord George Germain, the British secretary of state for the colonies, ordered General Frederich Haldimand, commander of British forces in Canada, to defeat the American and Spanish establishments on the Mississippi River. Patrick Sinclair, the lieutenant governor at Michilimackinac in northern Michigan, received the task of organizing the expedition. By the middle of February 1780, he reported that an assemblage of Menominee, Sioux, Sac and Fox Indians would be gathered to join a British regiment at the mouth of the Wisconsin River on March 10.

There, they would receive their orders to surprise Pencour (St. Louis) and, if successful, continue downriver as far as Natchez.[71] A total of 750 men, including traders, servants, and Indians left on the expedition. The force grew as they moved south.[72]

Of course, the approaching army lost the element of surprise even before forming. All during their movement southward, Leyba's scouts and American frontiersmen conveyed word of their progress toward St. Louis. An ailing Leyba dutifully reported the pending attack as he struggled to reinforce the defenses of his small village by recruiting soldiers and constructing a stockade with four planned towers. He took up a collection of money from the public and supplemented the sum with his own contribution.[73]

He must have been perplexed, for support was scarce, if any, from New Orleans. Gálvez, who clearly had conveyed that Leyba would not receive much support, was occupied with attacking Pensacola.[74] While preparing his defense, the very ill Leyba was rapidly losing his own physical strength.[75]

Help came from another quarter, for the Americans, including George Rogers

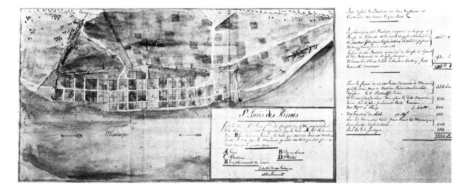

Fig. 19. St. Louis as fortified by Lieutenant Governor Cruzat in 1780. Photocopy in the State Historical Society of Wisconsin. Original in AGI, Seville. From McDermott, Spanish in the Mississippi Valley, 405.

Clark, sent him reports of enemy activity. Leyba received visits from Colonel Montgomery and Captain John Rogers, who proposed a counterattack. Leyba agreed to provide troops, artillery, and munitions. However, before Montgomery and Rogers could provide the necessary boats, Leyba heard that an invading force of three hundred Englishmen and nine hundred Indians was approaching.[76]

Leyba called in troops from St. Genevieve. Four days later, he received "about 150 men, all good shots" who added to the sixty men and two boats in St. Louis. He also brought in five cannon from the abandoned Fort Prince Charles.[77]

On May 23, Leyba's scouts informed him that the enemy was within twenty leagues, approximately fifty-four miles, of St. Louis. Three days later, the attack began.[78]

Leyba placed his cannon in the village's incomplete towers. He took command of the defense from the most complete tower and assigned his assistant, Lieutenant Silvio Francisco de Cartabona, in charge of twenty men, to guard the women and children. Leyba's fortitude is commendable. He was so ill and weak that he could not write his own letters, but gathered the strength to lead the defense of his village.[79]

The attackers, apparently feeling that they had surprised the Spanish settlement, or encouraged by the apparent lack of defenses, recklessly charged. They were surprised to find three hundred prepared defenders, hidden in two long trenches, who supplemented very effective cannon fire. Under Leyba's direction, the attack was defeated within a few hours. The soldiers refused to give ground and the artillery demoralized the attackers, especially the Indians. Haldimand blamed the loss and the lack of surprise on treachery by some Canadian traders.[80]

The failure to take St. Louis resulted in bitter frustration for the British soldiers and their allies. After quitting the attack, they began raiding at random throughout the countryside. The carnage amounted to "unheard of barbarity" wrote Leyba. "It was an affliction and general consternation to see these poor corpses cut into pieces, their entrails thrown out, their limbs, arms and legs scattered all over the field."[81] St. Louis had been defended, but not without cost, for the countryside had been devastated. Nor could the inhabitants of St. Louis rest, for they feared a second attack.

The disorganized British force with its out-of-control allies did not attack the town again. Fifteen days after the successful defense, Leyba agreed to a joint American-Spanish pursuit of the attackers. He provided one hundred soldiers to Colonel Montgomery's two hundred, but the force found only vacant Indian villages. Leyba's last letter to Gálvez, dated 20 June 1780, reported on this joint expedition as well as "*la maladie*," the sickness, with which he was burdened. He decided to put Cartabona in charge. Eight days later he died. He was buried the same day, in front of the altar of the parish church of the town he successfully defended.[82]

News of the victory in the upper Mississippi River, the capture of a 67-ship British convoy headed to the West Indies off the Azores[83] on August 8 and 9, the counteroffensive in Guatemala, and the government's encouragement with the arrival of Solano's armada all resulted in a more positive mood in Havana.[84] With the addition of Solano's reinforcements, Cuba's well-trained militia could defend the island while the regular troops could be used for the attack on Pensacola. In addition, José de Gálvez reported that France had offered to oversee defense of the islands, confirming what the local French officials told Navarro.[85]

Solano brought Royal Orders from José de Gálvez to Governor Navarro, to call a meeting in which the Royal desire for the defeat of Pensacola would be expressed. Navarro responded with a meeting that was held on September 13. Seven men attended: Navarro, Bonet, Solano, Bernardo de Gálvez, and three others. The men offered no opposition to the king's desire. Per earlier orders from Spain, Navarro had been holding meetings about the attack on Pensacola since May.[86] Gálvez would get his force.[87]

Not surprisingly, Navarro still felt that a smaller force would suffice. He remained hesitant to fulfill Gálvez's requests, despite troop reinforcements from Spain and additional supplies that had been solicited from the Continental Congress. In early October, three thousand barrels of wheat arrived from Maryland to help with the logistics.[88] However, neither Navarro nor his advisors seem to have much faith in Gálvez's strategy. In a second meeting six days later, a plurality voted ships and supplies for the expedition, even though the opposition argued against the expedition because of a rumor that a British fleet was close by. Havana needed protection. Gálvez's proponents successfully countered with the sentiment that Spanish strategy should not depend on rumors of British strategy.[89]

Navarro held at least a couple more meetings. Bonet complained about problems getting supplies and repeated that the British fleet, now off the Bahamas, was probably heading for Mobile or Pensacola. The tension between the Gálvez and Navarro factions was obvious. The fact that Navarro and Bonet had been forced into a position with which they did not agree was also clear. Gálvez himself, presented a constant and clear argument. Follow the Royal Orders, stop arguing, and let's "get started as soon as possible."[90]

Finally, on 16 October 1780, an armada of twelve warships and fifty-one transports, carrying 3,800 men with supplies, sailed out of Havana. They had been delayed, so the report reads, because of bad weather and the bad locations of the moon.[91] The October departure did avoid the summer heat, but, once again, put Gálvez's force at risk with inclement weather.

Many of Gálvez's men necessarily spent a great deal of time at sea, usually in small ships. Much of their time on these ships was spent in driving rainstorms and sometimes in hurricanes. It is difficult to imagine the conditions the men endured—wet, cold, and gray, with frequent sickness among members of the crew. Written words cannot convey the smell of drenched wood, the rain-drenched rope and canvas of the wooden ships, or the lot of the poor sailors, their hands raw and bleeding from working the wet rigging on ships tossed in the turbulent seas. To risk and accept such conditions to avoid being caught in the summer heat was a serious responsibility. Nothing in the documents suggests otherwise. Apparently, this was one issue over which Gálvez and Navarro could agree.

The biggest danger was not rain and constant storms, but hurricanes. Gálvez's previous two expeditions had been disrupted by bad weather and, ironically, his greatest endeavor, delayed for good weather, would suffer even worse. Despite the capable leadership of Commander José Solano, who issued worst-case scenario instructions in preparation for the feared hurricanes, a four-day hurricane hit and completely devastated the fleet on October 18. Ships were blown all over the Gulf of Mexico and survivors were washed ashore from Mobile to the Yucatán Peninsula. Local Indians annihilated one shipwrecked crew. The total dead could only be estimated, as reports came in. The British press boastfully overstated that two thousand had died.

This time the expedition could not be salvaged. Gálvez's ship survived and stayed at sea for a month during which time it captured two British frigates, the *Georgia* and the *Nancy,* which were on their way to New York.[92] The main part of the surviving armada struggled into Havana on 31 October 1780. This remnant included at least eleven ships, three of which were badly damaged.

General John Campbell, charged with defending Pensacola, could not have been more pleased upon hearing the fate of the Spanish fleet. Seeing an opportunity, he quickly organized and sent a force of 410 soldiers and 300 Indians, under Colonel Johan Ludvig Wilhelm von Haxleden, to surprise Mobile. This force included German soldiers from the Waldeck regiment and volunteer militia made up of royalists from Maryland and Pennsylvania. All of these men had been transferred to East Florida from New York. The Waldeck regiment, for example, had served at Fort Washington as well as in the defense of Staten Island against the Continental army. The regiment was shipped to Pensacola in October 1778, in anticipation of Spain's entry into the war.

The attack came on the evening of 7 January 1781, eight miles from Mobile, at La Aldea or "the Village which was on the east side of the bay."[93]

Colonel José de Ezpeleta had been left in charge of Mobile. He asked for reinforcements, but these were diverted to the Mississippi after weather prevented them from sailing up Mobile Bay. Ezpeleta had 190 men at the Village. These came from the regiments of the New Orleans Colonial Militia, including free Blacks. He had more troops in Mobile, but could not use them because they were needed to guard boats on the river that were loaded with provisions and supplies. He also lacked launches to transport the men.[94]

On a foggy night, the English force sneaked into the Spanish defense and the initial fighting began in the trenches with bayonets and knives. The outnumbered, but valiant, Spanish defenders repelled the attack. Ezpeleta recounted, "Our men, who had resolved to sell their lives dearly, opened a general volley against the enemy."[95] In the face of this desperate defense, the British were forced to retreat under the deadly fire of Ezpeleta's cannon shot from four, four-pound cannons.[96]

General Campbell's gambit failed, and among the casualties was Colonel Haxleden "who led the action and was the best officer in Pensacola." In another twist,

Haxleden's command was taken over by Captain Philip Barton Key of the Maryland Regiment, who ordered the retreat back to Pensacola. Key was an uncle of Francis Scott Key who later authored the *Star Spangled Banner*. Historical ironies aside, Mobile held, but remained threatened.

Ezpeleta proudly reported to Gálvez:

> With the greatest satisfaction, I can report to you that every one of the attacks thrown against us by the enemy has been repulsed, and with these small victories our men are gradually gaining a certain feeling of superiority over the enemy, which could be useful from now on.[97]

Even after Gálvez returned to Havana, reports continued to come in about the remnants of his expedition. Navarro and company, now aware that the king had sent a personal emissary to speed up Spanish activity, nevertheless felt vindicated enough to reassert their resistance to Bernardo de Gálvez. Gálvez wanted to organize another expedition, but Navarro had other ideas; this became evident in another series of meetings that he called. Besides, the king's emissary, Francisco de Saavedra, was overdue.[98] Saavedra's ship also had been swept off course and delayed by storms. A British warship captured his ship, at which time Saavedra threw all his papers overboard. He was taken prisoner to Jamaica where he remained from 15 November 1780 until his release on 2 January 1781. He did manage to secretly send a letter to Spain that informed his government of his plight.[99] The British never realized the importance of their Spanish prisoner.[100] So the king's emissary and military strategist was allowed to leave Jamaica and travel via Trinidad to Havana, where he arrived on January 22. Along with his royal authority to plan an invasion of Jamaica, he now had personal knowledge of the target.

The first line of Saavedra's instructions read, "the conquest of Jamaica is the most important and glorious goal that can be accomplished by His Majesty's arms."[101] But that action would not be attempted until after Pensacola had been defeated and money raised to assist with Guatemala.

Saavedra also had a letter from José de Gálvez that had been sent to Havana in anticipation of his release from Jamaica. Gálvez informed him that "his friend and my nephew" Bernardo de Gálvez had received a promotion to help expedite matters. In addition, a major French fleet had left Brest and, with these ships and reinforcements, the allies had a "considerable advantage over the English" to strike successfully at Jamaica.[102] The threat to Jamaica was a major concern to Great Britain, for here was the center of its West Indies trade, an industry far more lucrative than the businesses that had existed in the northern colonies.[103]

Spain, with the cooperation of France, was tightening a Caribbean noose around the English neck. A major knot presumed tied, in the new orders of Carlos III, was that Pensacola had been defeated. The leadership in Spain did not know of the tragic events that prevented the siege of Pensacola.

TWELVE

A Costly Blow to British Prestige, 1780–1781

⋰⋰⋱⋱

. . . with the promptness that His (Royal) orders prescribe and the situation demands.

Francisco Saavedra to J. Gálvez, Havana, 1781

*S*urviving, much less succeeding in war's turbulence, must have seemed like an impossible task to Bernardo de Gálvez. He had to work with colleagues who were not cooperating and weather that was even less dependable. Yet, within this hostile environment, Bernardo de Gálvez also had to concern himself with maintaining the Spanish possessions for which he was directly responsible—Louisiana, now with the addition of Mobile.

So, while organizing and campaigning for Pensacola, both during and after the disastrous first attempt, Gálvez constantly received reports from the commanders who were left in charge of posts in Louisiana. Letters came in from Manchac, Mobile, Fort Arkansas, New Orleans, and St. Louis, which included news of Leyba's death.[1] Pedro Piernas, appointed interim governor in New Orleans, had detailed, multi-page "instructions" on what his priorities should be.[2] To help, the leadership in Havana agreed to fulfill Gálvez's request, in December of 1780, for fifteen hundred men to defend Louisiana and Mobile. They were a welcome addition to the battle-weary province.[3]

Gálvez received reports of every matter—from supplies, Indian relations, the care and exchange of prisoners, an incident about detaining ships that had entered New Orleans and Pensacola under flags of truce, to reports of enemy fortifications and movements. Problems continued throughout the war. As late as the end of 1782, a rebellion in Natchez had to be suppressed.[4]

Gálvez seemed especially interested in the British use of Indian allies. Perhaps trying to negate an enemy advantage, Gálvez asked General John Campbell of Pensacola "not to employ Indians in our national quarrels," but was refused.[5] The neutralization of those tribes became important to Gálvez because they were major sources of information of British strength and troop movements.[6]

Gálvez acknowledged the importance of St. Louis in his instructions to Piernas and a letter to Silvio Francisco de Cartabona, the interim commander at St. Louis. Gálvez thanked Cartabona and his men for their valor and effort in the defense of St. Louis. He then nearly apologized for not sending help earlier. Distance and his pre-occupation with Pensacola, he wrote, "fatally retarded" the fulfillment of earlier requests. He added, "with God's help," he would be able to send the aid that the people of St. Louis and the area deserved. That help would be arriving with Francisco Cruzat, who had been appointed to fulfill Leyba's position on 25 July 1780. This would be Cruzat's second term in St. Louis.[7] Gálvez noted the post's need of aid and wanted Piernas to send as many supplies as the budget permitted, as quickly as possible.[8] Piernas complied with this instruction, for Francisco Cruzat, who took over from Commander Cartabona on September 24, acknowledged the receipt of supplies in January 1781. They were appreciated, he wrote, to "help maintain" the Indian alliances.[9]

The leadership in St. Louis, in cooperation with their French, American, and Indian counterparts across the river, plotted an incredible expedition.[10] How surprised and pleased Gálvez must have been when he heard about the activities of his people in St. Louis. Cruzat decided to send an expedition north into the Illinois country to counter British plans and activities. He already had Spanish contingents stationed at Sac Village above the mouth of the Moines River near modern Montrose, Iowa, and on the Illinois River near Peoria, under Jean Baptiste Malliet. Other individuals had been sent to various locations in what was considered disputed territory. Cruzat wanted to gather information on the British, while wooing the Sac, Fox, Oto, and Potowatami tribes.[11]

Aware of aggressive British attempts to ally Indians and, possibly, to attempt another offensive against St. Louis, Cruzat moved to take the momentum himself. He learned from Indian allies that St. Joseph, in the present-day state of Michigan, had become a gathering point as well as a location to stockpile enemy supplies and munitions. A surprise attack in the dead of winter on this northern post would fulfill his mission. In addition, such an act would satisfy his Indian allies and placate his field officers.[12]

The expedition was placed under the command of Captain Eugenio Pourré. Cruzat's report of the event, almost too casually, begins that on 2 January 1781 the contingent "left this town *(pueblo)* of Saint Louis of Illinois with the destination of St. Joseph." The report then describes the journey north into Michigan that Pourré, ninety-one militia, and sixty Indians from the Oto, Sotú, and "Potuatami" tribes with their chiefs, Heturnó and Naguiguen, accomplished, in spite of terrible hardships.

They started out in canoes, traveling up the Mississippi and Illinois rivers. The cold, snow, and ice prevented further water travel some eighty leagues (over two hundred miles) out, so they continued marching through snow and over ice. Along the way they stashed supplies and equipment, both to lighten their respective burdens and to assure a safe return trip.[13]

As they moved north they added another Spanish contingent, led by Jean Baptiste Malliet. On 12 February 1781, they surprised St. Joseph. Only a few people were there guarding the stockade and they quickly surrendered. The British hardly expected to encounter a Spanish contingent at that time and place. A Spanish flag was run up a pole as Pourré's men occupied the site for twenty-four hours. The next day, they lit fire to the munitions and remaining supplies and left, returning to St. Louis on March 6. News of the expedition was sent through New Orleans and Havana to Spain where it was met with approval.[14] The Spanish government was pleased enough to publish an account of the accomplishment in *la Gaceta de Madrid*, a Madrid newspaper.[15] John Jay then sent a copy of the article, with a translation, to Robert R. Livingston, the colonial secretary for foreign affairs, who, in turn, shared the story with Congress.[16]

Pourré's success has been a forgotten episode in United States history. The English dismissed the sacking of St. Joseph as of no importance. Early twentieth-century United States historian, Clarence W. Alvord, presented a paper to a conference of colleagues, which he subsequently published in 1908. His paper belittled the expedition's participants as "a band of marauders and of little importance." In addition, he incorrectly concluded that the expedition was sent in violation of instructions from New Orleans, and therefore was unofficial. Much of his information was based on Illinois historian Edward G. Nason. The only Spanish account used in Alvord's article was an account of the expedition published in *la Gaceta de Madrid,* which he trivialized as a "glorified account published to help Spain make territorial claims during the peace negotiations." Subsequent historians, and the documentation, refute Alvord's view, which was uncannily similar to the contemporary British position.[17]

Pourré's expedition was a local action, under the auspices of Cruzat. As a battle, the action is hardly worth mentioning. As an expedition, it was, as American historian Bruce Lancaster wrote, "a march that was in many ways comparable to [George Roger] Clark's move against Vincennes."[18] A Spanish contingent had marched into southern Michigan to make a point against their European enemy and its Indian allies. They succeeded, perhaps beyond their imagination.

As a strategy, the burning of St. Joseph ended all future British threats on St. Louis and the upper Mississippi River. Great Britain abandoned its plans to hem in the American colonies on the west. They now had been defeated in the north as well as the south, in the Mississippi River basin.[19]

Only the Gulf Coast and the Caribbean remained. Spain planned to concentrate on the Caribbean. Strategy and logistics became the priority in Havana and focused on Bernardo de Gálvez.

While Pourré's men trudged through the ice and snow in the north, Saavedra had arrived in Havana and immediately began to visit the individual members of the military and political leadership. On 23 January 1781, his first day in Havana, he visited Navarro, whom he described as "well intentioned, although somewhat weakened by his great age."[20] In fact, Saavedra's appearance, with royal authority and instructions, which he opened in front of Governor Navarro, seemed to discomfort the elderly man, who began to speak loudly, with energetic gestures, while turning red. The governor wanted to call a war meeting immediately, but Saavedra asked him to wait so he could speak to each of the principals personally. In addition, he could observe the state of affairs without interfering.[21]

As Saavedra reported in a letter to José de Gálvez, he was fairly direct with Bonet, who was commanding the navy and who remained especially opposed to attacking Pensacola. While trying not to offend the officer, Saavedra clearly laid out the concept that officials in Europe, meaning Spain and France, agreed on the importance of Pensacola. Saavedra told him that the leadership of both countries, including the king of Spain, knew that Bonet had not carried out the king's orders "with the promptness that his orders prescribe and the situation demands." However, Saavedra pressed, Bonet now had the opportunity to rectify "the unfavorable opinions of him." Bonet, according to Saavedra, wanted to seize the opportunity with "enthusiasm."[22]

Saavedra found the state of affairs in Cuba appalling. The army and navy were completely run-down, showing the negative affects of bad housing, disease, a lack of supplies and, not surprisingly, desertion. In addition, Saavedra learned that the treasury was three million *pesos* in debt. Although everyone involved had agreed that another attempt should be made to take Pensacola, they could not come to a consensus on strategy, finances, and who would command the expedition. Saavedra quickly realized that there was a problem.

> There was disagreement between the general of the land forces and the naval commandant, and among the general officers of each service, as could not fail to happen where each chief . . . argues in favor of the enterprise to which his personal glory is linked.[23]

On the first day of February, the first of at least six general meetings called *juntas de guerra* was held to discuss strategy. Saavedra presented papers of his authority, summed up his view of the state of the military, and presented his strategy, after clearly stating that he had "come in person to explain His Sovereign's will," which was to put into action the royal orders from the previous year.[24] Because the "season" was late before the onset of the summer hurricane season, he proposed that an attack on Jamaica should wait until the next year. On the other hand, the preparation for Pensacola should move ahead at an accelerated rate. Saavedra himself would travel to Mexico to assure that the funds would be available. After the expedition's departure for Pensacola, he continued, aid could be sent to Guatemala and a second fleet could be prepared to take extra funds to Spain. All of the men attending the meeting approved the plan.[25]

Saavedra spent part of his time and effort trying to soothe personalities and deal with egos. He noted that some divisive rivalries and jealousies were inflamed by "agitators." He also had to convince the cautious Bonet to move a little faster. He probably spent more time with Gálvez then anyone. At one point, he took a long walk with the general. The two men shared important positions and were roughly the same age. They were in their thirties and came from the same area in southern Spain. Saavedra listened to Gálvez explain that he had resolved to lead the siege of Pensacola with an undermanned force and did not want to ask for more troops. To request troops, reasoned Gálvez, would throw open debate and cause further delay in the enterprise. Gálvez felt that time was more important than men. Saavedra did not entirely agree. He understood Gálvez's reasoning, but felt that more men were needed to assure a Spanish victory. The strategist and general agreed to a plan wherein Gálvez would embark with his current force and Saavedra would bear the burden of securing reinforcements.[26]

Within weeks the expeditionary force was ready to embark. However, once again, the plans changed, for bad weather postponed the date of sailing for almost a week. Saavedra visited Gálvez on board his ship the *San Román* each day of that week. Finally, at an hour past midnight on 28 February 1781 the first ships left port for Pensacola. By mid-morning the whole fleet had unfurled sails.[27]

Before leaving, Gálvez sent orders to Colonel José de Ezpeleta, in Mobile, to begin transporting his troops to help at Pensacola. Ezpeleta and his men recently repulsed the Waldeck regiment and remained on edge for fear of an Indian attack.[28] They, no doubt, appreciated going on the offensive.

The siege of Pensacola, led by Bernardo de Gálvez, became the most known aspect of Spain's participation in the American Revolution. (See plates 16, 17, and 20.) Because of the victory and Gálvez's exploits, books and articles have been published in English about the event. Gálvez's battle journal has been translated and published twice. In addition, a short biography and a limited edition "tribute" to Gálvez have been published.[29] More recently, a highly illustrated and annotated edition of the journal was published in Spain.[30]

The Spanish attack on Pensacola was not a surprise to the English. Even Saavedra thought that attempts to disguise the fleet's preparation in Havana "seemed useless."[31] Besides, this effort marked the third attempt. If nothing else, Gálvez's exchange of correspondence with Campbell over the use of Indian allies was an open admission of his plans.

Not even the actual approach of the attacking force was a surprise, for one of Pensacola's frigates, the *Hound,* while escorting a merchant convoy, sighted Gálvez's approaching force early enough to give ample warning to Pensacola and to notify the people in Jamaica.[32]

This time the weather did not interfere. On 9 March 1781 the fleet arrived off the entrance to Pensacola Bay without incident. Confronted with British batteries on both sides of the mouth of the bay and an uncertain depth and route through the entrance, the expedition stalled as the old Havana rivalries began to surface.

To secure a safer entry into the port, Gálvez planned a landing on Santa Rosa Island and from there negating the guns on Sigüenza Point,[33] thus eliminating the potential of a cross fire at the bay's entrance, while possibly neutralizing any British warships assigned to help defend the port. They would then wait for the reinforcements from Mobile and New Orleans.[34]

Gálvez had 1,315 soldiers with his fleet. He faced a British force, sequestered behind a bay with the fortified entrance. The town of Pensacola sat on the backside of the bay with the fortress, named Fort George, next to it. Some 1,800 regular troops, aided by an unknown number of volunteers, Blacks, Indians, and at least two frigates prepared for the defense.[35]

On the same day of their arrival, the fleet's soldiers started disembarking on Santa Rosa Island at 8:00 P.M. By 3:00 P.M. the next day they had completed off-loading. The enemy provided no resistance, except for some harmless firing by the British frigates. Gálvez himself led the island's occupation and by 5:00 A.M. the next morning, Sigüenza Point had been occupied.[36] They captured seven British soldiers and some spiked cannon. A small battery was quickly set up and this forced the retreat of the two frigates. With the first part of his plan secure, Gálvez left Colonel Francisco Longoria in charge of the point. Gálvez retired to his ship to wait for expected reinforcements.

The next day, on March 11, the fleet's flagship made an attempt to enter the bay, but hit a sand bar and decided not to continue. Because of this ominous sign, the fleet's naval commanders, led by Captain Calvo de Irazábal, quickly decided that the operation was impracticable. A change in the weather, although not yet serious, made Gálvez anxious. Either the fleet would have to enter the bay or, if a storm hit, they would have to quit the siege and put out to sea. Gálvez, of course, wanted to move in, but Calvo refused to enter the bay.[37]

The problem of command had not been resolved. Governor Navarro placed Bonet in charge of the naval forces and Victorio de Navia in command of the army. Saavedra did not have the authority to countermand Navarro, so the force was left with a split command, led by officers who opposed the expedition. Navarro and his officers could not oppose Gálvez as the commander to lead the siege. Importantly, Navarro could not overrule the king's desire that Gálvez lead the siege. He could only limit Galvez's command.

With Gálvez's acquiescence, Saavedra partially resolved the matter by insisting that Gálvez take command of the army after the expedition left port. With the exception of his own ships from New Orleans and Mobile, Gálvez did not have any authority over the naval forces. The fleet command was assigned to José de Calvo Irazábal.

Aside from sending a harsh letter criticizing Navarro's failure to fully recognize and comply with Gálvez's position as field marshal and commander of the expedition to Pensacola,[38] Spain decided to do something about the situation. José de Gálvez, with the king's approval, had the authority to change the command in Havana. Apparently, Saavedra's reports were enough for the minister of the Indies.

In early February 1781, José de Gálvez sent two letters, one to his nephew and the other to Navarro. The similar letters announced the removal of Navarro, Bonet, and Navia from their positions. They were replaced by Field Marshal Juan Manuel Cagigal, as acting governor, José Solano, who was put in charge of the navy, and Bernardo de Gálvez, named to the command of all army operations. These same orders spelled out that the new appointees were to concentrate on taking and holding Pensacola.[39]

A subsequent letter from El Pardo in Spain, dated 17 February 1781, made clear why Navarro and his two colleagues had fallen into disfavor. These elderly men had become close-minded:

> those generals so addicted to their respective systems that they cannot open their minds to a new officer of less an age than themselves.[40]

Unfortunately, the two letters arrived in Havana long after the Pensacola flotilla had embarked. Had Spain acted a little faster, Bernardo de Gálvez could have avoided the potentially disastrous delay he now encountered. Neither he nor Saavedra knew of the change until late May or early June, after Pensacola had been defeated.[41]

Gálvez concentrated on the siege. While trying to convince Calvo to try entering the bay again, Gálvez sent the trusted Miró to Mobile to expedite the transfer of reinforcements. The troops in Mobile and Louisiana were under Gálvez's authority and beyond Navarro's reach. He also began unloading equipment in rough seas. As might be imagined, this last process was tedious and difficult. Five days after the failed attempt to enter the bay, Gálvez received word from his future brother-in-law, naval lieutenant Juan Antonio de Riaño, who had just traveled from Mobile, that nine hundred men would be arriving at any moment at the Perdido River, some eleven or twelve miles from Pensacola.[42] With the island occupied and the arrival of reinforcements, Gálvez secretly ordered his own brigantine, the *Galveztown*, to sneak into the bay one evening to get a sounding. Riaño took a second sounding. Still, the navy refused to move.[43]

Gálvez and his own officers then agreed on a course of action. On March 11, they decided that they would enter the bay, with or without the navy. Riaño was sent to find out what happened to Ezpeleta, who was expected from Mobile. He returned on March 16 with good news of the imminent arrival of troops from New Orleans and Mobile. This news, along with the bad living conditions of the troops on Santa Rosa Island and a fleet exposed on the open sea, was reason enough for their decision to act.[44]

They would take the vessels solely under their command and force the action. On March 18, they began to act. Gálvez sent a dispatch to José Calvo, challenging him to follow. Calvo replied that Gálvez was "a spoiled upstart and traitor to king and country" and if he repeated his disrespect, Calvo would hang him from a yardarm of the *San Ramón*.[45]

Gálvez boarded the *Galveztown*, captained by Pedro Rousseau. The *Galveztown* was a gift from his American colleagues in New Orleans, after they captured it from the British.[46] (See plates 18 and 19.) With two gunboats and Riaño's sloop, the *Valenzuela,* at his side, Gálvez ordered his pennant raised, fired a salute to his naval detractors, unfurled the sails and headed for the bay's mouth. It was in the middle of the afternoon, around 2:00 P.M. As the majority of the squadron watched, the four ships entered the opening under British artillery fire from Fort Barrancas. Obviously, the enemy had found their mark, for at the very least, the men in the fleet could see that the sails had been hit before they were lost in the smoke. Saavedra later commented that when the same guns were firing at Gálvez, at first glance "it seemed strange" that the Barrancas battery had not done more damage, and then observed that the distance was greater than it appeared and because of the battery's elevation, "the firing . . . was very inaccurate."[47]

When the artillery stopped and the smoke lifted, Gálvez's small, brave group had entered the bay. Moreover, they did not suffer one casualty![48]

With Gálvez setting the example, if not causing embarrassment, the rest of the fleet quickly followed suit. By the next day, the fleet sailed into the bay and anchored on the inside of Santa Rosa Island out of range of enemy cannon fire. They began a siege that lasted sixty-one days. Only Calvo's flagship did not enter the bay, primarily because there was no reason to do so. The navy commander was in open discomfort when he ordered his ship to return to Havana.[49]

Calvo did have a legitimate gripe with Gálvez. When the fleet left Havana, the strategy was to reinforce Mobile before proceeding to Pensacola. Gálvez arbitrarily changed the agreed-upon plan by heading to Pensacola instead of Mobile. After the fleet entered the port, Calvo was left with nothing to do but return. Calvo's ship, the *San Ramón,* was too big to enter the port and could not remain at risk outside the bay.[50]

The day after the squadron entered the harbor, Gálvez initiated a series of letters with the British commanders, General John Campbell, field marshal, and Governor Peter Chester. They agreed to terms of the siege, essentially stating that fighting would be limited to the military fortresses at Barrancas and, now, the main target, Fort George, with its attached crescent fort. The adjacent town and its citizens would be kept out of harm's way. Nor would British soldiers be allowed to endanger the town and its inhabitants by seeking shelter there.[51]

Campbell did not intend to capitulate, so the two sides prepared for siege. Artillery fire was exchanged and Spanish engineers began planning redoubts and trenches, the construction of which was difficult, for the enemy and their Indian allies initiated surprise counterattacks. On more than one occasion, the fighting resulted in hand-to-hand combat.

Through it all, Gálvez maintained an active command. He was heartened when a convoy from New Orleans arrived with another fourteen hundred men, mostly of the Navarra Regiment,[52] putting his total at over thirty-six hundred men.

He commanded an experienced army of regulars and militia. Like his previous campaigns, the force contained men of many colors and races, as well as from varied parts of the world.

On March 30, Gálvez personally led a column of eleven hundred men, who crossed a narrow passage to break up an ambush. They then occupied a beach, which was a cannon shot distance from Fort George. Twelve days later, Gálvez participated in the defense of one of many British and Indian counterattacks.

The participants found themselves involved in a furious battle. Gálvez, who was in the middle of the fighting, received two wounds. A bullet barely missed him, furrowing his stomach. Another bullet hit him on the finger on his left hand. This was not the first time he had received battle wounds during his career; he seemed to be a person who did not shy away from danger, but preferred to be with his men and share their risks.[53]

On this occasion, his wounds required medical attention and he was consigned to the field hospital, which was a series of tents set up out of the range of battle. Recently promoted Major General Ezpeleta, who had brought his troops from Mobile, took temporary command.

Gálvez must have been disappointed at being out of commission at such a crucial time, although there is no regret expressed in any existing record. The plan of the siege was his own and Ezpeleta was a trusted officer. Saavedra, who joined the attack soon thereafter, noted that the convalescing Gálvez was content.[54]

How Gálvez must have resented Campbell's refusal to exclude Indians from the fighting! Already, their benefit to the British defenders had become painfully evident. Without them, there would not have been counterattacks and the fighting would not have been as fierce. Pensacola would have been a much easier and less costly victory. The Spanish suffered the loss of a colonel, two junior officers, and more than a few soldiers combating such offensives. In addition, time and uncertainty played on the minds of those laying siege, as well as the besieged. On April 10, two deserters, one from the Louisiana Regiment and the other from the Regiment of the Prince, were executed for insubordination.[55]

As fighting continued, the siege appeared to be stalled. As usual, the weather did not help. Obviously, the act of getting into the bay and landing was influenced by rough seas and the threat of a storm. In addition, contemporary sources constantly refer to rain and the subsequent mud, as well as water-filled trenches and intermittent heat and humidity. The harshness of this environment and other problems, like mosquitoes and the perennially bad military clothing and food, contributed to the discomfort of the soldiers.[56]

A year later, after a storm helped save Jamaica from attack when it ruined a French attempt to send a convoy to the West Indies, a disappointed, but stoic Aranda wrote,

> It is not in man's power to contradict the weather. The sole recourse is to think of how best to repair the misfortune.[57]

Gálvez shared and practiced Aranda's philosophy.

As if nature had a decided to take sides, a major storm hit the area just two days after Gálvez had been wounded. Strong winds gusted through the camp, blowing down most of the tents, including those of the hospital. The shock of this episode, predicted camp surgeons, would result in many of the wounded dying from convulsions. Gálvez appeared to be one of the potential fatalities.[58]

At this moment of bad fortune, positive news and events began to occur. Not the least of the good news was that the forces of Gálvez's father had retaken the Castle of Nicaragua. Gálvez celebrated by firing the traditional artillery salute. Gálvez himself began to recover remarkably fast.[59] In Havana, Urriza had the pleasure of reporting to José de Gálvez about the success of the minister's brother and son; he reported the good news of the victory in Central America as well as Bernardo's successful entry into the Bay of Pensacola.[60]

On April 19, the day after the salute, the Spanish sighted a major fleet heading for the bay. This created real excitement, for the fleet carried sixteen hundred Spanish and eight hundred French reinforcements under Cagigal. Back in Havana, Saavedra and Solano apparently justified the transport because of a rumor that the British planned to send their own reinforcements from Jamaica. Squadron commander Solano and his French counterpart, chevalier de Montiel, put together a fleet that included fifteen ships-of-the-line, four of which sailed under French colors.[61] Saavedra, who had fulfilled his promise to Gálvez by helping arrange the reinforcements, used the opportunity to travel along.[62]

Three days later, the allied forces now vastly outnumbered the British defenders. Combined with a naval contingent manning a fleet of at least fifteen ships-of-the-line, four frigates, and over thirty vessels, Gálvez now had the seven-thousand-man force that he originally requested. The subsequent arrival of two companies of French light infantry and artillery put an exclamation point on the numbers.[63]

As Gálvez recuperated, Ezpeleta concentrated on positioning his artillery and letting it wear on the defenders. As was common in the warfare of that day, artillery barrages were a necessity. Superior artillery was as important as masses of men. At Pensacola, Spain had a well-supplied and well-manned artillery.

The Spanish soldiers were divided into four brigades to help mobilize the artillery. They had the responsibility of reconnaissance, digging trenches, and defending artillery positions against a counterattack. Meanwhile, the navy provided additional firepower as well as protection. By May 1, all British shipping in the bay had been captured or destroyed, some at the hands of their own crews.[64]

For each of the first three days of May, artillery fire was exchanged until nightfall. On the fourth day, the British surprised a company of grenadiers from the Mallorca Regiment and half a company from the Regiment of Hibernia. The Spanish forces retreated and, in the process, eighteen were killed and sixteen were wounded. In addition, some of their junior grade officers were captured. The British also spiked four Spanish cannons. But, by now, the vastly outnumbered and outgunned British were attacking out of desperation. Their Indian allies, sensing defeat, ceased to be a factor.

Gálvez, with his left arm in a sling, marshaled his forces for an attack on the Crescent Fort, which, if accomplished, would end the battle; but on May 7th, a scheduled attack was halted. The Spanish could afford to be cautious. The care paid off, for at 6:00 A.M. on the next day, the exchange of artillery began again. Spanish shot "set fire to the powder magazine, which, in turn, blew up the Crescent Fort with its garrison of 105 men."[65] The huge and devastating explosion created a major breach in the now unmanned fort. Campbell wrote that "in an instant" the blast "reduced the body of the redoubt to a heap of rubbish."[66] The Spanish infantry did not hesitate to move in, and they were quickly followed by the artillery, thus putting the Spanish guns in a much superior position for firing on Fort George.[67]

Brigadier General Girón and Ezpeleta commanded the occupation of the position. Their troops met some resistance in the form of small arms fire, but the quick placement of two howitzers and two campaign cannons checked that problem. An exchange of fire continued from the Spanish-occupied Crescent Fort and Fort George until three o'clock in the afternoon, when the British hoisted a "white flag."

Campbell sent a message requesting a cease-fire for one day "in order to capitulate." Gálvez countered with the offer that they capitulate at 1:00 P.M. on the next day. With both sides in agreement, the final surrender took place on May 10 at 3:00 P.M. Both of the forts were turned over to the Spanish forces. Pensacola was taken.[68] (See plates 20 and 21.)

This was a major victory. The ability and success of Spain to marshal its forces and successfully execute a strategy was disconcerting to the British. Coupled with Spanish success on the Mississippi River and the turn of events in Central America, Spain had become an important player in what became a world war. The Spanish had broken—in fact eliminated—the British hold and influence in the Mississippi Valley and the Gulf Coast. This was a costly blow to British prestige.

With only East Florida, the Bahamas, and Jamaica unquestionably under their control, the British had to rethink their strategy. They could see the possibility of losing everything in the West Indies. Already more troops were being shipped south to the Caribbean from New York. In fact, Great Britain shifted its war effort in the colonies to the south.[69] The allied strategy of nibbling at the British lion had begun to pay off.

But, as always, the price was not small. Excluding the many men and the equipment lost at sea during the hurricanes, Gálvez's forces suffered ninety-five killed and 202 wounded.[70] Great Britain lost 155 men. In addition, Spain took 1,113 prisoners and added 153 British artillery pieces to its own arsenal. Per the articles of capitulation, the townspeople, consisting of another 101 women and 123 children, were placed under Spanish care.[71] These British subjects later praised Gálvez to their king for his humane treatment of them.[72]

While Gálvez and his officers were compiling a final report and arranging for the

Fig. 20. The defeat of Panzacola (Spanish contemporary spelling) on the 9 of May 1781, by Lausan and printed by Nicolás Ponce, 1784(?) in Paris. From Reparaz, Yo Solo, 194–95.

welfare of their men and the British prisoners, including women and children, Solano used the opportunity to enter the port with his ships-of-the-line, two of which carried eighty cannons. This feat, according to Saavedra, had never been done before. Saavedra wrote of Solano's accomplishment, without commenting on Calvo's earlier refusal to do the same, in a letter to José de Gálvez that would accompany the final report.[73]

Gálvez entrusted his final report including his battle journal, articles of capitulation, the casualty list, and a letter to Navarro, to the care of Saavedra, who was about to return to Havana. Copies were forwarded to Spain.[74] News of the victory at Pensacola was very much welcomed in both Spain and the American colonies, for now the new country would not be limited to the eastern seaboard. Great Britain had lost its claim to the western frontier of the new republic. Now, the premature peace that had worried Washington earlier,[75] ceased to be a problem. Spain's victories greatly weakened England's negotiating position and led to England's loss of East Florida.[76]

Upon hearing of the victory at Pensacola, Pollock wrote to Gálvez from New Orleans how happy he was to hear that the latter confirmed his expectations. Gálvez, added Pollock, had "triumphed over the inconstancy and Caprice of your friends." Apparently surmising that Gálvez would not be returning to New Orleans, Pollock continued,

> As you are now upon the Eve of Departure from this Country, I come now to thank you for all your past favours & protection, which I have constantly experienced since our first meeting in the year 1777 as well in my public & private Character, but the Memory of one great instance of your Candour & justice I will carry to my Grave, that having been now four years acquainted with your Excelcy. it was never in the power of any publick or concealed Enemy to make you think ill of me, though malice & Envy were often employed to that End, a gratefull acknowledgement of which, is all Return I can make you, and believes that theres few men possessed with nobler qualities, to fulfill & adorn every office of a Subject, a friend & a protector than your Excelcy.
>
> You have a thousand people who can pretend they love you, with as much appearance of sincerity as I, so that according to Common Justice, I can have but a thousandth part in return of what I give, then will you only give me leave to say how I would desire to stand in your memory; as one who was truly sensible of the honor you did him, as one who was neither assuming, officious, nor teasing; who never willfully misrepresented persons or facts to you.

Pollock ended the letter with four lines of verse in praise of Gálvez and the capture of Pensacola.

> Leave me O'King to Calm the English Rage
> Rule thou thy self, as more advanced in Age
> Forbid it Gods; Gálvez should be lost
> The pride of Spain, a bulwark of his Court.[77]

The first of many royal acknowledgments of Gálvez's victory came in the renaming of Pensacola's bay. King Carlos III ordered that an old Spanish name for the bay be used, but with a recognition for the man who led the Spanish victory. Thus, the bay became Santa María de Gálvez, "in memory of the man who recovered it for the Crown of Spain."[78]

One loose end connected to Pensacola remained to be resolved. General Campbell, in an apparent attempt to divert resources from Pensacola, managed to supply and encourage British sympathizers in Natchez to rebel against the Spanish. Thus, while Gálvez was concentrating on Pensacola, a mob of about two hundred men, led by John Blommart, violated his oath of neutrality and attacked Spanish-held Fort Panmure under Captain de la Villebeuvre. After thirteen days of fighting, the Spanish capitulated.[79]

Blommart had hoped to parlay his initial victory into a movement that would result in the capture of New Orleans.[80] But Esteban Miró, who recently became the acting governor of Louisiana, sent a contingent of eighty men upriver, where they won a couple of skirmishes against the rebels.[81] The Spanish willingness to fight, coupled with the news that Pensacola had been defeated, ended the rebellion. Blommart surrendered on 23 April 1781 and thus avoided having to face Gálvez, who had decided to take a force of seven hundred men to deal with him.[82]

Blommart and his lieutenants were arrested and condemned to death. Bernardo de Gálvez later pardoned them on the occasion of a twenty-four-hour visit to Cap Français by Prince William, the duke of Lancaster and the future king of England.[83]

In keeping with his already-established reputation for treating prisoners well, Gálvez offered to send the captured British soldiers, including Blommart, from Pensacola to Charleston, or New York, or whatever place they wanted to go in Europe. He would grant them this choice if they agreed to be "sent under parole," on the promise that they would not fight against Spain, and by implication, its allies again.[84] Peter Chester was sent to London and two shiploads of men were sent to New York, which naturally set off protests from colonial leaders. Even Rendón was surprised. Only after sharing the articles of capitulation with other correspondence did he feel that the President of the Congress was satisfied.[85]

Now Saavedra, Gálvez, and the other newly promoted Spanish officials in Havana began to concentrate their attention toward completing the rest of their strategy. The first and easiest target would be New Providence in the British-held Bahamas and then, Jamaica. In the meantime, the French needed assistance as they helped the colonists in the north. Much work remained to be done.

THIRTEEN

Yorktown, the Bahamas, and Peace, 1781–1783

(We) could not waste the most decisive opportunity in the whole war.
Diary of Francisco Saavedra, 1781

*O*n 18 October 1781 Charles Lord Cornwallis surrendered his eight-thousand-man force at Yorktown, Virginia, after a nine-day bombardment by a French and American force under the joint command of Jean-Baptiste-Donatien de Vimeur, comte de Rochambeau, and George Washington. The British surrendered relatively quickly, not because of a lack of food and ammunition, but because they were being bombarded by superior artillery and the French fleet had blockaded the port to prevent any hope of aid. So, after scuttling his anchored supply ships, Cornwallis capitulated.[1]

Most students of the American Revolution know that this victory virtually secured the independence of the United States. They also know that the victory was made possible by the assistance of the French army on land, and the navy at sea, under Admiral François-Joseph-Paul de Grasse.

The role of Spain in this major episode of American history is not as obvious. There were no Spanish troops present. Nor did the French fleet include Spanish ships. Yet, Spain played an integral role in the ultimate victory at Yorktown. Without Spain, the opportunity of trapping Cornwallis's troops would have been lost and the war prolonged.

Great Britain's great advantage over the colonies was its navy. So long as the army stayed close to ports and did not venture inland it could count on the assistance of naval guns, supplies and, if necessary, a safe, rapid, and less stressful form of transportation. The allied forces were consigned to overland travel on a road system that is best described as nonexistent.

In addition, while the British irritated the local population by quartering its troops in houses and helping themselves to needed provisions, the allied forces tried not to alienate the population. From his arrival, Rochambeau warned his superiors

Fig. 21. An unflattering image of Admiral François Paul de Grasse at Yorktown. Published in London Magazine, *1782. Original in the New York Public Library, Prints Division. From Tuchman,* The First Salute, *center.*

"this is going to be an expensive war" because "we are paying even for our lodgings and campground." Another French officer added in 1780:

Here it is not as it is in Europe, where when the troops are on the march you can take horses, you can take weapons, you can issue billets for lodging, and with the aid of a gendarme overcome the difficulties the inhabitant might make.[2]

The reason was obvious for this hardship, for a good portion of the population had remained neutral over the separation from Great Britain. The allies did not want to alienate them. This is one reason why, in fact, the Continental army suffered through a winter at Valley Forge rather than impose on the population.

So, the importance of Spain joining France in the war was in its navy, which, when combined with France's, was larger than Great Britain's. Also, Spain's infusion of money, especially from Mexico, helped pay for the French forces in America. The benefit of Spanish aid is especially obvious in the story of Yorktown.

After the Spanish victory at Pensacola, Francisco Saavedra was sent to Cap Français, or Guarico, to work with Grasse in establishing a plan for the two European allies to follow for the next year.[3] (See plate 22.) Gálvez, who now had been promoted to commander of all forces including the French in the Caribbean, knew that the Spanish and French would have to cooperate to successfully attack Jamaica, the jewel of the British American possessions. Jamaica remained the primary goal. Grasse wrote Cagigal from Grenada, in the Caribbean, that he was aware of the cooperative planning begun by the two allies.[4] Meanwhile, Saavedra sailed to Cap Français to formulate strategy. He arrived a week before Grasse, who was bringing in a large armada of twenty-six ships-of-the-line including, noted Saavedra, fourteen that had copper hulls.[5] Saavedra used the time to visit with all the French officials as well as the Spanish troops who were on loan in the French port. Montiel, who was with Saavedra at Pensacola, did the introductions. Admiral Grasse and his fleet arrived on June 16 and, on the next day, Saavedra met with the French officer on board his ship Le Ville de Paris.[6]

After sharing each others' instructions, they determined that fate provided them an opportunity that could not be overlooked, for the chance before them played into their respective countries' general strategy, although the time to strike came much sooner than expected. Admiral Grasse reported that General Lord Cornwallis (see plate 23) occupied Yorktown on the Chesapeake Bay in Virginia, at a time when his country's navy was distracted elsewhere. Cornwallis moved south in compliance with Great Britain's new strategy to concentrate its war effort in the southern colonies without giving up New York. Great Britain did what Spain and France wanted it to do, extend itself. And, a major reason for Great Britain's risky strategy was the growing propensity for its two European enemies to cooperate, the result of which brought the recent string of victories. By the end of July 1781, Saavedra and Grasse had agreed on a campaign plan.[7]

Great Britain was taxed on two other fronts—the first in Guatemala and the second in Europe. Besides Gibraltar, which diverted more British attention than it deserved, Spain and France created a major diversion in England with a planned invasion. The presence of a combined fleet of sixty-six ships-of-the-line that might attack the English coast forced Great Britain to consider its own safety. The direct result of this was England's decision not to send any naval reinforcements to North America, at the very time Cornwallis occupied Yorktown. In other words, Great Britain's preoccupation with its own safety sacrificed naval parity in North America.[8]

Saavedra and Grasse knew this, for Great Britain's comparative naval weakness had already paid off. The formula for success was in place, but it would not last.[9]

Cornwallis's move to Yorktown was the opportunity that surpassed Jamaica. Here was the major part of the British North American army exposed at last. France and Spain, agreed Grasse and Saavedra, "could not waste the most decisive opportunity in the whole war."[10] After agreeing to an overall strategy that placed priority on Yorktown and included, per Grasse's desire, expelling the British from the Barbados, or Windward Islands, where British ships waited in protected ports to attack Spanish or French ships, the two men sent their strategy off for royal approval. However, they could not wait for an answer for the first part of their plan. A decision had to be made, on the premise that they would receive royal permission after the fact. However, the rebelling colonies, France, and Spain needed to act together, and quickly, to succeed—which they did.[11]

Bernardo de Gálvez, through Saavedra, released the French fleet from its West Indies obligation, to sail north and block the port at Yorktown. In addition, the fleet would transfer five thousand French soldiers to help in the siege. Meanwhile, the Spanish navy, under Solano, would protect French-held possessions in the Caribbean.

Saavedra first refused Grasse's suggestion that Spanish ships join the proposed exhibition so that some French ships could be left behind to protect Cap Français. Saavedra reasoned

that because Spain had not yet formally recognized the Anglo-Americans, there could perhaps be some political objection to taking a step that appeared to suppose this recognition.[12]

However, a major problem of financing the action surfaced. Upon learning of this, on the morning of June 22, Saavedra faced the problem of raising at least 500,000 *pesos* and, if possible, more. The French had been unable to come up with the money even among its own citizens. Grasse solicited private loans in a meeting with planters and merchants. He also posted printed notices in the streets requesting money in exchange for bills redeemable at the Treasury of Paris, at a profitable rate of interest. The reaction was negligible.[13] Spanish Puerto Rico and Santo Domingo provided an additional 100,000 *pesos*, but that was not enough.[14] With little time available, Saavedra decided to take action.

This is when he proposed the solution "to gain the same end with greater secu-rity." The French should take all of their ships-of-the-line, along with the money raised so far, and leave the Spanish fleet to protect the French colony, as previously planned. Grasse immediately accepted the idea.[15]

In the meantime, Saavedra would use one of the faster frigates to sail to Havana and, somehow, get the rest of the necessary funds, after which he would send them to the French admiral at a designated rendezvous, the "latitude of Matanzas." The plan was a long shot. Saavedra could not have known how he would get the funds, if at all. In addition, they faced another problem. As Saavedra put it, they had to act, "notwithstanding that now we find ourselves in the season of doldrums and hurri-canes." This was a risk the Spanish knew well. But action was better than nothing at all. Grasse agreed.[16]

This was a key decision, for Grasse then knew that he would be sailing north and he informed Rochambeau and Washington of his plans. Washington, who was in White Plains, New York, knew about Cornwallis's move to Yorktown and that the British under General Clinton were reinforcing New York City. He had not decided whether to move on New York or head south to Virginia, but Grasse's letter to Rochambeau made New York a moot point. He, like Grasse and Saavedra, would not, nor could not, miss this opportunity.[17]

The combined French and American armies marched south. Saavedra and Grasse sailed, each in different directions with separate tasks, but with the same goal—to trap and defeat the British army at Yorktown. After ten days at sea, Saavedra arrived at Havana on July 15. There, he learned that José de Gálvez had already ordered one million *pesos* be paid to the French. Unfortunately, the ships sent to Veracruz to pick up the money, most of which originated from the silver mines in Zacatecas and Chihuahua, had not returned. Saavedra could not wait, "because with-out the money the Conde de Grasse could not do anything and the delay . . . would put his fleet in jeopardy."[18] So he gave an account of what happened next.

> In this crises, the *intendente* resorted to the inhabitants. He declared the emergency in which he found himself, and in little more than six hours, they collected the five hundred thousand *pesos*, packaged it, and embarked it on the frigate, and set sail without having detained it for more than one day.[19]

Saavedra added that the French officials were "astonished" and a little embarrassed at the generosity of Havana's inhabitants in "the service of their king."[20]

Meanwhile, Saavedra received news that Grasse's fleet had progressed north without incident. Given the recent history of such ventures in the area, he could not help but comment:

> In truth, it was not without luck that in this season the fleet has departed well from the old channel, but it lets one know the excessive difficulty in

which the Conde de Grasse found himself when he resolved to make such a dangerous navigation with twenty-eight ships-of-the-line.[21]

At the moment the frigate embarked to take the money to Grasse, a ship with Bernardo de Gálvez entered port. The French frigate was held up to allow Gálvez to pen a letter that both recognized the mission's importance, and gave his official approval. Gálvez also wished Grasse good luck.[22]

Five days later, another French ship arrived at Havana to pick up the original one million *pesos* that had come from Mexico. Gálvez, Saavedra, and other Spanish officials resolved not to quibble over the money already transferred but "to give the whole million, forgetting about the part sent to Chesapeake Bay as a new service from Spain to help in our common cause."[23]

On 3 September 1781 Havana received word from Miralles in Philadelphia that Grasse had successfully arrived in the Chesapeake Bay on August 26 and delivered five thousand French soldiers as well as organized the blockade. Washington and Rochambeau's forces were approaching after a long journey. Cornwallis may have surmised that he would be surrendering.[24] (See plates 24 and 25.)

So, the battle of Yorktown was, in part, a Spanish strategy delineated by Saavedra, approved by Bernardo de Gálvez and, ultimately, by the king of Spain, within the general parameters laid out before Spain entered the war. In addition, the battle was funded by Spain with a line of credit that extended from Mexico through Cuba.

Grasse himself later wrote that the victory at Yorktown on 19 October 1781 happened because of the money supplied by Havana. That money, he wrote, might in truth be regarded as "the bottom dollars" upon which the edifice of American independence was raised.[25]

But the war did not end with Yorktown. Fighting continued on all fronts. Plans were quickly drawn up to invade the fort of Nassau on the island of New Providence in the Bahamas. Spain clearly intended to keep pressing the enemy. As early as March 30, a naval officer, Don Luis Huet, first submitted a "Plan of Attack with violent force in order to destroy, cut down and burn the Island of [New] Providence on the Channel of Bahama, and blow up their fortifications," which he based on various sources of information, including personal descriptions and a map of the island.[26] Huet had access to a couple of detailed, firsthand sources of information about New Providence, one compiled by Josef Casesnobes[27] and the other given in a verbal declaration by Captain Sebastián Aragonés and Joseph Cano Piloto, who were prisoners on the island.[28] As the plan developed, a force of one thousand men and twenty-one ships, the largest of which would be frigates, was designated for the attack. Had not the opportunity of Yorktown intervened, Spain would have launched an earlier attack on the Bahamas.

Bernardo de Gálvez, Saavedra, and their colleagues had some major decisions to make. As always, Jamaica remained as the ultimate goal. However, other objectives had not been fulfilled. In a twenty-eight-page letter to his uncle, Bernardo displayed a firm grasp of his options and possibilities. Bernardo's father, fighting in Central America, continued his offensive, which would not be completed until the victory at Caribe on the Río Tinto in April. Along with the allure of New Providence, East Florida remained a strong temptation.[29]

More money was needed, so Saavedra volunteered to go to Mexico, setting sail on October 24, just five days after the victory at Yorktown. Saavedra spent over two months in Mexico, where he met every official, including Viceroy Martín de Mayorga. He arranged for three shipments, totaling nine and one-half million *pesos,* plus supplies, to be transported to Cuba over a six-month period "because it did not appear prudent to me to stretch their [New Spain's] treasury out of shape" by asking for it all at once. He also arranged for supplies to be sent to Guatemala.[30]

Unsuspected problems arose in the form of rebellions in the South American regions of Venezuela, Colombia, and Peru. Antonio de Flores continuously called for aid and feared British-aided Indian rebellions.[31] These rebellions were mostly by Indians and mestizos, with some Creoles, primarily to oppose new taxes and government monopolies and, in some cases, to try to free themselves of Spanish rule. Many of these people called themselves *comuneros,* a Spanish term historically used to mean persons involved in a municipal rebellion.[32] The fighting proved costly as well as perplexing. While Bernardo de Gálvez tried to plan his war objectives, he had to heed the call for aid from his viceroy in Cartagena de Indies.[33]

The most spectacular of these rebellions was led by the mestizo leader, Tupac Amaru, who was involved in fighting that stood in stark contrast to the almost civilized warfare with the British. In the north-central part of South America, jungle and mountain warfare of the worst kind raged. Fighting extended into the Andes and to elevations of eighteen thousand feet.

It is not surprising that a document from the area, giving an account of the capture of Tupac Amaru, is included among the records of the Caribbean conflict, for both theaters were related. Tupac Amaru had been leading a successful and terrifying rebellion. After a pitched battle in knee-deep snow, involving nine thousand Spanish soldiers and a rebel army of "ten to twelve thousand men and nine cannons," Tupac Amaru and his family were captured.[34] He had become the focus of Spanish officials, and news of his capture and execution virtually ended native resistance during the period. Nevertheless, the influence of that resistance on Spain's wartime effectiveness in late 1781, cannot be stressed enough. Bernardo de Gálvez even considered going to Caracas himself to solve the problem. Wisely, he did not go, but sent troops and supplies instead. As a result, any consideration of attacking St. Augustine in East Florida, or mounting a rapid attack on Jamaica, had to be revised.[35]

At the same time, government leaders in Spain and France negotiated the chain of command for the attack on Jamaica. In Versailles, on 3 November 1781, the conde de Aranda signed an accord that officially put Bernardo de Gálvez in overall charge of the West Indies operation, and in direct command of all ground troops. Solano's squad was sub-delegated to the naval command of Admiral de Grasse. Cap Français was chosen as the staging place for the operation.

Earlier drafts of the accord demonstrate that the two countries were determined to take Jamaica; the Bahamas had been reduced in importance and not mentioned at all.[36] Furthermore, the two governments agreed that "a vigorous attack against Jamaica" take place in January.

Bernardo de Gálvez received the official correspondence from Spain in which the king "figured that" such an attack could occur on schedule. Gálvez would need to act quickly to assure that all the necessary troops and officers of both countries would be ready. At least, he had the encouragement of the two countries' monarchs.[37] The orders put him under pressure to move on Jamaica rapidly, for the Royal Order itself was not drafted in the Escorial in Spain until December 14, and could not have arrived in Havana before New Year's Day.[38]

At least, Gálvez knew that the South American rebellions had been defeated, the result of which rendered any Spanish attack on East Florida out of the question because of the energy expended in South America. New Providence and Jamaica remained as targets. Of these, he came to the obvious conclusion that Jamaica was much more important. He decided that he would personally concentrate on that British stronghold and assign Cagigal, his captain general of Havana, to the lesser plum in the Bahamas.

Gálvez began to shift more emphasis on Jamaica and less on the Bahamas. The plan, already delayed, called for Solano to have his ships and all the assigned troops transferred to Cap Français by the end of February 1782. The French were expected to arrive with their forces at the same time. By January, Solano was having problems. He could not embark from Havana until another expected treasure ship containing 1,000,000 *pesos* arrived from Veracruz. He was also short of crewmembers for three of his larger ships. He asked Gálvez if the French could help with transports, for he needed more men for these smaller ships as well.[39]

Gálvez was being pressed from many quarters. As alluded to by Solano, the planned invasion needed to be financed. Gálvez regretted not being able to send aid to Honduras in a timely fashion, because he opted to transfer a regiment to Cartagena. Now, his father's plans to move on the British along the north coast of Honduras and take the island of Roatán required special attention. He still planned to invade New Providence, but with Solano's approval, he suspended that operation to concentrate on the more pressing actions.[40]

Solano, under orders from Gálvez, needed every ship available to transfer soldiers and supplies, as well as provide transport to Jamaica. On March 5, Solano's flotilla of 5,282 soldiers and seventy-nine ships, including seven ships-of-the-line, finally sailed from Havana for Cap Français. This, combined with the forces that had already accompanied Gálvez, who transferred to the French port on February 1, left Cagigal in Havana with very few resources.[41]

Cagigal proceeded to organize for his assignment. The original plan called for simultaneous attacks on the two British-held bases, but the logistics dictated that Cagigal would go first. Fortunately, Alexander Guillon from South Carolina sailed into Havana seeking supplies. He had with him his own ship, the frigate *South Carolina,* which was "armed," as Bernardo de Gálvez wrote, "better than any boat of its class."[42] Guillon also had eight smaller warships, and twelve transports. The *South Carolina,* still on her maiden voyage, was the largest and most powerful ship under American command. She was part of the navy of South Carolina, hence her name.

Cagigal took the opportunity and quickly negotiated the use of the ships. Cagigal agreed to pay 10 *pesos* and four *reales* for each ton of capacity until eight days after the conquest. Guillon, who became the naval commander of the planned operation, and Francisco Miranda, Cagigal's aide-de-camp, both had firsthand knowledge of the Bahamas. They recommended a surprise attack through a little-used and relatively unknown channel. By March, Gálvez apparently felt that the planning for the attack on New Providence could continue.[43]

In Cap Français, Gálvez continued to plan for Jamaica and, conversely, to think less about the Bahamas. Troops and arms were being amassed for an invasion by as many as twenty thousand troops. Saavedra, in Mexico, organized the transfer of the Regiment of the Crown "mainly composed of Creoles," to Havana where it would replace the troops vacating Havana.[44]

But the plans went even less smoothly, even before Gálvez moved to Cap Français, for on 12 December 1781 the British intercepted and interfered enough with a French convoy transporting ten thousand troops, to leave them dispersed and at sea when, on Christmas evening, a great storm struck.[45] As a result, France reorganized its priorities, putting India and the European campaign ahead of Jamaica, which, after all, was more of a Spanish goal. Actually Spain's February victory on the Mediterranean island of Minorca prompted the Spanish government to lean more toward the European campaign, specifically Gibraltar.

In the West Indies, Grasse, who was unaware of any of the European nuances, had moved south and captured a number of Caribbean islands, the most significant of which was Saint Christopher, on February 12. His fleet, thought everyone, was critical to a successful invasion of Jamaica.

The news of Yorktown had a major impact in England. The British public openly expressed distaste for the continuing war. On February 27, the House of Commons voted to end all offensive military actions against the Americans. When the North ministry could not negotiate with the belligerents separately, the British Prime Minister resigned his government on March 20. The process of peace had begun.[46]

Even with the European distractions, Jamaica still seemed vulnerable, but the plan suffered another major setback when on 12 April 1782 Grasse and British Admiral George Rodney met in battle off the Îles des Saintes, south of Guadeloupe. Grasse had sailed south with his troop convoy to rendezvous at Santo Domingo. Unfortunately, a series of mishaps, including Grasse's decision to assign three of his ships-of-the-line elsewhere, left him with an inferior force before Rodney. The ensu-

Fig. 22. The frigate South Carolina *by John Phippen. The* South Carolina *was the flagship for the Spanish victory in the Bahamas. Original in the Peabody Museum, Salem, Massachusetts. Photograph by Mark Sexton. From James A. Lewis,* The Final Campaign of the American Revolution: Rise and Fall of the Spanish Bahamas, *frontispiece.*

ing battle was fierce, and left both fleets with severe damage. Rodney captured five ships-of-the-line, including Grasse in his flagship.[47] The remnants of the French fleet reached Santo Domingo with the bad news.

While Grasse's defeat did not completely negate plans for the invasion of Jamaica, it pushed any scheduled invasion late into the season of foul weather. Jamaica would have to wait. Gálvez, Solano, and the marquis de Vaudreuil of France proceeded to disperse their force of twenty thousand troops and at least thirty-nine ships-of-the-line.[48]

Bernardo de Gálvez, perhaps as a result of Grasse's capture, sent orders to Cagigal to abort the expedition to the Bahamas. Gálvez wanted all troops available for Jamaica when needed. Cagigal either ignored Gálvez's letter or embarked before receiving it. Instead, Gálvez received a series of detailed reports from Cagigal that, apparently, crossed Gálvez's order in transit. The reports listed soldiers by rank and regiments, and included lists of supplies, munitions, and ships organized for the attack on New Providence. Cagigal, his officers, and Havana's merchants had been thorough, devoting a lot of effort to the expedition's preparation.[49] By the time Gálvez received Cagigal's manifests, the latter was sailing toward the Bahamas.[50]

On 18 April 1782, four days after Gálvez penned his second letter to Cagigal to cancel the expedition, and ten days after Grasse's defeat, Cagigal wrote his superior that he had left Havana to attack the Bahamas. Cagigal's fleet left Havana with barely enough troops to defend the city, much less provide more help for the invasion of Jamaica.[51] Using the *South Carolina* as his flagship, the combined Spanish and American flotilla sailed the six hundred kilometers to Nassau, the capital of the Bahamas, without incident. Cagigal had 2,500 soldiers on board sixty-six ships, none of which were larger than the flagship.[52]

The force sighted Nassau on May 6 and anchored. Meanwhile, Guillon's ships had captured three British vessels to prevent word of the siege being revealed. Cagigal negotiated, through his aide Miranda,[53] and successfully convinced British Vice Admiral John Maxwell to accept terms of surrender without forcing an actual siege.[54] Maxwell drafted twelve articles and handed them to Miranda to take to Cagigal.[55] Cagigal revised the articles,[56] which Maxwell accepted, and the victory was complete.[57] The effort resulted in the best of all victories—one won without casualties.

Naturally, Cagigal was happy over his success. He had fulfilled another Spanish goal and he did it without loss of life or equipment. In another meticulous document, Cagigal reported that he had captured 612 soldiers, twelve ships including a frigate, weapons, and ammunition, listed by amount and caliber. He even listed 31,460 musket balls and 868 muskets. The new Spanish possession included five fortifications, 566 houses, 2,376 "white" and 847 "black" inhabitants.[58]

A conflict with the American, Guillon, slightly marred an otherwise joyous occasion. It appears that Guillon was more interested in getting paid and collecting booty, than in defeating his country's enemy. While Cagigal negotiated a capitulation, Guillon demanded 300,000 *pesos* before he put his ships at any more risk. Cagigal answered that they had an agreement and payment would come through proper channels in the Spanish government. Nonetheless, Cagigal apparently tried to placate the American by scraping together sixty or seventy thousand *pesos* for him.[59] Guillon then ordered his ships to lift anchor and leave on the day Maxwell agreed to surrender, and eight days before he and Cagigal had agreed that he should leave. Before leaving, the Americans did manage to supply themselves fully with provisions. Cagigal ordered his fiscal agent to summarize the expense of the supplies to be held against the debt that he incurred for Guillon's assistance.[60]

Cagigal dispatched Miranda with the articles of capitulation, a map of the town of Nassau, and the report to Bernardo de Gálvez.[61] Gálvez's reaction to this good news was less than happy. Perhaps disappointed over the failure to attack Jamaica, irritated because Cagigal did not obey his orders to cancel the Bahamas expedition, or jealous because, in spite of Gálvez's orders, Cagigal succeeded, Gálvez did not share Miranda's joy. Gálvez's irritation was exacerbated when the French press in Cap Français celebrated Cagigal's victory and slighted the news of Gálvez's father's success in Central America where he had just captured the island of Roatán and defeated the British at Caribe.[62]

Gálvez took revenge by using a complaint against Cagigal and Miranda that had been drawn up the previous year. The two men were criticized for their handling of Governor Campbell in Havana after he had been transferred from Pensacola. With Cagigal's blessing, Miranda toured the British governor around Havana. This apparent transgression combined with Gálvez's current irritation, resulted in an order for their arrest. With his uncle's backing, Gálvez's order was carried out. Subsequent misinformation from both Solano and Gálvez sealed Cagigal's fate. Cagigal eventually was incarcerated in Cádiz but, notably, fought for Miranda's honor. He even recommended his aide for promotion in a letter to the king.[63] After great expense and ten years, either imprisoned or under house arrest, Cagigal cleared his name, but his military career was in ruins. Miranda, not as well connected, suffered his insult as much as Cagigal and, apparently, developed bitterness toward his accusers that resulted in his subsequent leadership for Spanish American independence.[64]

The timing of Gálvez's treatment of Cagigal and Miranda does not speak well of him or his family. The whole episode hints at another side of the hero, which is petty and vain, very human traits indeed.[65] The irony of Cagigal's success and eventual treatment is that Gálvez eventually received credit for the victory. Like the sacking of Fort St. Joseph in Michigan, the victory of New Providence occurred under his command.[66]

Meanwhile, the state of war continued and so did planning. Saavedra was now sent to France to help keep the French interested in invading Jamaica.[67] In a telling letter to Montmorin, Vergennes described the Spanish strategist as a person of true merit who should be treated as if he were Vergennes himself.[68] Indeed, planning did continue, with more ships and troops being organized. Perhaps because of this, an even greater urgency for peace was impressed upon the European negotiators.

John Jay, who had finally been appointed United States' minister plenipotentiary to Spain, where he served an unproductive two and one-half years, had moved to Paris at Franklin's behest. He went to Paris with a true distaste for Spain and Spaniards that only was surpassed by that of his wife. He had gone to Spain late and unexpectedly, but was allowed to stay. Over the duration of his Spanish mission, he either refused to acknowledge or did not know of Spain's continuing aid to his country. A lack of knowledge is difficult to understand, for the Spanish press reported all the Spanish, French, and American military activities. Everything from publishing the journal of the expedition to St. Joseph to the battle at Yorktown was at Jay's or his secretary, William Carmichael's, disposal. Carmichael could read Spanish.[69] They did receive an up-to-date report on the battle of Yorktown, which was in progress. Unfortunately, the press omitted Spain's role in getting the French fleet there.[70] Perhaps an appreciation of Spain's contribution to the cause of his country's independence is too much to expect from the man who helped write a congressional anti-Catholic diatribe after Great Britain's Quebec Act permitted Canadian Catholics free worship and to have a bishop.[71]

Jay managed to alienate everyone, including members of his own delegation such as his secretary, Carmichael, whom he characteristically suspected. He became an embarrassment when Congress, perhaps repaying a political debt, announced that he should draw credit on the Spanish government for his living expenses, which involved paying for a huge delegation and an extravagant style of living. The Spanish government supported him for a while, but when they found out that Congress could not reimburse his expenses, he was cut off. He then moved his household to Paris to participate in the negotiations for peace.[72]

By the time he arrived in Paris, everyone's distaste for him was reciprocated. While his subsequent negotiations resulted in a preliminary peace between the colonies and Great Britain, they demonstrated distrust and betrayal of his ally France, as well as his distaste for Spain. He demonstrated a greater faith in Great Britain, his country's enemy. This last position was demonstrated to the point that Jay actually tried to collaborate with the English to retake West Florida from Spain. This act was, as one U.S. historian put it, "extraordinarily shortsighted." The same historian then went on to give examples of why he held this opinion. Not the least of these was that Jay overlooked Spain's "indispensable contribution" to American Independence. Jay's offer, in the final analysis, was an "act of bad faith."[73] Jay's activities were described by a later-day Spanish historian and diplomat as an "unfortunate and unhappy chapter" in Spanish-American relations, for he reneged on promises and spent on Spanish credit until he was told to stop.[74] In the final analysis, historian Jonathan Dull, in his seminal history of the French navy during the Revolutionary War, gave the best summary of Jay's actions:

> Jay provides an illustration of the vindictiveness to which disillusioned innocence is prone; however impressive was Jay's future service to his country, he set it a bad example by his diplomacy.[75]

Fortunately, Jay did not have a negative effect on the negotiations. The failure of Spain to take Gibraltar with the attack of the fireboats in September of 1782, coupled with the problems in preparing for the invasion of Jamaica, brought France and Spain, as well as the Netherlands, together for some serious negotiating. The Netherlands was a late entry into the war and a small player in the making of peace. Ironically, with the help of the captured Grasse, who had been transferred to England where he was allowed to act as a go-between with France, ideas seemed to be exchanged more rapidly. In Europe, there was less enthusiasm for an invasion of Jamaica. A French armada had gathered at the Spanish port of Cádiz waiting for orders to embark for the West Indies. Marie-Joseph-Paul-Yves-Roch-Gilbert du

Fig. 23. Cartoon celebrating the Bourbon alliance that won the war. From Reparaz, Yo Solo, *212.*

Motier, marquis de LaFayette, the newly designated French governor of Jamaica, was with them. However, Vergennes, hoping to negotiate a peace, delayed the fleet in the Spanish port.[76]

Vergennes's foresight was correct, for in Paris, the conde de Aranda circumvented Jay's audacity as well as his own instructions to fulfill a war goal of getting East Florida while retaining Minorca, by giving up on Gibraltar and trading the Bahamas back to Britain. An armistice and preliminary accord between the Europeans that included the preliminary agreement between the American colonies and Britain, was completed 20 January 1783.[77]

Hostilities ended and if there is any measure of success, then, after the United States, which gained an independence that was recognized by all, Spain was a big winner, for that country received the Floridas, Minorca, and control of the mouth of the Mississippi River. Spain successfully defended Central America from the British and did not lose Havana. Importantly, the success of Spain translated to the independence of the former British colonies, but this would be a connection quickly overlooked in the history of the new country. Nor was Spain surprised, for as the conde de Aranda wrote about the new United States at the time:

Fig. 24. British cartoon, February 24, 1783. Spain and France are leading a procession of the signers of the Preliminaries of Peace. Original in the British Museum, London. From Reparaz, Yo Solo, 230.

This Federal Republic was born a pigmy, as such, it needed the aid and strength of two powerful states like Spain and France to accomplish its independence. The day will come when it will grow up, become a giant and be greatly feared in the Americas. Then it will forget the benefits that it had received from the two powers and only think in its own aggrandizement.[78]

Francisco Saavedra, likewise realizing the implications of his country's involvement in a world war, cautioned as early as 1780, when he warned:

what is not being thought about at present, what ought to occupy the whole attention of politics, is the great upheaval that in time the North American revolution is going to produce in the human race.[79]

Both Aranda and Saavedra represented a country that had thought out a long-term plan for its participation in the war. Spain's role, irrespective of Jay's criticisms and subsequent centuries of American historical chauvinism, proved indispensable to the birth of the United States.

CONCLUSIONS AND EPILOGUE

. . . while mute guns were fired by the artillery.

Joseph M. Beatty, Jr., 1780

$\mathcal{S}$pain helped the United States gain its independence and that help came in the form of actual fighting, supplies, and money. In addition, the overall Spanish strategy is what finally resulted in the defeat of Great Britain. Conversely, without Spain's involvement, the consequences of that war would have been vastly different. All the leaders, from George Washington to the French minister of state, the comte de Vergennes, knew that Spain was vital to the cause.[1] The powerful Frenchman advised his king not to enter the war unless Spain was committed as well. France, he knew, needed Spain to assure victory.[2]

But because United States history is a story of a country born out of English colonies, the role of Spain has not been genuinely recognized. Nor, for that matter, have the sacrifices of Spain's colonies been acknowledged. Despite the publication of some very good articles and books, mostly produced as a result of the bicentennial celebration of the United States, Spain's role in the independence of the United States has remained relatively unknown. As mentioned in the preface, a salient point in presenting this history is that all Hispanics helped with American independence as a result of Spain's policy at that time. Evidence of that aid is present today in some unexpected ways.

First, look at financial help. Spain contributed hard specie and supplies originating in Spain, Mexico, and other parts of Latin America. One rather imaginative idea for collecting money for the war effort would be applauded by modern-day temperance people. In 1781, Mexico received word that a tax on *pulque,* an alcoholic drink derived from the maguey plant, was imposed on the purchase of drinks in bars called *pulquerías.* The tax was a surcharge of a half a *real* per drink "to help sustain the war." In this way, the order read, producers would not be directly affected, while the consumers, some of whom had a bad drinking habit called a *vicio,* would pay.[3] In New Spain, the tax did not result in much money because the people bought less.[4]

Eighteenth-century Spanish subjects who lived in areas that make up the present states of Texas, New Mexico, Arizona, and California answered Carlos III's call for a special tax to help with the war and, in the end, secure American independence. In March of 1780, Carlos III decreed that "his vassals in America contribute for a one-time donation of one *peso* ($30) per Indian and other castes, and two *pesos* for each Spaniard and noble, to sustain the present war."[5] In what is touted as the first cattle drive in Texas, cattle were herded overland to help feed Bernardo de Gálvez's troops.[6]

A copy of the declaration of war was sent to New Mexico on 7 October 1779, so the far northern province of New Spain received word within four months after Spain's actual entry into the war.[7] The commandant general of the Internal Provinces of northern New Spain (Mexico), Teodoro Cavallero de Croix, periodically mentioned the war to New Mexico's governor Juan Bautista de Anza. At one point, Croix reported that the last packet of letters from New Mexico did not get to Spain because they were thrown overboard when a British corsair pursued the ship on which they were being transported.[8]

In early August 1780, Croix sent a letter to Anza in which he wrote about voluntary contributions to help with the war. Then, on August 17, Croix officially notified Anza of the king's decree to collect for each person.[9] Anza proceeded to collect from his relatively poor, landlocked and sparsely populated province, but not from everyone. He received permission from Croix to exempt the Native American residents of Zuni and the Hopi pueblos from the tax.[10] After the end of the war, Felipe de Neve, who replaced Croix, acknowledged the receipt of 3,677 *pesos* or $110,300 by present standards, from New Mexico while ordering that the tax not be collected any more.[11]

Earlier, in California, the same Felipe de Neve was the governor who asked Fray Junípero Serra to collect the tax through the missions. The head Franciscan, whose statue is in the rotunda of the Capitol building in Washington, D.C., wanted to relieve this fiscal burden from the mission Indians, "without their realizing it," by paying out of church funds.[12] Father Serra referred to the English as "perfidious heretics"[13] on the one hand and then, in 1778, wrote in a document now lost:

> We prayed fervently last evening for the success of the colonists under one George Washington, because we believe their cause is just and that the Great Redeemer is on their side.[14]

Apparently, in Serra's mind, qualification for being a "perfidious heretic" had nothing to do with religion and everything to do with being an enemy of Spain. Nevertheless, a total of 4,216 *pesos* ($126,480), including 2,000 *pesos* ($60,000) from Neve, was collected. Approximately 25 percent, or around $30,000, of that total came from Serra's missions.[15]

During this time, Spanish influence in Arizona consisted of some sparse settlements and struggling missions, with a couple of *presidios,* or small forts, strung along the Santa Cruz River from Tucson southward. This area was administered as a part of Pimería Alta (today's Sonora). Like California, Texas, and New Mexico, the Sonorans collected funds for the war, which amounted to a resounding 22,420 *pesos* ($672,600), 429 ($12,870) of which came from the hard-pressed people of the little village of Tucson.[16]

Even in Spain, some noteworthy methods of support for the war should be mentioned. During the war, Seville, in southern Spain, had a large armory producing artillery pieces. That armory, although inactive, exists today. The main gate into the complex is flanked by two mortars, one of which contains the name "George Washington."[17] The artillery piece was named, as was the custom of the day, after a famous person. Apparently the war ended before it could be used and it became a decorative feature of the factory.

Spain is famous for its cathedrals and one of the most famous of these is in Toledo. When war was officially declared, the Church in Spain offered to help the government with some financial aid. The king, though appreciative, replied that he did not need the aid for the moment.[18] Three months later, Floridablanca notified the cathedral at Toledo that the time had come to contribute. Toledo responded with an interest-free loan and a donation of 500,000 *reales,* ($1,875,000) *"por vía de servicio,"* for their service to the king. The cathedral council then wrote to the archbishop and cathedral council of Málaga to notify them that help was needed.[19]

Málaga, while not as wealthy as Toledo, responded with a donation, and a loan of 200,000 *reales de vellon* ($37,500) each. They arranged with the government to pay back the loan, *"cuando se firme la paz,"* at the end of the war when the council's tax would be "reduced and excused" for the necessary years to make up the loan.[20] Both the king and Floridablanca were thankful for the support.[21] Whether or not other cathedrals and churches also contributed, as did Toledo and Málaga, in this fund raising effort is not known at this point. However, the scant sources used here seem to indicate that Málaga was not an isolated incident. If the seat of Spanish Catholicism gave money, it is certainly possible that many other cathedrals and parishes throughout the Spanish empire received an inquiry from Toledo and joined in the effort.[22]

Málaga's contribution to the effort gave rise to a legend that grew through the years, for the cathedral's towers were never completed. As a result, the story that the church's completion was sacrificed for American independence is commonplace today. The story is apocryphal, for construction did continue after the war, and was halted again to divert funds for road projects. How many times this type of scenario repeated itself through the years is a subject for a different study.[23] At the very least, though, the many American tourists who travel to the beautiful city of Málaga should visit the cathedral and note the incomplete tower and roof, and use it as a reminder of Málaga's contribution to their country's birth.

The irony of the Spanish Catholic Church, including officials like Fray Junípero Serra in California, aiding an effort that assisted in a revolution that, in part, justified itself because it objected to Great Britain's recognition of Catholics in Canada with the Quebec Act, is another of those quirks of history lost through the years.

Probably the most evident connection of Spain's financial help in the United States today is money. Reportedly traced to the account books kept by Oliver Pollock, the dollar sign comes from his simplistic rendering of a Spanish symbol to delineate Spanish currency versus others. For centuries, Spain has used the Pillars of Hercules to symbolize Spain's control of that geographical place where the continents of Europe and Africa come within sight of each other and separate the Mediterranean Sea from the Atlantic Ocean. The pillars, which symbolically look like Greek columns, usually flank the royal shield and have ribbon loosely wrapped around them. The Latin *non plus ultra*, "none beyond here" was changed to *plus ultra*, "beyond here" when Spain turned its attention to the west. Pollock and others used the two columns with their ribbons for the symbol for Spanish currency, which came out as an "s" with two lines run down through it. That evolved into today's dollar sign.[24]

Enough Spanish money filtered into the western frontier of the rebelling colonies, that the continental currency was sustained at par in the west, while it dropped to 12 cents per dollar in the east. American terminology still uses terms derived from the Spanish currency. "Two bits" for a quarter comes from Spanish coins that could be divided into eight pieces. Two bits or a *real* out of the original "piece of eight" amounted to one-fourth or a "quarter" of the whole piece.

The English term "dollar" came from the German *"Thaler"* and became the English word for the Spanish *peso* that was in use throughout Spain and the Spanish American colonies.[25] The English colonists had become accustomed to the use of the Spanish dollar and its convenient fractional parts. As such, it became the basis for the new country's national coinage. Various colonies, particularly Massachusetts, Connecticut, and Virginia made Spanish coins their legal tender. The first issue of Continental paper money on 10 May 1775, over a year before the Declaration of Independence, provided that the notes would be payable in "Spanish Milled Dollars or the value thereof in gold or silver."[26] Historian David Weber writes that the United States adopted the Spanish *peso* as their unit of currency in November 1776, just four months after the Declaration of Independence. Given all this information about the beginnings of our money, then the Spanish influence on United States terminology has been forever fixed in its heritage.[27]

Oliver Pollock, that patriot who secured so much critical aid and befriended Bernardo de Gálvez, went broke for his efforts. He was committed to jail in Cuba for his debts, where he stayed for eighteen months until Gálvez had him released.[28] In Philadelphia, Francisco Rendón petitioned Congress to pay him. Congress passed a resolution, which Rendón forwarded to the Virginia legislature with a suggestion that it pay its own debt to Pollock. Rendón tried to expedite the matter with a letter to Virginia's governor. Paying Pollock, the Spanish observer felt, was "the only honorable thing to do."[29]

With the war's end and with Cuba behind him, Pollock began petitioning

Congress in Philadelphia. He wanted to be paid for the debts he incurred to secure goods and supplies for his country. He had been incarcerated because he had secured loans on behalf of the United States and Virginia that he personally could not pay. While trying to remedy this personal affront, he did not forget his old friend as well, for he petitioned his own government to commemorate Gálvez with a portrait. He wanted Congress to recognize the Spanish officer most known for contributing to independence.[30]

In part, Pollock's persistence, with Rendón's support, paid off. In 1785, Congress voted to pay him $90,000 for his efforts. Unfortunately, he did not receive the money for another six years. Eventually, he received $108,605 from the Federal government, and the State of Virginia, which originally employed him, paid off his remaining accounts.[31]

While Pollock's petition for Gálvez's portrait did not receive the same attention as his request for funds, Gálvez did receive recognition. (See plate 26.) Almost two centuries later, the United States government accepted a statue of Bernardo de Gálvez on horseback, which was placed in front of the building in Washington, D.C. that houses the Department of State. Spain gave the statue to the United States as a bicentennial gift. The statue, which was done by Juan Avalos, has an uncanny likeness to Juan Carlos I, the king of Spain at the time of the gift. Pollock would have been proud.[32]

Along with his statue, Gálvez is remembered with a place name in the United States. In 1786, the year Gálvez died, José de Evia who had served as a young ensign under Gálvez in Louisiana, was ordered to chart the Gulf Coast west of New Orleans. His mission was to correct any errors made from earlier surveys. On July 23 he began to draft an uncharted "turbulent" bay. Upon realizing that the bay was unnamed, he recorded in his journal that, "I gave this point the name of Galveston Bay." The bay still retains that name as does the famous Texas resort town located there.[33]

Upon the Peace of Paris, Gálvez returned to Spain where, as the result of his exploits and the petitions of the citizens of Louisiana, he received many accolades, including a royal update of the Gálvez family shield. The new shield included an image of him on board the *Galveztown* with the saying "Yo Solo," "I alone," in reference to his entrance into Pensacola Bay.[34] (See plates 27 and 28.)

In Spain, he advised his government on Louisiana and Florida, then returned to Cuba as the newly appointed captain general of the island. He served in Havana for only a few months, releasing Pollock from jail in the process, before he was appointed viceroy of Mexico to replace his father Matías, who unexpectedly passed away.

Like his father, Bernardo would not serve long in Mexico for he, too, became ill and died in office. He took office in Mexico in June 1785, contracted an illness in the fall of 1786, and died on November 30. He was forty years old. While in office he used the plans drawn up under his father to begin construction of Chapultepec Castle.[35] His short administration was well received in Mexico and his passing was widely grieved. A poem by Manuel Antonio Valdés, praising his accomplishments and lamenting his death, was written a year after he died. That poem was recently published in the United States, both in the original Spanish and in English.[36]

Gálvez would never know that his fame would resurface in the twentieth century. Unfortunately, he left no descendants to enjoy the moment. His wife, the countess de Gálvez, gave birth to their third daughter, Guadalupe, after Gálvez's death. In honor of Gálvez, the archbishop of New Spain baptized the baby girl. Shortly thereafter, the countess moved the family to Spain. Within years, the countess and her

Fig. 25. Bernardo de Gálvez. Original in the Biblioteca Nacional, Madrid. From Reparaz, Yo Solo, 26.

three children were destitute. Her major benefactors had died. Uncle José, as mentioned, passed away in 1787. King Carlos III died in December of the next year. Bernardo's son died before reaching maturity, and his sister Matilde moved to Italy with the inherited titles.[37]

Bernardo de Gálvez is buried next to his father in the church of San Fernando in Mexico City.[38] His final resting place is visited frequently to this day.

Diego de Gardoqui (see plate 29), the Basque banker who helped funnel funds to the young struggling country and to whom Benjamin Franklin recommended John Paul Jones, also was honored as part of the United States bicentennial. King Juan Carlos I presented the City of Philadelphia with a statue of Gardoqui done by Luis Sanguino.[39] Gardoqui's knowledge of English was further utilized when he was appointed Spain's first minister plenipotentiary to the United States in 1784. He served more than four years in Philadelphia and New York. In addition to helping George Washington get his Spanish mule, which the future first president of the United States named "Royal Gift," Gardoqui spent a lot of time with John Jay, trying to negotiate a commercial treaty between Spain and the United States. They never succeeded, even though Jay, ironically, persuaded Congress to give up any rights of navigation on the Mississippi River. Representatives from the western and southern states rose up in Congress to block the treaty.[40]

Juan de Miralles, Spain's first diplomat sent to the United States, who went as an observer, also has been honored. A plaque has been placed on the site where his Philadelphia home was located. On 28 April 1780 Miralles died, after a brief illness, while visiting George Washington at his Morristown, New Jersey headquarters. The American general personally organized and presided over the sumptuous funeral for his Spanish friend. One of the soldiers described it, in part:

> The honorary pallbearers were six field officers and on the shoulders of four artillery officers in full uniform, the actual pallbearers, he was borne to the grave, while mute guns were fired by the artillery.[41]

Washington and his officers attended the funeral mass, which was officiated by a Spanish priest. Miralles was a respected and well-liked man among the colonial leaders. This was demonstrated a month later when Philadelphia society and many members of the Continental Congress attended a requiem mass in his memory.[42]

Miralles's assistant and successor, Francisco Rendón, continued in the same tradition. Rendón and Washington became good friends. He had a good understanding of the new country. Washington accepted the Spaniard's invitation to lodge at the latter's Philadelphia residence in the winter of 1781–82. Rendón became convinced of Washington's sincere desire to have Spain as a friend and protector of the newly created United States.[43] His desire to be Spain's first ambassador to the United States did not come to pass when Gardoqui accepted the position.[44]

Washington knew of Spain's importance to the birth of his country and had much for which to be thankful. Some of his memories would include that miserable winter spent at Valley Forge. He was desperate, and two Spanish sources of help were Major General Lafayette and Baron Friedrich von Steuben. The Frenchman had traveled to the colonies via northern Spain the summer before. The latter was Benjamin Franklin's recommendation for someone to properly train the Continental soldiers. Steuben was a Prussian officer who traveled to the United States with Spanish assistance. Steuben spent the spring at Valley Forge, training the troops so that they came out of the long winter more disciplined than they were the previous autumn.[45]

Apparently, the call for supplies went out too late to receive the aid at Valley Forge. But it did not go unheeded. Oliver Pollock, then in New Orleans, arranged to purchase over $60,000 worth of blankets for the army. After delays caused by the British blockade along the east coast, some of the blankets arrived. Part of the shipment was transported to Fort Pitt via the Mississippi and Ohio rivers.[46] Whether or not these were some of the blankets that Governor Patrick Henry of Virginia unwisely designated for his state's troops alone at Valley Forge, is a subject for further investigation.[47]

Diego de Gardoqui's company in Spain sent 18,000 blankets; 11,000 pairs of shoes, 41,000 pairs of stockings, as well as shirts and medical supplies. While Gardoqui's shipment went out in 1778, another account has $70,000 worth of supplies moving north out of New Orleans by the end of 1777. No doubt some of this last shipment was what Pollock arranged.[48]

Needless to say, George Washington did not want to put his men through another winter like the one at Valley Forge. He began preparing for the next winter early, and by October 1778, he was still looking for more blankets. Upon hearing that a Spanish ship with a large cargo had arrived in Baltimore, he wrote the Board of War requesting blankets from the shipment.[49]

Sometimes good intentions go astray. Answering the call for uniforms, Spain complied with a shipment in 1781. The uniforms arrived in Boston in June, and Washington requested them for immediate use.[50] Upon inspection, Major General William Heath, who apparently was in charge of the shipment, found the Spanish uniforms to be inadequate. As Washington wrote, "about 3,000 suits of clothes have arrived at Boston from Spain but unfortunately the Coats are scarlet."[51] This must have been lost on the Spanish, for some of their own regiments wore scarlet.[52]

After the death of Carlos III, Floridablanca remained in office to serve Carlos III's son. Carlos IV was a kindly, weak-willed, and simple-minded person. He wanted to continue his father's policies but could not. The outbreak of revolution in France as well as palace intrigue in Spain interrupted any plans. The aging and increasingly conservative Floridablanca was ousted and replaced with the conde de Aranda. Aranda did not last a year and was replaced by the ultimate palace politician as well as master of intrigue, the young Manuel de Godoy, who would rule Spain for many years to come.

Of all the personages from Spain who have passed over the pages of this history, perhaps Francisco Saavedra stands out for his later achievements. After the war, he was appointed intendant of Caracas where he initiated reforms and made some lasting acquaintances. He returned to Spain in 1788, where he served in a number of bureaucratic positions until 1797, when he became the minister of finance and, shortly thereafter, became the minister of state.

In Spain, he is most remembered for his role in the resistance to the French occupation in 1808. He was instrumental in forming a shadow government in Cádiz in 1810. Because of his refusal to accept Napoleon's brother as the king of Spain, he, like many others, took refuge in Ceuta on the northern coast of Africa.

After the French left Spain, he returned in 1813 to become involved with improving the channel of the Guadalquivir River to Seville. He took up residence in the city of his birth, where he presided over the Economic Society and the Academy of Medicine. He also convinced the government to help organize several free schools in Triana, a suburb of Seville. Saavedra died in Seville on 25 November 1819 and was buried in the church of La Magdalena, in the sacramental chapel.[53]

One interesting tidbit of Saavedra's later years is his connection with Simón Bolívar, the "George Washington" of South America. Saavedra apparently knew the Bolívar family from his days in Caracas, for when Bolívar, as a teenager, was sent to Spain, he sought out the well-connected and respected Saavedra, who at the time had replaced Godoy as minister of state. The one-time brilliant strategist, who helped engineer American independence, used his influence to help the future liberator of South America.[54]

And this is the final irony. Everything that Spain wanted to avoid while aiding the American colonies came to fruition. France's economic problems destroyed Vergennes and led to the revolution that brought down the French monarchy and replaced it with Napoleon. The would-be emperor of Europe invaded Spain and placed his brother Joseph on the throne. This act gave Spain's many colonies a reason to fulfill what Spain feared most with its participation in the rebellion of the English colonies. Although already moving toward independence, the colonies now claimed their sovereignty, for they saw no legal or other reason to maintain their loyalty to a French pretender.

Also, in one of history's twists of fate, the United States was able to solve the issue of free navigation of the Mississippi River because of Joseph Bonaparte. Napoleon had his brother, as king of Spain, give him Louisiana, and then Napoleon sold his ill-begotten property to the United States.

The young United States became a transcontinental country within seventy years after the end of the war. In the process, it annexed the Floridas, Louisiana, Texas, and the northern half of Mexico (New Mexico, Arizona, and California). And the United States never did pay its loans and debts to Spain and the countries, then colonies, from where the money and supplies that made independence possible originated. Spain's role in the independence of the United States was indeed, "a most intrinsic gift."

Habsburg to Bourbon Succession

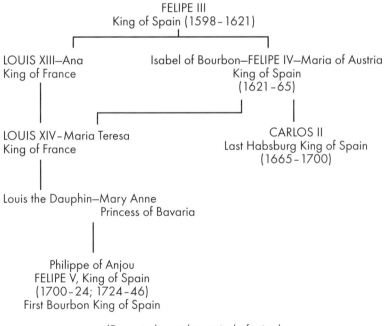

FELIPE III
King of Spain (1598-1621)

LOUIS XIII–Ana
King of France

Isabel of Bourbon–FELIPE IV–Maria of Austria
King of Spain
(1621-65)

LOUIS XIV-Maria Teresa
King of France

CARLOS II
Last Habsburg King of Spain
(1665-1700)

Louis the Dauphin–Mary Anne
Princess of Bavaria

Philippe of Anjou
FELIPE V, King of Spain
(1700-24; 1724-46)
First Bourbon King of Spain

(Dates indicate the period of reign)

APPENDIX 2

18th-Century European Wars

	In Europe	In America
1702-1714	War of Spanish Succession	Queen Anne's War
1719-1720	Spain vs France	no name
1733-1736	War of Polish Succession	no name
1740-1748	War of Austrian Succession	War of Jenkin's Ear
1756-1765	Seven Years' War	French and Indian War
	Great War for Empire	

APPENDIX 3

MONEY
at the time of the Independence of the United States

34 maravedíes	=	1 real de vellón
1 livres tounis (French)	=	4 reales de vellón (copper)
20 reales de vellón (copper)	=	1 real (silver)
8 reales	=	1 peso (fuerte)
1 peso (fuerte)*	=	1 dollar (American)
1 British pound sterling	=	3.354 dollars
1 dollar	=	30 dollars (1990)

Value of the Peso

1 dollar	=	1 peso
8 reales	=	1 peso
160 reales de vellón	=	1 peso
5,440 maravedies	=	1 peso
40 livres Tounis	=	1 peso
(libras in Spanish)		

*Peso, also known as the "peso fuerte," the "Spanish milled dollar," the "pillar dollar," and "piece of eight."

Sources: Leslie Bethell, editor, *Historia de América Latina Colonial; Economía,* (Barcelona; Editorial Crítica, S. A. 1990, originally University of Cambridge Press, 1984), p. X
    Randall, *Benedict Arnold,* p. 497.
    Fernández y Fernández, *Spain's Contribution,* p. 2.
    Yeoman, *A Guide Book of United States Coins,* pp. 2, 6-7.

APPENDIX 4

HAVANA RESIDENTS WHO LOANED MONEY FOR ADMIRAL DE GRASSE'S EXPEDITION TO YORKTOWN, AUGUST 16, 1781

NAME	AMOUNT IN REALES	INTEREST (ALL LOANS WERE TO BE REPAID FROM THE FIRST SHIPMENT OF SPECIE FROM MEXICO)	AMOUNT REPAID IN REALES (SEPT. 24–OCT. 2, 1781)
1. José Olazaval	160,000	2%	800,000 (plus 3,200 interest)
2. Francisco del Corral	200,000	2%	248,000 (plus 4,960 interest)
3. José Manuel López	320,000	2%	720,000 (plus 6,400 interest on 320,000)
4. Juan Dios de Muñoz	48,000	2%	48,000 (plus 960 interest)
5. Tomás de Evia[a]	264,000	none	264,000
6. Lorenzo Quintana	200,000	none	200,000
7. Manuel Quintanilla	600,000	2%	720,000 (plus 12,000 interest on 600,000)
8. Pedro Valverde[b]	160,000	none	160,000
9. Rafael Medina	160,000	2%	160,000 (plus 3,200 interest)
10. Juan Patrón	608,000	2%	816,000 (plus 12,160 interest on 608,000)
11. Juan Hogan[c]	240,000	none	240,000
12. Manuel Esteban[d]	200,000	none	200,000
13. Carlos Testona[c]	168,000	2%	289,000 (plus 5,972 interest on 289,000)
14. Fernero Brothers	160,000	2%	240,000 (plus 3,200 interest on 160,000)
15. Bartolomé de Castro	48,000	2%	48,000 (plus 960 interest)[g]
16. Nicolás Varela	48,000	2%	144,000 (plus 960 interest on 48,000)
17. Cristóbal de Nis	24,000	2%	88,000 (plus 480 interest on 24,000)
18. Pablo Serra	160,000	2%	320,000 (plus 3,200 interest on 160,000)
19. José Feu	160,000	2%	160,000 (plus 3,200 interest)
20. Pedro Figuerola	80,000	2%	80,000 (plus 1,600 interest)
21. Miguel Ibañez	112,000	2%	112,000 (plus 2,240 interest)
22. Doña Bárbara Santa Cruz[f]	80,000	none	80,000
23. Jaime Boloix	80,000	2%	240,000 (plus 1,600 interest on 80,000)
24. Francisco Asbert	48,000	2%	144,000 (plus 960 interest on 48,000)
25. Pedro Peraza	64,000	2%	144,000 (plus 1,280 interest on 64,000)
26. Pedro Martin de Leiba	64,000	2%	184,000 (plus 1,280 interest on 64,000)
27. Cristóval Murillo	16,000	2%	16,000 (plus 320 interest)
28. Francisco del Corral	48,000	2%	(See second name above)
	4,520,000		6,865,000	70,132 interest

Source: AGI, SD, 1849, exp. 191. Caja Cuenta de 1781. Ignacio Peñalver y Cárdenas, Havana, 30 June, 1782.

Notes: a) Paymaster, Regiment of Guadalajara. b) Paymaster, Infantry Regiment of Havana. c) Paymaster. Regiment of Ybernia. d) Paymaster, Regiment of Soria. e) Festona? f) Marquesa de Cárdenas. g) Paid to Andrés Fernero.

Note: The Exchequer turned over to the French 4,000,000 reales (500,000 pesos), evidently keeping the rest. Military units loaned approximately one-fifth of the total, and the treasury secured one-fourth of the total at no interest. It is quite possible that not all the creditors on this list were Spanish citizens (See nos. 17, 19, 23, and 24). Only one contributor was female (See no. 22).

NOTES

PREFACE

1. The three banners are copies of the originals in the Museo del Ejército (Army Museum) in Madrid, Spain. The banners are of the Regiments of Spain, the Prince, and Navarra, with respective catalog numbers of 4799/45, 4800/45, and 4801/45, all in the collections of the Palace of the Governors, Santa Fe, New Mexico.
2. See, for example, Fray Angélico Chávez, *Origins of New Mexico Families in the Spanish Colonial Period* (Santa Fe: Historical Society of New Mexico, 1954), and Beverly Becker, "Santa Fe: Est. 1610, 1607," *El Palacio* 100, no. 1 (winter 1994–1995): 14–16.

INTRODUCTION

1. William Carmichael to Floridablanca, San Lorenzo, 12 November 1784, Archivo Histórico Nacional (AHN), Madrid, Sección de Estado, legajo (leg.) 3885, expediente (exp.) 26, now in Carpeta 97 de Mapas y Planos.
2. Floridablanca to Carmichael, San Lorenzo, 24 November 1784, ibid. The offspring are sterile. "Jackass" translated to Spanish means a stallion ass, which is used to mate with a mare to create a mule or jackass, a sturdy but sterile work animal—which is what Washington wanted in the first place.
3. Washington to Floridablanca, 19 December 1785, ibid.
4. One of the animals did perish in transit, for Washington only received one. See "Bill of lading," 8 August 1789 in Richard M. Ketchum, *The World of George Washington* (New York: American Heritage Publishing Company, Inc., 1974), 198–99. The accompanying text notes that Washington named his mule "Royal Gift," and was frustrated because it took no interest in his mares. This is a confusing matter; clearly, the king did not intend to send breeders, yet it is inconceivable that Washington could not have known the difference.
5. Felipe V is rumored to have intrigued against his nephew, Louis XV, at one point, in an attempt to take the throne.
6. Debate continues as to whether or not Frenchmen participated with the Pawnee and Oto Indians in the ambush. Latest research and thought leans toward minimal French participation at most, and French influence at least. A recent exhibition of the Segesser Hide Paintings, one of which depicts the battle, indicates definite French participation. "The Segesser Hide Paintings," an exhibition at the Palace of the Governors, Santa Fe, N.Mex. The partial diary of the Spanish expedition, known as the Villasur expedition after its commander, has been published in Gottfried Hotz, *Indian Skin Paintings from the American Southwest: Two Representations of Border Conflicts Between Mexico and the Missouri in the Early Eighteenth Century* (Norman: University of Oklahoma Press, 1970). Also, see Alfred B. Thomas, trans. and ed., *After Coronado: Spanish Exploration Northeast of New Mexico,*

1696–1727 (Norman: University of Oklahoma Press, 1935); and Thomas E. Chávez, "The Segesser Hide Paintings: History, Discovery, Art," *El Palacio* (winter 1986): 18–27.

7. Mortimer Chambers et al., *The Western Experience Since 1640* (New York: Alfred A. Knopf, 1974), 629.

8. Arthur J. May, *A History of Civilization: The Mid-Seventeenth Century to Modern Times* (New York: Charles Scribner's Sons, 1964), 126.

9. Aranda to Floridablanca, Paris, 31 January 1778, AHN, Estado, leg. 3884, exp. 7, no. 1222; Jonathan R. Dull, *The French Navy and American Independence: A Study of Arms and Diplomacy, 1774–1787* (Princeton: Princeton University Press, 1975), 143; and Dull, *A Diplomatic History of the American Revolution* (New Haven: Yale University Press, 1985), 107–8, 146.

10. Dull, *Diplomatic History*, 143; and Richard B. Morris, *The Peacemakers: The Great Powers and American Independence* (New York: Harper & Row, Publishers, 1965), 455–57.

11. Dull, *Diplomatic History*, 43, 112, 121–22; and Dull, *French Navy*, 137.

12. Morris, *Peacemakers*, pp. 305–6, 395–96; and Enrique Fernández y Fernández, *Spain's Contribution to the Independence of the United States* (Washington, D.C.: Embassy of Spain, 1985. First published in *Revista/Review Interamericana* 10 (winter 1980): 3.

13. The best published work on José de Gálvez is Herbert I. Priestley, *José de Gálvez: Visitor-General of New Spain, 1765–1771* (Berkeley: University of California Press, 1916). Priestley's work concentrates on Gálvez as the visitor-general of New Spain and is not a true biography. Gálvez's first name is variously spelled Josef, Joseph, and José, the modern choice. He spelled his name "Joseph."

14. Priestley, *Gálvez*, 4; and José Rodulfo Boeta, *Bernardo de Gálvez* (Madrid: Publicaciones Españolas, 1977), 21.

15. Priestley, *Gálvez*, 8; and Dull, *French Navy*, 180.

16. Priestley, *Gálvez*, 5; and Eric Beerman, "Introduction," in *Yo Solo: The Battle Journal of Bernardo de Gálvez During the American Revolution*, trans. E. A. Montemayor (New Orleans: Polyanthos, Inc., 1978), xi.

17. Floridablanca and Aranda also achieved prominence and boosted their respective careers with the Jesuit expulsion. The conde de Aranda executed Carlos III's expulsion decree in Spain. Floridablanca successfully went to Rome to secure the abolition of the Jesuit Order everywhere.

18. Priestley, *Gálvez*, 6 and 7.

19. Ibid., 8.

20. The best biography of Bernardo de Gálvez is the classic and early John Walton Caughey, *Bernardo de Gálvez in Louisiana, 1776–1783* (Berkeley: University of California Press, 1934). A short and more recent contribution is Boeta, *Gálvez*. Also see Ralph Lee Woodward, Jr., "Bernardo de Gálvez and the American Revolution: An Introductory Essay," in *Tribute to Don Bernardo de Gálvez: Royal Patents and an Epic Ballad Honoring the Spanish Governor of Louisiana*, ed. R. L. Woodward, Jr. (Baton Rouge and New Orleans: The Historic New Orleans Collection, 1979), xvii–xviii.

21. Gálvez actually continued a policy of covert aid to the rebels at Fort Willing and Fort Pitt (name changed to Pitt from Ft. Duquesne, by the British). His predecessor, Luis de Unzaga, initiated the practice. James Alton James, "Oliver Pollock: Financer of the Revolution in the West," *Mississippi Valley Historical Review* (June 1929): 67–80; John Francis McDermott, ed. "The Myth of the 'Imbecile Governor'—Captain Fernando de Leyba and the Defense of St. Louis in 1780," in *The Spanish in the Mississippi Valley, 1762–1804*, 329–31, 360–61; José Montero de Pedro, *Españoles en Nueva Orleans y Luisiana* (Madrid: Ediciones Cultura Hispánica del Centro Iberoamericano de Cooperación, 1979), 32–33, 40–41; Beerman, "Introduction," xiii; C. Ward Bond, "Oliver Pollock: An Unknown Patriot," in *Tribute to Don Bernardo de Gálvez*, 136; Fernández y Fernández, *Spain's Contribution*, 4, 6–7; Woodward, "Gálvez," xxiv; Light Townsend Cummins, "Oliver Pollock's Plantations: An Early Anglo Landowner on the Lower Mississippi, 1769–1824," *Louisiana History* 29, no. 1 (winter 1988): 42–43.

22. Beerman, "Introduction," xiii–xiv; Robert L. Gold, "Governor Bernardo de Gálvez and Spanish Espionage in Pensacola, 1777," in *The Spanish in the Mississippi Valley,* 99; and Woodward, "Gálvez," xxiii.

23. The first published account of the journey to, and taking of, St. Joseph is based on newspaper accounts published in the *Madrid Gazette (la Gaceta de Madrid)* and is somewhat less than laudatory; the author concluded that the expedition was made up of "a band of marauders" and the result was "of little importance," Clarence W. Alvord, "The Conquest of St. Joseph, Michigan by the Spaniards in 1781," *Michigan History Magazine* 2 (1908): 196–210, based on a paper read before the State Historical Society of Missouri on 17 December 1907. The author did not have access to the expedition's journal. See also Lawrence Kinnaird, "The Spanish Expedition Against Fort St. Joseph in 1781: A New Interpretation," *Mississippi Valley Historical Review* 19, no. 2 (September 1908): 173–91; and Frederick J. Teggart, "The Capture of St. Joseph, Michigan, By the Spaniards in 1781," *Missouri Historical Review* 5, no. 4 (July 1911): 214–28. See Francisco Cruzat to Don Estevan Miró, 6 August 1781, Archivo General de Indias (AGI), Seville, Audiencia de Santo Domingo, leg. 2538, no. 154. A copy is in AGI, Audiencia de Santo Domingo, leg. 2084.

24. Carmen de Reparaz, *Yo Solo: Bernardo de Gálvez y la toma de Panzacola en 1781* (Barcelona, Spain: Ediciones del Serbal e Instituto de Cooperación Iberoamericana, 1986), 29–30, 35, 42–51; and Francisco Morales Padrón, ed., *The Journal of Don Francisco Saavedra de Sangronis During the comisión which he had in his charge from 25 June 1780 until the 20th of the same month of 1783,* trans. Aileen Moore (Gainesville: University Press of Florida, 1989), xxx, 99–127.

25. Her name is spelled different ways. The Spanish spelling apparently is María Felicitas de Saint-Maxent as in Reparaz, *Yo Solo,* 11, or María Feliciana de Saint-Maxent as in Boeta, *Bernardo de Gálvez,* 127. I use the French version of her name as she did, and the spelling of "St. Maxent." See Woodward, "Gálvez," xx. The name "d'Estrehan" comes from a previous marriage.

26. *Enciclopedia Universal Ilustrada Europeo-Americana,* vol. 52 (Barcelona: Hijos de J. Espasa, Editores, 1924), 132–33. The name of his dissertation is "Disertación sobre la dificultad de demostrarse matemáticamente el año fijo de la muerte de Cristo por la profecía de las semanas de Daniel."

27. The best work on Saavedra is Morales Padrón, ed., *Journal of Saavedra.*

28. Dull, *French Navy,* 287.

29. Ibid., 243–44; and James A. Lewis, "Las Damas de la Havana, El Precursor, and Francisco de Saavedra: A Note on Spanish Participation in the Battle of Yorktown," *The Americas* 37 (July 1980): 85–86, 90–98.

30. Francisco de Saavedra, *Mis Decenios,* Granada, Archivo Facultad de Teología, (Fondo Saavedra), tomo II, 252–74. An extract has been published in Spanish in Reparaz, *Yo Solo,* 208–12. Also see Dull, *French Navy,* 245.

31. Francisco de Saavedra to J. Gálvez, January 1782, AGI, Indiferente General, leg. 1578.

32. Dull, *French Navy,* 288.

33. Reparaz, *Yo Solo,* 137.

34. Dull, *French Navy,* 243.

35. Boeta, *Gálvez,* 35–36.

36. Ibid., 36.

37. Troy S. Floyd, "Bourbon Palliatives and the Central American Mining Industry, 1765–1800," *The Americas* 18, no. 2 (October 1961): 116; and Beerman, "Introduction," x–xi. Guatemala is spelled Goatemala in the documents of this period.

38. Instrucciones, 23 September 1779, AGI, Audiencia de Guatemala, leg. 451. Also see Floyd, "Palliatives," 116.

39. Floyd, "Palliatives," 106.

40. Gold, "Gálvez and Spanish Espionage," 87; and Woodward, "Gálvez," xxi–xxii, xxiv, and xx.

41. See numerous letters dated July 1778, in AGI, Guatemala, leg. 869; and Oakah L. Jones, "Matías de Gálvez: Spanish Ally of the American Revolution," unpublished paper, in which the author cites M. Gálvez to J. Gálvez, Omoa, 1 July 1778, and Martín de Mayorga to J. Gálvez, 6 August 1778, both in AGI, Guatemala, leg. 451.

42. Floyd, "Palliatives," 106 and 114; and Woodward, "Gálvez," xxii.

43. Floyd, "Palliatives," 106.

44. Diario general de los subcessos ocurridos en las expedicciones . . . dirigidas por el Mariscal de Campo . . . Matías de Gálvez . . . contra los Yngleses establecidos en el Golfo de Honduras . . . , 16 March 1782, Guatemala, AGI, leg. 869.

45. Juan Manuel de Cagigal to J. Gálvez, Havana, 10 April 1782, no. 222 with attachments; M. de Gálvez to Cagigal, Puerto de Roatán, 18 March 1782, both in AGI, Santo Domingo, leg. 1235.

46. Cagigal to J. Gálvez, 12 November 1782, no. 310 with attachment; M. Gálvez to Martín de Mayorga, viceroy of New Spain, 12 November 1782 (includes articles of capitulation), ibid.

47. Enciclopedia General Ilustrada del País Vasco, vol. 15 (San Sebastián: Editorial Aunamendi, 1983), 296–97.

48. Diego de Gardoqui to the Duke of La Alcudia, San Lorenzo del Escorial, 26 October 1794, AHN, Estado, leg. 3898; and Fernández y Fernández, Spain's Contribution, 24.

49. Diego de Navarro, captain general of Cuba to J. Gálvez, Havana, 17 December 1777, AGI, Santo Domingo, leg. 1598.

50. Fernández y Fernández, Spain's Contribution, 16.

51. For more on Francisco Rendón see William H. Broughton, "Francisco Rendón: Spanish Agent in Philadelphia, 1779–1786, Intendent of Spanish Louisiana, 1793–1796," Ph.D. diss., University of New Mexico, 1994.

52. Montero de Pedro, Españoles, 32–33; Woodward, "Gálvez," xxiv; and Gold, "Gálvez and Spanish Espionage," 91. For Pollock, see James Alton James, Oliver Pollock: The Life and Times of an Unknown Patriot (New York: Appleton-Century, 1937); and Cummins, "Pollock's Plantations," 38.

53. Diego José Navarro's story has yet to be published. See Reparaz, Yo Solo, 29, 30, 35, 43 and 45. Most of the documentation of Navarro's conflict with Bernardo de Gálvez is in AGI, Papeles procedentes de Cuba, legajos 1, 2, and 4a; and Santo Domingo, legajos 1598, 1659, 2082, and 2083 a and b. Research into the matter of Navarro's political survival is a topic for future study.

54. Various paintings of Carlos III exist. For example, portraits by Mengs reproduced in Reparaz, Yo Solo, 16; and by Francisco Goya in the Prado Museum, Madrid.

55. Dull, Diplomatic History, 50. In December 1775, Franklin wrote to Carlos's scholarly youngest son thanking him for a book the prince had translated and sent to the American. Franklin used the occasion to note America's desire for friendship.

56. B. Gálvez to Patrick Henry, New Orleans, 19 October 1778, AGI, Santo Domingo, leg. 2596.

57. Aranda to King Carlos IV, 1783, as quoted in Boeta, Gálvez, 137. Aranda predicted that the United States would seize the Floridas and New Spain (Mexico).

CHAPTER 1

1. Luis Angel García Melero, La Independencia de los Estados Unidos de Norteamérica a través de la prensa española: los precedentes (1763–1776) (Madrid: Ministerio de Asuntos Exteriores, Dirección General de Relaciones Culturales, 1977), 13–14.

2. Sidney B. Brinckerhoff and Pierce A. Chamberlain, Spanish Military Weapons in Colonial America, 1700–1821 (Harrisburg, Pa.: The Stackpole Co., 1972), 15; and Janet R. Fireman, The Spanish Royal Corps of Engineers in the Western Borderlands: Instrument of Bourbon Reform, 1764–1815 (Glendale: The Arthur H. Clark Co., 1977), 30–33.

3. Floyd, "Palliatives," 108.

4. James Alton James, "Spanish Influence in the West During the American Revolution," Mississippi Valley Historical Review 4 (1917): 193–94; and Light Townsend Cummins,

Spanish Observers and the American Revolution, 1775–1783 (Baton Rouge: Louisiana State University Press, 1991), 17–18.

5. General James Wolfe, as quoted in John M. Blum et al, *The National Experience: A History of the United States to 1877* (New York: Harcourt, Brace, Jovanovich, Inc., 1973), 83–84. Eric Williams, *From Columbus to Castro: The History of the Caribbean, 1492–1969* (New York: Vintage Books, 1984), 222–24. Williams demonstrates Britain's preference for its West Indies holdings and concludes: "Everyone was to bow down and worship king sugar. The mainland colonies refused."

6. Conde de Montmorin, the French ambassador in Madrid to Vergennes, the French foreign minister, as quoted in Bruce Lancaster, *The American Revolution* (New York: Houghton Mifflin Co., 1985), 234–35.

7. Juan Joseph Elegio de la Puente to J. Gálvez, 22 December 1777, AHN, Estado, leg. 3884, exp. 1, folio 1.

8. Puente to J. Gálvez, 20 December 1777, ibid., folio 2.

9. For a good study of the 1768 rebellion, see Carl A. Brasseaux, *Denis Nicolas Foucalt and the New Orleans Rebellion of 1768* (Ruston, La.: McGinty Publications, 1987).

10. Montero de Pedro, *Españoles,* 22–23.

11. Julián de Arriaga, the Spanish minister of the Indies to the captain-general of Havana, Madrid, 24 January and 24 March 1766 and from London, 26 December 1765, all in AGI, Santo Domingo, leg. 1194.

12. Letter from Madrid, 21 March 1766, ibid.

13. Arriaga to the conde de Ricla, captain-general of Havana, 22 September 1764, ibid.

14. Captain-general of Havana, February 1766, AGI, Santo Domingo, leg. 1211; Grimaldi to the captain-general of Havana, 30 April 1768 and 1 June 1768, both in AGI, Santo Domingo, leg. 1195. A group of one hundred British soldiers had to pass through Havana on their way to Louisiana. Why they actually had to stop at Havana is unclear.

15. A good assessment of Unzaga's administration is in Montero de Pedro, *Españoles.*

16. The captain-general of Havana to Arriaga, 30 September 1771, AGI, Santo Domingo, leg. 1211, no. 49. A *piragua* or *pirogue* is also a dugout canoe.

17. Arriaga to Unzaga, 21 March 1772, no number, ibid.

18. Unzaga to the marqués de la Torre, 21 and 27 March 1772, ibid.

19. Ibid.

20. Arriaga to Torre, 9 June 1772, ibid.

21. Cummins, "Pollock's Plantations," 36–43; and James, "Oliver Pollock: Financer," 68–69.

22. James, "Oliver Pollock: Financer," 71; James, "Spanish Influence," 197. Original is in *The Oliver Pollock Papers,* Library of Congress. O'Reilly is reputed to have won royal favor because he saved the life of Carlos III. Also see Bond, "Oliver Pollock: An Unknown Patriot," 135–39.

23. James, "Oliver Pollock: Financer," 70. For examples of the mentioned official correspondence, see correspondence cited in this chapter.

24. Arriaga to Unzaga, 20 June 1772, AGI, Santo Domingo, leg. 1211.

25. Solano to Arriaga, 26 April 1772, ibid., leg. 1095.

26. Letter from Havana, February 1776, ibid., leg. 1211.

27. Captain-general of Havana, 6 and 12 March 1771, ibid., leg. 1197.

28. Unzaga to Grimaldi, 30 June 1770; and Grimaldi to Arriaga, 19 October 1770, Archivo General de Simancas (AGS), Secretaría de Guerra; Florida y Louisiana (años 1779–1802).

29. Letter from Madrid, 21 March 1766, AGI, Santo Domingo, leg. 1194.

30. Unzaga to Arriaga, 2, 14, and 24 October 1772 (three letters), ibid., leg. 1211. Britain was in the process of trying to enforce its new "Quartering Act," which authorized the quartering of British troops within a town whenever their commanding officer thought it necessary. The previous "Quartering Act" of 1765 stipulated that the colonies provide barracks, as well as some supplies, for the troops.

31. Torre to J. Gálvez, 12 October 1776, copies in AGI, Santo Domingo, leg. 1224; and leg. 1598, no. 1236.

32. Ibid.; and anonymous to Torre, 16 July and 30 July 1776, ibid., leg. 1598.
33. Unzaga to Torre, 13 August 1776, leg. 1598; and 7 September 1776, leg. 1224; and Charles Lee to Unzaga, Williamsbourg, 22 May 1776, leg. 2596, all in ibid.
34. Lee to Unzaga, Williamsbourg, 22 May 1776 (two letters); and Unzaga to J. Gálvez, New Orleans, 7 September 1776, ibid., leg. 2596.
35. George Gibson to Unzaga, n.d., ibid.
36. Unzaga to J. Gálvez, 30 September 1776, ibid.
37. Torre to J. Gálvez, 9 October 1776, leg. 1224, ibid.
38. Unzaga to Torre, 7 September 1776, ibid.
39. James, "Oliver Pollock: Financer," 70.
40. Bruce Glascock, "Colonial Powder Problems or 'Then and Now,'" *Muzzle Blasts* (January 1973):10.
41. James, "Oliver Pollock: Financer," 70; James, "Spanish Influence," 196; Bond, "Oliver Pollock: An Unknown Patriot," 136; and ibid., 36.
42. James, "Oliver Pollock: Financer," 71; and Glascock, "Colonial Powder Problems," 36.
43. Glascock, "Colonial Powder Problems," 10.
44. Quoted in Bond, "Oliver Pollock: An Unknown Patriot," 136.
45. King George III, as quoted in Blum et al, *The National Experience,* 97.
46. J. Gálvez as quoted in Glascock, "Colonial Powder Problems," 18.
47. Ibid., 36; and J. Gálvez to Unzaga, 24 December 1776, AGI, Santo Domingo, leg. 2596.
48. Beerman, "Introduction," xii; and Woodward, "Gálvez," xx.

CHAPTER 2

1. Torre to J. Gálvez, 1 October 1776, AGI Santo Domingo, leg. 1211.
2. Woodward, "Galvez," xxii and xxiv.
3. The Revolutionary War helped, from the Spanish point of view, but the problem was not completely solved. See Cayetano Alcázar Molina, *"Los virreinatos en el siglo XVIII,"* in *Historia de América y de los pueblos americanos* (Barcelona and Buenos Aires: Salvat Editores, S.A., 1945), 75–76.
4. Among the first supplies requested by Charles Lee was quinine, which was an antibiotic indigenous to Spanish South America. J. Gálvez to the governor of Louisiana, 24 December 1776, AGI, Santo Domingo, leg. 2596. This is a marginal note attached to Unzaga's letter to J. Gálvez dated 30 September 1776, AGI, Santo Domingo, leg. 2596. Unzaga sent along Lee's request upon which he commented. For the story of American, meaning indigenous, contributions to Europe, see Jack Weatherford, *Indian Givers: How the Indians of the Americas Transformed the World* (New York: Crown Publishers, Inc., 1988). For quinine, see 77–78. Weatherford claims that Europeans did not use the word "quinine" until 1820, when French scientists Joseph Pelletier and Joseph Caventou succeeded in extracting the active ingredient from the bark of a Peruvian tree that grows at high altitude. This cannot be correct, for Spain was supplying quinine to the American colonists, and both people were using the word. Also, see B. Gálvez to J. Gálvez, New Orleans, 12 May 1777, AGI, Santo Domingo, leg. 2596, wherein young Gálvez repeats his orders to supply the "British Americans" . . . "[with] quinine," among other items.
5. Spain was the first European country involved in the slave trade to abolish the institution. Britain was the last European country to do so. Brazil was the last country overall.
6. The brother of George Rogers Clark, who received aid from Spain to support his campaigns against the British.
7. For an overview of the Dutch in the West Indies and their role in the American Revolution, see Barbara Tuchman, *The First Salute: A View of the American Revolution* (New York: Ballantine Books, 1988).
8. Arriaga to the conde de Ricla, 22 September 1764, AGI, Santo Domingo, leg. 1194.
9. Don José Solano to Arriaga, 26 April 1772, ibid., leg. 1095.

10. The relative incomes of the various areas are a subject worthy of further research. See, for example, Williams, *Columbus to Castro,* 217–36.
11. The conde de Aranda to the conde de Floridablanca, 7 March 1778, AHN, Estado, leg. 3884, exp. 7.
12. Joaquín Oltra and María Angeles Pérez Samper, *El Conde de Aranda y los Estados Unidos* (Barcelona: Promociones y Publicaciones Universitarias, S.A., 1987), 51–54 and 58–59.
13. Carlos III as quoted in ibid., 60. Also see 58–59 and 96.
14. Vergennes as quoted in ibid., 96. Also see 58–59.
15. Letter from London, 26 December 1765, AGI, Santo Domingo, leg. 1194.
16. Arriaga to the captain-general of Havana, 24 March 1776; and letter from Madrid, 24 January 1766, ibid.
17. Letter from Madrid, 21 March 1766, ibid.
18. Aranda to Grimaldi, 20 October 1775, AGI, Guatemala, leg. 665, sig. antigua 101-5-1.
19. Aranda to Grimaldi, 23 October 1775, ibid.
20. Ibid.
21. Aranda to Grimaldi, 20 October 1775, ibid.
22. Aranda to Grimaldi, 23 October 1775, ibid.
23. Matías de Gálvez to J. Gálvez, 6 January 1779, AGI, Guatemala, leg. 605, sig. antigua 101-5-1, no. 43. M. Gálvez wrote that the Archbishop of Nicaragua reported that the Spanish had not been able to safely navigate the San Juan River since 1728, because of Indian resistance, instigated by the English.
24. Flores to Arriaga, 27 February 1776, ibid.
25. Don Francisco Saavedra as quoted in *The Journal of Saavedra,* 39.
26. Fireman, *Spanish Royal Corps,* 58–60.
27. James Wright to the governor (of Teneninia [?]), 10 August 1775, AGI, Guatemala, leg. 665, sig. antigua 101-5-1.
28. Manuel Antonio Flores to Arriaga, 29 November 1775; and Arriaga to Flores, 22 November 1775, ibid.
29. Arriaga to Flores, 22 November 1775; and Arriaga to various officials, 22 November 1775, ibid.
30. Flores to Arriaga, 29 November 1775, ibid.
31. Flores to Arriaga, 13 February 1776, ibid.
32. For example, see Pedro Carbonell to Arriaga, 28 February 1776, ibid. There are many letters about this matter in AGI, Guatemala, legajo 665.
33. Flores to Arriaga, 27 February 1776; Governor Melchor Correa of Portobelo to J. Gálvez, 11 June 1776; and Extracto del diario formado por el Theniente de Navío D. Juan de Gastelu, Comandante de la Balandra Guarda, 11 July 1776, ibid.
34. Province of Costa Rica to J. Gálvez, 30 July 1776, no number, ibid. The name of the letter's writer is obscure in the document.
35. Agustín Pérez Guixano to Arriaga, 30 April 1776, ibid.
36. Arriaga to D. Donacio Cavello, governor of Nicaragua, 30 April 1776; letter to the president of Guatemala, the governor of Panama, and the governor of Portobelo, 28 February 1776; and letter to the president of Guatemala, 26 July 1776, all in ibid.
37. Flores to Arriaga, 15 April 1776, ibid.
38. Flores to Arriaga, 30 April 1776, ibid.
39. Ibid.
40. Resolution of the Council of the Indies, 26 April 1776, AGI, Santo Domingo, leg. 1059.
41. Grimaldi, 4 May 1776, ibid.
42. Saavedra, as quoted by Morales Padrón in "Editor's Introduction," *The Journal of Saavedra,* xx and xxiii. "Cevallos" is misspelled "Cavallos."
43. Woodward, "Gálvez," xxiv; and D. Antonio Ballesteros y Beretta, *Historia de España y su influencia en la Historia Universal,* tomo 5, (Barcelona: Salvat editores, S.A., 1929), 197.
44. Torre to J. Gálvez, 12 October 1776, AGI, Santo Domingo, leg. 1224.
45. Ballesteros y Beretta, *Historia,* 197.

46. Ballesteros y Beretta, *Historia,* 203.
47. Carbonell to J. Gálvez, 27 March 1777, no. 100 and Instrucción a Francisco de Navas, 8 February 1777, AGI, Guatemala, leg. 665, sig. antigua 101-5-1.
48. Letter to the president of Guatemala, 31 March 1778, ibid.

CHAPTER 3

1. Thomas Paine, *Common Sense* (1776; reprint, New York: Penguin Books, 1986), 81. Paine was an Englishman who had migrated to the colonies in 1774. Ironically, after the war he traveled to Europe where he participated in the French Revolution, thus aiding in the destruction of the government that helped the English colonies achieve independence.
2. *La Gaceta de Madrid,* 27 August 1776 and 10 September 1776, Biblioteca Nacional (BN), Madrid.
3. Ibid., 14 February 1775. A letter from the First Continental Congress in Philadelphia to King George III, in which the colonial position and possible solutions are explained, is quoted in full.
4. Second Continental Congress's petition to the king, as quoted in Blum et al, *National Experience,* 100.
5. *El Mercurio Histórico y Político* also published events as they occurred in the British colonies. For a good introduction to the Spanish press's coverage of the Independence movement, see García Melero, *La Independencia de los Estados Unidos.* The Spanish press, and publications dealing with the Revolutionary War, is a topic worthy of further research. A study of the English press and American Independence is Alfred Grant, *Our American Brethren: A History of Letters in the British Press During the American Revolution, 1775–1781* (Jefferson, North Carolina and London: McFarland & Company, Inc., Publishers, 1995).
6. For example, see letters to Torre, 16 July and 30 July 1776; Governor of Louisiana to Torre, 13 August 1776, all in AGI, Santo Domingo, leg. 1598.
7. The first Spanish settlement in California took place at San Diego in 1769. The San Francisco Bay was discovered by land later the same year. Franklin to William Temple Franklin, 10 September 1776, as quoted in Cummins, *Spanish Observers,* 29. The original was published in Paul H. Smith, ed., *Letters of Delegates to Congress, 1774–1789,* vol. 5 (Washington, D.C.: Library of Congress, 1976–1991), 132. This attitude continued through the peace negotiations. See Aranda to Floridablanca, Paris, 18 December 1782, "Observaciones topographiques," AGS, libro 172, nos. 384-rev 393.
8. Morris, *The Peacemakers,* 17, 221, and 224.
9. George Gibson to Unzaga, no date (1776), AGI, Santo Domingo, leg. 2596.
10. Morris, *The Peacemakers,* 13–14.
11. Reparaz, *Yo Solo,* 31.
12. Ibid.; and Woodward, "Gálvez," xvii and xxii.
13. Glascock, "Colonial Powder Problems," 10.
14. Letter from Madrid to the captain-general of Havana, 24 December 1776; letter from Madrid to the governor of Louisiana, 24 December 1776, both in AGI, Santo Domingo, leg. 2596.
15. J. Gálvez, as quoted in Glascock, "Colonial Powder Problems," 18.
16. Ballesteros y Beretta, *Historia de España,* 201. Ballesteros y Beretta also states that Grimaldi wanted to plan an attack on Ireland.
17. Dull, *Diplomatic History,* 50; and Celia López Chávez, "Benjamin Franklin, España y la diplomacia de una armónica," *Espacio, Tiempo y Forma: Revista de la Facultad de Geografía y Historia,* serie iv, 13 (2000), 329–30.
18. Benjamin Franklin to Don Gabriel de Bourbon, Philadelphia, 12 December 1775, Archivo General del Palacio Real, Madrid, Archivo del Infante Don Gabriel, Secretaría, leg. 738. Copy in Leonard W. Labaree et al, eds., *The Papers of Benjamin Franklin,* 24 vols. (New Haven and London: Yale University Press, 1959), vol. 22, 296–97.
19. Dull, *Diplomatic History,* 56.

20. Aranda to Grimaldi, 13 January 1777, AHN, Estado, leg. 3884, exp. 2, folio 4, no. 938. For a recent biography of Aranda, see Oltra and Pérez Samper, *El Conde de Aranda,* and specifically for Aranda's opinion of Vergennes, 92.

21. Oltra and Pérez Samper, *El Conde de Aranda,* 141.

22. Aranda to Grimaldi, 13 January 1777, AHN, Estado, leg. 3884, exp. 2, folio 4, no. 938.

23. Benjamin Franklin, Silas Deane, and Arthur Lee to Aranda, 28 December 1776, copy lettered C attached to Aranda to Grimaldi, 13 January 1777, ibid.

24. Aranda received the information after sending a direct inquiry. See Aranda to Vergennes, 28 December 1776, copy letter A attached to ibid.

25. Aranda to the marqués de Grimaldi, Paris, 13 January 1777, AHN, Estado, leg. 3884, exp. 2, folio 4, no. 938. The meeting took place on 29 December 1776, which would have been very soon after Franklin's arrival in Paris.

26. Oltra and Pérez Samper, *El Conde de Aranda,* 137–38.

27. Aranda to Grimaldi, 13 January 1777, AHN, Estado, leg. 3884, exp. 2, folio 4, no. 938.

28. Oltra and Pérez Samper, *El Conde de Aranda,* 143. Here, the Spanish documents are clear that, contrary to the views of some United States' historians, the American commissioners could not speak French. Aranda was adamant about the language problem after the first meeting, and arranged for a translator at the second meeting.

29. Aranda to Grimaldi, 13 January 1777, AHN, Estado, leg. 3884, exp. 2, folio 4, no. 938.

30. Ibid.

31. Ballesteros y Beretta, *Historia de España,* 196–97.

32. Ibid., 196; and Oltra and Pérez Samper, *El Conde de Aranda,* 136, 74 and 75.

33. Aranda to Grimaldi, 13 January 1777, AHN, Estado, leg. 3884, exp. 2, folio 4, no. 939.

34. Ibid.

35. María Pilar Ruigómez de Hernández, *El gobierno español del despotismo ilustrado ante la independencia de los Estados Unidos de América: Una nueva estructura de la política internacional, 1773–1783* (Madrid: Ministerio de Asuntos Exteriores, 1978), 127–29.

36. Richard B. Morris, in his landmark study of the making of peace in 1783, leads the reader to believe that the United States was unaware of Spain's interests in the war. Therefore, the devious Spaniards, with French complicity, tried to betray the Americans and, had it not been for John Jay, who learned of the conspiracy, peace, as we know it, would not have been accomplished. I take exception to that scenario. See Morris, *The Peacemakers,* passim.

37. Aranda to Grimaldi, 13 January 1777, AHN, Estado, leg. 3884, exp. 2, folio 4, no. 939. Aranda's second report was over thirty-seven pages, which, coupled with his first report written on the same day, totaled sixty-nine pages of information crucial to United States history.

38. Ballesteros y Beretta, *Historia de España,* 203.

39. Dictamen de Gálvez, 2 February 1777, AHN, Estado, leg. 3884, exp. 3, folio 16.

40. Dictamen de Grimaldi, 2 February 1777, ibid., exp. 3, folio 15.

41. Ibid.

42. Dictamen del conde de Ricla, 3 February 1777, ibid., exp. 3, folio 14.

43. Ibid.; and Dictamen de Gálvez, 2 February 1777, ibid., exp. 3, folio 16.

44. Grimaldi retired on 7 November 1776 but was not replaced until 18 February 1777. Ballesteros y Beretta, *Historia de España,* 201; and James, "Spanish Influence," 200–201.

45. Letter (Grimaldi) to Aranda, 14 February 1777, AHN, Estado, leg. 3884, exp. 3, folio 18. From the letter and other evidence, I have made the assumption that Grimaldi is the author. The other possible author of the letter is Floridablanca, who did not become the minister of state until 18 February 1777.

46. Spain, France, and Portugal all had historical claims to fishing off of the Newfoundland coast, because Portuguese, Galician, and Basque fishermen plied their trade in the area before Columbus sailed.

47. Morris, *The Peacemakers,* 219; Montero de Pedro, *Españoles,* 37; and Lancaster, *The American Revolution,* 125.

48. James, "Spanish Influence," 200–201.

49. Aingeru Zabala Uriate, "Bilbao y el comercio con el norte de América en el siglo XVIII," in *Los vascos y América,* eds. Ronald E. Mansilla et al (Bilbao: Fundación Banco de Viscaya, 1989), 193–95.

50. Diego de Gardoqui to Arthur Lee, 17 February 1777, in Juan Francisco Yela Utrilla, *España ante la independencia de los Estados Unidos* (1925; reprint, Madrid: Colegio Universitario de Ediciones Istmo, 1988), vol. 2, 618–20.

51. Ibid., 199–200; Ballesteros y Beretta, *Historia de España,* 204; *Enciclopedia universal ilustrada Europeo-Americana,* tomo 25 (Barcelona: Hijo de J. Espasa, editores, 1924), 846; and *Enciclopedia general ilustrada del país Vasco,* tomo 15 (San Sebastián: Editorial Aunamendi, 1983), 296–97. The story of Gardoqui and Sons is as important as that of Rodrique, Hortalez et Cie in France. There are indications of the extent of aid provided through these two companies. Gardoqui's company in Bilbao is the larger mystery. The archives in Bilbao might be a rich resource for this important research project. Cummins, *Spanish Observers,* 57–60 gives the best description of these meetings.

52. J. Gálvez to the governor of Louisiana, 24 December 1776, AGI, Santo Domingo, leg. 2596.

53. Glascock, "Colonial Powder Problems," 9.

54. Congressional Commission to Vergennes, March 1777, exp. 3, folio 35 in English and folio 19 in Spanish; and Franklin to Aranda, 7 April 1777, exp. 3, folio 23, all in AHN, Estado, leg. 3884.

55. Franklin to Aranda, 7 April 1777, ibid., exp. 3, folio 23.

56. Ibid.

57. Ballesteros y Beretta, *Historia de España,* 204.

58. Aranda to Floridablanca, Paris, 13 April 1777, AGN, Estado, leg. 3884, exp. 3, folio 20; copy in AGS, libro 162, nos. 170 rev. 174.

59. Congressional appointment signed by John Hancock, president of the Congress, 2 January 1777, AHN, Estado, leg. 3884, exp. 3, folio 21. The original certificate is oversized and in English. A French translation, which was provided by Vergennes, is included with it. Certificate of Appointment, 2 January 1777, AGN, Estado, leg. 3884, exp. 3, folio 21, exp. 3. John Hancock's signature, as it appears in all the documents I have seen, is very large. Apparently, the large size was his signatory. This trait would indicate that the traditional story of Hancock signing the Declaration of Independence with a signature larger than the other signers, to flaunt the British, is not true. Also, see Franklin to Aranda, 7 April 1777, Paris, no. 174 rev. 175 with an attachment, "Congressional Appointment," 2 January 1777, Baltimore, no. 174, all in AGS, libro 162.

60. Aranda to Floridablanca, 13 April 1777, Paris, AGS, libro 162, exp. 3, folio 20, ibid. A copy of this letter with attachments of Franklin's appointment is in AGS, libro, 162, nos. 170, rev. 174.

61. Ibid.

62. Ballesteros y Beretta, *Historia de España,* 204–5; James, "Spanish Influence," 200–201; Reparaz, *Yo Solo,* 32; Morris, *The Peacemakers,* 49; Dull, *Diplomatic History,* 92; and Ernest R. Dupuy and Trevor N. Dupuy, *The Encyclopedia of Military History From 3500 B.C. to the Present* (New York: Harper and Row, 1970), 715–16.

63. For disagreement, see Morales Padrón, "Editor's Introduction," xxv; for Saavedra's distaste, witness the following: "the condescension of Carlos III toward his sister contributed no less than did the want of vision of our Cabinet." In regard to the treaty itself, see Ballesteros y Beretta, *Historia de España,* tomo 5, 197. For examples of confusion or speculation see Archbishop of Cuba to Bucareli, 24 January and 27 June 1777; and Diego de Navarro, the governor of Havana to Bucareli, 20 August 1778, all in AGI, Santo Domingo, leg. 1214.

64. For example, see letter from Havana to Bucareli, 23 December 1777, ibid., leg. 1214.

65. Aranda to Floridablanca, 7 March 1778, AHN, Estado, 3884, exp. 7.

66. Commerce Committee, U.S. Congress to B. Gálvez, 12 June 1777, AGI, Santo Domingo, leg. 2596, no. 168.

67. Ibid.

68. Aranda to Floridablanca, 13 April 1777, AHN, Estado, leg. 3884, exp. 3, folio 26.

69. For example, the treason of Benedict Arnold, the rift between Alexander Hamilton and Thomas Jefferson and, of course, the feud between Hamilton and Aaron Burr that resulted in Hamilton's death.
70. Floridablanca to Aranda, 3 June 1777, AHN, Estado, leg. 3884, exp. 3, folio 27.
71. Aranda to Floridablanca, 27 September 1777, ibid.; and Memorie por Dr. Franklin, July 1777, ibid., folio 29.
72. Dull, *Diplomatic History,* 82–83.
73. Aranda to Floridablanca, 17 September 1777 (two letters), ibid., respectively, exp. 4, folio 32, no. 1136; and no. folio, 33, no. 1139.
74. Dull, *Diplomatic History,* 80–85.
75. A Memorial from the Commission of the United States, Benjamin Franklin, Silas Deane and Arthur Lee, September 1777, AHN, Estado, leg. 3884, exp. 4, folio 34.
76. Robert Morris and William Smith to B. Gálvez, 24 October 1777, York, Pennsylvania, AGI, Santo Domingo, leg. 2596. The American names were translated to Roberto and Guillermo in the document.
77. Morris and Smith to B. Gálvez, York, Pennsylvania, 21 November 1777; also see Congressional letter signed by John Hancock, president of Congress, York, Pennsylvania, 24 October 1777, both in AGI, Santo Domingo, leg. 2596.
78. Ballesteros y Beretta, *Historia de España,* tomo 5, 205; and Blum et al, *National Experience,* 109; and Letter directed to Franklin, 24 October 1777, Boston, AGS, libro 163, nos. 238 rev. 245. This letter was sent to Madrid by Aranda, attached to another Aranda sent to Floridablanca, 13 December 1777, Paris, AGS, libro 163, nos. 231–236.
79. Aranda to Franklin, 13 December 1777, ibid.

CHAPTER 4

1. Commission to Vergennes, March 1777, both in AHN, Estado, leg. 3884, exp. 6, folio 35; and Memorial, September 1777, exp. 4.
2. Woodward, "Gálvez," xviii–xix.
3. Royal Order, 26 August 1777, AGI, Santo Domingo, leg. 1598. Also, see Cummins, *Spanish Observers,* 32–34.
4. Cummins, *Spanish Observers,* 99.
5. Navarro to J. Gálvez, 11 November 1777, no. 127; Juan Elegio de la Puente, "Manifiesto de descubrimiento . . . de las Provincias de Florida . . . ," 12 September 1764, AGI, Santo Domingo, leg. 1598; and Juan Bautista Bonet to Marqués González de Castejón, 28 December 1777, AGN, Estado, leg. 3884, exp. 1, folio 3. The interesting Governor Navarro becomes a key person in this story of United States independence. He is deserving of a biography. Also, as might be surmised, the mysterious Puente is a subject worthy of more research. The best account of the activities of Miralles and Puente is in Cummins, *Spanish Observers,* passim.
6. Puente, "Manifesto," 4 May 1778, ibid.
7. B. Gálvez to J. Gálvez, 11 March 1778, AGI, Santo Domingo, leg. 2596.
8. Fernández y Fernández, *Spain's Contribution,* 14.
9. Navarro to J. Gálvez, December 1777, AGI, Santo Domingo, leg. 1598, no. 148.
10. Ibid.
11. "Instrucción reservada para el régimen y gobierno de Don Juan de Miralles . . . ," 17 December 1777, ibid.
12. Ibid.
13. Puente to J. Gálvez, 22 December 1777, AHN, Estado, leg. 3884, exp. 1, folio 1; and 20 December 1777, exp. 1, folio 2.
14. Navarro to B. Gálvez, 12 March 1778, AGI, Cuba, leg. 1, folio 239–363 III.
15. See previous chapter for the various colonial proposals.

16. Floridablanca sent two letters dated 23 December 1776 and 13 January 1777; also Floridablanca to Aranda, 13 January 1777, AHN, Estado, leg. 3884, folio 69, exp. 6.
17. Ibid.
18. Gold, "Gálvez and Spanish Espionage," 97.
19. Floridablanca to Aranda, 13 January 1778, El Prado, AHN, Estado, leg. 3884, folio 69.
20. Ibid.
21. Floridablanca to Aranda, 13 January 1778, El Prado, AHN, Estado, leg. 3884, folio 69.
22. Ibid.
23. Junta de los Señores Secretarios del despacho to Aranda, 22 January 1778, ibid., exp. 7.
24. Floridablanca to Aranda, 13 January 1778, El Prado, AHN, Estado, exp. 6, folio 69.
25. Aranda to Floridablanca, 31 January 1778, Paris, as quoted in Ruigómez de Hernández, *El gobierno español,* 127; original in AHN Estado, leg. 3884, exp. 7, no. 1222. Also see Dull, *The French Navy,* 127–28.
26. Aranda to Floridablanca, 31 January 1778, AHN, Estado, leg. 3884, exp. 7, no. 1222.
27. Floridablanca to Aranda, 2 February 1778, El Prado, ibid.
28. Dull, *The French Navy,* 97–98.
29. Ibid., 95–96.
30. Ibid., 100–101 and 104.
31. Ballesteros y Beretta, *Historia de España,* 205.
32. Ibid.; and Dull, *The French Navy,* 111 and 113.
33. Dull, *The French Navy,* 30.
34. Ibid., 110.
35. Ibid., 111 and 117.
36. Ibid., 117.
37. Ibid., 122.
38. Lancaster, *The American Revolution,* 237.
39. Ibid.; and Dull, *The French Navy,* 118–24.
40. Dupuy, *Encyclopedia of Military History,* 717.
41. Dull, *The French Navy,* 124.
42. Aranda to Floridablanca, 23 February 1778, AHN, Estado, exp. 8, folio 90.
43. Ibid.
44. Ibid.
45. Patrick Henry to B. Gálvez, 14 January 1778, AGI, Santo Domingo, leg. 2596.
46. B. Gálvez to Henry, 19 October 1778, Ibid. An "imperfect" French translation accompanied the English version.
47. Ibid.
48. Navarro to Bucareli, 8 November 1778; and Navarro to Bucareli, November 1778, AGI, Santo Domingo, leg. 1214.
49. Navarro to J. Gálvez, 13 June 1778, AHN, Estado, leg. 3884, exp. 1, folio 14; and Navarro to Bucareli, 22 September 1778, Ibid.
50. Navarro to J. Gálvez, 13 June 1778, AHN, Estado, leg. 3884, exp. 1, folio 14, [Reservado no. 42]; and Navarro to Bucareli, 16 May 1778, AGI, Santo Domingo, leg. 1214.
51. Navarro to J. Gálvez, 11 March 1779, AGI, Santo Domingo, leg.1229.
52. B. Gálvez to Robert Morris and William Smith, 3 April 1778, ibid., leg. 2596.
53. Henry to B. Gálvez, 14 January 1778, ibid.
54. George Washington to Navarro, 4 March 1779, AGI, Santo Domingo, leg. 1233, no. 82.
55. *Enciclopedia General Ilustrada del País Vasco,* 15, 296–97.
56. Navarro to J. Gálvez, 25 May 1779, AGI, Santo Domingo, leg. 1233, no. 71.
57. Miralles to J. Gálvez, May 1779, papeleta no. 1, attached to ibid.
58. Marcos Marreno Valenzuela, "Sobre la rebelión de las Colonias Ynglesas de América, 1778," AGI, Indiferente General, folio 17, 1791. The report is bound with green thread.
59. Ibid.
60. Marreno Valenzuela to J. Gálvez, 20 November 1778, ibid.

61. Francisco Alvarez, *Noticia del establecimiento y población de las colonias Inglesas en la America septentrional . . .* , (Madrid: A. Fernández, 1778). For New York, see 90–91. For Charleston, see 111.
62. Dull, *The French Navy*, 127–28.
63. Ibid., 128–29.
64. Ibid., 130.
65. Ibid., 131–32.
66. Vergennes to King Louis XVI, 5 December 1778 as quoted in ibid., 133. Original in the National Archives of France, Foreign Ministry Archives, *Memoirs and Documents,* France, Vol. 1897, no. 97.
67. Dull, *The French Navy*, 134–35.
68. Gold, "Gálvez and Spanish Espionage," 92.

CHAPTER 5
1. The best insight of Bernardo de Gálvez's spying system is Gold, "Gálvez and Spanish Espionage," 87–99; and Cummins, *Spanish Observers.* For Gálvez's new administration, see Gold, "Gálvez and Spanish Espionage," 91–92; Woodward, "Gálvez," xviii–xix; and Gilbert G. Din, "Lieutenant Raimundo DuBreüil, Commandant of San Gabriel de Manchac and Bernardo de Galvez's 1779 Campaign of the Mississippi River," *Military History of the West* 29, no. 1 (spring 1999): 1–30. Gálvez acknowledged his instructions and the work of Unzaga. See Bernardo de Gálvez to J. Gálvez, 12 May 1777, AGI, Santo Domingo, leg. 2596.
2. Woodward, "Gálvez," xxiii; and E. A. Montemayor, "Epilogue," in *Yo Solo: The Battle Journey of Bernardo de Gálvez during the American Revolution,* trans. by E. A. Montemayor (New Orleans: Polyanthos, 1978), 47.
3. Howard H. Peckham, *The War for Independence* (Chicago: University of Chicago Press, 1967), 125–26; and Lancaster, *American Revolution,* 240.
4. George Washington to Gouverneur Morris, 4 October 1778, in John C. Fitzpatrick, ed., *The Writings of George Washington from the Original Manuscript Sources, 1745–1799,* vol. 13 (Washington, D.C.: The United States Government Printing Office, 1944), 22. Reproduced in Yela Utrilla, *España ante la independencia,* vol. 2, 958.
5. Washington to the President of Congress, 11 November 1778, 231, ibid. Reproduced in Yela Utrilla, *España ante la independencia,* 958.
6. Washington to Henry Laurens, 14 November 1778, 256, ibid. Reproduced in Yela Utrilla, *España ante la independencia,* 958.
7. Royal Order to the Captain-General of Havana, no. 184 and to the Governor of Louisiana [attached to no. 184], 24 December 1776; and B. Gálvez to J. Gálvez, 12 May 1777, AGI, Santo Domingo, leg. 2596. Also, see the margin notes to this same letter. The notes are dated 15 August 1777.
8. Gold, "Gálvez and Spanish Espionage," 92; Ballesteros y Beretta, *Historia de España,* 199 and 201; and Cummins, *Spanish Observers,* 39, 78–79.
9. Din, "DuBreüil," 9.
10. Ibid., 3–4.
11. Ibid., 9 and 14.
12. Letters dated from El Pardo to B. Gálvez, 17 and 20 February (three letters) and 22 February 1777 (two letters), AGI, Santo Domingo, leg. 1598; and Ballesteros y Beretta, *Historia de España,* 201.
13. Ibid. The concept that Eduardo would be connected to *Gardoqui e Hijos* is my own and is based on the timing of shipments and their origins.
14. Torre to J. Gálvez, 9 May 1777; and B. Gálvez to J. Gálvez, 13 May 1777, AGI, Santo Domingo, leg. 1598.
15. Torre to J. Gálvez, 8 May 1777; and J. Gálvez to Torre, 6 May 1777, ibid. Here, there is some confusion, for Yela Utrilla has (Miguel Antonio) Eduardo, (Antonio) Raffelin and

(Luciano de) Herrera being assigned a year earlier in 1776. Then he correctly places Eduardo in 1777. The issue is further complicated when Yela Utrilla calls Eduardo "D. Eduardo de Miguel" and "D. Miguel Eduardo," and then writes that "Miguel Eduardo" and "Miguel Antonio Eduardo" are the same person. All the names are indexed under "Eduardo, Miguel Antonio." Yela Utrilla, *España ante la independencia*, 108, 150–51, 419 and 528. Also, Navarro to J. Gálvez, 8 November 1777 ibid., places Herrera in Florida in 1777; and see Cummins, *Spanish Observers*, 44 and 208.

16. B. Gálvez to J. Gálvez, 12 June 1777, BN, manuscripts, Louisiana Española, Signatura (sig.) 19247, nos. 43–46.

17. B. Gálvez to J. Gálvez, 2 June 1777, AGI, Santo Domingo, leg. 1598; and Cummins, *Spanish Observers*.

18. B. Gálvez to J. Gálvez, 9 August 1777; and 30 December 1778, AGI, Santo Domingo, leg. 1598. On both occasions, Bernardo de Gálvez requested permission to pay Eduardo from the Royal Treasury.

19. Cummins, *Spanish Observers*, 80–81.

20. B. Gálvez to J. Gálvez, 10 July 1777; and J. Gálvez to B. Gálvez, 13 October 1777, both in AGI, Santo Domingo, leg. 2596. Another copy of the letter dated 10 July 1777 is in BN, manuscripts, sig. 19247, nos. 41–42.

21. "Noticias de Pensacola," 1777, AGI, Santo Domingo, leg. 2596; and Gold, "Gálvez and Spanish Espionage," 92–93. The report, as sent to Spain, consisted of ten pages of clearly written information. Gold states that the report is dated 10 July 1777. Gálvez's accompanying cover letter is dated 10 July 1777. The report itself is undated, but completed by at least that date.

22. "Noticias," 1777, ibid.

23. Gold, "Gálvez and Spanish Espionage," 94.

24. The efforts of the Americans, British, and Spanish to win the allegiance of various Indian groups from Canada to South America is a fertile area for further research. In addition, the archives of these countries are strewn with information about Native Americans during this period.

25. "Noticias," 1777, AGI, Santo Domingo, leg. 2596; Gold, "Gálvez and Spanish Espionage," 95; and James, "Spanish Influence," 196.

26. Governor Peter Chester to B. Gálvez, 7 March 1777, AGI, Santo Domingo, leg. 2596; Gold, "Gálvez and Spanish Espionage," 95; and James, "Spanish Influence," 199.

27. Gold, "Gálvez and Spanish Espionage," 90–91 and 96; and James, "Spanish Influence," 198.

28. B. Gálvez to J. Gálvez, 12 May 1777, AGI, Santo Domingo, leg. 2596.

29. Chester to B. Gálvez, 10 June 1777, ibid.

30. Ibid. The first of a series of written exchanges between Bernardo de Gálvez and the British envoys did not take place until 31 July 1777. The envoys arrived on that date. Gálvez had received, read, and mailed the aforementioned report by 11 July 1777. B. Gálvez to Alexander Dickson and John Stephenson, 31 July 1777, ibid.

31. "Noticias," 1777, AGI, Santo Domingo, leg. 2596.

32. Chester to B. Gálvez, 10 June 1777; Dickson and Stephenson to B. Gálvez, 2, 17, and 19 August 1777, ibid. J. Barton Starr, *Tories, Dons, and Rebels: The American Revolution in British West Florida* [Gainesville: University Press of Florida, 1976], makes an argument that the ship's name was *Atalanta*, not *Atlanta*.

33. B. Gálvez to Dickson and Stephenson, 31 July and 26 August 1777, AGI, Santo Domingo, leg. 2596.

34. B. Gálvez to Dickson and Stephenson, 31 July 1777, ibid. One reason for the extent of time was the problem of translation. In fact, misunderstanding due to mistranslation was a convenient way for each side to make a point or delay, which was done more than once.

35. Dickson and Stephenson to B. Gálvez, 17 August 1777, AGI, Santo Domingo, leg. 2596.

36. B. Gálvez to Dickson and Stephenson, 26 August 1777, ibid.

37. B. Gálvez to Chester, 23 August 1777, ibid.

38. Ibid.; and B. Gálvez to J. Gálvez, 15 September 1777, AGI, Santo Domingo, leg. 2596.
39. B. Gálvez to J. Gálvez, 15 September 1777 (two letters), ibid. The report of this action along with copies of all the recent correspondence about seizing the British smugglers was mailed together to José de Gálvez in the middle of September.
40. "Noticias," 1777, and B. Gálvez to Chester, 23 August 1777, ibid.
41. Chester to B. Gálvez, 8 September 1777, AGI, Santo Domingo, leg. 2596.
42. B. Gálvez to J. Gálvez, 30 December 1777, ibid.
43. Ibid.; and James, "Spanish Influence," 96.
44. Gold, "Gálvez and Spanish Espionage," 96.
45. Colonel George Morgan to B. Gálvez, 22 April 1777; B. Gálvez to George Morgan, 9 August 1777, AGI, Santo Domingo, leg. 2596; and B. Gálvez to J. Gálvez, BN, manuscripts, Louisiana Española, sig. 19247, nos. 19–26. Another copy of the letter dated 9 August 1777 is in numbers 23–24, BN, manuscripts, Louisiana Española, sig. 19247.
46. Woodward, "Gálvez," xxiii; Montero de Pedro, *Españoles*, 41.
47. Letter to the Governor of Louisiana, 13 October 1777, AGI, Santo Domingo, leg. 2596.
48. Letter to the Governor of Louisiana, San Lorenzo del Escorial, 19 August 1777, ibid.
49. Letter to B. Gálvez, 23 December 1777, ibid.
50. B. Gálvez to J. Gálvez, 23 December 1777, ibid.
51. Letter to B. Gálvez, 22 April 1778, ibid. The amount reimbursed was 643 *pesos,* seven and a half *reales.*
52. B. Gálvez, 6 May 1777 as quoted in James, "Spanish Influence," 198.
53. Testimonio de las diligencias praticadas en el superior Govierno de esta Isla sobre la apre-hención de un paquebot Español nombrado *San Pedro Thelmo . . . ,* 30 July 1777; and Navarro to J. Gálvez, 3 August 777, AGI, Santo Domingo, leg. 1598.
54. B. Gálvez to J. Gálvez, 30 December 1777, ibid.; and E. Arnot Robertson, *The Spanish Town Papers: Some Sidelights on the American War of Independence* (New York: The Macmillan Co., 1959), 10–11, 14, and 20.
55. Navarro to J. Gálvez, 6 and 7 November 1777 (two letters), AGI, Santo Domingo, leg. 1227; and James, "Spanish Influence," 198.

CHAPTER 6

1. Cummins, *Spanish Observers,* 73.
2. Ibid. Gálvez was constructing cannon batteries and requested two cannons of twenty-four caliber and two cannons of twelve caliber.
3. Puente to J. Gálvez, 20 December 1777, folio 2; and 22 December 1777, folio 1, both in AHN, Estado, leg. 3884, exp. 1.
4. Bonet to Marqués González de Castejón, 28 December 1777, ibid., folio 3.
5. Declaración de Joseph Bermúdez, 22 December 1777, ibid, exp. 1; and Howard F. Cline, *Florida Indians I: Notes on Colonial Indians and Communities in Florida, 1700–1821* (New York and London: Garland Publishing, Inc., 1974), 129–32.
6. El comandante de departamiento to Bonet, 26 December 1777, AHN, Estado, leg. 3884 exp. 1, folio 4, exp. 1. The English spelling of Tunapé is Tonaby.
7. Navarro to J. Gálvez, 15 January 1778, AGI, Santo Domingo, legajo 2596; and Montero de Pedro, *Españoles,* 41.
8. B. Gálvez to J. Gálvez, 11 March 1778, AGI, Santo Domingo, leg. 2596; and Montero de Pedro, *Españoles,* 41.
9. B. Gálvez to Chester, 20 February 1778 (two letters), AGI, Santo Domingo, leg. 2596.
10. B. Gálvez to Navarro, 16 May 1778, ibid., leg. 1598.
11. Montero de Pedro, *Españoles,* 41; Gold, "Gálvez and Spanish Espionage," 98; and John Caughey, "The Panis Mission to Pensacola, 1778," *Hispanic American Historical Review* 10, no. 4 (1930): 480–89.
12. Navarro to ?, 30 April 1778, AGI, Santo Domingo, leg. 1598, no. 35.

13. Jurisdicción de Natchez, 21 February 1778, ibid., leg. 2596.

14. B. Gálvez to Willing, 24 and 26 March 1778 (two letters), ibid.; and Caughey, "The Panis Mission," 482.

15. B. Gálvez to Willing, 26 March 1778, New Orleans, AGI, Santo Domingo, leg. 2596, no. 264. Willing's activities were even criticized by his own people. For example, George Rogers Clark wrote to Fernando de Leyba in St. Louis about Willing's "bad conduct . . . when plunder is the prevailing Passion. . . ." Clark to Leyba, Kaskaskias, 6 November 1778, in Lawrence Kinnaird, "Clark-Leyba Papers," *The American Historical Review* 41, no. 1 (October 1935): 100–101.

16. B. Gálvez to Willing, 24 and 26 March 1778 (two letters); and Willing to B. Gálvez, 18, 24, 31 March and 1, 5 April 1778 (five letters); and B. Gálvez to Willing, 19, 24, 27 March and 6 April 1778 (four letters), all in AGI, Santo Domingo, leg. 2596.

17. Willing to B. Gálvez, 9 and 13 April 1778 (two letters), ibid.; and Stephen Watts to B. Gálvez, 31 May 1778, AGI, Cuba, leg. 1.

18. B. Gálvez to J. Gálvez, 11 March 1778; Harry Alexander to B. Gálvez, 15 March 1778, AGI, Santo Domingo, leg. 2596 no. 217; and B. Gálvez to Grand-Pré, 13 March 1778, AGI, Cuba, leg. 1.

19. Alexander to B. Gálvez, 15 March 1778, no. 217; and Jurisdicción de Nátchez, 21 February 1778, both in AGI, Santo Domingo, leg. 2596. Willing's ship is named in the "Letterbook of Brigadier General Edward Hand," 13 April–25 August 1778, vol. 1, no. 156, Record Group 93, National Archives of the United States of America, Washington, D.C.

20. Henry Stuart to B. Gálvez, 8 March 1778; and Willing to B. Gálvez, 13 April 1778, AGI, Santo Domingo, leg. 2596. Willing did capture a William Eason who was one of Stuart's assistants.

21. British subjects to B. Gálvez, 17 May 1778, ibid.

22. Yela Utrilla, *España ante la independencia,* 415; and B. Gálvez to Navarro, 16 May 1778, ibid., leg. 1598.

23. Yela Utrilla, *España ante la independencia,* 415; and B. Gálvez to J. Gálvez, 11 March 1778, ibid, leg. 2596.

24. Yela Utrilla, *España ante la independencia,* ibid.

25. Bando, Bernardo de Gálvez, 3 May 1778, AGI, Santo Domingo, leg. 2596.

26. B. Gálvez to J. Gálvez, 11 March 1778; and 12 April 1778 (two letters), both in ibid.

27. Letter to the Governor of Louisiana, 28 May 1778, ibid.

28. B. Gálvez to J. Gálvez, 11 and 24 March 1778 (two letters); Morris and Smith to B. Gálvez, 21 November 1777, ibid.; and Oliver Pollock to B. Gálvez, 13 May 1778, AGI, Cuba, leg. 1, (a copy is in AGI, Santo Domingo, leg. 1598).

29. B. Gálvez to Navarro, New Orleans, 16 May 1778, AGI, Santo Domingo, leg. 1598.

30. Ibid.; and B. Gálvez to J. Gálvez, New Orleans, 28 July 1778, AGI, Santo Domingo, leg. 2596. For Willing's activities see J. Barton Starr, "'Left as a Gewgaw,' The Impact of the American Revolution on British West Florida," in Samuel Proctor, ed., *Eighteenth Century Florida: The Impact of the American Revolution in British West Florida* (Gainesville: University Press of Florida, 1976), 14–27. For Willing's negative impact see 17–18.

31. Josef Petely to B. Gálvez, 19 May 1778; B. Gálvez to Carlos de Grand-Pré, 19 May 1778 and 19 June 1778, AGI, Cuba, leg. 1; B. Gálvez to Navarro, 13 June and 10 July 1778, AGI, Santo Domingo, leg. 1578; and Yela Utrilla, *España ante la independencia,* 434.

32. Din, "DuBreüil," 9 and 14.

33. Francisco Cruzat to B. Gálvez, 9 March 1778; Grand-Pré to B. Gálvez, 1, 4, and 13 March 1778 (three letters); B. Gálvez to Juan de Villebeuvre, 20 March 1778, AGI, Cuba, leg. 1. On 20 March, Navarro informed Gálvez that King Carlos III had elevated Louisiana to province status. See Navarro to B. Gálvez, 24 March 1778, AGI, Cuba, leg.

34. B. Gálvez to Navarro, 13 June 1778, AGI, Santo Domingo, leg. 1598; B. Gálvez to Grand-Pré, 19 June 1778 and 14 July 1778, AGI, Cuba, leg. 1.

35. Beerman, "Introduction," xiv; and Woodward, "Gálvez," xxiv.

242 NOTES TO PAGES 107-11

36. Morris and Smith to B. Gálvez, 21 November 1777, AGI, Santo Domingo, leg. 2596.
37. McDermott, "Leyba and the Defense," 329–34.
38. Receipt signed by James Willing, Oliver Pollock, and Bernardo de Gálvez, 2 May 1778, (copy translated into Spanish), AGI, Santo Domingo, leg. 2596; Leyba to B. Gálvez, 6 August 1778, AGI, Cuba, leg. 1; James, "Spanish Influence," 199; and McDermott, "Leyba and the Defense," 329.
39. Morris and Smith to B. Gálvez, 21 November 1777, AGI, Santo Domingo, leg. 2596.
40. Oliver Pollock to Spanish Officials, New Orleans, 13 May 1778, AGI, Cuba, leg. 1, (a copy is in Santo Domingo, leg. 1598).
41. Navarro to Pollock, 21 June 1778, ibid. (a copy is in AGI, Santo Domingo, leg. 1598).
42. Navarro to B. Gálvez, 17 June 1778, ibid.; and Cummins, *Spanish Observers,* 95.
43. For the amount of the debt, see James, "Oliver Pollock: Financer," 74–75; and Bond, "Oliver Pollock: An Unknown Patriot," 137.
44. McDermott, "Leyba and the Defense," 330–31; James, "Spanish Influence," 207; and James, "Oliver Pollock," 75.
45. Receipt signed by Willing, Pollock, and B. Gálvez, 2 May 1778; and B. Gálvez to J. Gálvez, 9 June 1778, AGI, Santo Domingo, leg. 2596, no. 169; and Yela Utrilla, *España ante la independencia,* 416.
46. The documents are not conclusive on whether or not the *Rebecca* and the *Morris* are the same. Nor are they clear on whether the ship was a corvette or frigate. Bond, "Oliver Pollock: An Unknown Patriot," 137; and Yela Utrilla, *España ante la independencia,* 417.
47. Pollock to B. Gálvez, 16, 17, and 18 June 1778 (three letters), AGI, Santo Domingo, leg. 2596.
48. Receipt signed by Willing, Pollock, and B. Gálvez, 2 May 1778; Pollock to B. Gálvez, 16 June 1778; letter dated 24 October 1778, ibid.; James, "Oliver Pollock: Financer," 72; and Yela Utrilla, *España ante la independencia,* 417.
49. B. Gálvez to Robert George, 18 August 1778; George and Richard Harrison to B. Gálvez, 18 August 1778, both in AGI, Santo Domingo, leg. 2596; and Yela Utrilla, *España ante la independencia,* 417.
50. Juan de la Villebeuvre to B. Gálvez, 6 July 1778, AGI, Santo Domingo, leg. 1598.
51. Grand-Pré to B. Gálvez, 6 July 1778, ibid.
52. B. Gálvez to Grand-Pré, 27 September 1778; and Navarro to B. Gálvez, 19 August 1778, AGI, Cuba, leg. 1, V, folio 569-803V.
53. James, "Spanish Influence," 208; and Leyba to B. Gálvez, 5 February 1779 in McDermott, "Leyba and the Defense," 335–36.
54. Henry Hamilton, as quoted in James, "Spanish Influence," 208.
55. Henry Hamilton, as quoted in McDermott, "Leyba and the Defense," 334–35.
56. Navarro to the Intendente de Ejército, Havana, 13 May 1778, AGI, Santo Domingo, leg. 2596.
57. Din, "DuBreüil," 14.
58. B. Gálvez to Navarro, New Orleans, 10 July 1778, ibid., leg. 1598.
59. B. Gálvez to J. Gálvez, New Orleans, 2 September 1778, ibid., leg. 2596, no. 199.
60. Letter dated 24 October 1778, AGI, Santo Domingo, leg. 2596; and Yela Utrilla, *España ante la independencia,* 417.
61. B. Gálvez to J. Gálvez, 28 July 1778, ibid.
62. B. Gálvez to J. Gálvez, 24 October 1778, no. 201; Patrick Henry to the Governor of Louisiana, 14 January 1778; and B. Gálvez to Henry, 19 October 1778, all in AGI, Santo Domingo, leg. 2596.
63. Relación de las cantidades . . . en las comisiones secretas del Real Servicio . . . , 24 October 1778, ibid.
64. B. Gálvez to J. Gálvez, 28 July 1778, ibid.
65. Navarro to B. Gálvez, 20 June 1778, folio 239–363 III; and 5 October 1778, folio 569–803 V, both in AGI, Cuba, leg. 1; and Navarro to J. Gálvez, 27 September 1778, AGI, Santo Domingo, leg. 1598. Navarro's letters of 27 September and 5 October show a little frustration on his behalf. Apparently, the Cuban captain-general was having trouble getting Bernardo de Gálvez to pay Eduardo on time.

66. Relación de las cantidades, 24 October 1778, leg. 2596; and B. Gálvez to J. Gálvez, 25 September 1778, no. 251, leg. 1598, both in AGI, Santo Domingo.

67. Miguel Eduardo to J. Gálvez, 13 April 1779; B. Gálvez to J. Gálvez, 25 February 1779, no. 251, AGI, Santo Domingo, leg. 1598.

68. Navarro to B. Gálvez, 30 March 1779, AGI, Cuba, leg. 1, folio 804–1000 VI; and Navarro to J. Gálvez, 14 April 1779, AGI, Santo Domingo, leg. 1598, no. 485.

69. Relación de las cantidades, 24 October 1778, AGI, Santo Domingo, leg. 2596.

70. B. Gálvez to Grand-Pré, 27 September 1778, AGI, Cuba, leg. 1, folio 569–803 V.

71. Navarro to J. Gálvez, 13 November 1778, leg. 1598; and Raymundo DuBreüil to B. Gálvez, 31 December 1778, leg. 2596, both in AGI, Santo Domingo.

72. B. Gálvez to J. Gálvez, 25 February 1779, AGI, Santo Domingo, leg. 2596. In reference to Gálvez's exaggeration see, Din, "DuBreüil," 15.

73. Navarro to B. Gálvez, 19 April 1779, AGI, Cuba, leg. 1, folio 1001–1132 VII; and Puente to Navarro, 29 March 1779, AGI, Santo Domingo, leg. 1598. Navarro added the rider that he did not know how accurate the news was, but he sent it along for Bernardo's informa- tion, nonetheless.

CHAPTER 7

1. McDermott, "Leyba and the Defense of St. Louis," 329; Fernando de Leyba to B. Gálvez, St. Louis, 11 July 1778, Missouri Historical Society (MHS), Papers From Spain, no. 63, St. Louis.

2. See Morris, The Peacemakers, 323.

3. B. Gálvez to Leyba, New Orleans, 13 January 1779, MHS, Papers from Spain, no. 10, (orig- inals in Papeles procedentes de la Isla de Cuba, AGI).

4. Allen Johnson and Dumas Malone, eds., Dictionary of American Biography, vol. 4 (New York: Charles Scribner's Sons, 1930), 127.

5. Jack M. Sosin, The Revolutionary Frontier, 1763–1783 (Albuquerque: University of New Mexico Press, 1967), 118.

6. Fernando de Leyba to George Rogers Clark, St. Louis, 8 July 1778, AGI, Cuba, leg. 1.

7. James, "Oliver Pollock: Financer," 73–74.

8. Clark to Leyba, 13 July 1778, AGI, Cuba, leg. 1; and Inventory, 2 May 1778, AGI, Santo Domingo, leg. 2596. The correspondence between Clark and Leyba reveals that Leyba's French was as bad as Clark's Spanish.

9. Carlos M. Fernández-Shaw, Presencia española en los Estados Unidos (Madrid: Ediciones Cultura Hispánica, 1987), 28, 74 and 373. The unconsummated love story of George Rogers Clark and Doña Theresa de Leyba is reputedly the basis for Henry Wadsworth Longfellow's poem, Evangeline, A Tale of Acadie.

10. Leyba to B. Gálvez, St. Louis, 16 November 1778; and Clark to Leyba, 26 October and 6 November 1778, all in AGI, Cuba, leg. 1.

11. McDermott, "Leyba and the Defense," 330.

12. Margin note dated 13 January 1779 in Leyba to B. Gálvez, St. Louis, 16 November 1778; and Patrick Henry to Leyba, 12 and 15 December 1778, all in AGI, Cuba, leg. 1.

13. McDermott, "Leyba and the Defense," 330.

14. Sosin, Revolutionary Frontier, 117.

15. B. Gálvez to Patrick Henry, New Orleans, 19 October 1778, AGI, Santo Domingo, leg. 2596.

16. McDermott, "Leyba and the Defense," 331.

17. Leyba to B. Gálvez, St. Louis, 18 October 1779 in Lawrence Kinnaird, ed., "Clark-Leyba Papers," The American Historical Review 41, no. 1 (October 1935): 11–12. Also see 93. Kinnaird presented some, but not all, of the papers pertinent to Clark and Leyba that he found in AGI.

18. Quoted in Abraham P. Nasatir, Borderland in Retreat: From Spanish Louisiana to the Far Southwest (Albuquerque: University of New Mexico Press, 1976), 25–26.

19. Sosin, Revolutionary Frontier, 118.

20. Ibid.
21. McDermott, "Leyba and the Defense," 334–35.
22. Ibid., 335–36, 339.
23. Ibid., 335; and Nasatir, *Borderland in Retreat,* 24.
24. Kinnaird, "Clark-Leyba Papers," 104, note 39.
25. Clark to Leyba, Kaskaskia, 25 January 1779, AGI, Cuba, leg. 1. Kinnaird dates this letter 23 January 1779 in "Clark-Leyba Papers," 104–5.
26. Sosin, *Revolutionary Frontier,* 119; McDermott, "Leyba and the Defense," 336; Clark to Leyba, 1 March 1779, ibid.
27. Clark to Leyba, St. Vincennes, 1 March 1779, AGI, Cuba, leg. 1.
28. Morris, *The Peacemakers,* 15; and Sosin, *Revolutionary Frontier,* 121.
29. George Washington [draft of a letter] to the Committee of Conference, Philadelphia, 13 January 1779, in John C. Fitzpatrick, ed., *Writings of Washington From the Original Manuscript Sources, 1745–1799,* vol. 14, 4 and 5. The draft is in Alexander Hamilton's hand.
30. Washington to John Augustine Washington, 12 May 1779, *Writings of Washington,* vol. 15, 61.
31. Sosin, *Revolutionary Frontier,* 121–23.
32. Letter to the Governor of Havana, Aranjuez, 20 April 1778, AGI, Santo Domingo, leg. 2082.
33. For example, see Floridablanca to Aranda, El Pardo, 13 January 1778; and Aranda to Floridablanca, Paris, 31 January 1778, no. 1222, both in AHN, Estado 3884, expediente 7.
34. Troy S. Floyd, *The Anglo-Spanish Struggle for Mosquitia* (Albuquerque: University of New Mexico Press, 1967), 128.
35. Morales Padrón, "Editor's Introduction," 240–41; and Matías de Gálvez to J. Gálvez, 6 January 1779, AGI, Guatemala, leg. 869. Mayorga succeeded despite the rumors of his lack of favor with the court, which may explain why many officials in his government in New Spain tended to work at cross-purposes with him. Guatemala is consistently spelled "Goatemala" in the 18th-century Spanish documents.
36. Jones, "Matías de Gálvez," in which the author cites M. Gálvez to J. Gálvez, Omoa, 1 July 1778; and Martín de Mayorga to J. Gálvez, 6 August 1778, both in AGI, Guatemala, leg. 451. Old Guatemala was destroyed by an earthquake.
37. Floyd, *Anglo-Spanish Struggle,* 120–21.
38. M. Gálvez to J. Gálvez, 6 January 1779, AGI, Guatemala, leg. 869.
39. Floyd, *Anglo-Spanish Struggle,* 129.
40. Ibid.
41. M. Gálvez to J. Gálvez, 6 January 1779, AGI, Guatemala, leg. 869.
42. Ibid.
43. Margin note to ibid.; J. Gálvez to M. Gálvez, 21 May 1779, ibid.; and Floyd, "Bourbon Palliatives and the Central American Mining Industry, 1765–1800," 116.
44. J. Gálvez to M. Gálvez, 21 May 1779, AGI, Guatemala, leg. 869.
45. Cummins, *Spanish Observers,* 60–61.
46. Juan Joseph de la Puente, "Manifiesto de descubrimiento," 4 May 1778, AGI, Santo Domingo, leg. 1578. This beautifully handwritten document, which was done in Havana, unabashedly argues that Spain should have possession of all of Florida, but emphasizes East Florida.
47. J. Leitch Wright, Jr., *Florida in the American Revolution* (Gainesville: University Press of Florida, 1975), 67.
48. Ramiro Guerra y Sánchez et al, *La historia de la nación cubana,* vol . 2 (Havana: Editorial Historia de la Nación Cubana, S.A., 1952), 129; and Allan F. Kuethe and G. Douglas Inglis, "Absolutism and Enlightened Reform: Charles III, The Establishment of the Alcabala, and Commercial Reorganization in Cuba," in *Past & Present, A Journal of Historical Studies,* no. 109 (November 1985): 120.
49. Navarro to B. Gálvez, 28 July 1779, AGI, Cuba, leg. 1, folio 1001–1132.
50. The original banners and records of these regiments are at the Museo del Ejército in Madrid, Spain. Copies of the banners and a synopsis of the regimental histories were sent

to the Palace of the Governors of the Museum of New Mexico in Santa Fe as Spain's bicentennial gifts to the State of New Mexico in 1976. Other states that were once part of the Spanish empire received the same gift. These reproduced flags, oil paint on silk, were the inspiration for this book.

51. Navarro to J. Gálvez, 8 March 1779; and "Regimiento de infantería de Navarra, estado de la fuerza . . . ," 1 March 1779, both in AGI, Santo Domingo, leg. 1229. The troop numbers are added incorrectly in the document and it is hard to decipher the total available troop strength, which ranges from 1,370 to 1,468. Internal evidence points to the higher number.

52. Relación de los pertrechos y municiones . . . , 14 February 1779; and Relación de la artillería . . . , 11 July 1779, both in ibid.

53. The gathering and compilation of all troops and equipment, being prepared for war under Havana's command, is a study waiting to be done.

54. Account of payment, 24 October 1778, AGI, Santo Domingo, AGI, Santo Domingo, leg. 2596.

55. B. Gálvez to Navarro, New Orleans, 16 May 1778, ibid.

56. Dull, *Diplomatic History,* 108–9.

57. Navarro to J. Gálvez, Havana, 14 February 1779, AGI, Santo Domingo, leg. 1598.

58. See, Fitzpatrick, *Writings of Washington,* vol. 13, pp. 10, 89, 117, 129, 169, and 236; vol. 14, 5, for samples of Washington's thought process concerning the eventuality of Spain entering the war. Washington's letters range from October 1778 to March 1779.

59. B. Gálvez to Navarro, New Orleans, 5 February 1779, AGI, Santo Domingo, leg. 1598.

60. Navarro to B. Gálvez, Havana, 19 April 1779, AGI, Cuba, folio 1001–1132 VII. Here, Navarro warns Gálvez of a British buildup in Florida in anticipation of war with Spain.

61. Bonet to B. Gálvez, 28 March and 7 April 1779, AGI, Santo Domingo, leg. 2081.

62. B. Gálvez to Bonet, New Orleans, 5 March 1779, ibid.

63. Bonet to B. Gálvez, Havana, 28 March and 16 April 1779; Bonet to J. Gálvez, 16 April 1779, leg. 2081, ibid.

64. Bonet to J. Gálvez, Havana, 16 April 1779, ibid.; and Navarro to J. Gálvez, Havana, 19 April 1779, AGI, Cuba, leg. 1, folio 1001–1132 VII.

65. J. Gálvez to Bonet, 25 June 1779, Aranjuez, AGI, Santo Domingo, leg. 2081.

66. Navarro to B. Gálvez, Havana, 28 July 1779, AGI, Cuba, leg. 1, folio 1001–1132 VII; and Bonet to J. Gálvez, Havana, 12 August 1779, AGI, Santo Domingo, leg. 2081.

67. Navarro to J. Gálvez, Havana, 11 November 1779; William Campbell to Captain Anthony Forstel, 9 September 1779; Charles Stewart to Forstel, 1 October 1779; letter of the captain of the artillery, William McJohnston, 2 October 1779, all in ibid., Santo Domingo, leg. 2082.

68. B. Gálvez to Bonet, New Orleans, 17 August 1779, ibid., leg. 2081.

CHAPTER 8

1. For example, see Morris, *The Peacemakers,* 14–17. Morris's book is a more recent, but mild version that describes Floridablanca's diplomatic ability as an attempt to "blackmail" France and England. See also the earlier work, Samuel Flagg Bemis, *Diplomacy of the American Revolution* (Bloomington: Indiana University Press, 1957), 110–12. Din, "DuBreüil," misprints the pages as 411–12.

2. *The Pennsylvania Packet,* 9 February 1779, reprinted in Smith, *Letters of Delegates,* vol. 11, 304–5.

3. Gouverneur Morris to *The Pennsylvania Packet,* 27 February 1779, in Smith, *Letters of Delegates,* vol. 12, 114–20.

4. Samuel Adams to Caleb Davis, 5 December 1778, 287; and Henry Laurens to Patrick Henry, 6 December 1778, 291, ibid.

5. Rhode Island Delegates to William Greene, 8 December 1778, 304–5, ibid.

6. Dull, *Diplomatic History,* 108.

7. Conrad Alexandre Gerard to the President of Congress, 9 February 1779, *Diplomatic Correspondence,* vol. 3, 39–40; and William Henry Drayton's Notes to the Proceedings of the Committee of the Whole of Congress, 9 February 1779, in Smith, *Letters of Delegates,* vol. 12, 71–72; and footnote 1, 38.
8. Cummins, *Spanish Observers,* 151.
9. Samuel Adams to Caleb Davis, 5 December 1778, in Smith, *Letters of Delegates,* vol. 11, 287–88.
10. Samuel Adams to Samuel Cooper, 21 February 1779, in ibid., vol. 12, 101–3. Underline is in the original.
11. William Whipple to Josiah Bartlett, 7 February 1779, ibid., vol. 12, 28–29; Gerard to Congress in Drayton's Notes, 9 February 1779, ibid., vol. 12, 71–72; John Armstrong to Horatio Gates, 3 April 1779, ibid., vol. 12, 179–80; and Gouverneur Morris to *The Pennsylvania Packet,* 27 February 1779, ibid., vol. 13, 114–20.
12. Drayton to King George III, 13 February 1779, ibid., vol. 12, 61–69. Emphasis is in the original.
13. William Whipple to Josiah Bartlett, 7 February 1779, ibid., 29; 28 February 1779, ibid., 122; John Armstrong to Horatio Gates, 3 April 1779, ibid., 279–80; Richard Henry Lee to Thomas Jefferson, 15 March 1779, ibid., 197; and William Whipple to Joseph Whipple, 16 April 1779, ibid., 342–43.
14. Ultimatum proposed by the court of Madrid to the courts of France and England, dated 3 April 1779, 466, 481–82; and extract of an answer of the court of London to the proposition contained in the ultimatum of Spain, dated 4 May 1779, *Diplomatic Correspondence,* vol. 3, 483. The Spanish ultimatum is in English translation. A version in Spanish may be found in El Marqués de Almodóvar to Floridablanca, London, 16 April 1779, AGS, leg. 7021, Secretaría de Estado; Inglaterra (años 1750–1820), atado 2, no. 13. The nine-page document is included with Almodóvar's acknowledgement thirteen days from the date of the ultimatum. Britain's reply was sent through the Spanish ambassador. See Almodóvar to Floridablanca and Vergennes, as cited above, AGS.
15. Almodóvar to Floridablanca, London, 17 April 1779, ibid., no. 14.
16. Richard Henry Lee to John Page, 29 March 1779, *Diplomatic Correspondence,* vol. 12, 261–62; and John Fell's Diary of the Commercial Committee of Congress, 17 March 1779, *Diplomatic Correspondence,* vol. 12, 204–5.
17. William M. Dabney and Marion Dargan, *William Henry Drayton and the American Revolution* (Albuquerque: University of New Mexico Press, 1962), 164–65.
18. William Paca and William Henry Drayton to Congress, 30 April 1779, *Letters of Delegates,* vol. 12, 410–11; and William Carmichael to Congress, 3 May 1779, *Letters of Delegates,* vol. 12, 417–21. Subsequent historians have taken both sides of the debate, even to the point of agreeing to the counter charges of complicity with the British. Could it be that the whole delegation, each member in his individual way, was passing information to the enemy? See *Letters of Delegates,* vol. 12, 11 and 12.
19. Dabney and Dargan, *Drayton,* 166; and Morris, *The Peacemakers,* 11.
20. As quoted in Morris, *The Peacemakers,* 12.
21. John Fell's Diary, 8 May 1779, Letters of Delegates vol. 12, 438; and 19 May 1779, *Letters of Delegates,* vol. 12, 448.
22. Jesse Root to Jonathan Trumball, Sr., 23 August 1779, ibid., vol. 13, 400; Thomas Burke's Draft Report for the U.S. Minister to the Court of Spain, August 1779, ibid., vol. 13, 328; James Lovell to Abigail Adams, 9 August 1779, ibid., vol. 13, 340.
23. Morris, *The Peacemakers,* 12 and 13.
24. Cummins, *Spanish Observers,* 119, 131 and 151; and Morris, *The Peacemakers,* 13.
25. Washington to Jay, 16 August 1779, West Point, *Writings of Washington,* vol. 16, 115.
26. Dull, *Diplomatic History,* 108, 121–22. Dull writes that Britain's problem was its inability to keep Spain neutral because of Gibraltar, the possession of which was "a dubious blessing."
27. Carlos Álvarez García et al, eds., *Documentos relativos a la independencia de Norteamérica* . . . in *Archivo General de Simancas* (Madrid: Ministerio de Asuntos Exteriores, 1976), xii.

28. Cummins, *Spanish Observers*, 113.
29. "Proceedings of Congress . . . , Report of the Committee Assigned to Deal With Letters of Lee and Gerard," 23 February 1779, Francis Wharton, ed., *The Revolutionary Diplomatic Correspondence of the United States* (Washington, D.C.: United States Government Printing Office, 1889), vol. 3, 58–61.
30. Benjamin Franklin to Patrick Henry, Paris, 26 February 1779, ibid., 67–68; and B. Franklin to the Committee of Foreign Affairs, Paris, 26 May 1779, ibid., 193.
31. John Adams to the President of Congress, 3 August 1779, ibid., 282–83. Adams's opinion and the preponderance of evidence runs contrary to historian Barbara W. Tuchman, who argues that the Dutch had a significant, even key, role in the outcome of the war. She downplays, even belittles, Spain. See Tuchman, *The First Salute*.
32. Washington to Navarro, Philadelphia, 4 March 1779, AGI, Santo Domingo, leg. 1233.
33. Navarro to J. Gálvez, Havana, 25 May 1779, ibid. This is a cover letter for a packet in which Navarro included two transcribed letters written by Miralles and forwarded for José de Gálvez's information.
34. Dull, *Diplomatic History*, 107–8.
35. Dull, *The French Navy*, 90–91; and Fernández y Fernández, *Spain's Contribution*, 9.
36. Fernández y Fernández, *Spain's Contribution*, 9.
37. Dull, *Diplomatic History*, 109.
38. Morris, *The Peacemakers*, 13–15. Morris uses the term "blackmail" on two different occasions, in describing Spain's diplomatic position. Also, see Dupuy and Dupuy, *Encyclopedia of Military History*, 716, in which Floridablanca is called "wily," in a negative sense, because of his success.
39. Dull, *Diplomatic History*, 109.
40. Ibid., 110.
41. Morales Padrón, "Editor's Introduction," 4 and 5.
42. J. Gálvez to Roberto Ribas Betancourt, 18 May 1779; and Betancourt to J. Gálvez, 25 May 1779, both in AGI, Indiferente General, leg. 1582.
43. D. Diego Joseph Navarro, "Real Orden [Royal Order]," 22 July 1779, AGI, Santo Domingo, leg. 1229.
44. Morales Padrón, "Editor's Introduction," 4. Navarro wanted Miralles to urge Congress to conquer San Agustín [St. Augustine] in East Florida "as soon as possible."
45. Navarro to the Governor of Charlestown, Havana, 6 August 1779; and Navarro to J. Gálvez, Havana, 8 August 1779, both in AGI, Santo Domingo, leg. 2082.
46. Cummins, *Spanish Observers*, 134 and 140.
47. Miralles to Congress, 24 November 1779, *Diplomatic Correspondence*, vol. 3, 412–14. Miralles, unlike Navarro, brought up the strategy of using East Florida as a diversion for Spanish activity in West Florida.
48. Navarro to J. Gálvez, Havana, 28 July 1779, AGI, Santo Domingo, leg. 1229.
49. Fernández y Fernández, *Spain's Contribution*, 7; and "La declaración de guerra," 12 August 1779, as printed and published in Mexico City, in David Marley, ed., *Documentos novo-hispanos relativos a la guerra entre España e Inglaterra, 1779–1784* (México, D.F: Ralston-Bain, 1985), 3 and 4. There is a question about the coincidence of the news reaching New Orleans on the same date when war was declared in Europe; this means that Bernardo de Gálvez received word before his superior, Navarro. This is entirely possible because José de Gálvez wrote his nephew directly on 18 May 1779, and sent letters out to most of the other officials on 20 May. See J. Gálvez to the Governor of Louisiana, 18 May 1779, AGI, Cuba, leg. 569; and see 11 herein.
50. Bonet to B. Gálvez, Havana, 7 April 1779; J. Gálvez to Bonet, Aranjuez, 25 June 1779; Bonet to J. Gálvez, Havana, 12 August 1779; B. Gálvez to Bonet, New Orleans, 17 August 1779, all in AGI, Santo Domingo, leg. 2081.
51. "La declaración de guerra," 12 August 1779, 3 and 4.
52. Quoted in Morris, *The Peacemakers*, 14.

53. Samuel Adams to Samuel Cooper, 21 February 1779, Smith, *Letters of Delegates*, vol. 12, 102–3. Adams notes that if Britain does not acknowledge U.S. independence, Spain will go to war, in which case the British will need to withdraw their troops from the colonies to face graver threats.

54. For a concise description of the debates see Morris, *The Peacemakers*, 12–13. For a good sampling of the details see Smith, *Letters of Delegates*, vol. 12, passim. Especially see William Paca and William Henry Drayton to Congress, 30 April 1779, *Letters of Delegates*, vol. 12, 410–11 in which they claimed that Gerard shared a letter sent to him from Vergennes, which stated that neither Paris nor Madrid had any trust in Arthur Lee. The two congressmen recommended Lee's recall. Statement of William Carmichael to Congress, 3 May 1779, *Letters of Delegates*, vol. 12, 417–21.

55. Arthur Lee, Memorial to the court of Spain, Paris, 6 June 1779, *Diplomatic Correspondence*, vol. 3, 209. In Spain there is a document written in English that is titled "The Way to Bring England to Her Sense," n.d. and no name, AGS, Estado, leg. 8162, seg. 5. This document appears to be one of Lee's missives, but needs to be compared.

56. Ibid.

57. Floridablanca to Arthur Lee, Madrid, 6 August 1779, *Diplomatic Correspondence*, vol. 3, 290. Lee's two letters are dated 7 and 25 June 1779 in Floridablanca's reply. The assumption here is that June 7 is a mistake for June 6. The second letter has not been found yet. Copies of the June 6 Lee "memorial" and Floridablanca's reply made it into the U.S. National Archives and eventually both were published. This leads one to assume that the correspondence was made available to the Continental Congress. How, and why, is a subject for further research.

58. John Fell's Diary, 8 and 10 May 1779, ibid, 438 and 448. Gerard, according to Fell, actually suggested that the Congress send a minister plenipotentiary to Spain, which implies full diplomatic recognition. Was this just Gerard's idea or did it originate from the Spanish court? The nuances of official Spanish recognition are a subject in need of further research. Note, too, that Benjamin Franklin carried papers from Congress, naming him minister plenipotentiary to Spain when he first traveled to Paris in 1777. He did not press the matter beyond initial formalities. See Official Certificate of Appointment of Benjamin Franklin, Signed by John Hancock, 2 January 1777, folio 21; and Franklin to the conde de Aranda, 7 April 1777, folio 23, both in AHN, Estado, leg. 3884, exp. 3.

59. Dull, *A Diplomatic History*, 116; Cummins, *Spanish Observers*, 149, 151–53; and Morris, *The Peacemakers*, 20.

60. Morris, *The Peacemakers*, 12 and 13. Smith, *Diplomatic Correspondence*, vol. 3, passim, provides an excellent first-hand account of how the Lee-Deane feud evolved into and delayed the election of a commissioner or minister to Spain.

61. George Washington to Lord Stirling, West Point, 28 and 29 August 1779; and G. Washington to the President of Congress, West Point, 29 August 1779, both in Fitzpatrick, *Writings of Washington*, vol. 16, 198–200. Washington described the Spanish entry into the war as "most interesting and agreeable."

CHAPTER 9

1. Floyd, "Bourbon Palliatives," 108; and Kuethe and Inglis, "Absolutism and Enlightened Reform," 118 and 142.

2. Francisco Cruzat to Estevan Miró, 6 August 1781, leg. 2084 and 2548 (two copies of the same document), both in AGI, Santo Domingo; and Clarence W. Alvord, "The Conquest of St. Joseph, Michigan by the Spaniards in 1781," *Michigan History Magazine* 14 (1930): 398–414.

3. Willard Sterne Randall, *Benedict Arnold: Patriot and Traitor* (New York: William Morrow & Co., Inc., 1990), 338 and 421. Arnold proposed that a joint French-American naval force invade the English possessions in the Caribbean. He also proposed attacks on Mobile and Pensacola.

4. Kuethe and Inglis, "Absolutism and Enlightened Reform," 118–19.
5. Most U. S. historians have not given Spain credit for its planning. Recent exceptions are Light Townsend Cummins, *loc. cit.;* Jonathan Dull, *loc. cit.;* Francisco Morales Padrón, *loc. cit.;* Eric Beerman, *España y la independencia de Estados Unidos* (Madrid: Editorial MAPFRE, S.A., 1992); and among many other historians in Spain. The most notable of these last is the very first publication, Yela Utrilla, *España ante la independencia.*
6. Jesse Root to Jeremiah Wadsworth, 9 September 1779, 289–90; Nathaniel Peabody to Meshech Weare, 10 August 1779, 353–55; William Flemming to Thomas Jefferson, 10 August 1779, 344; John Armstrong, Sr. to Horatio Gates, 16 August 1779, 371–72, all in Smith, *Letters of Delegates,* vol. 13; Arthur Lee to Committee of Foreign Affairs, 10 August 1779, 292 and 24 August 1779, 307, in Wharton, *Diplomatic Correspondence,* vol. 3. Armstrong, Peabody, and Flemming all wrote of the invasion going to Ireland.
7. Dull, *The French Navy,* 136–40.
8. Ibid., 150–56.
9. Ibid., 157. Floridablanca wanted to reorganize and try again. Vergennes wanted to concentrate his forces in the Americas. The Dutch did not help at all in this episode. They refused even to convoy merchant ships carrying desperately needed Scandinavian and German wood and masts through the North Sea, destined for France. See Dull, *The French Navy,* 143–44.
10. Arthur Lee to Committee of Foreign Affairs, 10 August 1779, 292 and 24 August 1779, 307, both in Wharton, *Diplomatic Correspondence,* vol. 13. Dull also compiled the figures of ships from the French archives and notes that the rendezvous off of Cape Finisterre was a late strategy change. His figures for ships-of-the-line are twenty Spanish and thirty or thirty-one French. He also notes that Floridablanca agreed to send sixteen ships to be held in reserve, including eight cruising at the Azores to intercept British shipping. Dull, *The French Navy,* 140, 147–50, and 153–54.
11. Some histories of the siege of Gibraltar are Tom Henderson McGuffie, *The Siege of Gibraltar, 1779–1783* (London: B. T. Batsford Co., 1965); and Jack Russell, *Gibraltar Besieged, 1779–1783* (London: William Heinemann, Ltd., 1965). Neither of these books used Spanish sources. Beerman, *España y la independencia,* 261–65, is a history based on Spanish documents and contains a section on the siege of Gibraltar.
12. For contemporary British points of view, see John Drinkwater, *A History of the Siege of Gibraltar* (London: John Murray, 1905, originally in 1785); and John Spilsbury, *A Journal of the Siege of Gibraltar, 1779–1783,* B. T. H. Frere, ed. (Gibraltar: Gibraltar Garrison Library, 1908).
13. Gibraltar's name came from a Moorish leader whose name was Tariq, who occupied the site in 711 A.D. He built a castle at the base of the hill by 725 A.D. The site became known as Gibel-Tariq or Jeber Tariq, meaning the mountain of Tariq. Over the years, the name became corrupted to Gibraltar.
14. Russell, *Gibraltar Besieged,* 41.
15. Sir Charles Petrie, *King Charles III of Spain: An Enlightened Despot* (New York: The John Day Company, 1971), 186–87.
16. Ibid., 186
17. Ibid., 190. The Spanish lost six ships-of-the-line, two of which were destroyed.
18. Dull, *The French Navy,* 178; and J. Gálvez to Sr. Gobernador de la Havana, 27 January 1780, AGI, Cuba, leg. 1.
19. Petrie, *King Charles III,* 190. Petrie is a British historian. Dull, *The French Navy,* 180, notes that Montmorin felt that Lieutenant-General Córdova was senile. Córdova was Lángara's superior. [A note on the spelling of Córdova. I have chosen to use the "v" as it appears in the Spanish documents of the time. Other published sources have replaced the "v" with a "b".]
20. The Spanish naval minister, the marqués de Castejón, as quoted in Petrie, *King Charles III,* 195. Castejón was in Floridablanca's camp. Montmorin considered Castejón a

"cipher" who was kept in office by Floridablanca. See Dull, *The French Navy,* 180. A history of the opinionated Montmorin is a good subject for further study.

21. J. Gálvez to the Governor of Havana, 27 January 1780, AGI, Cuba, leg. 1. The exact quote reads, "dearly sell the enemy the victory," *vender cara a los enemigos una victoria.*

22. Governor of Havana to the King, Havana, 14 January 1780, AGI, Santo Domingo, leg. 2082.

23. Ibid.; and Beerman, "Introduction," xiii–xiv. Correspondence generally took a minimum of five weeks to travel from Havana to the Court. José de Gálvez and Carlos III would have received the report in mid-November.

24. Floyd, "Bourbon Palliatives," 116–17.

25. J. Gálvez to the Governor of Havana, 27 January 1780, AGI, Cuba, leg. 1.

26. Dull, *The French Navy,* 179.

27. Petrie, *King Charles III,* 191.

28. J. Gálvez to the Governor of Havana, 27 January 1780, AGI, Cuba, leg. 1.

29. Petrie, *King Charles III,* 195.

30. Ibid., 191.

31. Dull, *The French Navy,* 179.

32. Beerman, "Introduction," xiv. Mobile was defeated on 14 March 1780. See chapter XI, herein.

33. *La Gaceta de Madrid,* 23 June 1780, BN. The articles were published in a supplement for this date. There is an undated eleven-page report on Bernardo de Gálvez's successful campaign on the Mississippi River that was sent to the Crown. "Noticia individual del Éxito que han recivido las armas de nuestro Católico e monarca don Carlos III dirigidas por el Señor Brigadier de los Reales Exercitos Governador de la Provincia de la Louisiana . . . ," no date, BN, Manuscripts, Louisiana-Española, sig. 19248, no. 177–82.

34. Floyd, "Bourbon Palliatives," 116–17; and M. Gálvez to J. Gálvez, 12 January 1780; J. Gálvez to the President of Guatemala, 20 April 1780, AGI, Indiferente General, leg. 1582.

35. Petrie, *King Charles III,* 191–92.

36. Dull, *The French Navy,* 187.

37. Ibid., 188.

38. Ibid., 190–91.

39. The whole question of Spanish (and French) strategy, regarding Gibraltar, needs further study. In addition, we need to determine exactly what was Rodney's goal. Was he to lift the siege or merely supply the besieged garrison? If the former, he failed. If the latter, he partially succeeded. But in the larger picture, the cost of success was exceeded by eventual loss of the war.

40. Floridablanca, as quoted in Petrie, *King Charles III,* 192–93.

41. Dull, *The French Navy,* 207.

42. Petrie, *King Charles III,* 147; and Desmond Gregory, *Minorca, the Illusory Prize: A History of the British Occupations of Minorca Between 1708 and 1802* (New Jersey: Fairleigh Dickinson University Press, 1990), 187.

43. Dull, *The French Navy,* 232.

44. Ibid., 232–33. An interesting undated document written in French exists in the Archive of the Indies in which the "articles" that were agreed upon between Spain and France "for the service . . . at the Island of Minorca" are listed. The troops would be kept separate with their own officers and system of rewards. Pay was kept equal. The commander of the French troops would be second in command to the Spanish general and would "receive word separately and solely" from the Spanish general. The Spanish commander would determine the disposition of any captured prizes. Other details dealt with desertion, prisoner exchange, and daily reporting. This document suggests that the preparations for Minorca, between Spain and France, may not have been as secret as imagined. "Articles concertes pour le service de troupes . . . ," no date, AGI, Santo Domingo, leg. 2083a.

45. Dull, *The French Navy*, 232; Gregory, *Minorca, the Illusory Prize*, 188; and Arthur Foss, *Ibiza and Minorca* (London: Faber and Faber, 1975), 158–59.
46. Gregory, *Minorca, the Illusory Prize*, 183–84.
47. Ibid., 187; and Foss, *Ibiza and Minorca*, 159.
48. Gregory, *Minorca, the Illusory Prize*, 188.
49. Ibid., 187; and Dull, *The French Navy*, 235.
50. Gregory, *Minorca, the Illusory Prize*, 191.
51. Dull, *The French Navy*, 235; and Petrie, *King Charles III*, 198–99.
52. Gregory, *Minorca, the Illusory Prize*, 189; and Foss, *Ibiza and Minorca*, 160.
53. Gregory, *Minorca, the Illusory Prize*, 190.
54. Petrie, *King Charles III*, 194.
55. Ibid., 199–200.
56. Ibid., 201. For a detailed description of d'Arcon's floating batteries see W. Johnson, "The Siege of Gibraltar; Mostly Relating to the Shooting of Hot Shot and Setting Fire to A Besieging Fleet," *International Journal of Impact Engineering* 6, no. 3 (1987): 184–85.
57. Johnson, "The Siege of Gibraltar," 185–89.
58. John Drinkwater, as quoted in ibid., 189. Drinkwater claims "about 2,000 losses" while Dull, *The French Navy*, 308 cites a Frenchman named Bessiere who estimated the casualties at 1,500.
59. Johnson, "The Siege of Gibraltar," 202 and 207.
60. John Spilsbury, as quoted in ibid., 207.
61. Drinkwater, as quoted in Johnson, "Siege of Gibraltar," 202.
62. Ibid., 206.
63. Ibid., 203.
64. Ibid., 206.
65. Dull, *The French Navy*, 271.

CHAPTER 10
1. Any veteran who has been on reconnaissance in Vietnam will quickly understand the accomplishments of these early-day jungle fighters. One image that comes to mind is the march of the Spanish soldiers to get beyond the Falls of Iguazú, as depicted in the movie *"The Mission."* The movie gives a correct view of the kinds of hardship these men would endure, but it does not, nor could it, convey the additional problem of constantly being on the alert for fear of ambush.
2. J. Gálvez to Navarro, El Pardo, 11 February 1780; and J. Gálvez to M. Gálvez, 22 April 1780, both in AGI, Santo Domingo, leg. 2082; and Francisco Saavedra to J. Gálvez, Havana, 12 February 1781, AGI, Indiferente General, leg. 1578.
3. Letter to the Governor of Havana, El Pardo, 12 February 1781; also see letter to B. Gálvez, El Pardo, 12 February 1781, both in AGI, Santo Domingo, leg. 2083a.
4. Saavedra to J. Gálvez, Havana, 19 February 1781, AGI, Santo Domingo, leg. 1578. "Que tienen los ingleses en abrir por aquella parte comunicación de la mar del Norte a la del Sur, y sorverse [resolverse] por este medio el comercio de las dos Américas."
5. Saavedra to J. Gálvez, Havana, 19 January 1782, ibid.; M. Gálvez to J. Gálvez, Nueva Guatemala, 6 January 1779 and J. Gálvez to M. Gálvez, Aranjuez, 21 May 1779, AGI, Guatemala, leg. 869; Floyd, "Bourbon Palliatives," 106; Eric Beerman, *España y la Independencia*, 239; and Jones, "Matías de Gálvez," 5, citing Floyd, *The Anglo-Spanish Struggle*, 131, 139–40.
6. M. Gálvez to J. Gálvez, Guatemala, 6 October 1779, AGI, Santo Domingo, leg. 2082.
7. As quoted in Jones, "Matías de Gálvez," 3 and cited as M. Gálvez to Martín de Mayorga, Nueva Goatemala, 9 September 1778, Archivo General Centroamerica (AGCA), Guatemala City, leg. 299, exp. 6692, A2.5.
8. Beerman, *España y la Independencia*, 237–46 gives the most recent and clear overview of

the fighting in Central America. *La Gaceta de Madrid,* in various editions during this time, published fairly extensive and accurate reports of the fighting. For example, April 1880; February and June 1781; July 1782, *la Gaceta de Madrid,* Biblioteca Nacional, Madrid.

9. Floyd, *The Anglo-Spanish Struggle,* 138–39.
10. Beerman, *España y la Independencia,* 238–39.
11. M. Gálvez to Navarro, Valle de los Llanos de Gracias, 29 October 1779, AGI, Santo Domingo, leg. 2082.
12. Navarro to M. Gálvez, Havana, 29 December 1779; Navarro to J. Gálvez, Havana, 28 December 1779; and J. Gálvez to Navarro, Aranjuez, 20 April 1780, all in ibid.
13. Beerman, *España y la Independencia,* 240.
14. Ibid.; and M. Gálvez to J. Gálvez, San Pedro Sula, 12 January 1780; and letter to the president of Guatemala, 20 April 1780, both in AGI, Indiferente General, leg. 1582.
15. Navarro to J. Gálvez, Havana, 12 February 1780; J. Gálvez to Navarro, El Pardo, 11 February 1780; Urriza to J. Gálvez, 20 February 1680; Urriza to J. Gálvez, Havana, 4 January 1780; and J. Gálvez to Urriza, 28 April 1780, all in AGI, Santo Domingo, leg. 2082. Navarro's shipment was less than had been requested and, perhaps, explains the simultaneous shipment from Spain.
16. Beerman, *España y la Independencia,* 240–41.
17. Floyd, *The Anglo-Spanish Struggle,* 142–43.
18. Ibid., 145–47.
19. The full account of the attack and loss of the Castle of Immaculate Conception is in Juan de Ayssa, "Diario del Ataque y defensa del Castillo de la Inmaculada Concepción del Río de San Juan, Provincia de Nicaragua, su rendición, y demás que ocurrió a los defensores hasta su Capitulación," 29 April 1780, AGI, Santo Domingo, leg. 2083b. The "Diario" gives various and detailed accounts of the cannons. At one point, the besieged saw two batteries of five cannons each. They destroyed another battery of the same size. A couple of days later, the Spanish reported seeing two howitzers.
20. Ibid.
21. Ibid.
22. Antonio Ramón Bosque to Navarro, Havana, 14 June 1780; Navarro to Victorio de Navia, Havana, 30 May 1780; Navarro to Navia, Havana, 15 June 1780, all in AGI, Santo Domingo, leg. 2083a.
23. *Noticias recibidas de Jamayca el 13 de junio de este año,* Havana, 14 June 1780; and Bonet to Navarro, Havana, 30 May 1780, Havana, both in ibid.
24. Floyd, *The Anglo-Spanish Struggle,* 145–47.
25. Ibid., 149–50.
26. Floyd, *The Anglo-Spanish Struggle,* 150.
27. Dalling to Kemble, Kingston, 10 August 1780, as quoted in ibid., 151. Originals are in vol. 17 of the Collection of the New York Historical Society and are published as Stephen Kemble, *The Kemble Papers,* vols. I and II (New York: New York Historical Society, 1932).
28. *Extracto de las noticias adquiridas en Jamayca por D. Juan de Ayssa . . . ,* Havana, no date (circa 1 December 1780), AGI, Santo Domingo, leg. 2083b.
29. Letter to B. Gálvez; and to the president of Guatemala, El Pardo, 9 March 1781, AGI, Santo Domingo, leg. 2083b.
30. Josef de Nava to M. Gálvez, Fort San Carlos, 7 January 1781; M. Gálvez to Navarro, Nueva Guatemala, 19 January 1781; Navarro to J. Gálvez, Havana, 2 April 1781, all in ibid., leg. 2083b; M. Gálvez to Victorio de Navia, Nueva Guatemala, 10 March 1781; M. Gálvez to Navarro, Nueva Guatemala, 5 April 1781, all in ibid., leg. 2083a. The number of prisoners is the Spanish version. The British count is six prisoners. See Floyd, *The Anglo-Spanish Struggle,* 52.
31. M. Gálvez to Navarro, Nueva Guatemala, 5 April 1781; Cagigal to J. Gálvez, Havana, 30 June 1781, both in AGI, Santo Domingo, leg. 2083b.
32. Beerman, *España y la Independencia,* 243.
33. Letter to the Governor of Havana, Aranjuez, 1 June 1781, AGI, Santo Domingo, leg. 2083b.

34. M. Gálvez to Navia, Nueva Guatemala, 10 March 1781, ibid. leg. 2083a.
35. Francisco Saavedra to J. Gálvez, Havana, 19 February 1781; and Correspondencia de D. Francisco de Saavedra, años 1780–1782, both in AGI, Indiferente General, leg. 1578.
36. Saavedra to J. Gálvez, 4 April 1781, ibid. The quote reads, in part, *Me parece que debemos contar por una de las maiores ganancias de esta guerra. . . .*
37. M. Gálvez to Navia, Nueva Guatemala, 10 March 1781; M. Gálvez to Cagigal, Nueva Guatemala, 23 June 1781, both in AGI, Santo Domingo, leg. 2083a.
38. Navarro to J. Gálvez, Havana, 26 February 1781, ibid., leg. 2083b.
39. Navarro to J. Gálvez, Havana, 8 March 1781, ibid., leg. 2083a; and, for the boats, see Navarro to J. Gálvez, Havana, 28 February 1781, ibid.
40. M. Gálvez to J. Gálvez, 25 May 1780, AGI, Guatemala, leg. 869.
41. The two reports are Cayetano de Ansoátegui to M. Gálvez, Mouth of the Limón River, 14 April 1780; and Vicente Arizabalaga to Ansoátegui, 6 May 1780, both in ibid. Detailed accounts of these two expeditions were published in *la Gaceta de Madrid,* 20 February 1781, BN.
42. It is clear that Ansoátegui was in command, and all reports imply, but do not state, that they left from Comayagua. The routes and strategy are pretty clear from the narratives of the two officers, ibid.; and specifically, Ansoátegui to M. Gálvez, 12 May 1780, AGI, Guatemala, leg. 869.
43. Ansoátegui to M. Gálvez, 14 April 1780, ibid.
44. Ibid.
45. Ibid.
46. Arizabalaga to Ansoátegui, 6 May 1780, ibid.
47. Ibid.
48. Beerman, *España y la Independencia,* 241.
49. Cagigal to J. Gálvez, Havana, 6 September 1782, AGI, Santo Domingo, leg. 2084.
50. Letter from San Lorenzo, 17 November 1781, ibid., leg. 2083a.
51. Cagigal to Martín de Mayorga, Havana, 16 October 1782, ibid., leg. 2084.
52. Miguel Antonio Eduardo to Cagigal, Havana, 18 October 1782; Cagigal to J. Gálvez, Havana, 19 October 1782, both in ibid. The source in Baltimore was Samuel Purviance.
53. Letter to the Governor of Havana, Madrid, 14 December 1782, ibid.
54. Floyd, "Bourbon Palliatives," 106. Floyd cites a document in AGI, Guatemala, legajo 422 to state that Mexico gave 300,000 pesos and Peru another 100,000 pesos. Also, see Urriza to J. Gálvez, Havana, 28 October 1781, AGI, Santo Domingo, leg. 1657.
55. Matías de Gálvez, "Diario General de los sucesos ocurridos en las expediciones de mar, y tierra, dirigidas por el Mariscal de Campo el Señor Don Matías de Gálvez . . . contra los Yngleses establecidos en el Golfo de Honduras, y sus aliados los Yndios Zambos, y Moscos . . . ," Trujillo, 18 April 1782, AGI, Guatemala, leg. 869. Arizabalaga's force is listed as "one thousand four hundred trained soldiers and one hundred infantry veterans."
56. Ibid.; and Beerman, *España y la Independencia,* 243–45. Beerman's account is based on the publication of Gálvez's account, the Diario, in *la Gaceta de Madrid,* 5 July 1782, BN.
57. Ibid.
58. M. Gálvez, Diario. Gálvez wrote that the distance "from the capital of the New Kingdom of Guatemala to the port of Trujillo" was 209 leagues. Beerman, *España y la Independencia,* 243, converts this to a distance of 600 kilometers.
59. M. Gálvez, Diario, 18 April 1782.
60. Ibid. A small detachment of two hundred soldiers was dispatched under Captain Cristóbal Bernal to open roads to help with the attack on the British from the "leeward," or opposite direction of the wind, which is the side protected from the wind. Heavy rains prevented the operation.
61. Ibid.; Beerman, *España y la Independencia,* 244; and Floyd, "Bourbon Palliatives," 117.
62. M. Gálvez, Diario; Beerman, *España y la Independencia,* 244, adds the corsair *Purísima Concepción,* and a total of twenty-seven ships. The list above, with Beerman's additional corsair, would indicate at least thirty boats.

63. M. Gálvez, Diario. A great subject for future study is the identification of the many Spanish soldiers and sailors who had non-Spanish surnames. Many were Irish, whose historical and religious differences with Great Britain gave them cause to fight with Spain.

64. Urriza to J. Gálvez, Havana, 20 February 1782, AGI, Santo Domingo, leg. 2084.

65. The order is copied into M. Gálvez, Diario. The officers are Captain Miguel Alfonso de Sousa; frigate captains Andrés Tacón and Enrique Reinaldo Macdonell; lieutenant of the ship, Josef Astigárriga; ensigns Francisco Ontañón, Josef Roca and Josef Salomón; from the Infantry Regiment, Francisco Ayala; from the Navy, Joseph Ruiz; the first pilot, Ensign Ramón de Evia, and Gálvez.

66. M. Gálvez, Diario; M. Gálvez to Cagigal, Puerto de Roatán, 18 March 1782, leg. 1235; M. Gálvez to Urriza, Roatán, 20 March 1782, leg. 1659, both in AGI, Santo Domingo; and Beerman, *España y la Independencia*, 244.

67. The British claimed that there were more than five hundred slaves. According to M. Gálvez, in the "Diario," The British captives were allowed to keep one slave of each sex.

68. Ibid.; and Beerman, *España y la Independencia*, 244.

69. M. Gálvez, Diario; and M. Gálvez to Cagigal, Puerto de Trujillo, 18 April 1782, leg. 2084, AGI, Santo Domingo. The casualties are listed as "a sailor and a grenadier," and four others slightly wounded, all of whom were on "the admiral's ship." Evidently, Gálvez was not any more averse to putting himself at risk than his son Bernardo, whose story is in the next chapter.

70. Ibid.

71. Ibid., leg. 2084, AGI, Santo Domingo.

72. Ibid.

73. Beerman, *España y la Independencia*, 245, uses the name based on J. Calderón Quijano, "Un incidente militar en los establecimientos ingleses de río Tinto en 1782," *Anuario de Estudios Americanos*, (1945). M. Gálvez, Diario, uses a name that looks like "Misternic."

74. M. Gálvez, Diario.

75. M. Gálvez to Cagigal, Puerto de Trujillo, 18 April 1782, AGI, Indiferente General, leg. 1583; Urriza to J. Gálvez, Havana, 10 April 1782, AGI, Santo Domingo, leg. 1659; and Urriza to J. Gálvez, Havana, 4 May 1782 (two letters), AGI, Santo Domingo, leg. 2084. M. Gálvez asked for more supplies, which were sent for the "recently reconquered forts on the Gulf of Honduras."

76. Beerman, *España y la Independencia*, 246.

77. M. Gálvez to Cagigal, Guatemala, 21 September 1782, AGI, Indiferente General, leg. 1583; a copy is in AGI, Santo Domingo, leg. 1235. See chapter XII, herein, for Cagigal in disfavor.

78. Cagigal to J. Gálvez, Havana, 12 November 1782, AGI, Santo Domingo, leg. 1235.

79. Cagigal to Solano, Havana, 8 November 1782, ibid., leg. 2081.

80. Luis de Unzaga to J. Gálvez, Havana, 3 February 1783, ibid.; and Urriza to J. Gálvez, Havana, 4 May 1782, ibid., leg. 1659. In this last letter, Urriza wrote that M. Gálvez now has greater needs. Also, see Solano to M. Gálvez, Havana, 12 November 1782; Unzaga to Solano, Havana, 29 January 1783; Solano to Unzaga, 30 January 1783; and Unzaga to Solano, 19 February 1783, all in AGI, Santo Domingo, leg. 2081.

81. Solano to J. Gálvez, Havana, 10, 17, and 18 November 1782, all in AGI, Santo Domingo, leg. 2081.

82. Letter to M. Gálvez, El Pardo, 29 January 1783, ibid., leg. 1235; Also, see Solano to Unzaga, Havana, 20 February 1783; and Solano to M. Gálvez, Havana, 6 March 1783, both in ibid., leg. 2081.

83. Gálvez's predecessor, the elderly Martín de Mayorga, mysteriously died on his return passage to Spain. See Floyd, "Bourbon Palliatives," 241–42; and Priestley, *Gálvez*, 10.

84. Boeta, *Gálvez*, 39–40. Matías palace, the Castle of Chapultepec stands today in Mexico City. It is Mexico's national museum of history.

NOTES TO PAGES 166-71 ❧ 255

CHAPTER 11

1. Alvord, "The Conquest of St. Joseph," 404; McDermott, "Leyba and the Defense," 339; Peckham, *The War for Independence*, 115. Also see Rabin F. A. Fabel, "West Florida and British Strategy in the American Revolution," in *Eighteenth Century Florida and the Revolutionary South*, Samuel Proctor, ed. (Gainesville: University Press of Florida, 1976), 49–67.
2. Woodward, "Gálvez," xxiii, and Caughey, "The Panis Mission," 487. Morris, *The Peacemakers*, 220, correctly argues that the United States posed future threats to Spain.
3. Beerman, "Introduction," xiv. Gálvez's father-in-law, St. Maxent, delivered his plan to the governor and son-in-law before war had been declared.
4. Bond, "Oliver Pollock: An Unknown Patriot," 137; and Frances Poussett et al (thirty-four others) to B. Gálvez, n.d., AGI, Santo Domingo, leg. 2596.
5. B. Gálvez to Navarro, 3 July 1779, AGI, Santo Domingo, leg. 1229. Not only did Gálvez report that Manchac had received four hundred new troops and Natchez had a total of eight hundred troops, he even observed that Pensacola was planning to transfer an additional three hundred men. A copy of the same document is in AGI, Santo Domingo, leg. 2082. Bettie Jones Conover, "British West Florida's Mississippi Frontier Posts, 1763–1779," *Alabama Review* 29 (1976): 177–207, claims that the total British Mississippi River troop strength was 457, excluding officers.
6. Navarro to B. Gálvez, Havana, 28 July 1779, AGI, Cuba, leg. 1; Navarro to Juan Bautista Bonet, Havana, 7 August 1779, AGI, Santo Domingo, leg. 1229; and Navarro to B. Gálvez, Havana, 12 August 1779, AGI, Santo Domingo, leg. 1229.
7. Navarro to J. Gálvez, Havana, 29 September 1779, AGI, Santo Domingo, leg. 1229. The frigates *Santa Marta* and *Santa Matilde*, along with the brigantine, *El Renombrado*, convoyed the troops to Louisiana. Navarro to J. Gálvez, Havana, 11 August 1779; and J. Gálvez to Navarro, 11 October 1779, both in AGI, Santo Domingo, leg. 2082; Navarro to B. Gálvez, Havana, 22 September 1779, AGI, Cuba, leg. 1. Also see Din, "DuBreüil," 22.
8. Gold, "Gálvez and Spanish Espionage," 99; and Montero de Pedro, *Españoles*, 40. See Gilbert C. Din, *Francisco Bouligny: A Bourbon Soldier in Spanish Louisiana* (Baton Rouge & London: Louisiana State University Press, 1993), 110, for an account that Gálvez had less than enthusiastic support from his city council.
9. Caughey, "The Panis Mission," 488–89. Gálvez, in fact, credits Panis for forming the plan of attack on Pensacola.
10. B. Gálvez to Bonet, New Orleans, 17 August 1779, AGI, Santo Domingo, leg. 2081.
11. Navarro to J. Gálvez, Havana, 11 September 1779, ibid., leg. 2082. Navarro understated his difference of opinion with Bernardo de Gálvez in the estimated number of troops needed for laying siege to Pensacola. A copy of this letter is in ibid., leg. 1233.
12. Navarro to J. Gálvez, Havana, 11 August 1779, ibid.
13. B. Gálvez to Carlos de Grand-Pré, New Orleans, 16 August 1779, AGI, Cuba, leg. 1; and Din, "DuBreüil," 25.
14. Din, "DuBreüil," 17.
15. B. Gálvez to Bonet, Havana, 29 August 1779, AGI, Santo Domingo, leg. 2081; and B. Gálvez to Grand-Pré, Havana, 21 August 1779, AGI, Santo Domingo, leg. 2081.
16. Report of the expedition on the Mississippi River, attached to Navarro to J. Gálvez, Havana, 11 November 1779, AGI, Santo Domingo, leg. 2082; and Montemayor, "Epilogue," 47. The report erred in the addition by using the same numbers but totaling twenty more.
17. As quoted in Bond, "Oliver Pollock: An Unknown Patriot," 137.
18. James, "Spanish Influence," 205; and Bond, "Oliver Pollock: An Unknown Patriot," 137.
19. Din, "DuBreüil," 24.
20. Din, *Francisco Bouligny*, 103–4.
21. Din, "DuBreüil," 25, 26, and 28.
22. Report of the expedition, 11 November 1779, AGI, Santo Domingo, leg. 2082; and Beerman, "Introduction," xiv.

23. Anonymous undated report in BN, Manuscritos, Signatura 19248, no. 177–182. This report notes that Baton Rouge was defended by two companies and 110 grenadiers from the German Waldek Regiment.

24. As quoted in Din, "DuBreüil," 29.

25. For a glimpse of Delavillabeuvre's, or de la Villabeuvre's, activities during the war, see Jack D. L. Holmes, "Juan de la Villebeuvre, Spain's Commandant of Natchez during the American Revolution," *Journal of Mississippi History* 37 (1975): 97–130.

26. Wright, Jr., *Florida in the American Revolution,* 76. The link between the actions of Gálvez and E'staing, if any, needs further study.

27. Anonymous undated report, BN, Manuscripts, Sig. 19248, no. 177–182.

28. Albert W. Haarmann, "The Spanish Conquest of West Florida, 1779–1781," *Florida Historical Quarterly* 39 (1960): 107–34; Beerman, "Introduction," xiv; "Royal Patents," in Woodward, ed., *Tribute to Don Bernardo de Gálvez,* 105; and Woodward, "Tribute to Gálvez," xxiv.

29. Din, *Francisco Bouligny,* 104.

30. "Royal Patents," in Woodward, ed., *Tribute,* 105. It is unclear whether the boats captured on the Amite River are included in this tally. Also see Anonymous Report, BN.

31. Navarro to J. Gálvez, Havana, 11 November 1779, AGI, Santo Domingo, leg. 2082. Navarro wrote, "I send to you the letters that I have received from the Governor of Louisiana. Letters taken from the English in Natches. . . ." Among the letters enclosed in the packet were William Campbell, governor of Pensacola, to Captain Anthony Forstel, 9 September 1779; Charles Stewart to Forstel, 1 October 1779; Mr. Elias Bunnford to Judge William Hicorn [this last is a Spanish spelling], 2 October 1779; and Captain of the Artillery William McJohnstone to ?, 2 October 1779, all in AGI, Santo Domingo, leg. 2082.

32. J. Gálvez to the governor of Havana, 6 January 1780. ibid.

33. Bonet to J. Gálvez, 12 August 1779, ibid., leg. 2081.

34. Marginal note, dated 22 April 1780, on Navarro to J. Gálvez, 22 February 1780, ibid., leg. 2082. Such notes were usually written for the king's eyes; he could read the shorter notes and avoid reading the letter. Obviously then, the minister who forwarded the information had great influence on royal thought. In return, Carlos III had great confidence in his ministers, and had no problem keeping informed and delegating authority.

35. J. Gálvez to the governor of Havana, 11 January 1780, ibid., leg. 2087.

36. Floridablanca to J. Gálvez, 11 May 1780 and 18 May 1780; attached is a copy of a letter from France, 28 April 1780, all in ibid., leg. 2082.

37. Cummins, *Spanish Observers,* 133; and Notes on a Conference between Chevalier de la Luzerne and General Washington, Headquarters, West Point, 16 September 1779, in Fitzpatrick, *Writings of Washington,* vol. 16, 294–99.

38. Conference, West Point, 16 September 1779, Fitzpatrick, *Writings of Washington,* vol. 16, 299.

39. Lancaster, *The American Revolution,* 240–41.

40. Royal Orders to Juan de Miralles, 31 December 1779, AGI, Santo Domingo, leg. 2082.

41. Montero de Pedro, *Españoles,* 44; and Navarro to J. Gálvez, Havana, 6 June 1780, AGI, Santo Domingo, leg. 2082.

42. Montero de Pedro, *Españoles,* 43 and 44. Washington repeated that Spain's activity would have a positive effect for him.

43. Conference, West Point, 16 September 1779, in Fitzpatrick, *Writings of Washington,* vol. 10, 298; and Navarro to J. Gálvez, Havana, 6 June 1780, AGI, Santo Domingo, leg. 1233.

44. J. Gálvez to Navarro, 29 August 1779, quoted in Reparaz, *Yo Solo,* 38; and Navarro to J. Gálvez, Havana, ibid.

45. The extracts are included in Navarro to J. Gálvez, AGI, Santo Domingo, leg. 1233. The two cited letters are dated 7 April 1780 and 12 April 1780.

46. J. Gálvez to Navarro, 29 August 1779, quoted in Reparaz, *Yo Solo,* 35. Original in AGI, Cuba, leg. 1290. This is the letter in which José de Gálvez refers to Mobile and Pensacola as "the keys to Mexico proper."

47. Navarro to J. Gálvez, Havana, 10 April 1780, AGI, Santo Domingo, leg. 1233.
48. Urriza to J. Gálvez, 20 February 1780, leg. 2082; Acuerdo [agreement] de los Excmos.[Excellencies] señores don Diego Joseph Navarro, Bonet y Miró, Havana, 31 January 1780; Navarro to J. Gálvez, Havana, 22 February 1780, all in AGI, Santo Domingo, leg. 2082. Miró did not sign the agreement.
49. Diario formado por Don Estevan Miró, January to February 1780, AGI, Cuba, leg. 2. The diary is thirteen hand-written pages. Another, or perhaps different, version of the tirade has another Navy commander exclaiming, "What do we want with Mobile and Pensacola? Havana is fifty times more important than Mobile and Pensacola ... and I do not know if sometimes it is not suitable to disobey the orders of the king when you understand if his Majesty would be here, he would do the same." See Colonel José de Ezpeleta y Galdeano quoting Navy Commander Gabriel de Aristizábal as printed in Reparaz, *Yo Solo*, 42
50. Acuerdo de los Excmos, 31 January 1780 and Navarro to J. Gálvez, 22 February 1780, both in AGI, Santo Domingo, leg. 2082. Navarro and Bonet agreed to spare 1,966 troops and ninety-nine officers, to be sent on thirty ships. These included men from the regiments of the *Príncipe, Navarra, Havana Fixo*, and *Cataluña*.
51. Gerónimo Girón to Navarro, 29 May 1780, AGI, Cuba, leg. 113; Acuerdo, 31 January 1780, AGI, Santo Domingo, leg. 2082, in which Bonet noted that Gálvez had embarked and was on his way to Mobile.
52. Quoted from "Royal Patents," in Woodward, *Tribute*, 105.
53. Ibid.; and Beerman, "Introduction," xiv. An interesting account of the siege is Coker and Coker, *The Siege of Mobile, 1780, in Maps* (Pensacola: Perdido Bay Press, 1981).
54. Navarro to J. Gálvez, 23 April 1780, AGI, Santo Domingo, leg. 1230.
55. A three-day storm and contrary winds delayed the planned embarkation of the reinforcements. The same storm cut back the numbers of soldiers. See Navarro and Bonet to J. Gálvez, Havana, 31 January 1780; Navarro to J. Gálvez, Havana, 26 February 1780; and Bonet to Navarro, 24 February 1780, all in ibid., leg. 2082. Also see, Diario por . . . Miró, January to February 1780, AGI, Cuba, leg. 2.
56. Starr, "'Left as a Gewgaw,'" 20. Actually the defenders had other munitions in their arsenal, but they were the wrong caliber.
57. B. Gálvez as quoted in Boeta, *Gálvez*, 96. Also, Beerman, "Introduction," xiv; and "Royal Patents," in Woodward, *Tribute*, 106.
58. B. Gálvez to Bonet, 28 March 1780, AGI, Santo Domingo, leg. 2081. Also, see Starr, "'Left as a Gewgaw,'" 21.
59. Ibid.
60. Ibid.; and Bonet to B. Gálvez, 6 April 1780, AGI, Santo Domingo, leg. 2081. Gálvez wrote that two frigates guarded the mouth of Pensacola's Bay. Pensacola had a force of 1,300 regular troops, 600 "arms-trained hunters and inhabitants," at least 300 "gun-carrying Negroes" and, maybe, 2,500 Indians. He claimed to have 2,700 men. Also, see Reparaz, *Yo Solo*, 43–44. Actually, Gálvez's figure for the Indians appears to be too high, for Cline (*Florida Indians*, I, 159) notes that only about a thousand Indians came to Pensacola's aid.
61. Bonet to J. Gálvez, 19 July 1780 (two letters), AGI, Santo Domingo, leg. 2081.
62. Bonet to J. Gálvez, 19 July 780 and 29 August 1780, both in ibid.
63. Dull, *French Navy*, 188–89.
64. J. Gálvez to Urriza, 20 June 1780; Urriza to J. Gálvez, 16 February 1780, both in AGI, Santo Domingo, leg. 2082.
65. Dull, *French Navy*, 188–89.
66. J. Gálvez to Navarro, 20 April 1780, AGI, Santo Domingo, leg. 2082.
67. Montero de Pedro, *Españoles*, 42.
68. B. Gálvez, Extracto de las noticias de Panzacola . . . , 2 September 1780, AGI, Santo Domingo, leg. 2082.
69. McDermott, "Leyba and the Defense," 341–42; and Urriza to J. Gálvez, 27 August 1780, AGI, Santo Domingo, leg. 2082.

70. Sosin, *Revolutionary Frontier,* 123.
71. McDermott, "Leyba and the Defense," 339; and Alvord, "The Conquest of St. Joseph," 405.
72. McDermott, "Leyba and the Defense," 342.
73. Ibid., 341 and 384. Leyba collected one thousand *piastres* from the inhabitants of St. Louis and contributed four hundred himself.
74. Dull, *A Diplomatic History,* 147, writes that the Illinois country was not that important to Spain. Woodward, "Gálvez," xxiv, states that Gálvez sent aid; and B. Gálvez to Leyba, New Orleans, 13 January 1779, MHS, Papers from Spain, no. 10. The matter of Gálvez's involvement with, and whether he deserves credit for, the successes at St. Louis is a subject awaiting more research. This author tends to believe that Gálvez was not concerned about St. Louis at the time. He deserves some credit for the success of a victory under his general command, but not for his direct participation or concern.
75. McDermott, "Leyba and the Defense," 346.
76. Colonel Montgomery to George Rogers Clark, 15 May 1780, quoted in McDermott, "Leyba and the Defense," 342–44.
77. Quoted in ibid., 342. Also, see 340–41.
78. Ibid., 344; and Leyba to B. Gálvez, St. Louis, 20 June 1780, AGI, Cuba, leg. 13. Curiously, this letter is in French. McDermott notes that the ill Leyba did not have the strength to write and therefore dictated his last letters to a secretary who could only write in French. McDermott, "Leyba and the Defense," 346, footnote 40.
79. Abraham B. Nasatir, "St. Louis During the British Attack of 1780," in *New Spain and the Anglo American West,* George P. Hammond, ed., vol. 1 (Los Angeles and Lancaster, Pa.: Private Printing, 1932), 242–43. Nasatir quotes Leyba as explaining that he could not find anyone who could write Spanish well enough to take his dictation, so he had to call on his French secretary.
80. Both McDermott, "Leyba and the Defense," 344–46 and Nasatir, "St. Louis During the British Attack," 239–61, are good accounts of this episode.
81. Leyba's Report, 8 June 1780, is translated in part in McDermott, "Leyba and the Defense," 344–46.
82. Leyba to M. Gálvez, St. Louis, 20 June 1780, AGI, Cuba, leg. 13; and McDermott, "Leyba and the Defense," 348. Inbentario estimado de los bienes del difunto Don Fernando de Leiba, 5 July 1780, MHS, St. Louis Archives, no. 2362. Leyba's report was forwarded to Spain by Martín Navarro, the intendant in New Orleans. José de Gálvez wrote Matías de Gálvez on 3 February 1781, that Leyba's successful defense of *"San Luis de Ylinoeses"* encouraged the king to reward Leyba with a promotion to lieutenant colonel, and Cartabona to the rank of captain. The former received his promotion posthumously.
83. Dull, *French Navy,* 193.
84. Junta de Guerra, Havana, 13 September 1780, AGI, Santo Domingo, leg. 1230.
85. Reparaz, *Yo Solo,* 38; Kuethe and Inglis, "Absolutism and Enlightened Reform," 141; Peralta y Rojas to J. Gálvez, 3 August 1780, leg. 1087; Mr. Reynaud to Navarro, 14 June 1780, leg. 1230, all in AGI, Santo Domingo. Navarro also reported that some supplies arrived from Mexico. See Navarro to J. Gálvez, Havana, 17 July 1780, AGI, Santo Domingo, leg. 1230.
86. J. Gálvez to Navarro, 17 April 1780; Navarro to J. Gálvez, Havana, 6 September 1780, AGI, Santo Domingo, leg. 2082.
87. Junta de Guerra, Havana, 13 September 1780, ibid., leg. 1230. The other three attendees were Victorio de Navia, the "Commander General of the Army of Operation," Guillermo Weigham, the "Field Marshal," and Juan Manuel de Cagigal, also listed as a field marshal. Juan Tomaseo, an officer with Solano, was invited, but missed the meeting because of sickness.
88. Urriza to J. Gálvez, 5 October 1780, ibid., leg. 1657. Navarro had requested arms, meats, and other supplies.
89. Junta de Guerra, Havana, 19 September 1780 and 22 September 1780, ibid., leg. 1230.

90. Quoted in Junta de Guerra, 15 October 1780, ibid. Also see Junta de Guerra, 28 September and 3 October 1780, all ibid.; Navarro to J. Gálvez, Havana, 18 October , ibid., in which Navarro includes accounts for five meetings and mentions seven. This report was submitted two days after the expedition sailed. The listed dates for the meetings are September 13, 15, 19, 22 and 28, and October 1 and 3, 1780. Historians owe a debt of gratitude to the Spanish legal or bureaucratic custom, as well as to Navarro, who wrote honest reports of these meetings. In some cases, minutes were written for the meetings. The politics, rivalries, and arguments leading up to the Pensacola expedition is a subject worth more in-depth research.

91. Letter from some of Solano's officers to Navarro, Havana, 30 October 1780, ibid., leg. 1230; and Beerman, *España y la Independencia*, 107.

92. Urriza does not give credit to Gálvez's ship, which he identifies as *La Sonda*, for the capture of the two frigates. Beerman, *España y la Independencia*, 107–14, is the best-documented account of this disastrous expedition. He identifies Gálvez's ship as the *Nuestra Señora de la O*, and credits it with the capture of the British ships; see page 107. Urriza to Gálvez, 26 November 1780, Santo Domingo, AGI, leg. 1657; "Royal Patents," in Woodward, *Tribute*, 106; and Montero de Pedro, *Españoles*, 42.

93. Jack D. L. Holmes, "Alabama's Bloodiest Day of the American Revolution: Counterattack at the Village, 7 January 1781," *The Alabama Review* 29, no. 3 (July 1976): 209.

94. Ibid., 209–10, 216.

95. Ezpeleta to Piernas, Mobile, 15 January 1781, as quoted in Holmes, "Alabama's Bloodiest Day," 214.

96. Holmes, "Alabama's Bloodiest Day," 214.

97. Ezpeleta to B. Gálvez, Mobile, 20 January 1781, as quoted in Holmes, "Alabama's Bloodiest Day," 219.

98. J. Gálvez to Navarro, 24 June 1780, AGI, Indiferente General, leg. 1578. This letter is in a folio titled "Correspondencia con el Gobernador de la Havana año 1780." After an adventurous trip, Saavedra finally arrived in Havana on 22 January 1781.

99. J. Gálvez to Saavedra, El Pardo, 29 March 1781, AGI, Indiferente General, leg. 1578.

100. Morales Padrón, "Editor's Introduction," xxx.

101. Letter from Aranjuez to Navarro, 24 June 1780, with attached Royal Orders, AGI, Indiferente General, leg. 1587, folio: Correspondencia con el Governador de la Havana, Año 1780. José de Gálvez earlier had written to his king, "the conquest of Jamaica is the most important and splendid objective which Your Majesty's armed forces can undertake in this war," J. Gálvez to the king, undated, AGI, Indiferente General, legajo 1578 as translated and published in Morales Padrón, *Journal of Saavedra*, 8–9, footnote 14.

102. J. Gálvez to Saavedra, El Pardo, 29 March 1781, AGI, Indiferente General, leg. 1578.

103. Letter from Aranjuez to Navarro, 24 June 1780, with attached Royal Orders, folio: Correspondencia con el Gobernador de la Havana, Año 1780, ibid. Also, see Williams, *From Columbus to Castro*, 217–236. Williams argues that British preference for the "sugar islands" was the reason for the revolution.

CHAPTER 12

1. Cartabona to B. Gálvez, St. Louis, 29 September 1780, AGI, Cuba, leg. 1.

2. B. Gálvez to Pedro Piernas, New Orleans, "Instructions", n.d., ibid.

3. Navarro to Navia, Havana, 14 December 1780, AGI, Santo Domingo, leg. 2083a.

4. Esteban Miró to Cagigal, New Orleans, 2 November 1782, ibid., leg. 1235.

5. B. Gálvez to John Campbell, 19 May 1780; Campbell to B. Gálvez, 20 April 1780, AGI, Cuba, leg. 1.

6. Villasure to ?, 21 January 1780; Cruzat to B. Gálvez, 13 February 1780; letter from St. Louis, 2 September 1780; Piernas to B. Gálvez, 1 May 1780; Ezpeleta to B. Gálvez, 27 September 1780, all in ibid.

7. B. Gálvez to Silvio Francisco de Cartabona, 25 July 1780, MHS, Papers from Spain, no. 52 (original in Papeles procendentes de la Isla de Cuba, AGI).

8. B. Gálvez to Piernas, Havana, n.d. "Instructions," AGI, Cuba, leg. 1. The importance of St. Louis is spelled out in section 17 of the instructions.

9. Cruzat to B. Gálvez, St. Louis, 16 January 1781, ibid. For Cruzat's appointment see Nasatir, *Borderland in Retreat*, 30–31.

10. Clarence Alvord, "The Conquest of St. Joseph," 398–414. Also see Nasatir, *Borderland in Retreat*, 31–32.

11. Nasatir, *Borderland in Retreat*, 30–31.

12. Cruzat to B. Gálvez, 13 January 1781, AGI, Cuba, leg. 1.

13. Cruzat to Estevan Miró, St. Louis, 6 August 1781, (two copies), leg. 2084 and 2548, both in Santo Domingo, AGI. The copy in 2548 has an attached report written in French from Pourré and his officers, in which they announce the defeat of Fort St. Joseph. The report is signed by and cited as, Charles Tayon, Louis Chavlier, Joseph Labussiere, Louis Honosí, and Eugene Pourrí, St. Joseph, 12 February 1781.

14. Ibid.; and Nasatir, *Borderland in Retreat*, 33.

15. Alvord, "Conquest of St. Joseph," 398.

16. Kinnaird, "A New Interpretation," 175.

17. Alvord, "The Conquest of St. Joseph," 398–414; Edward G. Mason, *Chapter From Illinois History* (Chicago: H. S. Stone & Co., 1901), 293. For Alvord, parroting the British position see Nasatir, *Borderland in Retreat*, 2. Dull, *A Diplomatic History*, 147, states that the Illinois country was of little importance during negotiations, but does not demean the expedition as a military act. Morris, *The Peacemakers*, does not mention the area as a significant, or any, part of the peace negotiations. Also, see Dupuy and Dupuy, *Encyclopedia of Military History*, 717. The two primary articles to take Alvord to task were Frederick J. Teggert, "The Capture of St. Joseph, Michigan, By the Spaniards in 1781," *Missouri Historical Review* 5, no. 4 (July 1911): 214–28; and Kinnaird, "A New Interpretation," 173–191.

18. Lancaster, *The American Revolution*, 266.

19. Nasatir, *Borderland in Retreat*, 32.

20. Saavedra, *Journal*, 99.

21. Saavedra to J. Gálvez, Havana, 16 February 1781, AGI, Indiferente General, leg. 1578.

22. Ibid.

23. Ibid., 107. This journal entry was written on 23 January, which is to say that Saavedra drew this conclusion within a couple of days after his arrival.

24. Saavedra to J. Gálvez, Havana, 16 February 1781, AGI, Indiferente General, leg. 1578.

25. Ibid., 108–15. According to Saavedra, the meetings leading up to the Pensacola expedition took place on the following dates: 1, 3, 6, 13, and 19 February 1781.

26. Saavedra, *Journal*, 116. The discussion took place on 4 February 1781.

27. Ibid., 126–28; Beerman, "Introduction," xv; "Royal Patents," in Woodward, *Tribute*, 107. For the ship's name, see "Estado que manifiesta los Buques en que se han embarcado las Tropas destinadas a las órdenes del Mariscal de Campo D. Bernardo de Gálvez . . . ," Havana, 28 February 1781, AGI, Santo Domingo, leg. 2083a. The *San Román* is listed as the only ship-of-the-line in the fleet of thirty-two ships that included three frigates.

28. Saavedra, *Journal*, 118–20. See chapter XI, herein. Ezpeleta was colonel in the Regiment of Navarra.

29. The Battle Journal has been published as "Diary of the Operations of the Expedition against the place of Pensacola conducted by the Arms of His Catholic Majesty, under the Orders of the Field Marshall Don Bernardo de Gálvez," edited by Gaspar Cusachs, *Louisiana Historical Quarterly* 1, no. 1 (1917): 45–84; and Montemayor, *Yo Solo*. The biography is Boeta, *Gálvez*; and the tribute is Ralph Lee Woodward, Jr., *Tribute to Gálvez*. Also, see James A. Servies, *The Siege of Pensacola, 1781: A Bibliography* (Pensacola: The John C. Pace Library, 1981).

30. Reparaz, *Yo Solo*.

31. Saavedra, *Journal,* 114.
32. Ibid., 119–20, n. 88.
33. Named after Carlos Sigüenza y Góngora, a 17th-century Mexican mathematician, historian, and genius, who late in his life surveyed the Gulf Coast. His findings were challenged. Sigüenza y Góngora wrote a detailed reply to his critic and was so confident of himself that he invited that person to match the value of his library as a wager. See Irving A. Leonard, *Baroque Times in Old Mexico* (Ann Arbor: University of Michigan Press, 1973), 211–13.
34. Montemayor, *Yo Solo,* 2.
35. "Royal Patents," in Woodward, *Tribute,* 108; Dull, *French Navy,* 233; and Montemayor, *Yo Solo,* 3.
36. Montemayor, *Yo Solo,* 344.
37. Montero de Pedro, *Españoles,* 42; "Royal Patents," in Woodward, *Tribute,* 107; and Montemayor, *Yo Solo,* 4.
38. J. Gálvez to Navarro, El Pardo, 12 February 1781, AGI, Santo Domingo, leg. 2083a.
39. J. Gálvez to B. Gálvez; and J. Gálvez to the Governor of Havana, both from El Pardo, 12 February 1781, AGI, Santo Domingo, leg. 2083a. The first of these letters states that Cagigal is named interim governor in place of Navarro.
40. Letter from El Pardo to Saavedra, 17 February 1781, AGI, Indiferente General, leg. 1780. The original reads " . . . aquellos generales demasiado adictos a sus propios sistemas para ceder a las luces de un oficial de menos graduación y años que ellos."
41. Saavedra, *Journal,* 191. Saavedra heard the news on his return to Havana 26 May 1781.
42. Montemayor, *Yo Solo,* 5. For brother-in-law, see Eric Beerman, "'Yo Solo' not 'Solo': Juan Antonio de Riaño," *The Florida Historical Quarterly* 58, no. 2 (October 1979): 174 and 182.
43. Ibid., 5. The sounding took place on the night of 5 March.
44. Beerman, "Not 'Solo,'" 179–80.
45. Ibid., 180.
46. Beerman, *España y la Independencia,* 51–52. The *Galveztown* was the British brigantine *West Florida,* which was captured by the American frigate *Morris,* captained by William Pickles, on 10 September 1779. The battle and subsequent capture took place on Lake Pontchartrain near the Mississippi River. Bernardo de Gálvez underwrote the *Morris* and was happy to see the pesky *West Florida* eliminated. Captain Pedro Rousseau was a native of France.
47. Saavedra, *Journal,* 153. Beerman, *España y la Independencia,* 141, notes that Riaño became Gálvez's brother-in-law after the siege of Pensacola. See Beerman, "Not 'Solo,'" 182. St. Maxent's four daughters all married Spaniards.
48. Beerman, "Introduction," xv; Montemayor, *Yo Solo,* 7; and Saavedra, *Journal,* 143, footnote 99.
49. Montero de Pedro, *Españoles,* 42, claims that Calvo left in the *San Ramón.* Reparaz, *Yo Solo,* 56, 74, 82, 87 and 268, has the *San Ramón* as the flagship. Beerman, "Introduction," xv, lists the flagship's name as the *Commandante.*
50. Saavedra, *Journal,* 141, footnote 98, and page 143. The dispute between Calvo and Gálvez is best treated by Jack D. L. Holmes, "Bernardo de Gálvez, 'Man of the Hour' During the American Revolution," *Cardenales de dos Independencias,* Francisco de Solano, ed. (México: Fomento Cultural Banamex, A.C., 1978).
51. The terms are summarized in Montemayor, *Yo Solo,* 8–13. Also see, Peckham, *The War for Independence,* 185. Campbell agreed to neutralize the town by withdrawing into Fort George.
52. Montemayor, *Yo Solo,* 13.
53. Ibid., 20. Gálvez received his first wounds in action while fighting Apaches in north-central Mexico as a young junior officer. He also received minor wounds fighting in Morocco. See Boeta, *Gálvez,* 44.
54. Saavedra, *Journal,* 154. For a biography of Ezpeleta, see Francisco de Borja Medina Rojas, *José de Ezpeleta, Gobernador de la Mobila, 1780–1781* (Sevilla: Escuela de Estudios Hispanos Americanos de Sevilla, 1980). This is a very large and detailed book.

55. Montemayor, *Yo Solo*, 19.
56. Reparaz, *Yo Solo*, 131, 150, and 168.
57. Quoted in Dull, *French Navy*, 263.
58. Montemayor, *Yo Solo*, 20.
59. Ibid., 21.
60. Urriza to J. Gálvez, Havana, 7 April 1781, AGI, Santo Domingo, leg. 2083b.
61. Ibid., 21–22; Dull, *French Navy*, 235; Saavedra, *Journal*, 145; and Reparaz, *Yo Solo*, 138 and 140. The people in Havana had not yet heard about the new appointments. The French ships-of-the-line were the *Palmier, Destin, L'Intrepide and Tritón.*
62. Saavedra, *Journal*, 144–45.
63. Ibid., 144–45, 155. Saavedra states that the total number of troops was 7,806.
64. Montemayor, *Yo Solo*, 18, 22–23. At least ten ships were captured. Captain Robert Deans incinerated his own frigate, the *Mentor.* Also, see James A. Servies, ed., *Log of H.M.S. Mentor, 1780–1781* (Gainesville: University Press of Florida, 1982), 20–23.
65. Quoted in Montemayor, *Yo Solo*, 29. For Gálvez's arm in a sling see the contemporary illustration by Lausan, engraved by the conde de Artois in Paris, ca. 1784. For the best reproduction of this image, see Reparaz, *Yo Solo*, 194–95. The use of this image as historical fact is a stretch, for the image is a romantic version. At the very least, we know that Gálvez was able to retake command while still convalescing from the wound on his left hand.
66. Campbell, 8 May 1781, as quoted in Starr, "'Left as a Gewgaw,'" 22.
67. Beerman, "Introduction," xvi.
68. Ibid., xvi; Montemayor, *Yo Solo*, 30; "Royal Patents," in Woodward, *Tribute*, 108; and Reparaz, *Yo Solo*, 200.
69. Woodward, *Tribute*, xxiv; Lancaster, *The American Revolution*, 240; and Montero de Pedro, *Españoles*, 43.
70. Relación de los muertos y heridos, 12 May 1781, in Reparaz, *Yo Solo*, 206–7. Reparaz explains in a footnote that different reports list the dead in a range from ninety-one to one hundred. The figure used herein is derived from seventy-four given in the cited "Relación," plus twenty-one naval deaths noted in Reparaz's accompanying footnote.
71. Saavedra, *Journal*, 173.
72. See "Royal Patents," in Woodward, *Tribute*, 109.
73. Saavedra to J. Gálvez, 14 May 1781, transcribed in Reparaz, *Yo Solo*, 224–26. Original in Archivo, Fondo Saavedra, Facultad de Teología, Granada.
74. B. Gálvez to Navarro, 15 May 1781, transcribed in Reparaz, *Yo Solo*, 202. Also see 201–2; and Saavedra, *Journal*, 185. The battle journal, articles of capitulation, and the casualty lists have been translated in Montemayor, *Yo Solo*, 1–44. The articles of capitulation also have been published in Spanish in Reparaz, *Yo Solo*, 239–45.
75. J. Gálvez to Saavedra, 31 August 1781 as quoted in Reparaz, *Yo Solo*, 227. Original in Archivo, Fondo Saavedra, caja 16, Facultad de Teología, Granada.
76. Peckham, *The War For Independence*, 185; and Woodward, "Gálvez," xxiv.
77. Pollock to B. Galvez, New Orleans, 7 July 1781, MHS, Oliver Pollock Papers, 57–0050.
78. J. Gálvez to B. Gálvez, 9 August 1781, AGI, Cuba, leg. 1. The British Fort George was renamed San Miguel, because the day of its surrender was the day of the Apparition of Saint Michael (*Miguel*), the Archangel.
79. Miró to Navarro, New Orleans, 25 May 1781, AGI, Santo Domingo, leg. 2083b; and Beerman, *España y la Independencia*, 190. Beerman states that the defense lasted one day.
80. Beerman, *España y la Independencia*, 190.
81. B. Gálvez to J. Gálvez, Havana, 26 October 1781, AGI, Santo Domingo, leg. 2084.
82. Miró to Navarro, New Orleans, 19 July 1781; and Cagigal to J. Gálvez, Havana, 22 June 1781, both in ibid., leg. 2083b.
83. Beerman, *España y la Independencia*, 227. The visit took place on 2 April 1783.
84. Quote from Saavedra, 9 May 1781 in *Journal of Saavedra*, 172.
85. Beerman, *España y la Independencia*, 169; and *Journal of Saavedra*, 172–73, footnote 122. Rendón reported that *The New York Gazette*, 15 October 1781 contained protests as well.

CHAPTER 13

1. John D. Broadwater, "Yorktown Shipwreck," *National Geographic* 173 (1988): 804–23 provides an interesting account of the excavation of one of those scuttled ships. Along with ships, Cornwallis scuttled munitions.
2. Rochambeau to the French minister of war, The Prince de Montbarey, 19 July 1780; and the chevalier de Coriolis, n.d., both quoted in Lee Kennett, *The French Forces in America, 1780–1783*, (Westport, Conn.: Greenwood Press, 1977), 72–73.
3. Francisco de Saavedra to King Carlos III, "Diario inédito," transcribed, in part, in Reparaz, *Yo Solo*, 247–52. Original in *Mis Decenios*, Granada, Archivo Facultad de Teología, Fondo Saavedra, tomo 2, 252–74. Also see Saavedra, *Journal*, 200.
4. Grasse to Cagigal, Grenada, 12 June 1781, AGI, Santo Domingo, leg. 2083b.
5. Saavedra, "Diario inédito," in Reparaz, *Yo Solo*, 248. See Dull, *French Navy*, 256, 257, 279, in which he notes the importance of copper-hulled ships.
6. Saavedra, "Diario inédito," Reparaz, *Yo Solo*, 248–49.
7. Saavedra to J. Gálvez, 18 August 1781, AGI, Indiferente General, leg. 1578. The plan was sent to Spain on 31 July 1781.
8. Dull, *Diplomatic History*, 111; and Dull, *French Navy*, 237.
9. Saavedra, *Journal*, 200–201.
10. Saavedra, "Diario inédito,"in Reparaz, *Yo Solo*, 248. "... *para que no se malograse el golpe más decisivo de toda la guerra. . . .*"
11. Ibid.
12. Saavedra, *Journal*, 202.
13. Ibid., 207–8. The French came up with 50,000 *livres*.
14. Saavedra, "Diario inédito," in Reparaz, *Yo Solo*, 249–50.
15. Saavedra, *Journal*, 202.
16. Saavedra to J. Gálvez, 18 August 1781, AGI, Indiferente General, leg. 1578.
17. Saavedra, *Journal*, 200–201, footnote 142.
18. Saavedra, "Diario inédito," in Reparaz, *Yo Solo*, 250; and *Journal*, 211.
19. Ibid. An interesting legend grew out of this episode, that the women of Havana had contributed their jewelry to raise the money. In truth, the citizens of Havana, most of them merchants, expected to be repaid, either from American wheat or from the money expected from Mexico. At the very least, they had more confidence in their government than the French in Guarico had in theirs. A good description of the event that dispels the myth and gives a good, detailed account is James H. Lewis, "Las Damas de la Havana, El Precursor, and Francisco de Saavedra: A Note on the Spanish Participation in the Battle of Yorktown," *The Americas* 37 (July 1980): 83–99. A graph in the Appendix is derived from Lewis's article and lists the actual contributors.
20. Saavedra, "Diario inédito," in Reparaz, *Yo Solo*, 250.
21. Saavedra to J. Gálvez, 18 August 1781, AGI, Indiferente General, leg. 1578.
22. B. Gálvez to de Grasse, Havana, 17 August 1781, ibid. Saavedra almost decided to accompany the money to Yorktown where he could confer with "los generales Washington, Rochambeau, y LaFayette," but he and Gálvez concluded that he was of more value in Havana. See Saavedra, "Diario inédito,"in Reparaz, *Yo Solo*, 250–51.
23. Saavedra, "Diario inédito," in Reparaz, *Yo Solo*, 251. "[Y] al fin se resolvió mediante un informe mío que se le diese todo el millón, mirando la entrega hecha para la Bahía de Chesapeake como un nuevo servicio de la España a la causa común."
24. Ibid., 252.
25. Quoted in Stephen Bonsal, *When the French Were Here* (Garden City, N.Y.: Doubleday & Co., 1945), 119–20.
26. Luis Huet, "Plan de Ataque," 30 March 1781, AGI, Santo Domingo, leg. 2083a.
27. Report given by Josef Casesnobes of the state of the Island of Providencia, Havana, 3 February 1781, ibid.
28. Declaración del capitán Sebastián Aragonés y de Joseph Cano Piloto, Havana, 27 March 1781, ibid.

29. B. Gálvez to J. Gálvez, Havana, 26 October 1781, ibid., leg. 2084.
30. Saavedra to J. Gálvez, January 1782, AGI, Indiferente General, leg. 1578; and Morales Padrón, *Journal of Saavedra*, 235–72.
31. Flores to Cagigal, Cartagena, 10 July 1781; and Cagigal to J. Gálvez, Havana, 8 August 1781, both in AGI, Indiferente General, leg. 2083a.
32. John Edwin Fagg, *Latin America: A General History* (New York: Macmillan Publishing Co., Inc., 1970), 271–72. Like the revolt of Tupac Amaru, the effect of the *comunero* rebellions on the war with Great Britain and the eventual independence of the United States have yet to be thoroughly studied. For that matter, how the war contributed to the causes of the revolts is another interesting subject for further study.
33. Beerman, *España y la Independencia*, 201.
34. For a firsthand report of the capture of Tupac Amaru, listed as Josef Gabriel Tupac Amaru, see Report from the Viceroy of Santa Fe to Havana, Cuzco, 8 April 1781, leg. 2083b, Santo Domingo, AGI. For accounts in English, see Fagg, *Latin America*, 260–61; and Lillian Estelle Fisher, *The Last Inca Revolt, 1780–1783* (Norman: University of Oklahoma Press, 1986). Tupac Amaru, who is a legendary figure in South America, was drawn and quartered while alive. His execution speaks to the mean-spirited nature of the time. He was as vicious as the people who captured him. At one time, he executed a prisoner by making him drink molten gold.

Tupac Amaru was an inherited name from the last Inca emperor. In the end, he was turned over by defectors among his own people. For a Latin perspective, see María del Carmen Cortés Salinas, "Benito de la Mata Linares: Juez y Testigo en la rebelión de Tupac Amaru," *Quinto Congreso Internacional de Historia de América* 1 (1972): 230–57; Luis Durand Florez, ed., *La Revolución de los Tupac Amaru* (Lima, Perú: Comisión Nacional del Bicentenario de la Rebelión Emancipadora de Tupac Amaru, 1981); Eulogio Zudaire Huarte, "Análisis de la rebelión de Tupac Amaru en su bicentenario (1780–1980)," *Revista de Indias*, no. 60 (1980): 13–79; and Boleslao Lewin, *Tupac Amaru: su época, su hado* (Buenos Aires: Editorial Leviatán, 1995). This last book is a popular, unfootnoted publication, by a well-known historian, that notes the very active role of Tupac Amaru's wife in his revolutionary activities.
35. The influence of the South American rebellions on the war is a good subject for further research. Beerman, *España y la Independencia*, 200–202, is one historian who tries to make the connection.
36. Convention entre (His Most Catholic Majesty) et (His Most Christian Majesty) concernant les operation, et le service des troupes combineés des deux couromes dans les Indes Occidentales, Versailles, 7 October 1781; and Reponse aux diverses proproutions contenies dans un memoire de la Cour d' Espagne, 3 November 1781, both in AGI, Santo Domingo, leg. 2083a.
37. A fin de proporcionar en la campaña próxima la expedición proyectada contra Jamayca, San Ildefonso, 27 September 1781, ibid., leg. 2083b.
38. Royal Order to B. Gálvez, 14 December 1781, ibid., leg. 2549.
39. Solano to B. Gálvez, Havana, 3 January 1782, AGI, Indiferente General, leg. 1578.
40. B. Gálvez to J. Gálvez, Havana, 22 January 1782, ibid.; and Urriza to J. Gálvez, Havana, 17 January 1782, AGI, Santo Domingo, leg. 2084.
41. Beerman, *España y la Independencia*, 175–77.
42. Quoted in Beerman, *España y la Independencia*, 176. Original is in B. Gálvez to J. Gálvez, 23 January 1782, AGI, Santo Domingo, leg. 1234. Also, see Cagigal to J. Gálvez, Havana, 15 March 1782, AGI, Santo Domingo, leg. 2084.
43. Urriza to J. Gálvez, Havana, 6 March 1782, AGI, Santo Domingo, leg. 2084.
44. Saavedra to B. Gálvez, 19 January 1782, AGI, Indiferente General, leg. 1578; and A fin de proporcionar en la campaña próxima la expedición proyectada contra Jamayca, San Ildefonso, 27 September 1781, AGI, Santo Domingo, leg. 2083b.
45. Dull, *French Navy*, 259–61.

46. Ibid., 271.

47. Ibid., 283.

48. Ibid., 284.

49. Juan Nepomuceno de Quesada, Estado que manifiesta los oficiales y tropa de que se compone la expedición del mando del Excmo. Señor don Juan Manuel de Cagigal, Havana, 8 April 1782 (two copies), AGI, Santo Domingo, leg. 2084; and AGI, Indiferente General, leg. 1583. The last is signed by Urriza. Also, Estado que manifiesta los Viveres, y untencilios embarcados en los Buques de la presente expedición del mando *de . . . Cagigal,* Havana, 10 April 1782, AGI, Santo Domingo, leg. 2084; and Relación de las Embarcaciones destinadas para la inmediata salida del Real servicio, Havana, April 1782, AGI, Indiferente General, leg. 1579. Compiled by Juan Martín Galiano and signed by Urriza. Copies of both are in AGI, Santo Domingo, leg. 1659. For merchants, see Urriza to J. Gálvez, Havana, 12 April 1782, AGI, Santo Domingo, leg. 1659. For more preparations, Urriza to J. Gálvez, Havana, 18 November 1781, AGI, Santo Domingo, leg. 2084.

50. Beerman, *España y la Independencia,* 177; Urriza to J. Gálvez, Havana, 12 April 1782, AGI, Santo Domingo, leg. 2084. Urriza reports the number of ships at fifty-seven. Of that total, forty-five were Spanish and twelve were *"Angloamericanos."*

51. Cagigal to Juan Daban, acting governor of Havana, 27 April 1782 and Daban to J. Gálvez, Havana, 6 May 1782, both in AGI, Santo Domingo, leg. 2084.

52. Beerman, *España y la Independencia,* 177.

53. Cagigal to John Maxwell, on board the *South Carolina,* 7 May 1782, AGI, Indiferente General, leg. 1583.

54. The best account for the Spanish occupation of the Bahamas is James A. Lewis, *The Final Campaign of the American Revolution: The Rise and Fall of the Spanish Bahamas* (Columbia, S.C.: University of South Carolina Press, 1991). Beerman, *España y la Independencia,* 179–81 has a good account of the taking of New Providence or the Bahamas. For a contemporary description with good detail, see Juan Martín Galiano to Urriza, Nueva Providencia, 19 May 1782, AGI, Santo Domingo, leg. 2084.

55. Maxwell to Cagigal, N. Providencia, 7 May 1782, AGI, Indiferente General, leg. 1583.

56. Cagigal to Maxwell, on board the *South Carolina,* 7 May 1782 (two letters), ibid.

57. Artículos de Capitulación estipulados en Nassau de Nueva Providencia, 8 May 1782, AGI, Santo Domingo, leg. 2084.

58. Estado que manifiesta las Fuerzas de Tierra y Mar, Artilleria, Municiones de Guerra, etc., con que ha capitulado la Ysla de Providencia y sus adyacentes en 8 de mayo de 1782, n.d., Nueva Providencia, AGI, Indiferente General, leg. 1583.

59. Juan Martín Saliano to J. Gálvez, Nueva Providencia; Urriza to J. Gálvez, Havana, 10 June 1782, both in AGI, Santo Domingo, leg. 2084.

60. Ibid.; and Beerman, *España y la Independencia,* 181. Beerman has a list of the supplies taken by Guillon. Two years later, Congress passed a resolution, presented by the delegates of South Carolina, that Spain be petitioned to pay that state "adequate compensation . . . for the service performed by the *South Carolina* in the reduction of [New] Providence." Resolution of Congress, 3 May 1784, AHN, Estado, leg. 3885, exp. 19.

61. Cagigal to B. Gálvez, Nueva Providencia, 20 May 1782, AGI, Santo Domingo, leg. 2085b.

62. M. Gálvez, Diario, Trujillo, 18 April 1782, AGI, Guatemala, leg. 869. Lewis, *Final Campaign,* has a very good, detailed summary of Cagigal's success and Bernardo de Gálvez's displeased reaction.

63. Cagigal to His Majesty, Havana, 2 January 1782, AGI, Santo Domingo, leg. 1234. This whole episode between Cagigal and Gálvez, as well as what finally became of Cagigal and Miranda, is a fine subject for future study. Cagigal, who was promoted to his position of influence, along with Bernardo de Gálvez and Solano, when they replaced Navarro, Bonet, and Navia, was not alone suffering the wrath of "Los Gálvez." Solano, too, came under fire for his constant delays. In August 1783, he was charged with disobeying his orders when he delayed the fleet destined for Cádiz. The real reason for the charge seems

to point to his constantly independent decision-making that, in part, grew out of his fear of an invasion of Havana. J. Gálvez to B. Gálvez, San Ildefonso, 10 August 1783, AGI, Santo Domingo, leg. 2081. Also, see the end of chapter X, herein.

64. Lewis, *Final Campaign,* 40 and 104.

65. Beerman, *España y la Independencia,* 182–83. Beerman paints Gálvez as petty in this matter and he criticizes the family as well. Gilbert Din, *Francisco Bouligny,* paints the same picture of Gálvez and his family, over a different matter.

66. For example, see Beerman, "Introduction," xvii; and Dull, *French Navy,* 299.

67. B. Gálvez to Aranda, Guarico (Cape François), 26 April 1782, AGI, Santo Domingo, leg. 2084.

68. Dull, *French Navy,* 287, note 21.

69. Morris, *The Peacemakers,* 44. Beerman, *España y la Independencia,* passim. Specifically for St. Joseph, see Alvord, "Conquest of St. Joseph," 398. Alvord quotes and bases his article on *La Gaceta de Madrid.* For Yorktown, see *La Gaceta de Madrid,* 11 and 14 December 1781, BN.

70. Richard Harrison to John Jay, Cádiz, 20 November 1781, AHN, Estado 38842, exp. 20, no. 4.

71. Randall, *Benedict Arnold,* 146. Jay's co-authors were John Dickenson and Thomas Cushing. See William Chancy Ford, ed., *The Journals of the Continental Congress* (Washington, D.C.: U.S. Government printing Office, 1904), vol. 1, 82–90 and vol. 2, 6, 8–70.

72. Morris, *The Peacemakers,* 236–37. Morris's account of Jay's diplomatic mission in Europe is pro-Jay and anti-Hispanic, although he describes Jay as standoffish, vain, touchy, and self-righteous. A more noncommittal account of Jay's activities in Spain can be found in Rafael Sánchez Mantero, "La misión de John Jay en España (1779–1782)," *Anuario de Estudios Americanos* 23 (1966): 1389–1431. Sánchez Mantero based his article solely on United States sources and, surprisingly, did not use the many Spanish resources at his disposal. Dull, *Diplomatic History,* passim, corrects and revises Morris, basically through the use of United States and French sources. For a history of Jay during the peace negotiations, from a Spanish point of view, see Oltra and Pérez Samper, *Aranda,* 197–217.

73. Dull, *A Diplomatic History,* 149.

74. Fernández y Fernández, *Spain's Contribution,* 11–12.

75. Dull, *French Navy,* 329.

76. Ibid., 319.

77. Ibid., 323–24.

78. Aranda, Memorial, 1783, as quoted in Reparaz, *Yo Solo,* 23.

79. Saavedra, 4 December 1780, *Journal,* 54.

CONCLUSIONS AND EPILOGUE

1. For example, Washington to B. Franklin, May 5–7, 1779, vol. 1, 6–7; Washington to the Congressional Committee of Conference, 13 January 1779, vol. 14, 4–5, both in *Writings of Washington.*

2. Quoted in Lancaster, *The American Revolution,* 234–35. Also, see Vergennes to Louis XVI, 5 December 1778, quoted in Dull, *French Navy,* 133; see also 97.

3. Copia de Expediente formado sobre arreglo de Pulquerías, sobre el nuevo impuesto de seis granos en cada arroba, y sobre medidas, in "Cedulas Reales, Ordenes y Novissimas Disposiciones de Gobierno, año 1780," folios 347–348, Fray Angélico Chávez History Library, Palace of the Governors, Santa Fe, N.Mex. The quote reads, "ayuda de sostener la Guerra."

4. José Jesús Hernández Palomo, *La Renta del Pulque en Nueva España, 1663–1810* (Sevilla: Escuela de Estudios Hispanoamericanos, 1979), 214–221. Hernández Palomo notes that the collected money was used to support the local militias in Mexico.

5. Quoted in Martín Morgado, *Junípero Serra's Legacy* (Pacific Grove, Calif.: Mount Carmel Press, 1987), 183.

6. Two books on the subject are Robert H. Thonhoff, *The Texas Connection With the American*

Revolution (Burnet, Tex.: Eakin Press, 1981); and Robert S. Weddle and Robert H. Thonhoff, *Drama and Conflict: The Texas Saga, 1776* (Austin: Madrona Press, 1976).

7. Cavallero de Croix to the governor of New Mexico, Chihuahua, 7 October 1779, no. 769, Spanish Archives of New Mexico (SANM), New Mexico State Records and Archives (NMSRA), Santa Fe, N.Mex.

8. Cavallero de Croix to the governor of New Mexico, 11 February 1780, no. 785; and regarding the corsair, 30 March 1779, no. 790, both in ibid. The last letter is missing from the archive, but is listed with a translated extract in Ralph E. Twitchell, *Spanish Archives of New Mexico*, 2 (Cedar Rapids, Iowa: Torch Press, 1914), SANM, NMSRA, Santa Fe, N.Mex., 282.

9. Cavallero de Croix to Anza, 1 August, no. 827 and 17 August 1780, no. 828, both in ibid.

10. Ibid.

11. Felipe de Neve to the Governor, 13 January 1783, no. 850, ibid. For conversion rates, see the index.

12. Morgado, *Serra's Legacy,* 183. According to Morgado, this idea originated from the governor and worked smoothly.

13. The quote is dated 15 June 1780 and is in Francis J. Weber, *A Bicentennial Compendium of Maynard J. Geiger's The Life and Times of Fray Junípero Serra* (Mission Hills, Calif.: By the Author, 1984), 53. Fernández y Fernández, *Spain's Contribution,* 10, states that the money went directly to General Rochambeau, but this claim is not documented.

14. Letter dated 7 May 1778 in Weber, *Bicentennial,* 68. The document was discovered by Benjamin Cummings Truman and noted in 1867 at Mission San Juan Capistrano, and is now lost.

15. David J. Langum, "The Caring Colony: Alta California's Participation in Spain's Foreign Affairs," *Southern California Quarterly* 22 (fall, 1980): 218–19. Langum reports the following contributions: the presidio of Monterey, fifty-three soldiers, 833 *pesos;* presidio of Santa Barbara, thirty-four soldiers, 249 *pesos;* presidio of San Diego, fifty-four soldiers, 515 *pesos.*

16. David J. Weber, *The Spanish Frontier in North America* (New Haven and London: Yale University Press, 1992), 266.

17. The cast mortar is located at the west entrance of the Fábrica de Artillería de Sevilla. The documentation pertinent to the mortar has been deposited in the Archivo General de Andalucía, in Seville.

18. For example, see Archbishop of Málaga to the King, 3 December 1779; and the King to the Archbishop of Málaga, 15 December 11779, both in Archivo Histórico del Cabildo de la Santa Iglesia Catedral de Málaga, leg. 13, pieza no. 52, Actas Capitulares de 1777 a 1781, Acta Capitular de 23 de diciembre de 1779.

19. Cabildo (Council) Catedralicio de Toledo to the Archbishop and Cabildo Catedralicio de Málaga, 1 March 1780, ibid., Acta Capitular de 9 de marzo de 1780.

20. Council of the Cathedral of Málaga to the King, 14 March 1780; Ministro de Hacienda (Finance) to the Archbishop of Málaga, 23 March 1780, both in ibid., Acta Capitular del 27 de marzo de 1780. "[Y] se descontará de lo que el Cabildo debería pagar por subsidio y escusado en los años necesarios para cubrir la deuda."

21. King to the Archbishop and Council of the Cathedral of Málaga, 28 May 1780; and Floridablanca to the Archbishop and Cabildo of the Cathedral of Málaga, 30 May 1780; both in ibid. Floridablanca's letter was the cover letter for the king's letter.

22. This is a great subject for further research. A church-by-church or cathedral-by-cathedral survey would prove very interesting.

23. For a discussion refuting the legend, see María Victoria Campos Rojas, "El por qué de la inconclusa Catedral," *Revista Jabega, Revista de la Diputación Provincial de Málaga* 16 (4th trimestre 1976): 23–28. Documents demonstrating that construction continued are in Archivo Histórico del Cabildo de la Santa Iglesia Catedral de Málaga, leg. 610–612 and 708.

24. Bond, "Oliver Pollock: An Unknown Patriot," 139; and James, "Spanish Influence," 207. Another interpretation of the dollar sign is that it evolved from the "Ps" for *pesos* to the

"$," familiar to us today. For a survey of all these interpretations, see Carlos M. Fernández-Shaw, *Presencia española en los Estados Unidos* (Madrid: Instituto de Cooperación Iberoamericana, 1987), 102–3. A *peso fuerte* was equivalent to one U.S. dollar, so it was easy to switch a dollar sign. A *peso fuerte* also could be divided into eight parts called *reales*. For an equivalency table, see Leslie Bethell, ed., *Historia de América Latina; América Latina Colonial: Economía* (University of Cambridge Press, 1984; reprint, Barcelona: Editorial Crítica, S.A., 1990), x.

25. *The Compact Oxford English Dictionary,* 2nd ed. (Oxford: Clarendon Press, 1992).
26. Richard S. Yeoman, *1990: A Guide Book of United States Coins* (Racine, Wis.: Western Publishing Co., Inc., 1989), 6–7.
27. Weber, *Spanish Frontier,* 266.
28. Ward, "Oliver Pollock," 138.
29. Rendón to Estevan Miró, Philadelphia, 1 November 1782, AGI, Cuba, leg. 104A, folio 1–16I, año 1782 a 1783. Miró, at the time, was governor of Louisiana.
30. Montero de Pedro, *Españoles,* 40.
31. James, "Oliver Pollock," 79–80
32. Fernández y Fernández, *Spain's Contribution,* 8. See illustration herein. The statue was dedicated on 3 June 1976. See Montemayor, *Yo Solo,* viii.
33. Quoted by Robert A. Nesbitt, "Historian Unfolds History of Bernardo de Gálvez in Recent Lecture," *The Saccarappa* 14, no. 4 (May 1981), n.p. Evia became the director of the port of New Orleans, where he stayed until 1803 when Louisiana was sold to the United States. He died in Havana on 24 November 1815.
34. "Explicación del escudo de armas, Precedente que por su Familia y Persona pertenece al agraciado Don Bernardo de Gálvez," 28 July 1783, Madrid, in Woodward, *Tribute,* 4–6; and "Reales Cédulas en que el Rey se sirve hacer merced de Título de Castilla con la Denominación de Conde de Gálvez, y la Adición de una Flor de Lis de Oro en Campo Azul para el Escudo de sus Armas, al Teniente General de los Reales Exércitos, Don Bernardo de Gálvez, 20 May 1783," reproduced and translated in Woodward, *Tribute,* 3–135 [originals in the Historic New Orleans Collection]. The motto has been used in the titles of two books. See Reparaz and Montemayor. Also, see William S. and Hazel P. Coker, *The Siege of Pensacola in 1781 in Maps* (Pensacola: Perdido Bay Press, 1981).
35. Boeta, *Gálvez,* 39–40. The Castle of Chapultepec stands today in Mexico City. It is Mexico's national museum of history.
36. The poem is "Apuntes de algunas de las gloriosas acciones del Exmo. Señor D. Bernardo de Gálvez . . . ," and is published in the original with an English translation in Woodward, *Tribute,* xxiv, 65–94, 116–135.
37. Montemayor, "Epilogue," 48. Perhaps further research will locate descendents from the daughters.
38. There is an organization in the United States called Los Granaderos de Gálvez, which is dedicated to Bernardo de Gálvez's memory, and the role of Spain in the Revolutionary War. The organization has chapters in Texas, Louisiana, and Florida. For the burial, see Beerman, "Introduction," xvii.
39. Fernández y Fernández, *Spain's Contribution,* 21. The statue was placed at the northeast section of Logan Circle at 18th Street and Benjamin Franklin Parkway.
40. Bailey, *A Diplomatic History,* 60–62. Congress tied the issue of Spain's control of the Mississippi River or free (United States) navigation of the river to French access to cod fishing off the New England coast. The northern states had little interest in the Mississippi River issue, whereas the southern states had little concern over French fishermen in New England's waters. The central states tended to join the southern states in their concern for free navigation. All seemed in agreement that Florida was less important than either free navigation of the Mississippi or New England's cod fishing.

41. Joseph M. Beatty, Jr., "Letters of the Four Beatty Brothers of the Continental Army, 1774–1794," *Pennsylvania Magazine* 44 (1920): 218–19; and Fernández y Fernández, *Spain's Contribution,* 14–16. Miralles was buried in a scarlet suit embroidered with gold lace, a gold-laced hat, cued wig, white silk stockings, and diamond shoe and knee buckles.

42. Cummins, *Spanish Observers,* 162. This is the best account of Miralles's death and funeral.

43. Fernández y Fernández, *Spain's Contribution,* 16.

44. See Broughton, "Francisco Rendón."

45. Fernández y Fernández, *Spain's Contribution,* 3.

46. James, "Oliver Pollock," 72.

47. Lancaster, *The American Revolution,* 185; and Montemayor, "Epilogue," 47. Montemayor states that some of the supplies sent through New Orleans got to Washington's army.

48. James, "Spanish Influence," 201.

49. Washington to the Board of War, 18 October 1778, *Writings of Washington,* vol. 13, 105–6.

50. Washington to Major General William Heath, 8 June 1781, vol. 22, 182–83; and 13 June 1781, vol. 22, 209–10, both in *Writings of Washington.*

51. Washington to the Superintendent of Finance, 13 July 1781, *Writings of Washington,* vol. 22, 365–67.

52. For example, the Regiment of Hibernia. See Reparaz, *Yo Solo,* 176.

53. Francisco Morales Padrón, "Editor's Introduction," xxxii–xxxiii.

54. Demetrio Ramos Pérez, *Simón Bolívar: El Libertador* (Madrid: Biblioteca Iberoamericana, 1988), 11 and 14. For a survey of Saavedra's life, archives and published works about him, see Miguel Molina Martínez, "El 'Fondo Saavedra' del Archivo de los Jesuitas en Granada," *Archivo Hispalense: Revista Histórica, Literaria y Artística,* nos. 207 and 208 (January–August 1985): 373–80.

SELECTED BIBLIOGRAPHY

Manuscript Collections

SPAIN

GRANADA:
Facultad de Teología
  Archivo, Fondo Saavedra

MADRID:
Archivo General del Palacio Real
  Archivo del Infante don Gabriel, Secretaría
Archivo Histórico Nacional (AHN)
  Sección de Estado
  Sección Mapas, Planos y Dibujos
Biblioteca Nacional (BN)
  Manuscritos, Louisiana-Española
  La Gaceta de Madrid
Museo del Ejército
Museo Naval

MÁLAGA:
Archivo Histórico del Cabildo de la Santa Iglesia Catedral de Málaga

SEVILLE:
Archivo General de Indias (AGI)
  Sección Gobierno
    Audiencia de Guatemala
    Audiencia de Santo Domingo
  Indiferente General
  Papeles procedentes de Cuba
    Sección Mapas y Planos
      Florida y Louisiana
      Guatemala
      Monedas
Archivo General de Andalucía
  Fondos Documentales de la Fábrica de Artillería de Sevilla

VALLADOLID:
Archivo General de Simancas (AGS)
Secretaría de Estado: Inglaterra (años 1750–1820)
Secretaría de Guerra: Florida y Louisiana (años 1779–1802)

UNITED STATES
NEW MEXICO:
New Mexico State Records Center and Archives, Santa Fe (NMSRCA)
The Spanish Archives of New Mexico
Fray Angélico Chávez History Library, Palace of the Governors Museum, Santa Fe
(History Library, POG)
Cedulas, Reales Ordenes y Novissimas Disposiciones de Gobierno, 1680–1791,
compiled by José Antonio López Frías. Vols. 1 and 2. Catalog no. 972s.
The Palace of the Governors Museum, Santa Fe (POG)

SAINT LOUIS:
Missouri Historical Society
Oliver Pollock Papers
Papers from Spain
St. Louis Archives

WASHINGTON, D.C.:
National Archives
Letterbook of Brigadier General Edward Hand, 9–18 October 1776;
13 April to 25 August 1778, Record Group 93 (Microfilm 853, Roll 17)

Published Sources

Actas del Congreso de Historia de los Estados Unidos. Madrid: Universidad de la Rábida y
Servicio de Publicaciones del Ministerio de Educación y Ciencia, 1976.
Alcázar Molina, Cayetano. *Los virreinatos en el siglo XVIII.* In *Historia de América y de los pueb-
los americanos.* Vol. 13. Barcelona and Buenos Aires: Salvat Editores, S.A., 1945.
Alvarez, Francisco. *Noticia del establecimiento y población de las colonias inglesas en la América
septentrional. . . .* Madrid: A. Fernández, 1778.
Alvarez García, Carlos; María Francisca Represa Fernández; and Miguel Represa Fernández,
eds. *Archivo General de Simancas: Secretaría de Estado: Inglaterra (años 1750–1820),* 2 vols.
Madrid: Ministerio de Asuntos Exteriores, 1976.
Alvord, Clarence W. "The Conquest of St. Joseph, Michigan by the Spaniards in 1781," *Michigan
History Magazine* (1930): 398–414. First published in *Missouri Historical Review* 2 (1908):
195–210.
Bailey, Thomas A. *A Diplomatic History of the American People.* 1940. Reprint, Englewood
Cliffs, N.J.: Prentice-Hall, Inc., 1974.
Ballesteros y Beretta, Antonio. *Historia de España y su influencia en la historia universal.* Tomo
V. Barcelona: Salvat editores, S.A., 1929.
Beatty, Jr., Joseph M., ed. "Letters of the Four Beatty Brothers of the Continental Army,
1774–1794," *Pennsylvania Magazine* 44 (1920): 218–19.
Becker, Beverly. "Santa Fe: Est. 1610, 1607." *El Palacio* 100, no. 1 (winter 1994): 14–16.
Beerman, Eric. *España y la Independencia de los Estados Unidos.* Madrid: Editorial MAPFRE ,
S.A., 1992.
———. "Introduction." In *Yo Solo: The Battle Journal of Bernardo de Gálvez During the American
Revolution.* Translated by E. A. Montemayor, x–xvii. New Orleans: Polyanthos, 1978.
———. "The 1782 American-Spanish Expedition." *Proceedings: United States Naval Institute*
104 (December 1978): 86–87.

———. "'Yo Solo' Not Solo: Juan Antonio Riaño at Pensacola in 1781." *Florida Historical Quarterly* 58, no. 2 (1979): 174–84.

Beeson, Lewis. "Michigan News." *Michigan History* 39 (1955): 119.

Bemis, Samuel Flagg. *The Diplomacy of the American Revolution.* Bloomington: Indiana University Press, 1957.

Bethell, Leslie, ed. *Historia de América Latina; América Latina colonial: Economía.* University of Cambridge Press, 1984. Reprint, Barcelona: Editorial Crítica, S.A., 1990.

Blum, John M., et al. *The National Experience: A History of the United States to 1877.* New York: Harcourt Brace Jovanovich, Inc., 1973.

Boeta, José Rodulfo. *Bernardo de Gálvez.* Madrid: Publicaciones Españoles, 1977.

Bond, C. Ward. "Oliver Pollock: An Unknown Patriot." In *Tribute to Don Bernardo de Gálvez.* Edited and translated by Ralph Lee Woodward, Jr. Baton Rouge and New Orleans: The Historic New Orleans Collection, 1979.

Bonsal, Stephen. *When the French Were Here.* Garden City, N. Y.: Doubleday and Co., 1945.

Bradford, Ernie Dugate Selby. *Gibraltar: The History of A Fortress.* London: Rupart Hart-Davis, 1971.

Brasseaux, Carl A. *Denis Nicolas Foucalt and the New Orleans Rebellion of 1768.* Ruston, La.: McGinty Publications, 1987.

Brinckerhoff, Sidney B. and Pierce A. Chamberlain. *Spanish Military Weapons in Colonial America, 1700–1821.* Harrisburg, Pa.: The Stackpole Co., 1972.

Broadwater, John D. "Yorktown Shipwreck," *National Geographic* 173 (1988): 804–23.

Broughton, William H. "Francisco Rendón: Spanish Agent in Philadelphia, 1779–1786, Intendant of Spanish Louisiana, 1793–1796." Ph. D. diss., University of New Mexico, 1994.

Butler, Albert F. "Rediscovering Michigan's Prairies." *Michigan History* 33 (1949): 117–30.

Campos Rojas, María Victoria. "El por qué de la inconclusa Catedral." *Revista Jabega, Revista de la Diputación Provincial de Málaga* 16, 4th trimestre (1976): 23–28.

Caughey, John Walton. *Bernardo de Gálvez in Louisiana, 1776–1783.* Berkeley: University of California Press, 1934.

———. "The Panis Mission to Pensacola, 1778." *Hispanic American Historical Review* 10, no. 4 (1930): 480–89.

———. "Willing's Expedition Down the Mississippi, 1778." *Louisiana Historical Quarterly* 15 (January 1932): 5–36.

Chambers, Mortimer, Raymond Grew, David Herlihy, Theodore K. Rabb, and Isser Woloch. *The Western Experience Since 1640.* New York: Alfred A. Knopf, 1974.

Chávez, Fray Angélico. *Origins of New México Families in the Spanish Colonial Period.* Santa Fe: Historical Society of New Mexico, 1954.

Chávez, Thomas E. "The Segesser Hide Paintings: History, Discovery, Art." *El Palacio* (winter 1986): 18–27.

Cline, Howard F. *Florida Indians I: Notes on Colonial Indians and Communities in Florida, 1700–1821.* New York and London: Garland Publishing, Inc., 1974.

Coker, William S. and Hazel P. *The Siege of Mobile, 1780 in Maps: With Data on Troop Strength, Military Units, Ships, Casualties, and Prisoners of War, including a brief history of fort Charlotte (Condé).* Pensacola: Perdido Bay Press, 1982.

———. *The Siege of Pensacola, 1781 in Maps with Data on Troop Strength, Military Units, Ships, Casualties, and Related Statistics.* Pensacola: Perdido Bay Press, 1981.

The Compact Oxford English Dictionary. Second edition. Oxford: Clarendon Press, 1992.

Conover, Bettie Jones. "British West Florida's Mississippi Frontier Posts, 1763–1779." *Alabama Review* 29 (1976): 177–207.

Cortés Salinas, María del Carmen. "Benito de la Mata Linares: Juez y Testigo en la rebelión de Tupac Amaru." *Quinto Congreso Internacional de Historia de América* 1 (1972): 230–57.

Cummins, Light Townsend. "Oliver Pollock's Plantations: An Early Anglo Landowner on the Lower Mississippi, 1769–1824." *Louisiana History* 29, no. 1 (1988): 35–48.

———. *Spanish Observers and the American Revolution, 1775–1783.* Baton Rouge and London: Louisiana State University Press, 1991.

Cusachs, Gaspar, ed. "Diary of the Operations of the Expedition against the place of Pensacola conducted by the Arms of His Catholic Majesty, under the Orders of the Field Marshall Don Bernardo de Gálvez." *Louisiana Historical Quarterly* 1, no. 1 (1917): 45–84.

Dabney, William and Marion Dargan. *William Henry Drayton and the American Revolution.* Albuquerque: University of New Mexico Press, 1962.

Diccionario Enciclopédico Hispano-Americano de Literatura, Ciencias, Artes, etc., Vol. VII. Barcelona: Montaner y Simón, n.d.

Din, Gilbert C. *Francisco Bouligny: A Bourbon Soldier in Spanish Louisiana.* Baton Rouge and London: Louisiana State University Press, 1993.

———. "Lieutenant Raimundo DuBreüil, Commandant of San Gabriel de Manchac and Bernardo de Gálvez's 1779 Campaign on the Mississippi River." *Military History of the West* 29, no. 1 (spring 1999): 1–30.

Documentos relativos a la independencia de Norteamérica existentes en archivos españoles. Vols. 1–11. Madrid: Ministerio de Asuntos Exteriores, 1977–1985.

Drinkwater, John. *A History of the Siege of Gibraltar.* 1785. Reprint, London: John Murray, 1905.

Dull, Jonathan R. *A Diplomatic History of the American Revolution.* New Haven: Yale University Press, 1985.

———. *The French Navy and American Independence: A Study of Arms and Diplomacy, 1774–1787.* Princeton: Princeton University Press, 1975.

Dupuy, R. Ernest, and Trevor N. Dupuy. *The Encyclopedia of Military History From 3500 B.C. to the Present.* New York: Harper and Row, 1970.

Durand Florez, Luis, ed. *La Revolución de los Tupac Amaru.* Lima, Peru: Comisión Nacional del Bicentenario de la Rebelión Emancipadora de Tupac Amaru, 1981.

Emery, B. Frank. "Fort Saginow." *Michigan History Magazine* 30 (1946): 476–503.

Enciclopedia General Ilustrada del País Vasco. Vol. 15. San Sebastián: Editorial Aunamendi, 1983.

Enciclopedia Universal Ilustrada Europeo-Americana, Vols. 18, 25, and 52. Barcelona: Hijos de J. Espasa, Editores, 1907–30.

Escobedo Mansilla, Ronald; Ana María Rivera Medina; and Alvaro Chapa Imaz, eds. *Los vascos y América.* Bilbao: Fundación Banco de Vizcaya, 1989.

Fabel, Robin F. A. "West Florida and British Strategy in the American Revolution." In *Eighteenth Century Florida and the Revolutionary South.* Edited by Samuel Proctor. Gainesville: University Press of Florida, 1976.

Fagg, John Edwin. *Latin America: A General History.* New York: Macmillan Publishing Co., Inc., 1977.

Ferguson, Wallace K. and Geoffrey Bruun. *A Survey of European Civilization.* Boston: Houghton Mifflin Co., 1969.

Fernández y Fernández, Enrique. *Spain's Contribution to the Independence of the United States.* Washington, D.C.: Embassy of Spain, 1985. First published in *Revista/Review Interamericana* 10, no. 3 (1980).

Fernández-Shaw, Carlos M. *Presencia española en los Estados Unidos.* Madrid: Ediciones Cultura Hispánica, Instituto de Cooperación Iberoamericana, 1987.

Fireman, Janet R. *The Spanish Royal Corps of Engineers in the Western Borderlands: Instrument of Bourbon Reform, 1764–1815.* Glendale, Calif.: The Arthur H. Clark Company, 1977.

Fisher, Lillian Estelle. *The Last Inca Revolt, 1780–1783.* Norman: University of Oklahoma Press, 1986.

Fitzpatrick, John C., ed. *The Writings of George Washington From the Original Manuscript Sources, 1745–1799.* Vols. 13–16, 19, and 22. Washington, D.C.: United States Government Printing Office, 1931–44.

Floyd, Troy S. "Bourbon Palliatives and the Central American Mining Industry, 1765–1800." *The Americas* 18, no. 2 (October 1961): 103–25.

———. *The Anglo-Spanish Struggle for Mosquitia.* Albuquerque: University of New Mexico Press, 1967.

Ford, William Chauncy, ed. *The Journals of the Continental Congress,* Vols. 1 and 2. Washington, D.C.: U.S. Government Printing Office, 1904.

Foss, Arthur. *Ibiza and Minorca.* London: Faber and Faber, 1975.

Franco, José Luciano. "Diego de Gardoqui y las negociaciones entre España y Norteamérica, 1777–1790." In *Libro jubilar de Emeterio S. Santovenia en su cincuentenario de escritor,* 138–75. Havana: Garcia Vear, 1957.

García Melero, Luis Angel. *La Independencia de los Estados Unidos de Norteamérica a través de la prensa española: los precedentes (1763–1776).* Madrid: Ministerio de Asuntos Exteriores, Dirección General de Relaciones Culturales, 1977.

Gardiner, C. Harvey. "The Mexican Archives and the Historiography of the Mississippi Valley in the Spanish Period." *The Spanish in the Mississippi Valley, 1762–1804.* Edited by John F. McDermott, 38–50. Chicago: University of Illinois Press, 1974.

Glascock, Bruce. "Colonial Powder Problems or 'Then and Now.'" *Muzzle Blasts* (January 1973): 9–10, 18 and 36.

Gold, Robert L. "Governor Bernardo de Gálvez and Spanish Espionage in Pensacola, 1777." *The Spanish in the Mississippi Valley, 1762–1804.* Edited by John F. McDermott. Chicago: University of Illinois Press, 1974.

Grant, Alfred. *Our American Brethren: A History of Letters in the British Press During the American Revolution, 1775–1781.* Jefferson, North Carolina: McFarland and Co. Inc., Publishers, 1995.

Gregory, Desmond. *Minorca, The Illusory Prize: A History of the British Occupations of Minorca Between 1708 and 1802.* Rutherford, N.J.: Fairleigh Dickinson University Press, 1990.

Guerra y Sánchez, Ramiro; Pérez Cabrera, José M.; Remos, Juan J.; and Santovenia, Emeterio S. *La historia de la nación cubana.* Tomo II. Havana: Editorial Historia de la Nación Cubana, S.A., 1952.

Haarmann, Albert W. "The Spanish Conquest of West Florida, 1779–1781." *Florida Historical Quarterly* 39 (1960): 107–34.

Hernández Franco, Juan. *La gestión política y el pensamiento reformista del Conde de Floridablanca.* Murcia: Universidad de Murcia, 1984.

Hernández Palomo, José Jesús. *La renta del pulque en Nueva España, 1663–1810.* Sevilla, Spain: Escuela de Estudios Hispanoamericanos de Sevilla, 1979.

Hills, George. *Rock of Contention: A History of Gibraltar.* London: Robert Hale and Co., 1974.

Holmes, Jack D. L. "Alabama's Bloodiest Day of the American Revolution: Counterattack at the Village, January 7, 1781." *Alabama Review* 29, no. 3 (July 1976): 208–19.

———. "Bernardo de Gálvez, 'Man of the Hour' During the American Revolution." In *Cardenales de dos Independencias.* Edited by Francisco de Solano. Mexico: Fomento Cultural Banamex, A. C., 1978.

———. "The Historiography of the American Revolution in Louisiana." *Louisiana History* 19, no. 3 (1978): 309–26.

———. "Juan de la Villebeuvre, Spain's Commandant of Natchez During the American Revolution." *Journal of Mississippi History* 37 (1975): 97–130.

Hotz, Gottfried. *Indian Skin Paintings from the American Southwest: Two Representations of Border Conflicts Between Mexico and the Missouri in the Early Eighteenth Century.* Norman: University of Oklahoma Press, 1970.

James, James Alton. *Oliver Pollock: The Life and Times of an Unknown Patriot.* New York: Appleton-Century, 1937.

———*The Life of George Rogers Clark.* Chicago: University of Illinois Press, 1928.

———. "Oliver Pollock: Financer of the Revolution in the West," *Mississippi Valley Historical Review* (June 1929): 67–80.

———. "Spanish Influence in the West During the American Revolution," *Mississippi Valley Historical Review* 4 (1917): 193–208.

Johnson, Allen and Dumas Malone, eds. *Dictionary of American Biography.* Vol. 4. New York: Charles Scribner's Sons, 1930.

Johnson, W. "The Siege of Gibraltar: Mostly Relating to the Shooting of Hot Shot and Setting Fire to A Besieging Fleet." *International Journal of Impact Engineering* 6, no. 3 (1987): 175–210.

Jones, Oakah L. *Guatemala in the Spanish Colonial Period.* Norman: University of Oklahoma Press, 1994.
————"Matías de Gálvez: Spanish Ally of the American Revolution." Paper presented at the Phi Alpha Theta convention in St. Louis, Missouri, 30 December 1989.
Kemble, Stephen. *The Kemble Papers, Vols. 1 and 2.* New York: New York Historical Society, 1932.
Kennett, Lee. *The French Forces in America, 1780–1783.* Westport, Conn. and London: Greenwood Press, 1977.
Ketchum, Richard M. *The World of George Washington.* New York: American Heritage Publishing Co., Inc., 1974.
Kinnaird, Lawrence. "The Spanish Expedition Against Fort St. Joseph in 1781: A New Interpretation." *The Mississippi Valley Historical Review* 19, no. 2 (1932): 173–91.
Kinnaird, Lawrence, ed. "Clark-Leyba Papers." *The American Historical Review* 41, no. 1 (1935): 92–112.
Kinsbruner, Jay. *The Spanish-American Independence Movement.* Huntington, N.Y.: Robert E. Krieger Publishing Company, 1976.
Kuethe, Allan F. and G. Douglas Inglis. "Absolutism and Enlightened Reform: Charles III, the Establishment of the Alcabala, and Commercial Reorganization in Cuba." *Past & Present: A Journal of Historical Studies* 109 (1985): 118–43.
Labaree, Leonard W., William B. Wilcox, and others, eds. *The Papers of Benjamin Franklin,* 24 vols. New Haven and London: Yale University Press, 1959–.
Lancaster, Bruce. *The American Revolution.* New York: Houghton Mifflin Company, 1985.
Langum, David J. "The Caring Colony: Alta California's Participation in Spain's Foreign Affairs." *Southern California Quarterly* 22 (fall 1980): 218–19.
Leonard, Irving A. *Baroque Times in Old Mexico.* Ann Arbor: University of Michigan Press, 1973.
Lewin, Boleslao. *Tupac Amaru: su época, su hado.* Buenos Aires: Editorial Leviatán, 1995.
Lewis, James A. "Las Damas de la Havana, El Precursor, and Francisco de Saavedra: A Note on Spanish Participation in the Battle of Yorktown." *The Americas* 37 (July 1980): 83–99.
————. *The Final Campaign of the American Revolution: Rise and Fall of the Spanish Bahamas.* Columbia, S.C.: University of South Carolina Press, 1991.
Loomis, Noel M. and Abraham P. Nasatir. *Pedro Vial and the Roads to Santa Fe.* Norman: University of Oklahoma Press, 1967.
López Chávez, Celia. "Benjamin Franklin, España y la diplomacia de una armónica." *Espacio, Tiempo y Forma: Revista de la Facultad de Geografía y Historia,* serie iv, 13 (2000): 319–37.
Marley, David, ed. *Documentos novohispanos relativos a la guerra entre España e Inglaterra, 1779–1784.* Mexico City: Windsor/Mexico, 1985.
Mason, Edward G. *Chapter From Illinois History.* Chicago: H. S. Stone and Co., 1901.
May, Arthur J. *A History of Civilization: The Mid-Seventeenth Century to Modern Times.* New York: Charles Scribner's Sons, 1964.
McDermott, John Francis. "The Myth of the 'Imbecile Governor'—Captain Fernando de Leyba and the Defense of St. Louis in 1780." In *The Spanish in the Mississippi Valley, 1762–1804.* Edited by John F. McDermott. Chicago: University of Illinois Press, 1974.
McGuffie, Tom Henderson. *The Siege of Gibraltar, 1779–1783.* London: B. T. Batsford, 1965.
Medina Encina, Purificación, ed. *Archivo General de Indias: Sección de Gobierno (años 1752–1822).* Vols. 1 and 2. Madrid: Ministerio de Asuntos Exteriores, 1977.
Medina Rojas, F. de Borja. *José de Ezpeleta: Gobernador de la Mobila, 1780–1781.* Sevilla: Escuela de Estudios Hispanoamericanos de Sevilla, 1980.
Molina Martínez, Miguel. "El 'Fondo Saavedra' del Archivo de los Jesuitas en Granada." *Archivo Hispalense: Revista Histórica, Literaria y Artística* 68, nos. 207 and 208 (1985): 373–80.
Montemayor, E. A. "Epilogue." In *Yo Solo: The Battle Journal of Bernardo de Gálvez During the American Revolution.* Translated by E. A. Montemayor. New Orleans: Polyanthos, 1978.
Montemayor, E. A., trans., *Yo Solo: The Battle Journal of Bernardo de Gálvez During the American Revolution.* New Orleans: Polyanthos, Inc., 1978.

Montero de Pedro, José. *Españoles en Nueva Orleans y Luisiana*. Madrid: Ediciones Cultura Hispánica del Centro Iberoamericano de Cooperación, 1979.

Morales Padrón, Francisco. *Participación de España en la independencia política de los Estados Unidos*. Madrid: Publicaciones Españolas, 1952.

Morales Padrón, Francisco, ed. and Introduction, and Aileen Moore Topping, trans., *Journal of Don Francisco Saavedra de Sangronis During the Commission, which he had in his charge from 25 June 1780 until the 20th of the same month of 1783*. Gainesville: University Press of Florida, 1989.

Morgado, Martin. *Junípero Serra's Legacy*. Pacific Grove, Calif.: Mount Carmel, 1987.

Morris, Richard B. *The Peacemakers: The Great Powers and American Independence*. New York: Harper and Row, Publishers, 1965; Reprint, New York: Harper Torchbooks, 1970.

Nasatir, Abraham P. *Borderland in Retreat: From Spanish Louisiana to the Far Southwest*. Albuquerque: University of New Mexico Press, 1976.

———. "The Anglo-Spanish Frontier in the Illinois Country During the American Revolution, 1779–1783." *Journal of Illinois State Historical Society* 21 (1928): 291–358.

———. "St. Louis During the British Attack of 1780," *New Spain and the Anglo American West*. Vol. I . Edited by George P. Hammond. Los Angeles, Calif. and Lancaster, Pa.: Private Printing, 1932.

Nesbitt, Robert A. "Historian Unfolds History of Bernardo de Gálvez in Recent Lecture." *The Saccarappa* 14, no. 4 (May 1981).

Nevins, Allen and Henry Steele Commager. *A Pocket History of the United States*. New York: Washington Square Press, 1966.

Nihart, Brooke. "Spanish Support of the American War of Independence, 1775–83." *Militaría: Revista de Cultura Militar* 7 (1995): 313–44.

Nunis, Jr., Doyce B. *The 1769 Transit of Venus: The Baja California Observations of Jean-Baptiste Chappe d'Auteroche, Vicente de Doz and Joaquín Veláquez Cárdenas de León*. Translated by James Donahue, Maynard J. Geiger, O.F.M., and Iris Wilson Engstrand. Los Angeles, Calif.: Natural History Museum of Los Angeles County, 1982.

Oltra, Joaquín, and María Angeles Pérez Samper. *El Conde de Aranda y los Estados Unidos*. Barcelona: Promociones y Publicaciones Universitarias, S.A., 1987.

Paine, Thomas. *Common Sense*. 1776. Reprint, New York: Penguin Books, 1986.

Payne, Stanley G. *A History of Spain and Portugal*. Vols. I and II. Madison: University of Wisconsin Press, 1973.

Peckham, Howard H. *The War for Independence*. Chicago: University of Chicago Press, 1967.

Pérez Samper, María de los Angeles. *La vida y la epoca de Carlos III*. Barcelona: Editorial Planeta, S.A., 1998.

Petrie, Sir Charles. *King Charles III of Spain: An Enlightened Despot*. New York: John Day Company, 1971.

Priestley, Herbert Ingram. *José de Gálvez: Visitor-General of New Spain (1765–1771)*. Berkeley: University of California Press, 1916.

Proctor, Samuel, ed. *Eighteenth Century Florida: The Impact of the American Revolution in British West Florida*. Gainesville: University Press of Florida, 1978.

Quijano, J. Calderón. "Un incident militar en los establecimientos ingleses de río Tinto en 1782." *Anuario de Estudios Americanos* (1945).

Ramos Pérez, Demetrio. *Simón Bolivar: El Libertador*. Madrid: Biblioteca Iberoamericana, 1988.

Randall, Willard Sterne. *Benedict Arnold: Patriot and Traitor*. New York: William Morrow & Co., Inc., 1990.

Reparaz, Carmen de. *Yo Solo: Bernardo de Gálvez y la toma de Panzacola en 1781*. Barcelona, Spain: Ediciones del Serbal, S.A., 1986.

Robertson, E. Arnot. *The Spanish Town Papers: Some Sidelights on the American War of Independence*. New York: The Macmillan Co., 1959.

Ruigómez de Hernández, María Pilar. *El gobierno español del despotismo ilustrado ante la independencia de los Estados Unidos de América: una nueva estructura de la política internacional (1773–1783)*. Madrid: Ministerio de Asuntos Exteriores, 1978.
Russell, Jack. *Gibraltar Besieged, 1779–1783*. London: William Heinemann, Ltd., 1965.
Sánchez Mantero, Rafael. "La misión de John Jay en España (1779–1782)." *Anuario de Estudios Americanos* 23 (1966): 1389–1431.
Servies, James A. *The Siege of Pensacola, 1781: A Bibliography*. Pensacola: The John C. Pace Library, 1981.
Servies, James A., ed. *Log of H. M. S. Mentor, 1780–81*. Gainesville: University Press of Florida, 1982.
Smith, Paul H., ed. *Letters of Delegates to Congress, 1774–1789*. Vols. 4 and 5. Washington, D.C.: Library of Congress, 1976–1991.
Solano, Francisco de, ed. *Cardenales de dos Independencias*. México: Fomento Cultural Banamex, A. C., 1978.
Sosin, Jack M. *The Revolutionary Frontier, 1763–1783*. Albuquerque: University of New Mexico Press, 1967.
Spilsbury, John. *A Journal of the Siege of Gibraltar, 1779–1783*. Edited by B. T. H. Frere. Gibraltar: Gibraltar Garrison Library, 1908.
Starr, J. Barton. "'Left as a Gewgaw:' The Impact of the American Revolution on British West Florida." *Eighteenth Century Florida: The Impact of the American Revolution in British West Florida*. Edited by Samuel Proctor. Gainesville: University Press of Florida, 1976.
———. *Tories, Dons and Rebels: The American Revolution in British West Florida*. Gainesville: University Press of Florida, 1976.
Teggart, Frederick J. "The Capture of St. Joseph, Michigan, By the Spaniards in 1781." *Missouri Historical Review* 5, no. 4 (1911): 214–28.
Thomas, Alfred B., ed. and trans. *After Coronado: Spanish Exploration Northeast of New Mexico, 1696–1727*. Norman: University of Oklahoma Press, 1935.
Thonhoff, Robert H. *The Texas Connection With the American Revolution*. Burnett, Tex.: Eakin Press, 1981.
Tuchman, Barbara. *The First Salute: A View of the American Revolution*. New York: Ballantine Books, 1988.
Twitchell, Ralph E. *Spanish Archives of New Mexico*, Vol. 2. Cedar Rapids, Iowa: Torch Press, 1914.
Weatherford, Jack. *Indian Givers: How the Indians of the Americas Transformed the World*. New York: Crown Publishers, Inc., 1988.
Weber, Francis J. *A Bicentennial Compendium of Maynard J. Geiger's The Life and Times of Fray Junípero Serra*. Mission Hills, Calif.: By the author, 1984.
Weber, David J. *The Spanish Frontier in North America*. New Haven: Yale University Press, 1992.
Weddle, Robert S. *Changing Tides: Twilight and Dawn in the Spanish Sea, 1763–1803*. College Station: Texas A & M University Press, 1995.
———. *Spanish Sea: The Gulf of Mexico in North American Discovery, 1500–1685*. College Station: Texas A & M University Press, 1985.
———. *The French Thorn: Rival Explorers in the Spanish Sea, 1682–1762*. College Station: Texas A & M University Press, 1991.
Weddle, Robert S. and Robert H. Thonhoff. *Drama and Conflict: The Texas Saga, 1776*. Austin: Madrona Press, 1976.
Wharton, Francis, ed. *The Revolutionary Diplomatic Correspondence of the United States*. Vols. 1–6. Washington, D.C.: United States Government Printing Office, 1889.
Williams, Eric. *From Columbus to Castro: The History of the Caribbean, 1492–1969*. New York: Vintage Books, 1984.
Woodward, Jr., Ralph Lee, ed. *Tribute to Don Bernardo de Gálvez: Royal Patents and an Epic Ballad Honoring the Spanish Governor of Louisiana*. Baton Rouge and New Orleans: The Historic New Orleans Collection, 1979.

Wright, Jr., J. Leitch. "British East Florida: Loyalist Bastion." *Eighteenth Century Florida: The Impact of the American Revolution in British West Florida.* Edited by Samuel Proctor. Gainesville: University Press of Florida, 1976.

———. *Florida in the American Revolution.* Gainesville: University Press of Florida, 1975.

Yela Utrilla, Juan Francisco. *España ante la independencia de los Estados Unidos.* 1925. Reprint, Madrid: Colegio Universitario de Ediciones Istmo, 1988.

Yeoman, Richard S. *1990: A Guide Book of United States Coins.* Racine, Wis.: Western Publishing Co., Inc., 1989.

Zabala Uriate, Aingeru. "Bilbao y el comercio con el norte de América en el siglo XVIII." *Los vascos y América.* Edited by Ronald Escobedo Mansilla and others, 171–202. Bilbao: Fundación Banco de Vizcaya, 1989.

Zudaire Huarte, Eulogio. "Análisis de la rebelión de Tupac Amaru en su bicentenario (1780–1980)." *Revista de Indias,* no. 60 (1980): 13–79.

Zuñiga y Ontiveros, Felipe de. "Notes of Some of the Glorious Actions of His Excellency Don Bernardo de Gálvez, Count of Gálvez, Who was Viceroy, Governor and Captain General of this New Spain, etc., Rendered As An Epic Ballad." 1787. In *Tribute To Don Bernardo de Gálvez,* edited and translated by Ralph Lee Woodward, Jr. Baton Rouge and New Orleans: The Historic New Orleans Collection, 1979.

INDEX